Landscape in INK *and* COLOURED PENCIL

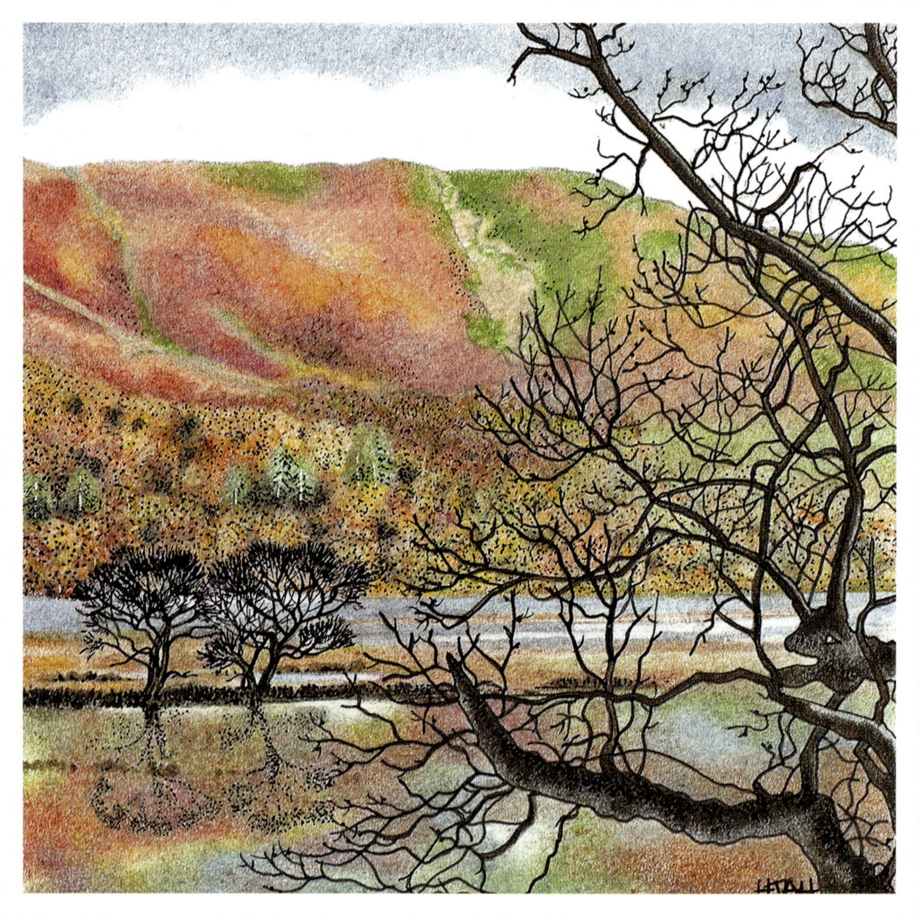

Derwentwater Morning.

Helen Hanson

Landscape in INK *and* COLOURED PENCIL

THE CROWOOD PRESS

First published in 2022 by
The Crowood Press Ltd
Ramsbury, Marlborough
Wiltshire SN8 2HR

enquiries@crowood.com
www.crowood.com

This impression 2025

British Library Cataloguing-in-Publication Data
A catalogue record for this book is available from the British Library.

For product safety - related questions, contact:
productsafety@crowood.com

ISBN 978 0 7198 4066 1

Cover design: Sergey Tsvetkov

Dedication
For my sister, Sylvia, with grateful thanks

Acknowledgements
I would like to thank the team at The Crowood Press for inviting me to write about this unusual mix of media, and for their support throughout the project. I am indebted to the Society of Botanical Artists, who made a place for me as a printmaker and then as a coloured pencil artist and brought me many friends. My grateful thanks are also due to all the artists and colleagues who taught and encouraged me on my artistic journey, including Felicity House who introduced me to the delights of ink, and Roger Reynolds who supervised my first tentative steps in coloured pencil. My special thanks go to my sister, to whom this book is dedicated, for her unfailing support since my earliest printmaking days, and whose most recent kindness was the early proofreading of this book.

Graphic design and typeset by Peggy & Co. Design
Printed and bound in India by Thomson Press

Contents

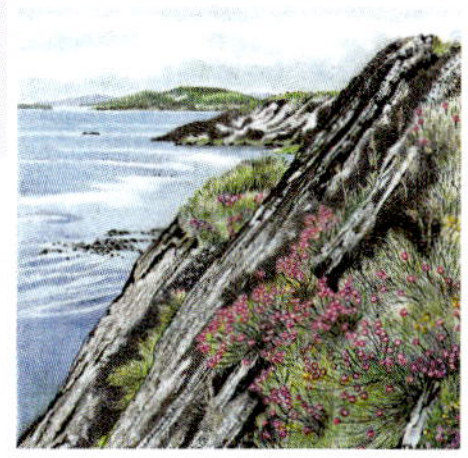
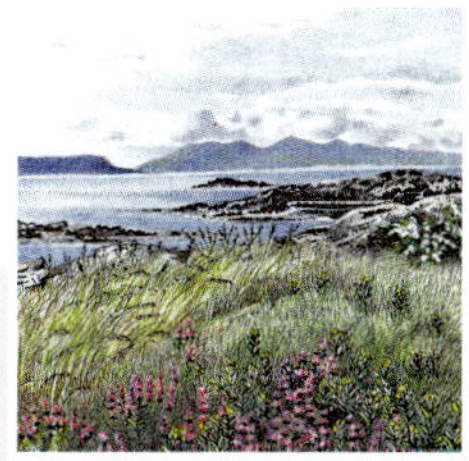
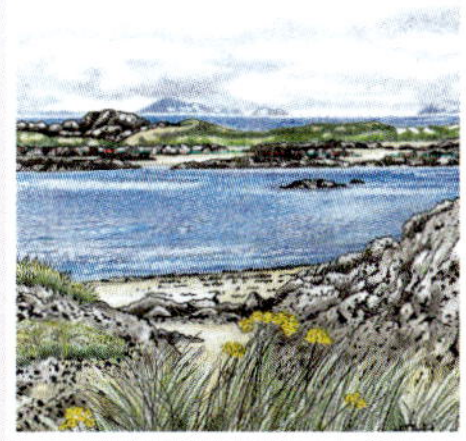
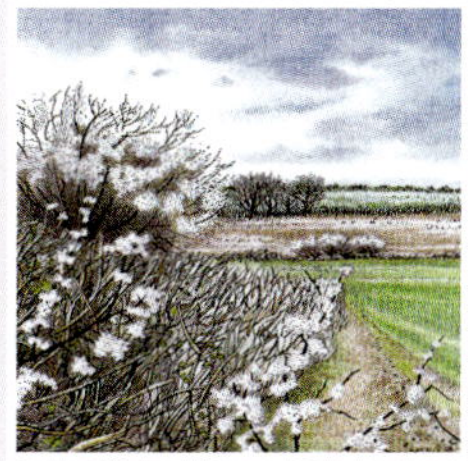
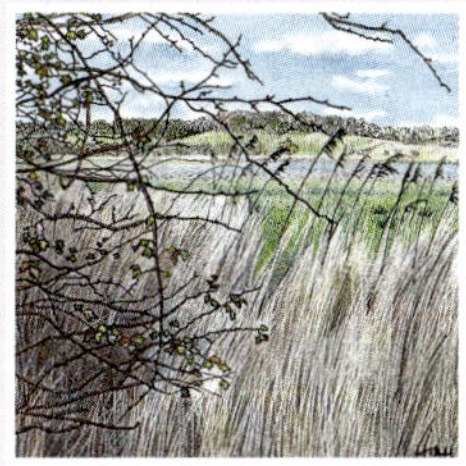
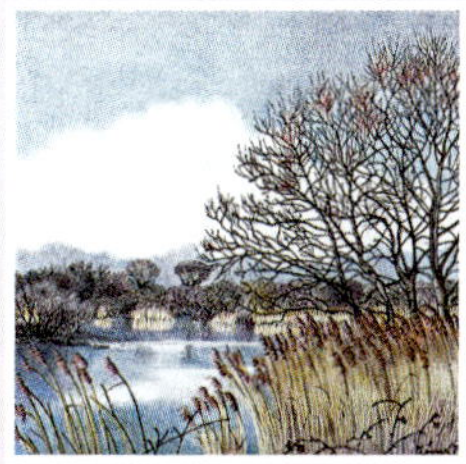
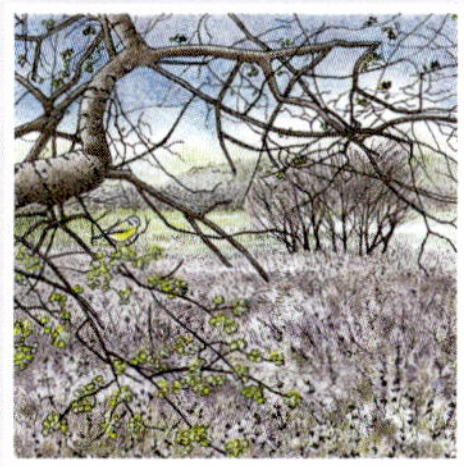
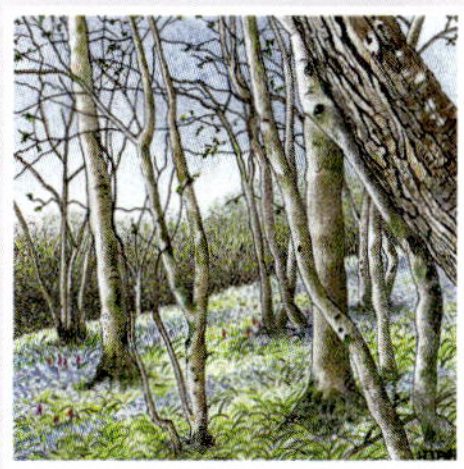
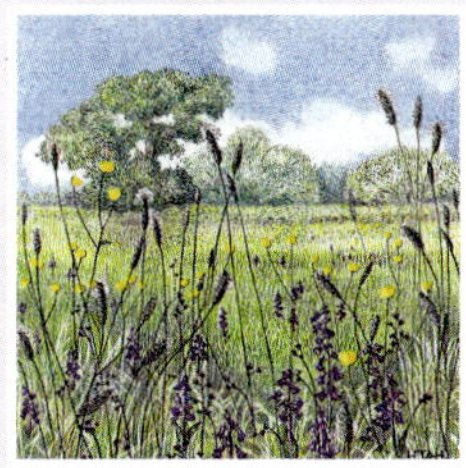
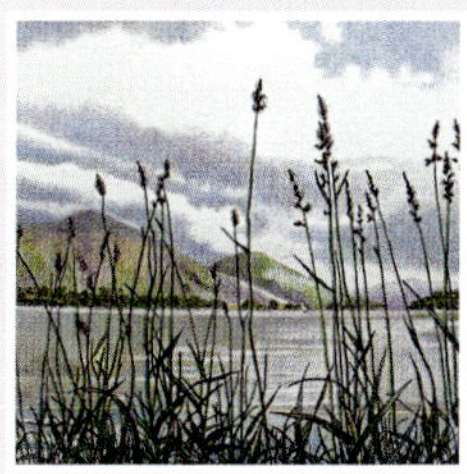
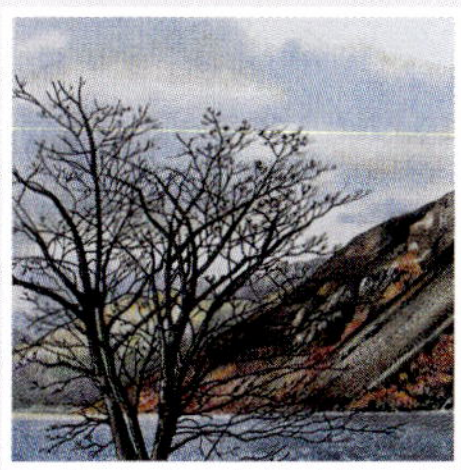
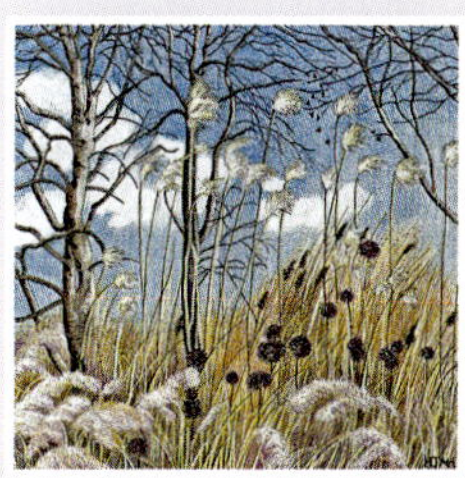

Introduction

In writing this book I became aware that the steps I had taken to arrive at my current method of working had led me full circle, reconnecting me firmly with my early interests. There is something pleasing about this circularity, and I hope that my personal journey and this book will encourage you to follow what you enjoy, to be creative and maybe break new ground.

My enthusiasm for art goes back to early childhood. Thanks to an excellent natural history teacher, I also developed an interest in the flora of Britain. Grass of Parnassus, Bee Orchid and Ploughman's Spikenard were just some of the poetic names that lodged in my memory from our class trips to the local Ainsdale dunes to identify its noted wildflowers.

I became a Modern Languages teacher, but retained an interest in both art and wild plants. In my mid-twenties I enrolled for a printmaking evening class, turning up hopefully with a dried artichoke head, and produced my first linocut. I became fascinated with the process of printmaking, joined an etching class the following year, and was soon hooked. It quickly became clear what inspired me as I turned my attention to landscape, incorporating many of the plants I knew would give a sense of place. I started working seriously in my spare time and gradually built up a portfolio.

In the 1980s I joined Greenwich Printmakers, an artists' co-operative gallery. Membership changed everything for me and set me on a path of exhibiting, selling my work in galleries throughout the UK, and an increasingly busy life as a printmaker.

REINVENTING MYSELF

After about thirty years of printmaking, I sold my press and decided to embark on a self-education project. I began a roller-coaster few years of attending courses in any art medium that appealed. I am grateful to all my tutors, as I show in my acknowledgements. I tried and tested everything. One day I introduced coloured pencil into one of my landscape etchings, then tried a smaller version of the same image using ink and coloured pencil, the two media I had found most appealing.

I began a series – and a whole new lease of life creatively. I had managed to reinvent myself, and a bonus followed in the form of new teaching opportunities. I was presenting an unusual mix of media, both easy to learn and apply, and felt enthusiastic and motivated. It allowed me to teach both local and residential courses and to work with consenting adults – a real joy!

WHAT TO EXPECT

The combination of ink and dry coloured pencil is unexpected. Most internet searches produce examples of pen and wash or pen and watercolour pencil. These are usually created in the traditional way, by tinting an ink drawing, either before or after depicting the scene. My approach is not one of 'colouring in', although I use it very sparingly for emphasis; instead, I integrate the two media as I work, using them to *translate* the landscape. I include techniques such as embossing and lifting out colour, interpreting the landscape through the methods at my disposal.

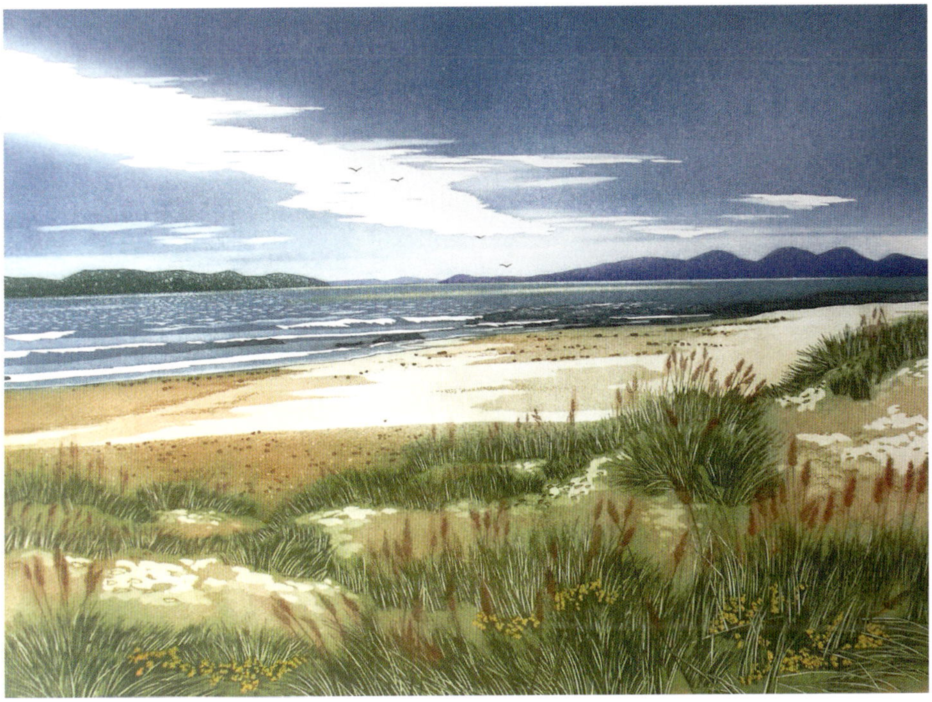

Sky, Sea and Sand was an etching of Machrihanish Bay, Kintyre. At the end of a walk along the shore, the clouds broke into a dramatic diagonal formation. With the foreground dunes and machair, the breakers and the Paps of Jura, I had my image. The edition of 150 was printed using one plate and ten colours, with additional hand-colouring.

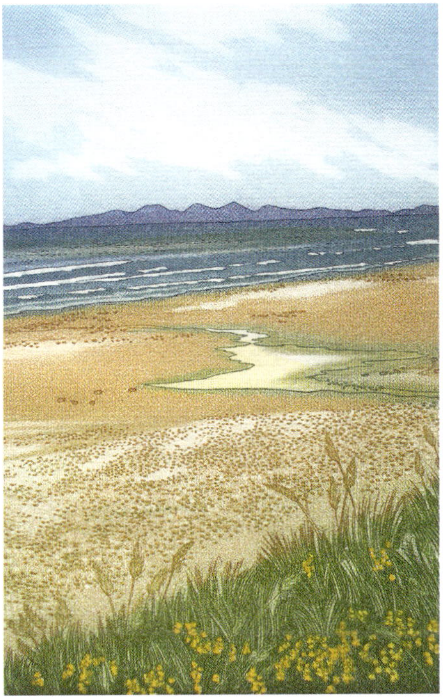

Breaking Waves. This small etching was a companion to *Sky, Sea and Sand*, depicting the same stretch of Kintyre shoreline. It was also on one plate, inked in several colours, and the foreground flowers were added in watercolour.

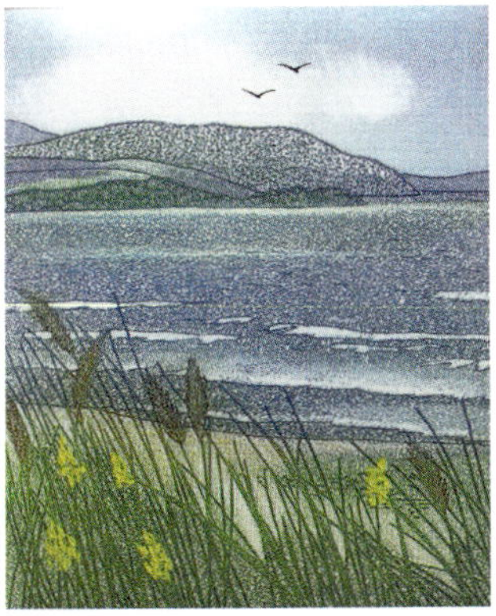

Kintyre. I often etched one or two miniatures to go with a larger series. This one was also of Kintyre and the same stretch of machair, using the same palette but with fewer colours.

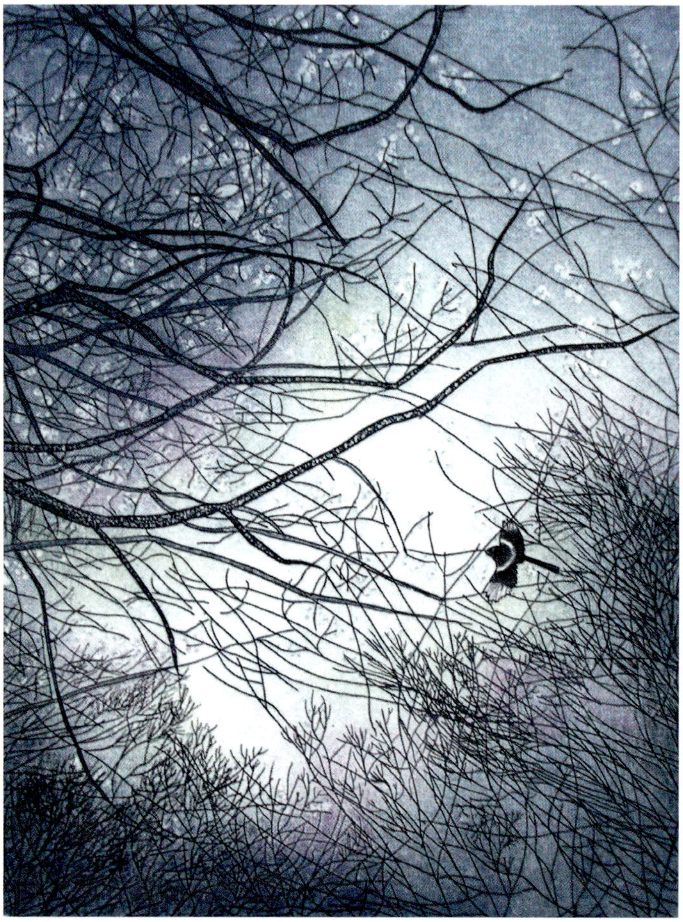

First Light. The last of a series of three etchings, which prompted my change to ink and coloured pencil. I editioned the plate in a deep indigo, using Faber-Castell pencils to add drifts of colour to the print when dry. I liked the combination so much that new ideas started flowing fast – and have not stopped.

It is a thoughtful, slow-growing process that feels like putting together a mildly challenging jigsaw.

Both media are straightforward in application, and neither requires years of practice. Mark-making in ink is easily done and can be as creative as you wish. Coloured pencil work is simple but effective, and the results hold few unwelcome surprises for the beginner. I encourage students to develop their own style, and never cease to be delighted by the resulting individuality. The only rules are those that apply generally to artwork, such as considerations of format, composition and perspective.

The activity itself is therapeutic, as the image is built up gradually through a process that is both absorbing and meditative. It helps to accept that this is slow art, and that the process is to be enjoyed as much as the result. It fits in well with most routines, lending itself to a couple of hours here and there as much as to a concentrated effort. Like knitting and plants, it grows slowly but surely.

I hope this book will encourage you to take a fresh look at landscape, plant life, and how you might interpret them. Set off on your own journey of discovery with no rules and expectations, and get ready to enjoy the creative process at every stage!

Spring Dawn. This was my first work in ink and coloured pencil, based on the previous etching. I chose a smaller, square format, using the branches and foreground as a frame to enclose the bird. It is predominantly ink, but the blended coloured pencil was ideal for the dawn sky.

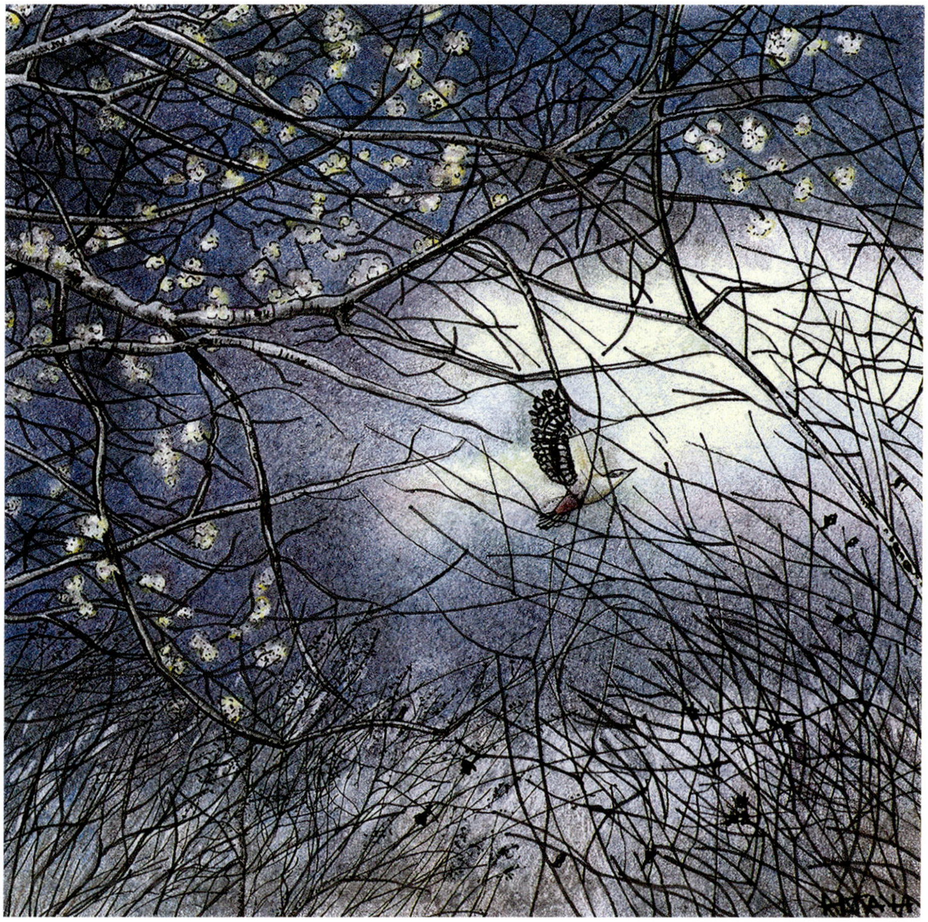

Small Signs of Spring. This was my second attempt at ink and coloured pencil, introducing a more integrated approach. I experimented with Frisket on the sky and created more shadow mixes, adding highlights with a battery eraser. It was more successful as a learning piece than as an artwork, but a very useful exercise.

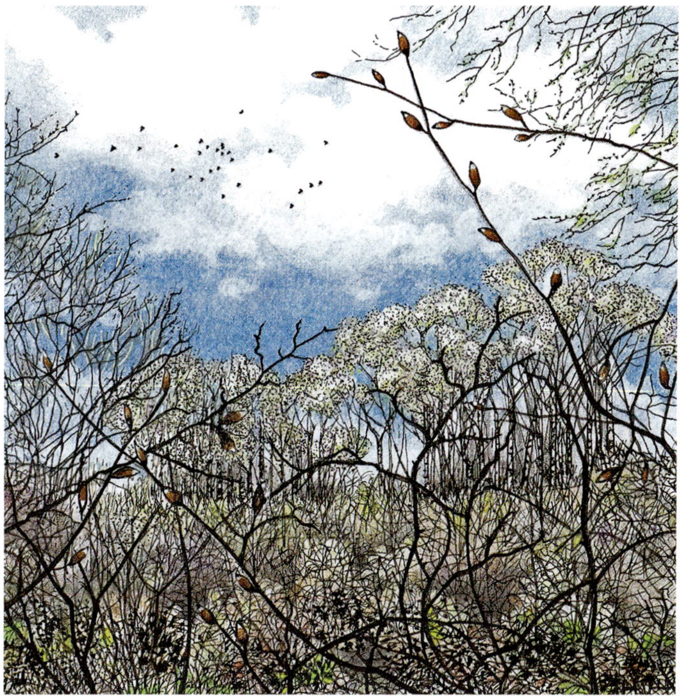

CHAPTER 1

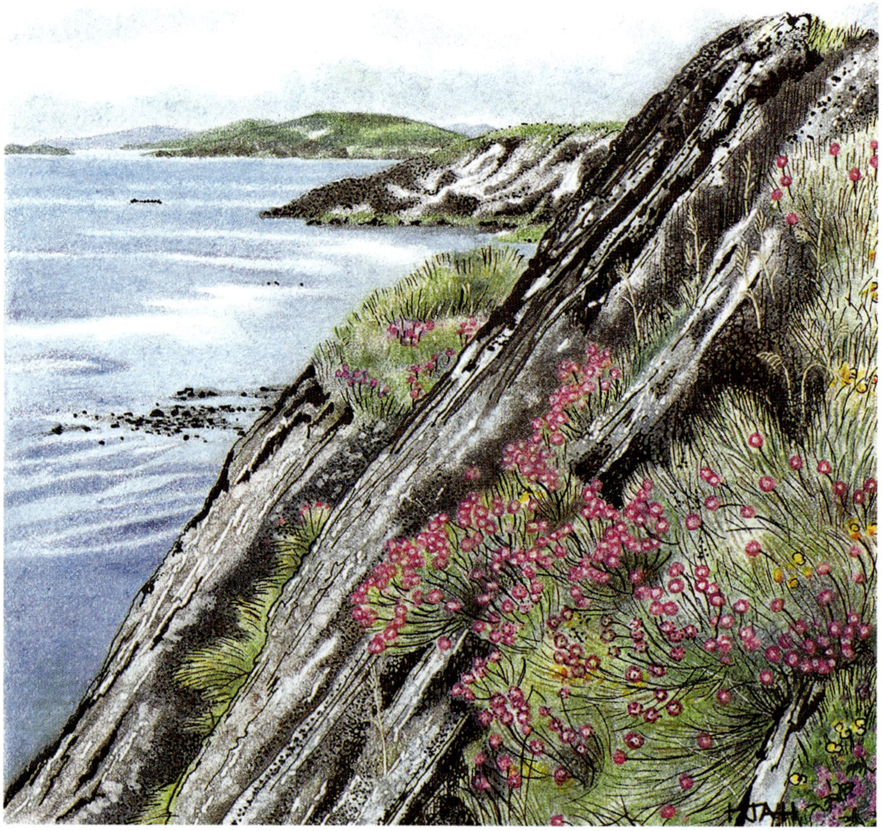

Gigha Shore.

Materials and Equipment

Much of the success of an individual piece of work depends on a happy combination of ink, pencil and paper. When we first take up any art form, we may underestimate the contribution of good materials, but with practice and experience their importance becomes more obvious. For the beginner, expense is often a factor, particularly on discovering the real cost of good art materials. You may not want to invest in something if you are not sure you will continue. I always encourage my students to buy just a few of the best they can afford once they have tried and tested materials in class. A small selection of well-chosen materials will start you off and provide the best chance of a successful result.

It is better to make an informed choice than to impulse buy, as a large set of high-quality coloured pencils can cost as much as a washing machine – a much less enjoyable purchase. Different makes suit different people and styles of working. Some artists continue to experiment with pens, pencils and papers, but many discover their favourites and stick to them, so that surface, texture and palette become an integral part of their style.

DRAWING PENS AND INKS

Ink is a wonderfully expressive medium. It flows, literally and creatively, almost seeming to encourage the artist. I also think it leads to better observation: if you can't rub out, you try harder. Technical pens are available for extremely precise, controlled work, but fine sketching pens of the sort found in most stationery outlets are perfect for combining with coloured pencil. There are pen sizes to suit all requirements, from a 0.03 fine line to a wide brush marker, and new brands are appearing on the market all the time. If their regular, predictable marks do not appeal to you, or you want more 'accidentals', you can use a traditional dip pen or even make your own improvised version. I use artists' fibre-tip drawing pens in my current landscapes, but would not rule out the use of brush pens or traditional dip pens with coloured pencil for an alternative look.

Artists' Sketching Pens

Modern fibre-tip drawing pens have revolutionized the way we draw in ink, introducing a constancy of line that was not available to earlier artists. The result is much more controlled and predictable mark-making, which has its advantages for certain types of work. Many of the fibre-tip drawing pens on the market are made by well-known art brands such as Faber-Castell, Derwent and Staedtler, with others coming from pen manufacturers like Pentel, Pilot, Sakura and Edding. When you are choosing pens, do check whether they are waterproof or not. For line and wash with a watercolour component, waterproof ink is necessary; however, non-waterproof inks can be used with dry, wax-based coloured pencils. Allow the ink sufficient drying time, keep away from any water that might splash, do not wipe the surface with a brush (or your hand) until quite dry, and try not to sneeze!

The question of lightfastness also arises if you want to exhibit and sell your work. Some ink pens, especially coloured ones, are dye based; dyes disperse evenly in the ink binder and are more water soluble, offering greater flow and vibrancy of colour.

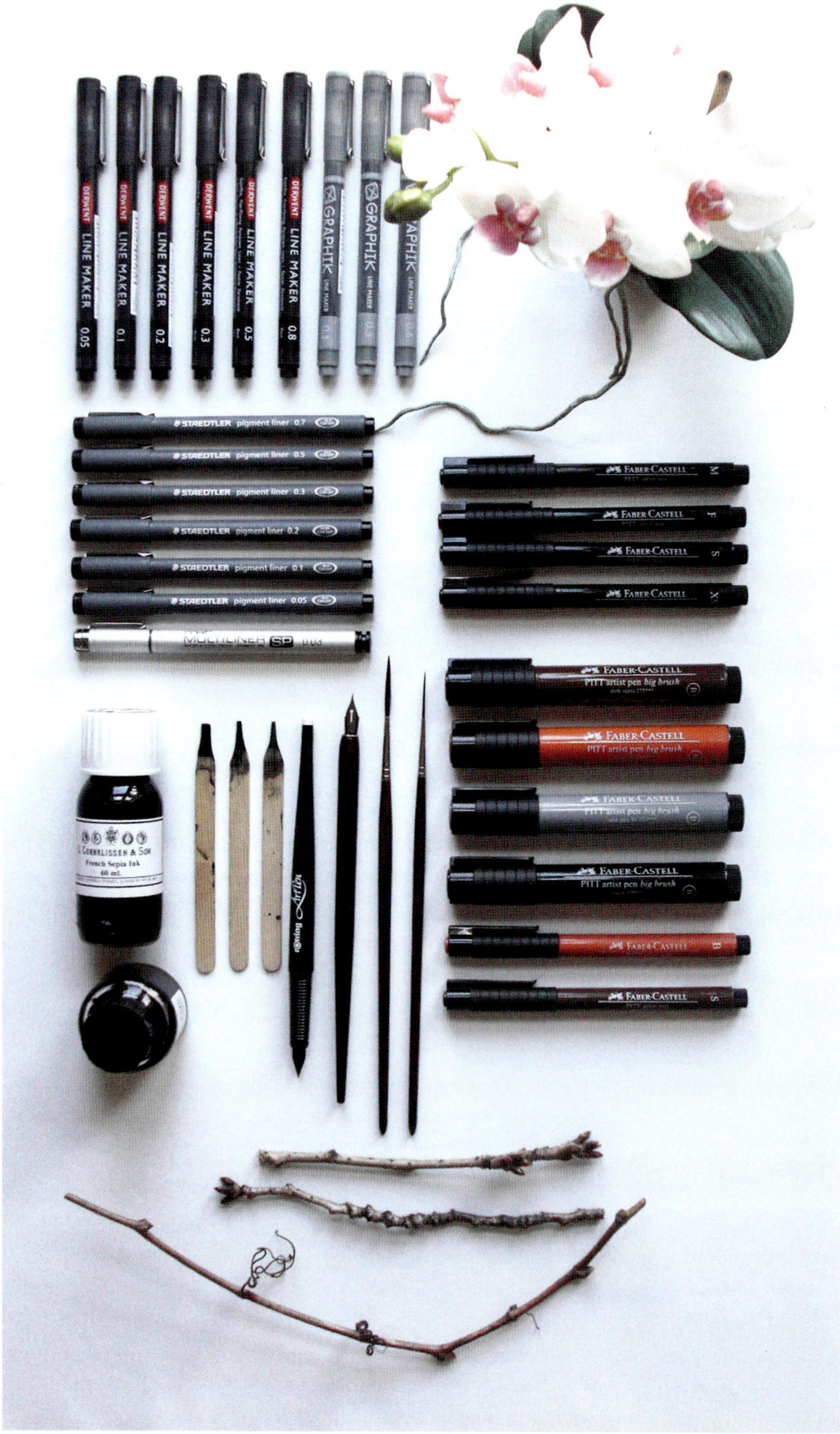

Inks and pens. For this collection of drawing pens and inks, I have limited myself to the ones I use regularly: Staedtler, Copic and Faber-Castell waterproof pens, plus Derwent Linemaker. I have also included some dip pens, a Rotring drawing pen, some home-made lolly-stick pens, a couple of rigger brushes and a few interesting twigs.

However, they are less lightfast and therefore better suited to work that is intended for immediate reproduction, as they scan and print very well. In pigment-based ink, particles are suspended in the ink binder and both flow and vibrancy are reduced. The main advantage of pigment-based ink is that it has much higher lightfastness ratings, so work can be put on display without fear of fading. Most of the black drawing pens you will need for work in ink and coloured pencil are likely to be pigment based, but it is a good idea to be aware of the difference. I shall not attempt to review all the brands currently available, as these change rapidly; instead, I shall limit myself to a few comments and recommendations regarding the ones I use most frequently.

Staedtler Pigment Liner

This fine liner for writing, sketching and drawing is sold in most stationery and art shops. It is available in nine sizes, from 0.8–0.05mm, and has a long metal-encased tip, keeping it firm for use. The ink is pigment based, waterproof, lightfast and indelible, making it an inexpensive and reliable sketching tool.

Copic Black Multiliner

This is a slightly more expensive technical pen with a range of sizes from 0.7 to 0.03. I use the smallest nib size for minute detail such as tiny dots. The ink is pigment based, waterproof and lightfast, with refillable cartridges.

Faber-Castell Pitt Artist Pens

Pitt Artist pens are Indian ink pens with four very different nib sizes: super fine, fine, medium and brush. They are available in sepia, sanguine and a very intense black. The inks are fast drying, waterproof and smudge-proof and can be used with watercolour and other media. I find that the SX does not meet my requirements for extremely fine work, but the set mixes and matches very well with other makes, and the Indian ink has a real richness. I like to use the sepia and sanguine ranges in autumnal landscapes as an addition to black ink.

Derwent Linemaker

Derwent describes these pens as 'superfine, free-flowing fine liners… which will not move once dry.' They contain permanent, fast-drying pigment ink, but I cannot find any references to them being completely waterproof. I use them because they flow beautifully, but I do proceed with caution, making sure that everything is perfectly dry before adding coloured pencil. The graphite-coloured range is useful for some softer mark-making in winter landscapes.

There are, of course, many other brands of sketching pen, and you can experiment once you have decided on your style and the sort of paper that you prefer. Finer nibs are available if you explore the technical pen ranges, but these require a very smooth paper and can scuff the surface if it is too textured. Brush pens, which bridge the gap between pen and paint, can be used if you want to pursue a less detailed, more freestyle approach. Either should be compatible with coloured pencil.

Dip Pens

Dip pens are an ancient but exciting way of applying ink. They are much more artist-dependent than fibre-tip drawing pens (although some might say they take on a life of their own). The difference lies in the fact that they have no ink barrel and consequently no measured flow. The consistent, identical ink marks delivered by the fibre-tip pen cannot be replicated, because each act of dipping will inevitably alter the thickness and quality of the deposited line. If you are unlucky, dip pens can deliver an unexpected blot that you will have to fashion into something. During my time as a printmaker I became familiar with 'accidentals': unplanned happenings on the surface of the metal, which add to the drama. Working with a dip pen takes practice and will probably deliver surprises. Nevertheless, the results look spontaneous and full of life and could work very well with rich coloured pencil.

Dip pens come in different sizes with a range of nibs, from the small and delicate to the huge wooden pens used in some Japanese painting. I shall not be using the dip-pen method in this book, but I am aware that some readers might like to work in a different way, using the same combination of media. There is no reason why you should not experiment to the full.

Types of Drawing Ink

The waterproof, pigment-based sketching pens I have described are the simplest and most readily available type of ink for the methods described in this book. I use these most of the time, but also like the rich Indian ink versions from Faber-Castell. If you are working with a dip pen, Winsor and Newton and Jackson's both produce an Indian ink with a base of high-quality shellac medium and purified water. These can be diluted before use to achieve washes and subtle tones, preferably with distilled water,

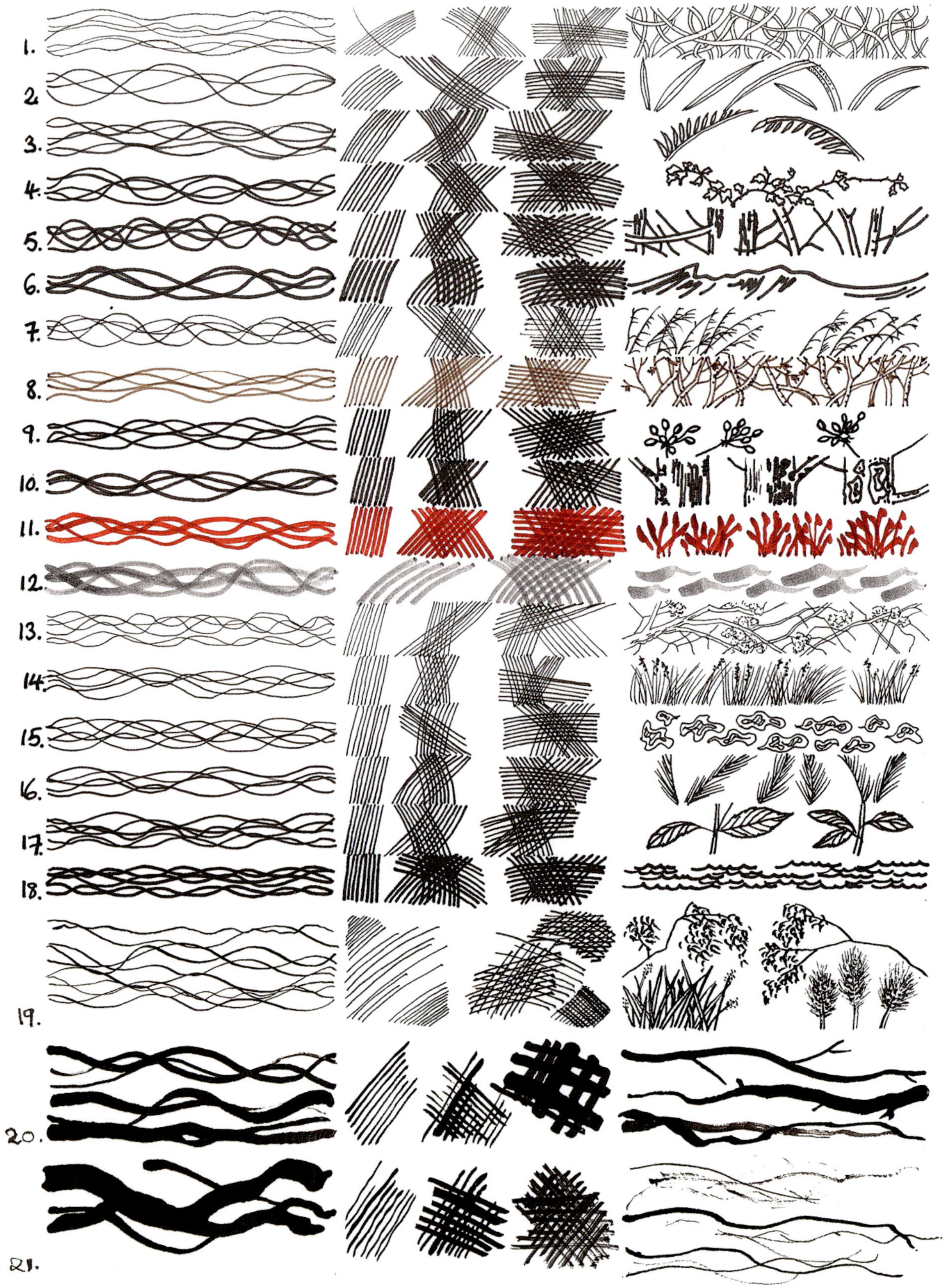

The inked line.
1: Copic Multiliner 0.03. **2–6:** Staedtler Pigment Liner 0.05, 0.1, 0.3, 0.5 and 0.7. **7–12:** Faber-Castell Pitt Pens SX, S, F, M and B and Big Brush (including examples in Dark Sepia, Sanguine and Cold Grey IV. **13–18:** Derwent Line Maker 0.05, 0.1, 0.2, 0.3, 0.5 and 0.8. **19–21:** Dip pens, home-made stick pens and twigs with Indian ink.

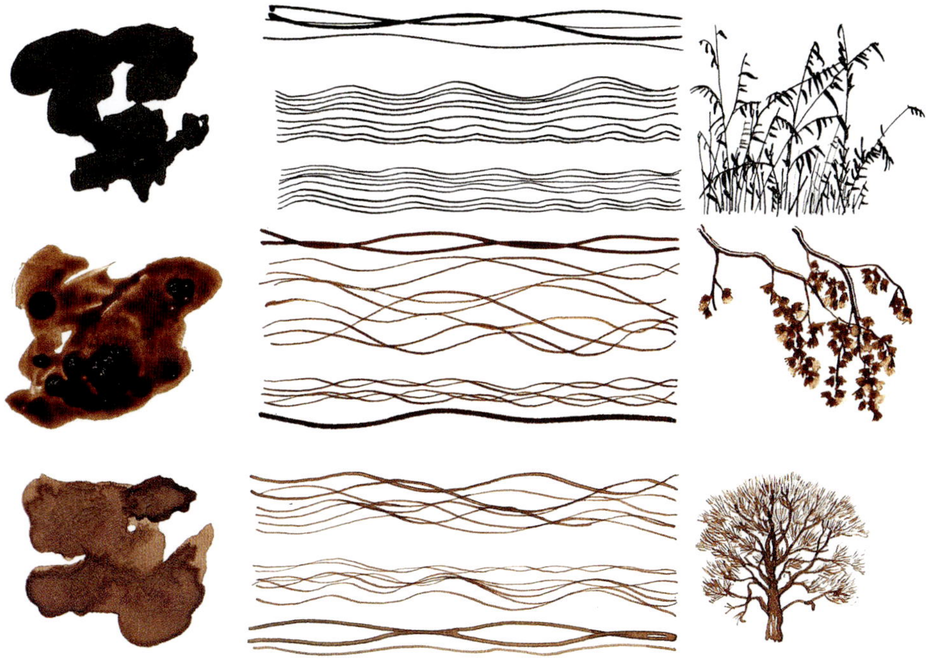

Dip-pen inks. **1:** Winsor and Newton waterproof Indian ink. **2:** Cornelissen 'French Sepia' ink. **3:** Daniel Smith 'Walnut' ink. The central panels demonstrate lines drawn with medium and fine dip pens and with a Jakar ruling pen. The small images show the inks on Strathmore Bristol board. All will combine with coloured pencil to give an unusual look.

as tap water may cause the dye to separate from the binder. When dry, the ink forms a water-resistant film that will work with coloured pencil. Do check that the Indian ink you buy is water-resistant as water-soluble versions are also available.

One of my personal favourites is Cornelissen's 'French Sepia' ink. This is a traditional shellac ink with a transparent satin finish, which perfectly complements autumnal coloured-pencil shades. This is a very unusual mix of the two media, ideal for creating a rustic look reminiscent of Samuel Palmer. Another speciality ink is Daniel Smith's 'Walnut', a transparent, finely pigmented ink made from walnut husks. It flows easily, and its warm sepia colour gives an antique look.

Home-Made Pens

Having pushed back the boundaries a bit, you could be truly adventurous and create your own pens. If you want to combine ink and coloured pencil and progress through freestyle towards abstraction, try improvising with carved lollipop sticks, coffee stirrers, cocktail sticks and twigs in different shapes and sizes. Wood tends to absorb the ink and will produce quite an extended and variable line. However, if these wilder excesses of mark-making are not for you, there will be plenty of guidance to follow on working in ink in a more traditional way.

COLOURED PENCILS

It is no coincidence that pencil manufacturers developed in areas where wood was plentiful and of good quality. Historically, Germany, Switzerland and the Lake District in the UK all became centres of excellence in the production of pencils and coloured pencils. Artists' coloured pencils are now made by a wide range of manufacturers employing high quality pigments and are used by artists, illustrators and designers worldwide. As with most art materials, better quality results in superior performance, and this is usually the result of a higher pigment concentration combined with durable wood casing. The best pigments in the world will be unsatisfactory inside inferior wood casings that split and break when sharpened. Student coloured-pencil ranges are more affordable, but they do have a weaker pigment concentration. They are fine for school use but may be disappointing if you are hoping for powerful colour that is reliably lightfast. I always recommend buying a smaller number of artists' pencils in colours that will mix and match rather than a larger selection of cheap ones.

Professional coloured pencils are designed to blend, so you can create your own mixes as you would with paint. You may prefer to choose a palette of colours that suits the type of work you do, such as landscape, botanical or animal studies, selecting pencils from different ranges. A complete set of colours from one manufacturer will inevitably include shades you rarely use, so if you do specialize, this may be a better option.

Different makes and collections of artists' coloured pencils vary in their consistency and in their use. Extremely hard pencils such as Prismacolor 'Verithin' are good for precise work, ultra-fine lines and outlining. Hard pencils such as Derwent 'Artists' suit fine detail and light coverage but also layer well, building up to very rich colour if required. Medium ranges such as Faber-Castell 'Polychromos' and Derwent 'Procolour' are excellent all-purpose pencils and will suit most needs. Caran D'Ache's 'Pablo' range has a wonderful selection of subtle, 'in-between' shades, and their award-winning 'Luminance' collection is the most lightfast available. Softer pencils with a waxier consistency such as Derwent 'Coloursoft' and the American brand Prismacolor 'Premier' can be used as a pop of colour or a final, rich layer. They burnish well and will produce a good shine.

As different collections of pencils suit different stages, you might like to build up a landscape and flower collection that includes various makes. The main manufacturers all have companion ranges of watercolour pencils: Faber-Castell's 'Albrecht Dürer', Derwent's 'Watercolour Pencils' and Caran D'Ache's 'Museum Aquarelle'. If you have these already, they can be used dry, but do keep away from water. One drip can make a lot of difference!

I have noted some of my personal favourites after each section, but you will also discover your own. The pencil collections are introduced in order, from the hardest to the softest. I should add that as well as being a tutor, I am a self-confessed coloured pencil addict; however, I have not tried every make on the market, so will confine myself to the ones I know and use. Please do not feel that you need them all (although you may want them all). Start with a few or one set, and build up as and when you can.

Prismacolor 'Verithin' (very hard)

The name says it all: made by the American firm Prismacolor, and at the other end of the scale from their 'Premier' collection, these slim pencils have a thin, hard wax core. They are not suitable for layering or covering large areas, but they deliver very sharp detail when required, with plenty of pigment. I use them mainly for minute detail, occasional outlining, and for sharpening edges in botanical work. 'Verithin' are not all-purpose pencils and the colour range is limited to thirty-six, but some shades may be a useful addition for specific tasks.

05 Indigo Blue
21 Carmine Red
34 Pine Green
55 Scarlet Red
62 Sienna Brown
75 Violet

Derwent 'Artists' (hard)

These are quite hard and are the original Derwent coloured pencils produced in their Keswick factory, which now houses the modernized Pencil Museum. Unsurprisingly, they have a wonderful range of subtle landscape colours with names such as Teal Blue, Spruce Green, Storm Grey and Fell Mist, which are ideal for recreating the surrounding countryside. They may appear pale at first, but it is possible to build up considerable depth of colour with careful layering. I have chosen some of their muted shades that suit the British landscape like no other collection, many of which also appear in their 'Procolour' series.

0400 Primrose Yellow
0410 Champagne
1630 Ash Rose
2120 Grape
2210 Heather
2410 Slate Violet
2700 Blue Violet Lake
2830 Teal Blue
3610 Ash Blue
4120 Fir Green
5010 Green Grey
5130 Chartreuse
5140 Green Earth
5150 Parchment
5310 Felt Grey
6440 Light Rust
6480 Taupe
6490 Bistre
6910 Storm Grey
7110 Fell Mist

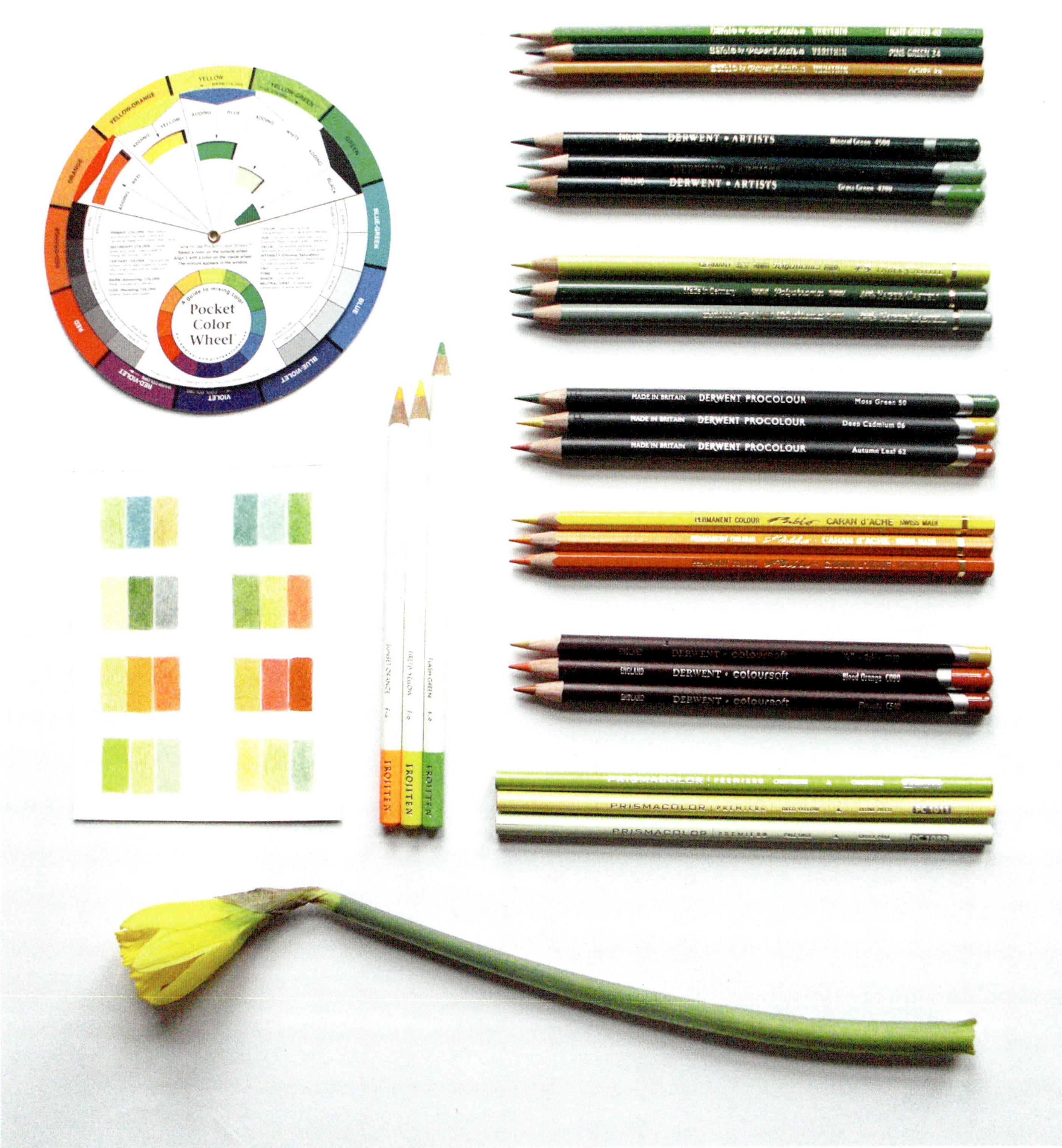

Coloured pencil ranges. From top to bottom in order of hardness, a selection of greens, yellows and oranges: Prismacolor 'Verithin', Derwent 'Artists', Faber-Castell 'Polychromos', Derwent 'Procolour', Caran D'Ache 'Pablo', Derwent 'Coloursoft' and Prismacolor 'Premier'. *Left*: 'Irojiten' Tombow Fluorescents. Note the increasing strength and waxiness, as shown on the colour chart.

Faber-Castell 'Polychromos' (Medium Hard)

Made in Bavaria by a firm established in 1761, these excellent quality pencils are medium hard, very easy to use, and a good choice for a first collection. They have some good greens for botanical and landscape work and an excellent range of warm and cool greys from I to VI.

205 Cadmium Yellow Lemon
107 Cadmium Yellow
113 Orange Glaze
118 Scarlet Red
226 Alizarin Crimson
133 Magenta
119 Light Magenta
249 Mauve
157 Dark Indigo
120 Ultramarine
140 Light Ultramarine
146 Sky Blue
167 Permanent Green Olive
267 Pine Green
278 Chrome Oxide Green
165 Juniper Green
173 Olive Green Yellowish
268 Green Gold
170 May Green
168 Earth Green Yellowish
174 Chromium Green Opaque
172 Green Earth
194 Red Violet
187 Burnt Ochre
183 Light Yellow Ochre
182 Brown Ochre
280 Burnt Umber
283 Burnt Sienna
177 Walnut Brown
175 Dark Sepia
272 Warm Grey III
271 Warm Grey II
231 Cold Grey II
233 Cold Grey IV

Derwent 'Procolour' (Medium Hard)

Derwent developed 'Procolour' after the original 'Artists' and 'Coloursoft' ranges. They are between soft and hard, easy to use and have a silky feel. They are a good starter collection with the added advantage of Derwent's subtle landscape colours. Almost all the colours are also available in the Artists range, but a few (below) are new.

12 Primary Red
20 Cerise Pink
44 Racing Green
51 Foliage Green
65 Nutmeg
69 Felt Grey

Caran D'Ache 'Pablo' (Medium Hard)

These coloured pencils are also medium hard with a slightly pastel-like texture. Made in Switzerland, they have a beautiful range of colours, especially for botanical artists. For landscape work I like their 'in-between' shades such as Brownish Orange, Khaki Green, Olive Grey and Greyish Green.

025 Green Ochre
033 Golden Ochre
031 Orangeish Yellow
040 Reddish Orange
063 English Red
043 Brownish Orange
089 Dark Carmine
493 Granite Rose
091 Light Purple
350 Purplish Red
100 Purple Violet
131 Periwinkle Blue
159 Prussian Blue
169 Marine Blue
145 Bluish Grey
155 Blue Jeans
151 Pastel Blue
470 Spring Green
015 Olive Yellow
016 Khaki Green
225 Moss Green
018 Olive Grey
249 Olive
039 Olive Brown
019 Olive Black
065 Russet
053 Hazel
055 Cinnamon
047 Bistre
405 Cocoa
045 Vandyke Brown
404 Brownish Beige
006 Mouse Grey

Tombow 'Irojiten' (Medium Hard)

These exquisitely packaged Japanese pencils resemble a little set of nine volumes. They are medium hard with a silky feel, and are easy on the paper. Unusually they are arranged by tone: Pale Tone 1 and 11, Deep Tone 1 and 11, Vivid Tone, Light Greyish Tone, Very Pale Tone, Dull Tone and Fluorescence. I find the 'Light Greyish Tone' selection very useful for grasses, especially Fawn, Cork, Sallow, Wax Yellow and Sea Fog. The 'Deep Tone' colours such as Crimson, Autumn Leaf, Plum and Maroon are a rich addition to an autumn palette. I sometimes use the Fluorescents to add a powerful beam of sunlight or dazzling highlights. 'Irojiten' are more of a treat than an all-purpose collection, and certainly look very elegant on the shelf.

Caran D'Ache 'Luminance 6901' (Medium Soft)

This more recent range of pencils by Caran D'Ache has a very high lightfast rating. 'Luminance' pencils are award-winning, intensely saturated coloured pencils designed for fine artists and illustrators. They have a smooth, creamy feel, virtually unbreakable leads, and layer well with no waxy deposit. They share some of the colours found in the 'Pablo' range, but have many new ones, with some excellent 'in-between' shades and neutrals.

Derwent 'Coloursoft' (soft)

This range is Derwent's softest, with a rich, creamy consistency. In landscape work I prefer to use them as a top layer or for adding a pop of colour, often on quite small areas. Despite their consistency, 'Coloursoft' pencils still sharpen to a very fine point. Their richness adds a powerful final layer of colour, and they can be used effectively as a burnisher. Most of the colours are not in the 'Artists' or 'Procolour' ranges, and there are some good additions for landscape. They also have excellent autumn berry colours such as Loganberry, Blackberry and Cranberry.

020 Acid Yellow
090 Blood Orange
130 Deep Red
150 Cranberry
160 Loganberry
220 Grey Lavender
230 Pale Lavender
280 Blackberry
360 Cloud Blue
390 Grey Green
450 Yellow Green
480 Lincoln Green
500 Lichen Green
540 Pimento
550 Ginger
580 Light Sand
610 Dark Terracotta
660 Persian Grey
690 Steel Grey

Prismacolor 'Premier' (soft)

The American 'Premier' range pencils by Prismacolor have a very soft, creamy consistency. They are favourites with botanical artists because some of their unusual colours, such as Ginger Root, Artichoke, Chartreuse and Limepeel, are exactly right for certain plants. In addition to these, I use the berry shades – Black Raspberry, Black Cherry and Black Grape – and the sky shades Powder Blue and Cloud Blue, and find Greyed Lavender and Parma Violet excellent for a final bit of shadow on grassland. As with other richly pigmented, waxy pencils I tend to use them as a last layer or to add vivid splashes of colour.

1084 Ginger Root
1098 Artichoke
1034 Goldenrod
1032 Pumpkin Orange
1019 Rosy Beige
1080 Beige Sienna
1030 Raspberry
1095 Black Raspberry
1078 Black Cherry
1026 Greyed Lavender
1008 Parma Violet
996 Black Grape
1087 Powder Blue
1023 Cloud Blue
289 Grey Green Light
1089 Pale Sage
989 Chartreuse
1005 Limepeel
1020 Celadon Green
1021 Jade Green

If this dazzling selection of what is available has left you bewildered, go back to basics. Derwent 'Procolour' and Faber-Castell 'Polychromos' are good starter sets, suitable for most of the work you will be doing. You can always add individual colours when you need them, and move on to other collections as you progress.

PAPERS

Hot Pressed Watercolour Paper

In general, the more texture a paper has, the more likely it is that a first layer of coloured pencil will skim its surface rather than penetrate the fibres. Some American styles of coloured pencil work make use of this grainy look, in which the colour surface resembles aquatint on an etching. If you want a finer, closer look with more layers and complete coverage, it is better to select a smooth surface. Hot pressed watercolour paper is one possibility, but I do recommend trying out a sample before committing yourself. Check its smoothness, and experiment with the coloured pencils you intend to use. The composition of the paper, the nature of the pigment, and even the angle at which you hold the pencil will all affect the coverage and the result. There are many different makes and thicknesses of paper, and in addition, manufacturers change their processes; I used Fabriano 5 hot pressed paper for most of my small, square landscapes, but have found their newer version disappointing.

Bristol Board

I now prefer to use Bristol board, and favour Strathmore series 300 or series 400. They are different weights but both give reliably good results with coloured pencil, and I recommend them to my students to be sure of success. Both are high-quality, multi-ply Bristol board, available in two finishes. The smooth finish is harder and excellent for both fine line drawings using pen and ink and for coloured pencil work, making it the ideal choice for landscape in ink and coloured pencil. The vellum finish has slightly more 'tooth' (texture) and can be used for pencil, charcoal and pastel as well as coloured pencil. Other

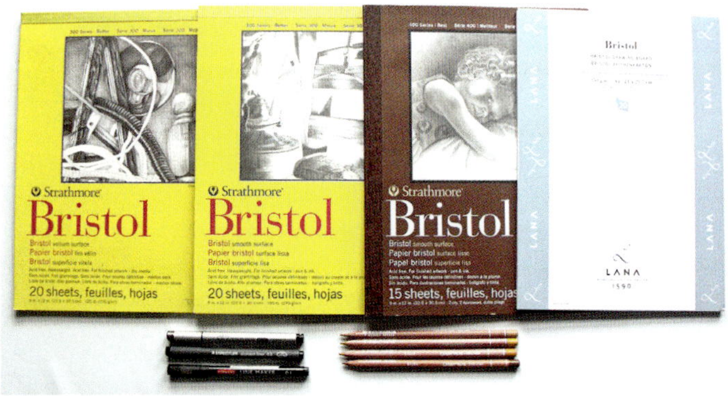

Paper selection. These are the papers that I find most suit my way of working in ink and coloured pencil, but do try others until you find your own favourites: Strathmore Bristol Board Series 300 smooth and vellum, Series 400 for a heavier weight, and Lana ultra-white satin finish for light coverage or predominantly ink subjects.

manufacturers producing Bristol board are Canson, Winsor and Newton, Frisk and Daler-Rowney.

It is worth trying out various makes and colours of Bristol board, as you may find that different types suit different subjects. The shades of white and the surfaces do vary. They are suitable for coloured pencil but also for other media, so are not all identical. I bought some French 'Lana' Bristol board for its pure whiteness, but found the surface too smooth for waxier pencils, which had a tendency to slide. However, it was perfect for a series of snow images in which the ink predominated. It flowed very smoothly across the surface, and I used both Staedtler waterproof sketching pens and Derwent 'Linemaker' in graphite. The coloured pencil work was minimal, so I successfully added touches of Derwent 'Artists' hard pencils in muted shades – and the snow was brilliantly white.

Tracing Paper

You may need to trace if you have a successful preliminary drawing and want to transfer it before you start working. Even with simple art materials such as tracing paper, quality affects performance. Cheap tracing paper may be difficult to see through and tear easily. Look for a light weight (about 60gm, varying according to the make) as thicker papers from 90gm upwards may not show the image as clearly. Goldline and Daler-Rowney are both suitable, and various art suppliers produce their own versions.

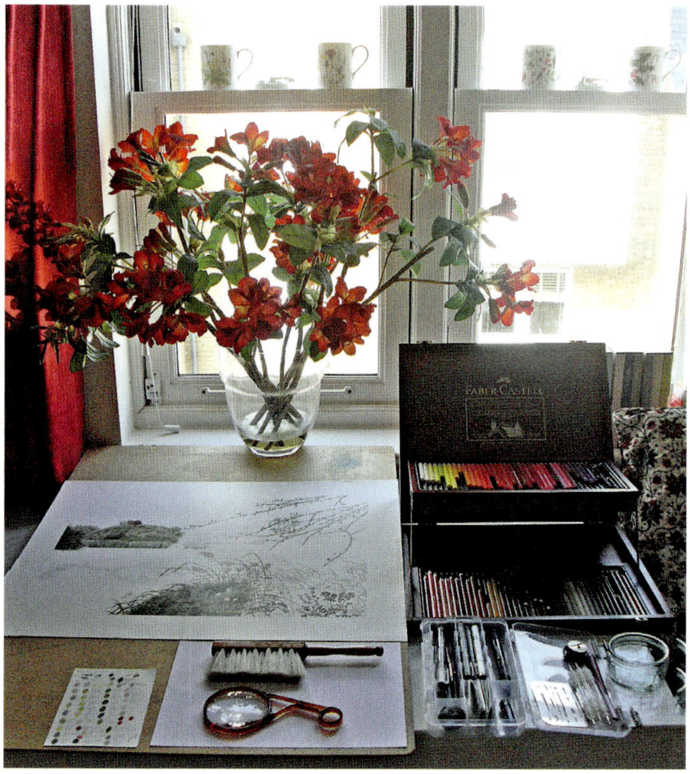

Studio space. It is not necessary to have a vast studio. Mine is now quite small but comfortable, with north light and enough space for a drawing board, pens and pencils. I keep the pencils I have chosen for a current piece of work alongside, in colour-coded jamjars for easy access.

OTHER EQUIPMENT

Finding Your Space

It is not necessary to have a fully equipped studio to work in ink and coloured pencil. In my studio I have a large drawing board to keep the paper flat, especially if I am working on a sizeable image. I slant it slightly, often just resting it on a windowsill or a rolled towel. A lamp with a magnifier and daylight bulb fitting is useful for detailed work but not essential. I have pens, coloured pencils and reference books to hand, but generally keep things uncomplicated. Ink and coloured pencil work is quite user friendly; if you can find a table somewhere where you can leave your work, it lends itself to an hour or two of activity as well as hours of concentrated effort. You can return refreshed and it will still look the same. If you want to do preliminary sketches and colour matches outdoors, a few pens, a putty rubber and a roll of selected coloured pencils will suffice.

Pencil Sharpeners

I have tried out many types of pencil sharpener and come to some simple conclusions: it is not the length of the point that matters but its sharpness, and the blade is crucial to this. If pencils break in a sharpener, it may be for various reasons: the pencil may have been dropped and the core broken in places; the blade may need replacing; or inferior wood has been used for the casing. The latter happens sometimes if the pencils are produced cheaply, or if a manufacturer changes the source of the wood or its type. Furthermore it is easy to ruin your pencils and think that a sharpener is useless when it simply needs a change of blade. These are mostly standard and can be replaced with the help of a small screwdriver.

Table pencil sharpeners look professional and produce an impressively long point, but tend to eat pencils, which can prove expensive. Electric versions save time but positively devour them. Once the very fine point has been worn down even slightly with use, you may feel the need to resharpen them, thus eating away even more of the pencil. Some artists prefer a scalpel blade to revive the point. A few table sharpeners have metal claws that create notches on the barrel of the pencil, so choose a rubber version if you want to avoid this.

I have been most impressed by a small, inexpensive, solid brass sharpener made by Möbius and Ruppert. It accommodates two pencil sizes, is portable in a pocket, and can be purchased with a set of spare blades. It delivers a very sharp point without eating up much pencil, and I have found it perfect for all my requirements. Other makes are available, but remember that none of them will work properly with a blunted blade!

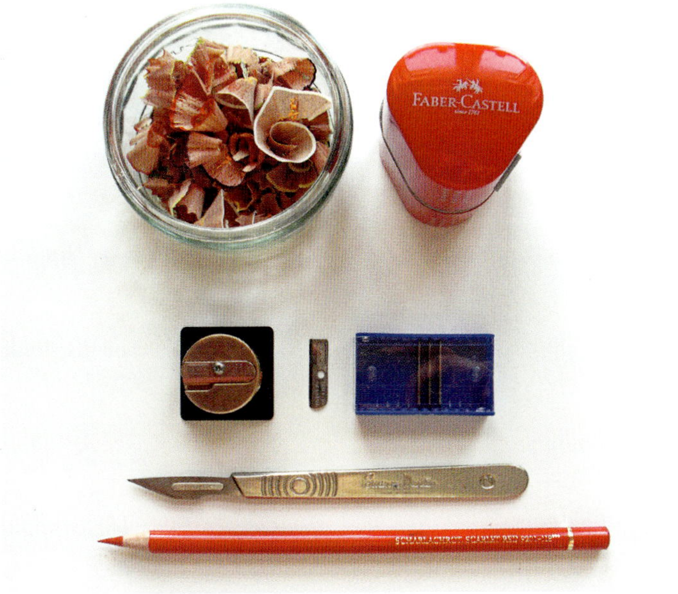

Sharpeners and blades. There are many varieties of sharpener, all of which will need replacement blades for continued efficiency. Some artists swear by a scalpel blade, but my favourite is Möbius and Ruppert's circular, two-holed brass sharpener, which produces a very sharp point (shown here) without wasteful length.

Erasers

A putty rubber and a plastic (standard) rubber are important basics for your toolkit. A plastic rubber is useful at the sketching stage, but once you have started using your chosen paper, a much gentler, malleable putty rubber is essential. Putty rubbers are designed to be rolled, squashed and manipulated into useful shapes for mark-making and erasing. They seem to eat dirt as if by magic: you can remove a lot of graphite, then you squeeze and squash the rubber and it comes out clean again. Do this as soon as you get it: remove the plastic and don't try to use it in its oblong form. It can be rolled into a sausage shape to lighten graphite marks and can then be used to shape and lift out coloured pencil work.

An eraser shield, sold in most art shops, will allow you to tidy edges with a putty rubber without damaging any colour. Most also include a selection of cut-out shapes and lines for erasing small areas. Some manufacturers, such as Tombow, produce pens with a tiny eraser shape at the end for taking out shapes and lines. I am very fond of my Derwent battery eraser, which buzzes into action and lifts out little highlights or wider patches of light at the press of a button. If any marks seem too shaped, the edges can be softened with a putty rubber. The kit includes replacement erasers that slot in easily, and the tips can be cleaned by running them along fine sandpaper.

Frisket

I always tell my beginners that 'Frisket' is their friend. This low adhesion film is generally used for stencilling and airbrushing, but is also invaluable for lifting out large or small areas of coloured pencil. It can be used to correct mistakes, remove colours or to lift out creatively. It is available in gloss or matt; the gloss makes it easier to see where you are working, but the matt accepts pencil more readily.

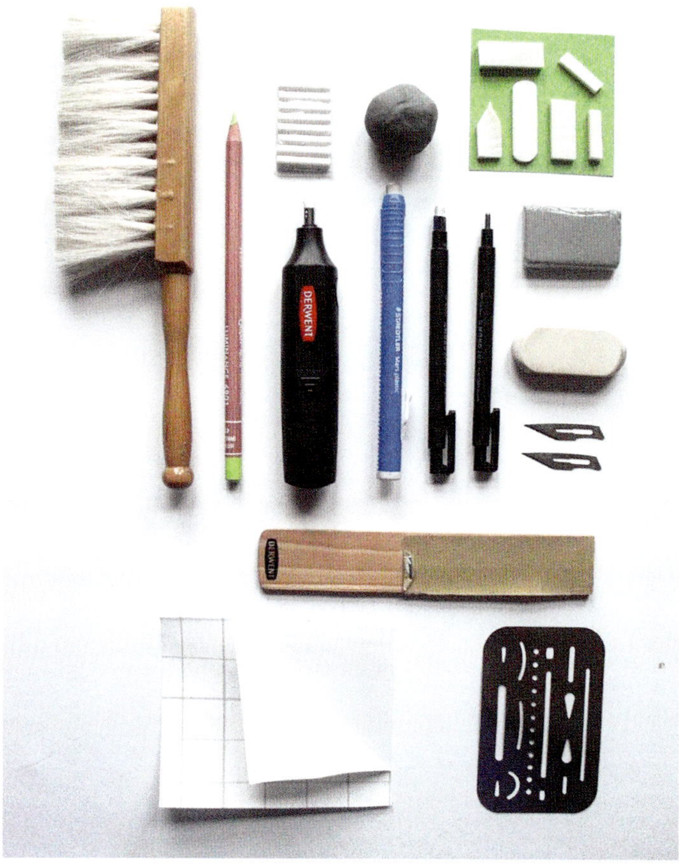

Erasers and Frisket. This collection for erasing and lifting out includes a soft brush; a coloured pencil for use with Frisket; a Derwent battery eraser with spares and sandpaper block; assorted small, pen-style rubbers; a grey putty rubber (and used squashy version); a standard plastic eraser and chopped pieces; scalpel blades; an eraser shield, and squared Frisket showing the peel-away covering.

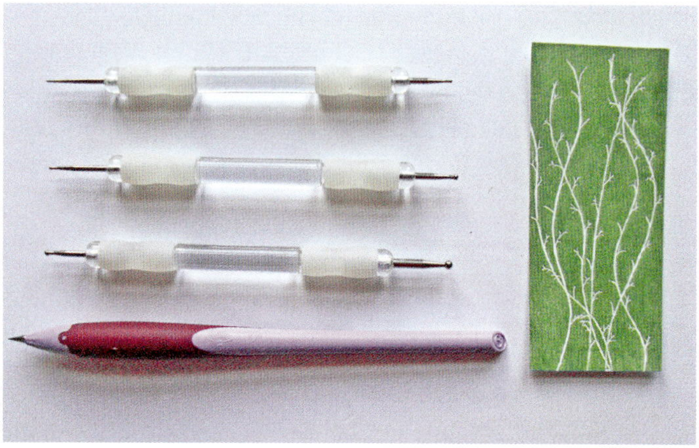

Embossing tools. This picture shows a set of three standard embossers, all double-ended and increasing in size. The fourth is a fine pergamano tool suitable for very thin lines. For the stylized drawing I used a wide embosser for the main stem, a smaller one for the branches, and the pergamano tool for the fine twigs.

Embossing Tools

These tools are mainly associated with crafting and pergamano or parchment embossing, and can be obtained from their specialist suppliers. I have one fine line version and a pack of assorted plastic embossers with circular metal tips that I found in a local craft shop. It is worth looking around in hobby shops and online as packaged sets do turn up. Bear in mind that you will be embossing paper, and not leather or parchment, so avoid anything that is likely to be too sharp or to tear the surface. You can create your own embossing tools; a 'dead' biro will make indentations, but avoid anything that will damage the paper, and always do a test.

Blenders and Burnishers

A blender is a soft, colourless pencil made from the binder used for coloured pencils. It helps blend two or more colours to create a new one, mixing and smoothing them so that individual strokes and hard edges are softened.

A burnisher is also a colourless pencil but is harder. It is used as a final process over layers of pigment to create a rich, polished shine. Burnishing pushes the pigment into the paper and leaves a very well blended, almost photographic finish. It makes the colours look brighter and can give an image a polished or reflective look by sealing it with a heavy layer of colourless wax. It should be applied at the end, as a burnished area will not accept any more layers of colour. Derwent, Lyra, Koh I Noor, Caran D'Ache and Staedtler all produce coloured pencil blenders and/or burnishers.

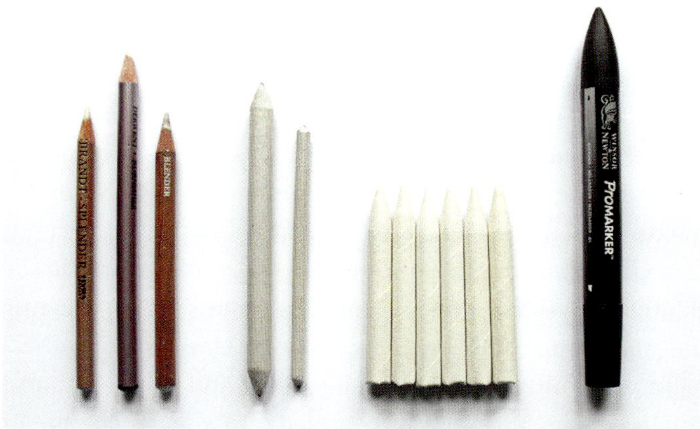

Blenders, burnishers and tortillions. This collection shows (*from left to right*) two different makes of blender, a burnisher, paper stumps, a pack of tortillions and an alcohol-based blender by Winsor & Newton.

Travel kit. I take a sketchbook, a roll of likely coloured pencils, a few drawing pens, a rubber, sharpener and embosser, plus a mini paintbox and retractable brush with eight essential mixers: two yellows, reds, blues and browns. This gives me scope for pencil or pen and watercolour sketches. The mini magnifier goes round my neck. All very portable and adaptable.

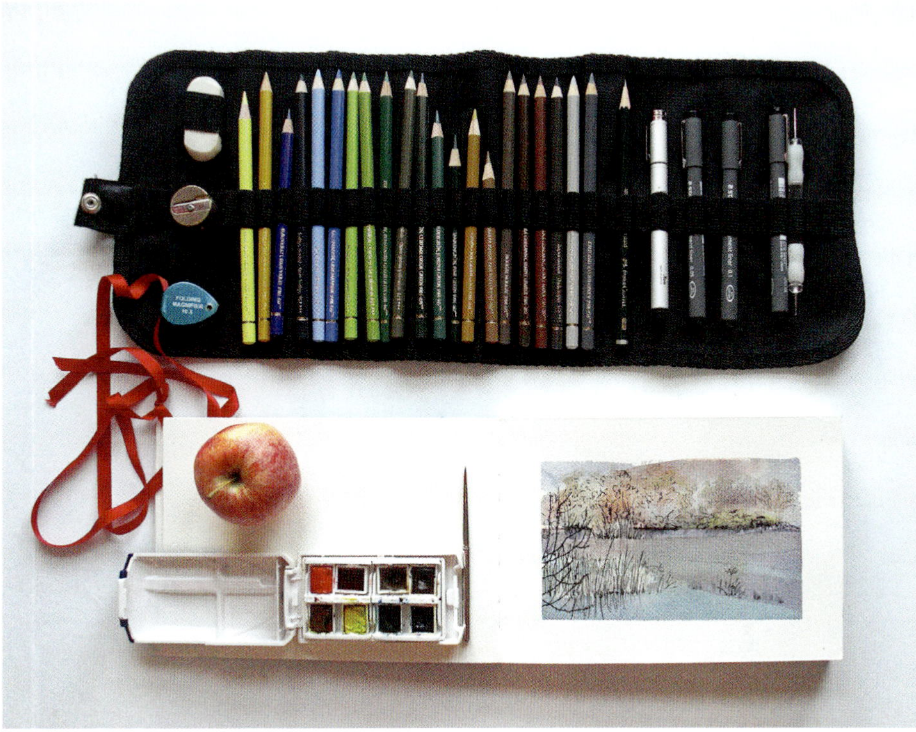

Tortillions and Paper Stumps

A tortillion is a hollow tube of tightly rolled paper that can be used to blend charcoal, pastel or pencil drawings. It is used in much the same way as a paper stump, but is slightly sharper at the tip and is therefore less suitable for blending large areas.

A paper stump is similar but has a rounded end, and was specifically designed for use with coloured pencils. It can be cleaned and sharpened with sandpaper, a knife or even a large pencil sharpener for precision, and is used for gently blending colours and softening edges. Both will move colour on the surface without pressing into or flattening the fibres of the paper. The result is subtle and misty, ideal for clouds, water and weather. Both are available in a range of sizes from art shops, craft shops and pencil manufacturers.

Sandpaper

Fine sandpaper is a useful extra. It can be used for cleaning paper stumps and battery erasers, and will create a point on a difficult-to-sharpen pencil. Faber-Castell and Derwent both make neat little sandpaper blocks that will fit in your travelling kit.

THE NEXT STAGE

Once you have chosen pens, paper, coloured pencils and sundries, you are ready to progress to the next stage. Do not worry if your collection is quite small, as you can still make a start and see how the materials work for you. Discovering which pencils have the consistency that best suits your work, which colours you use most frequently, and which ones you would like next are all part of the learning process. The following chapter will deal with that very important matter, the subject: where to find it, what to do with it and how to make it your own.

CHAPTER 2

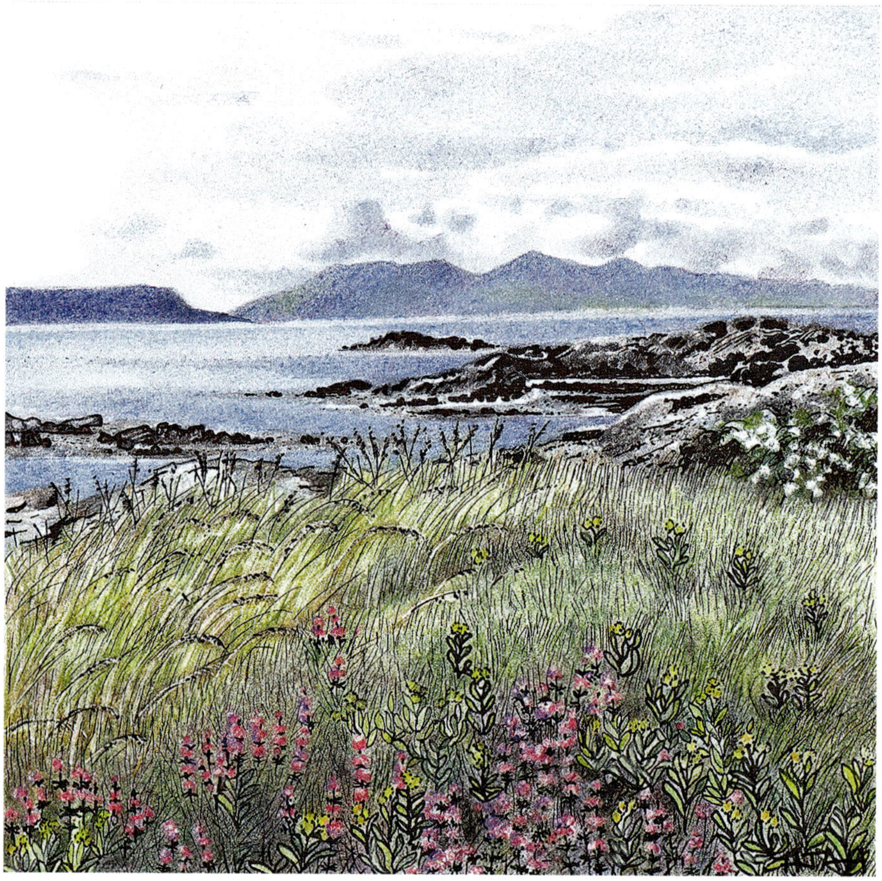

Western Isles.

Translating the Landscape

WALKING THE TERRITORY

Interpretation, Translation and the Importance of Memory

When we draw or paint, we try to represent what we see to the best of our ability. Most of us are not aiming at exact reproduction, even if we could achieve it. Experienced or not, we *interpret* what we see, making use of our personal style, colour preferences and the skill with which we handle our chosen medium. In the process, we create something unique that could only have been done by us.

Owning Your Work

When I first started to tutor courses in landscape in ink and coloured pencil, I made the decision not to use a step-by-step, follow-the-teacher approach throughout the course, with all students working from the same image. I felt that this method worked better for a medium such as watercolour, in which guidance through a series of stages can be a helpful part of the learning process. Although it is inevitably based on the tutor's own interpretation and timing, it teaches transferable skills and delivers a finished piece of work. Having worked on numerous pieces of my own, I realized that there was no definitive, step-by-step way of working in ink and coloured pencil. Each image needed a different approach and method of construction; there were also few, if any, precedents for this combination of media. There were no rules that could be established, beyond the basic guidelines for holding the pencil, creating ellipses, layering and so on.

I start with a few short, step-by-step exercises to give beginners a guided approach to working in two media. Once they have tried these out, I teach a way of looking, introducing the materials and practising the techniques, encouraging students to use them to interpret what they see. I came to this conclusion principally after observing my first few groups, and delighting in the diversity of the images that appeared when they had more individual freedom. Over the course of a week's workshop, as they completed two or three images, strongly personal styles started to emerge, all refreshingly different. Until then I had relied on my own way of depicting the landscape as a guide, and it was fascinating to see other possibilities appearing in the work of my enterprising students.

I noticed how they would bring their experience of working in other creative areas to their interpretations. Those without much experience of pen and paint often found it easier to resist the tendency to draw and colour in. Some chose images that were more design than landscape, producing a tapestry of colour and ink. Potters, stained-glass artists and printmakers all had a different take on the landscape, drawing on their own artistic experience in combining the two media. A student who had worked in textiles instinctively used a combination of ink strokes and threads of colour so that her bluebell wood resembled embroidery. I saw this individuality as a fruitful starting point.

The techniques involved in the application of ink and coloured pencil to paper are relatively easy and do not require lengthy practice. However, this does not mean that the work itself is easy: the simpler the techniques, the more their success lies in the vision and interpretation that the artist brings to the picture. Our work is inevitably an expression of ourselves,

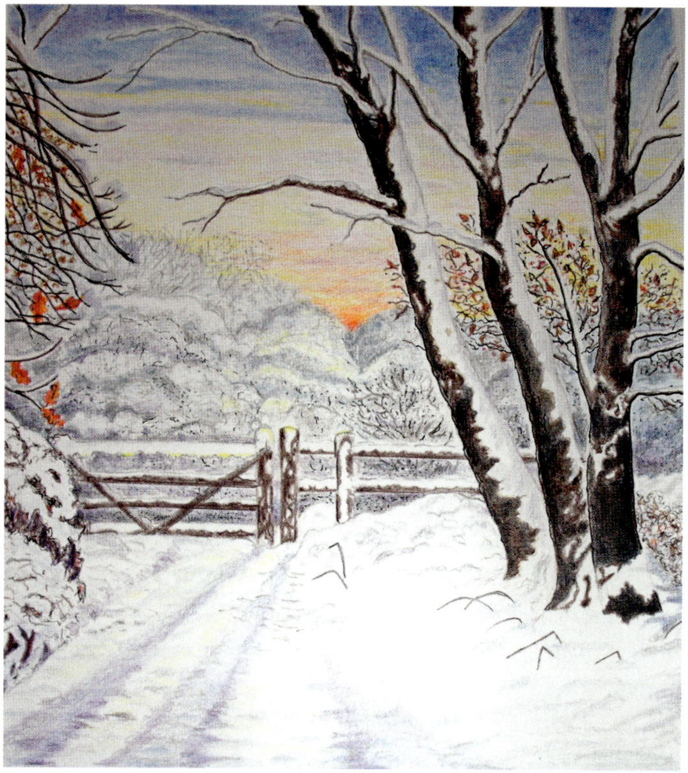

Gate in the Snow: cool and warm palette. Janet Leeder's landscape from the course 'Winter Fells' has a contrasting winter palette with cool blue shadow set against warm brown and orange tones. A biologist, teacher and plant enthusiast, Jan's work is refined and accurately observed.

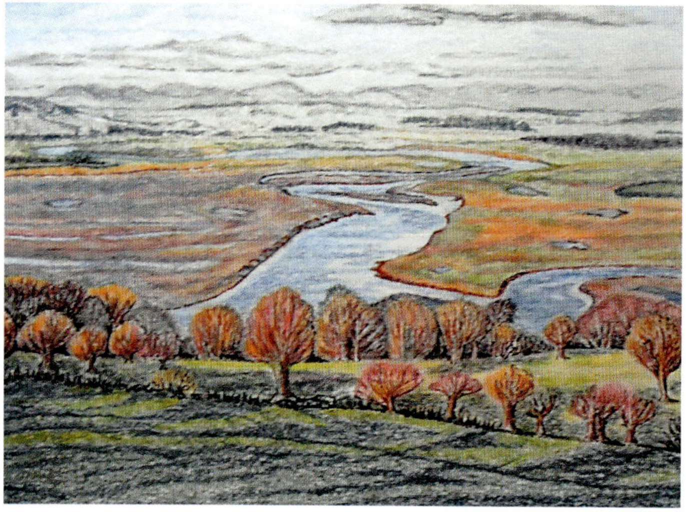

Milnthorpe Sands: knowing the territory. Lynne Farrell is an expert botanist and really knows the lie of the land. This is evident in all her work, notably in this knowledgeable panorama of Milnthorpe Sands. She has a very robust style that is perfectly suited to the stone walls and windblown tree shapes she depicts so well.

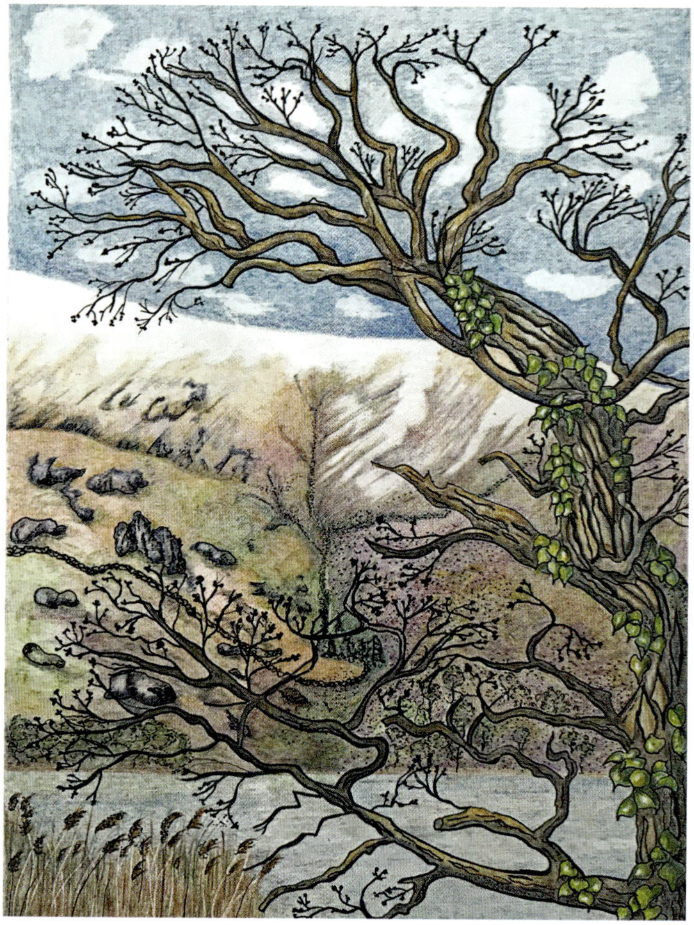

Tree by the Lake: illustrative style. Valerie Lowe's work, also from the 'Winter Fells' course, has a pleasingly illustrative quality. Framed by the twists of ivy, it could have stepped out of a fairy tale. She has handled the integration of ink with coloured pencil very well throughout, and kept to a subtly blended palette of colours.

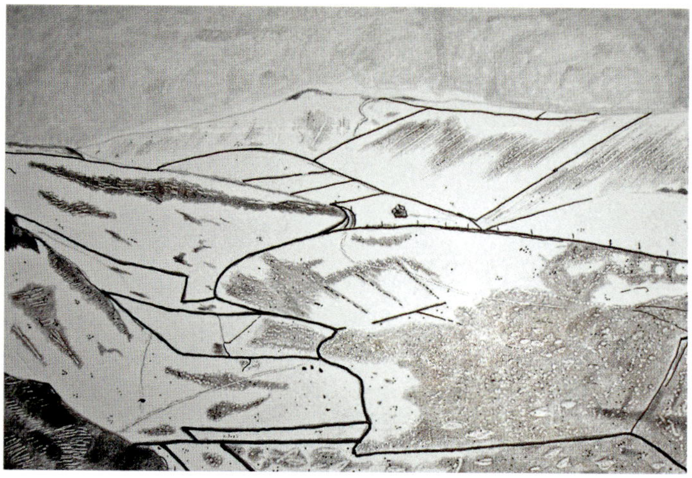

Whiteout Landscape: less can be more. It is quite possible to use the two media to produce a beautifully understated image. Mark Corner's spare but perfectly observed piece for the 'Winter Fells' workshop uses minimal ink, coloured pencil and embossing to capture a winter whiteout.

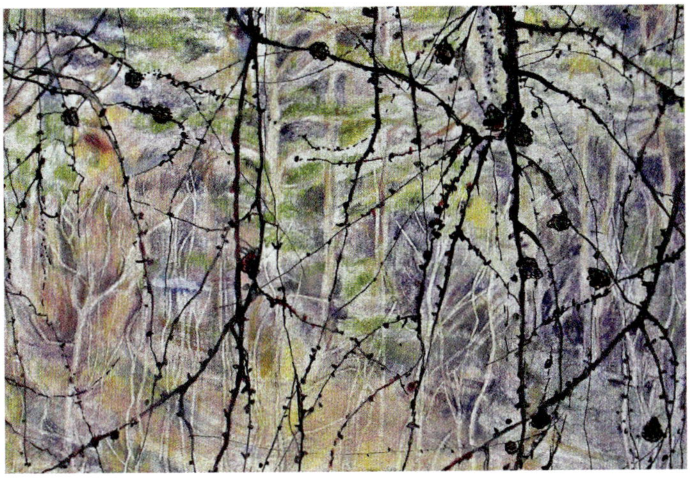

Through the Larches: almost abstraction. Created on a course entitled 'Winter Into Spring', Dinah Brown's landscape uses ink and coloured pencil, but keeps them separate. This works well for an image that might otherwise have appeared confusing. The hazy woodland was blended in coloured pencil and tree shapes were lifted out, leaving the larch branches to create an inky framework.

coupled with the influences we have absorbed. The very fact that we have chosen certain influences over others says something about our nature. Sometimes our art reveals a side rarely seen by other people; it emerges in our choice of materials, our marks on the paper, our tolerance of accidentals, our colour preferences and in many other ways. The question we may need to ask as we start is this: if the techniques are simple, how will my interpretation be unique?

Choosing Your Sources

You may be reading this book with the intention of working from a favourite photo or magazine image just for enjoyment. There is no compulsion to work directly from nature or even from your own photographs, and it is not always possible to head for the hills in search of the ideal subject. Even if you find it easier to use an available image, you will be able to use all the compositional ideas and techniques in this book and will end up with your own unique version. Nowadays we have instant access to millions of images for inspiration, so where you source yours depends on the photographer's copyright, your reasons for working, and what plans you have for your picture. If you are thinking of exhibiting, for copyright reasons I would strongly advise you to use your own material right from the start. This means choosing your own subject and taking your own photos. If you are already a working artist, you will certainly want to do this. For this reason, and to illustrate my own way of working from start to finish, I have begun the story 'in the field'.

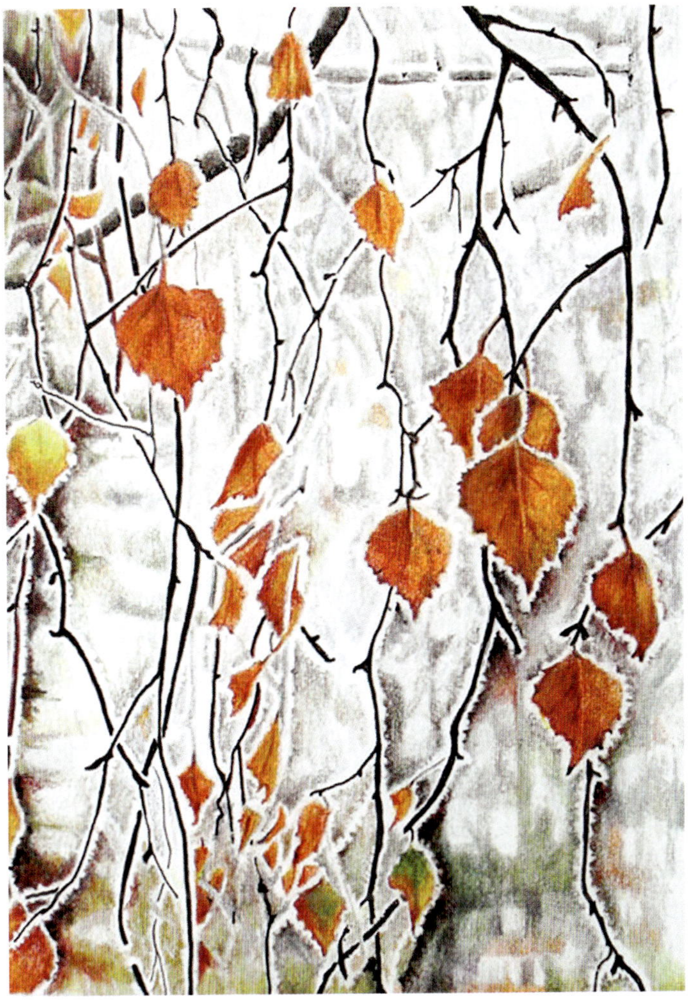

Autumn Leaf Design: using pattern. Patricia Faraday has taken a magazine image showing bright, frozen leaves against a misty background and interpreted it in ink and coloured pencil. The inked branches and coloured pencil leaves have their sharpness accentuated by frosted borders. The background colours are neutral, with a hint of ink and echoes of the leaf colour.

I have always seen my own landscape work as a translation process. Because I always start from scratch and need to own all the processes, my first rule is to know the territory. I like to walk the paths, smell the air and get close to the plants and trees I will be depicting. This familiarization is invaluable: everything is stored in the visual memory, and once I am back in the studio it can be retrieved. It is literally 'a sense of place', and as your work on an image progresses, you can check whether you are achieving it. Sometimes, after walking and

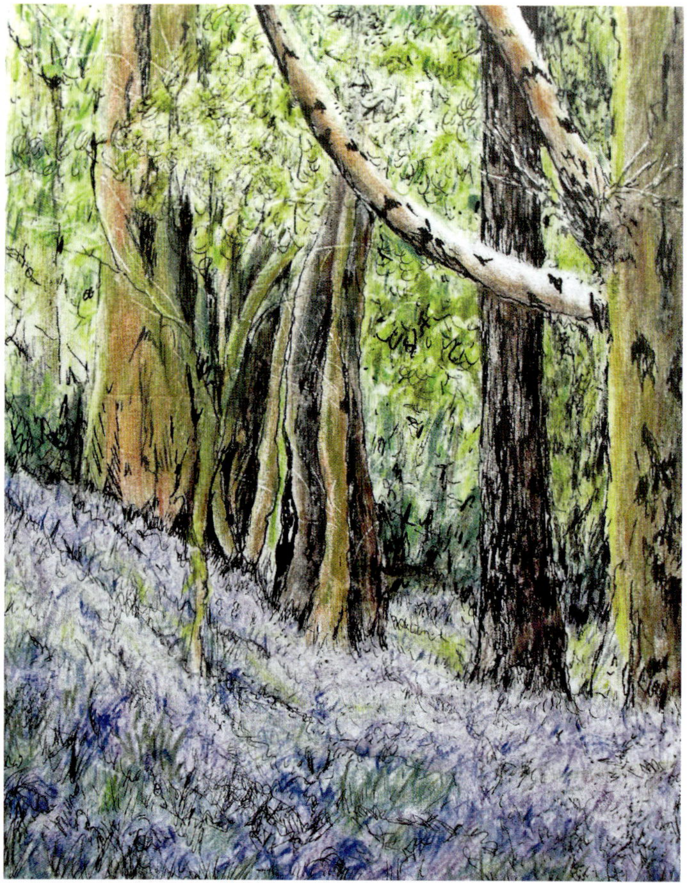

Bluebell Wood: textile influence. Ink and coloured pencil does not have to be precise and controlled. Done on a 'Spring Woodlands' course, this multi-layered image of a bluebell wood resembles a textile piece. Liz Jones has applied different shades of coloured pencil in a relaxed style, seeming to thread the ink markings through the foliage and tree trunks.

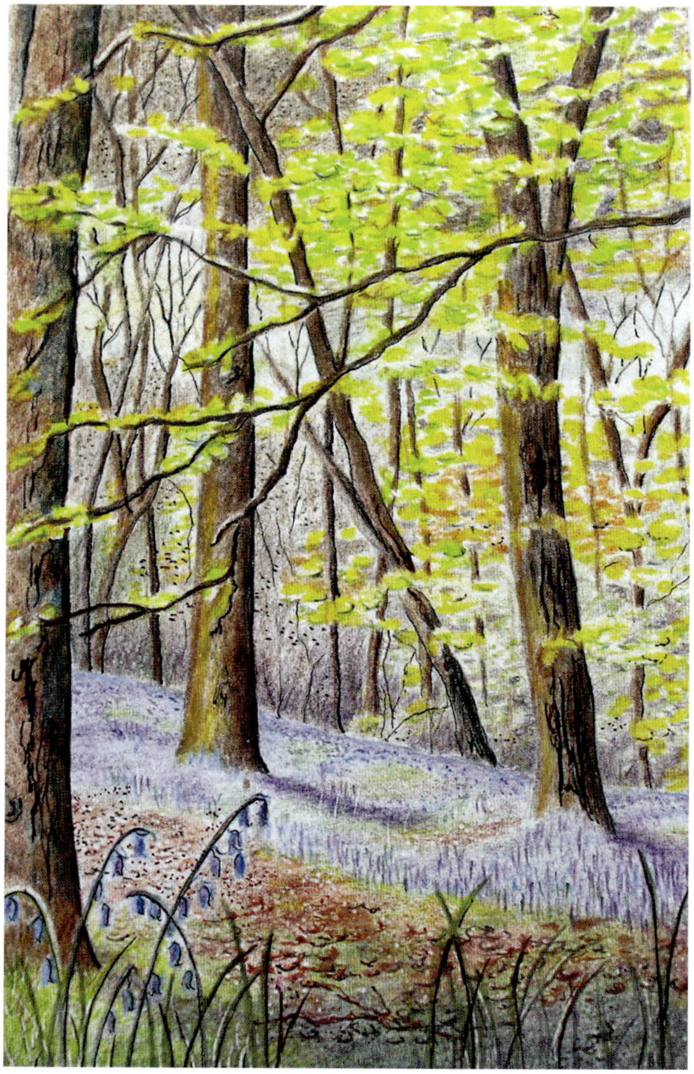

Bluebell Path: harmony and balance. This image by Penelope Picken also came from the 'Spring Woodlands' course. She has taken the difficult subject of a bluebell wood and made it work by featuring a slope and bright overhanging branches. She has kept the balance between ink and coloured pencil harmonious throughout.

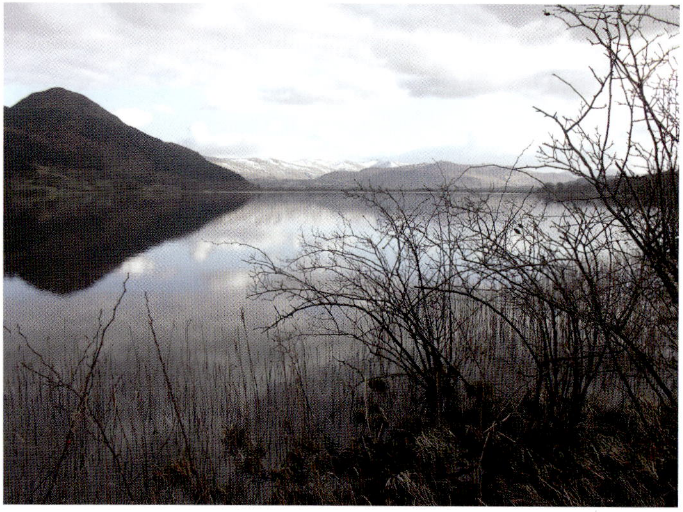

Walking the territory. Choosing your own viewpoint from the start allows you to capture a specific moment, time of day and mood. Seeing and experiencing the landscape and its vegetation at first hand will fix it firmly in your visual memory, whether you work on site or from your own photograph. Just observe, and your brain will do the rest.

photographing an area, I would drive past a stunning bit of scenery on the way home and leap out to take a photo. I soon realized that I would never make use of these extra pictures: I never remembered where I had been or why I had stopped. The territory was meaningless, it had no sensory associations, and my visual memory saw no reason to store it.

Reading the Season, Light and Mood

How Seasonal Are You?

I have always been aware that I am an intensely seasonal person, whose moods and energies fluctuate with the time of year and levels of light. The seasons have certainly figured prominently in my work. I find inspiration in them all and particularly like the transition period from one to the next, when elements of both are present. My sensitivity to changes in light and season has both helped and hindered my work. It requires great effort on my part to get out into the winter gloom, but I know that once there, I can really see and feel the mood of the landscape. It is this atmosphere, more than any topographical or picturesque features, that I try to create in my images and to convey to the viewer. I love wilderness and rarely include signs of human life or habitation, often using birds as a focal point in a remote environment that belongs strictly to nature. That is my personal choice, and explains why I do not include recognizable landmarks; I prefer an anonymous piece of landscape that viewers can make their own. Please do not feel that you must embrace the wild if it is not your choice; you are quite free to depict whatever landmarks and scenery you choose in your own images.

Seasons and times of day bring different kinds of light to the countryside. The colour palette changes with the seasons, and weather adds its impact, giving artists many ways of determining the mood of a picture. It is our job to capture a moment: something that will spark a sense of time, place and recognition. Sometimes, someone will identify a landscape from your picture. This is pleasant but coincidental; a more meaningful response for me would be 'I know that moment'. Something about the time of year, time of day and slant of the light will have touched a chord.

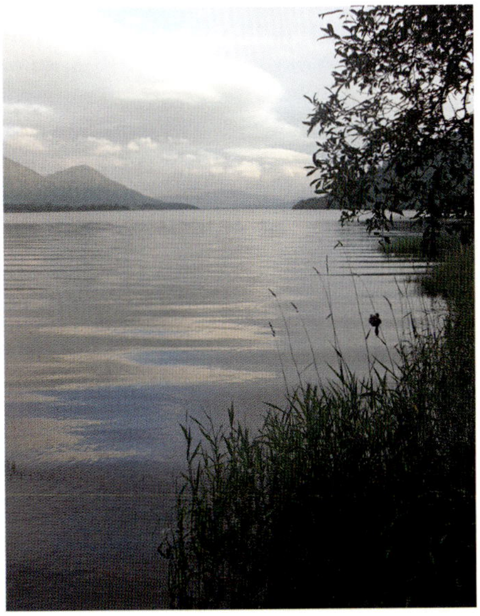

Summer light. Bassenthwaite Lake photographed in late afternoon August sunshine. The light is misty but mellow, gleaming on the surface of the water and the fells opposite. The shade of the trees and the foliage at the water's edge appear very deep in contrast.

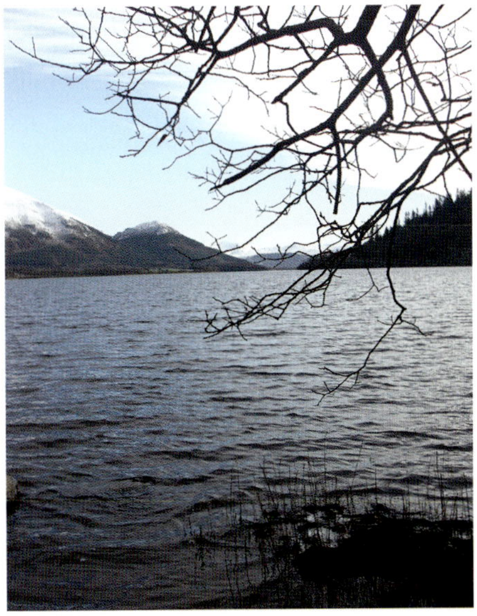

Winter light. This is the same stretch of the lake on an afternoon in February. It is icy, the light is already failing, and the steely colours lack warmth. The location and time of day are the same, but the season and weather conditions have dramatically altered the mood.

What to Look For in a Season

So how do we convey what we can see and feel in a landscape? Start with some basic observations and jot them down if this helps. Establish the season and how far advanced it is. Is it moving towards the next one or just emerging from the last? How much foliage is about? Are the trees evergreen or deciduous? Can you identify them by their shapes? What sort of flowers and grasses can you see? What is the weather like? Is it settled or is there an incoming change? What sort of clouds are visible?

Make some decisions about the light. Where is its source? How low/high is it in the sky? Where are the shadows? Photographers know that the light is often at its most interesting early in the morning or late in the afternoon, and that overhead sun at noon can be harsh and unflattering to its subject. Light is also bluer and more energizing in the early morning, making it the best time for a walk to wake us up for the day ahead. Compare the mellow light of a summer's evening with the early dusk of a winter's day. The more you observe, the more you will learn how the light changes, first with the season and then with the time of day.

Deconstructing Mood

Mood is a more subjective consideration. It helps to ask yourself how *you* feel about the landscape. The mood it evokes in *you* is important if you want to convey this to other people. Mood may be what attracts us to a particular image, even more than content, and the job of the artist is to deconstruct how this happens. We are visual creatures, and images engage the emotions; for this reason, one technically accomplished work may not appeal as much as another of the same standard. If it seems devoid of any discernible mood, it may not engage us or manage to hold our attention for very long.

When you look at your chosen landscape or image, try to pinpoint what it is that produces the feeling you are experiencing. If you are outdoors, add a few notes to your seasonal observations and sketches. In botanical coloured pencil groups, I always ask students to start by writing down briefly what they like about a subject and what they feel makes it unique. This is a wholly unscientific exercise, designed to keep in mind the essence of the subject, the better to convey it. They can then check whether the finished piece ticks all the boxes. A similar approach can be taken with landscape, either in the wild or as seen in an image. Ask yourself what is creating the mood you are experiencing. Is it the low light and misty colours? The dazzlingly bright sun and new leaves? The cold stillness, bare trees and steely sky? Recreating these elements in your picture, in the right colours, will elicit the desired mood.

Sketches, Colour Notes and Botany

Sketching on Site

If you are an outdoor sketcher, a little book will help you to record your chosen landscape. You can use the minimal ink and coloured pencil kit as described in Chapter 1, or pen and watercolour. Detailed work in ink and coloured pencil is essentially a studio-based activity, but the sort of spontaneous sketches you can do on site will help with composition and mood; most importantly, they will fix the scene in your memory. I often use waterproof drawing pens with a watercolour wash. I like to put colour down first and draw freely over the top, but you may prefer the more traditional approach of pen first, then wash. Alternatively, if you enjoy graphite sketches, these will help you to work out a composition; they are also a good way of fixing the tonal values in your picture. Make use of whatever method you prefer; if you are not an outdoor worker, use your eyes to take everything in, soak up the atmosphere and let the visual memory store it.

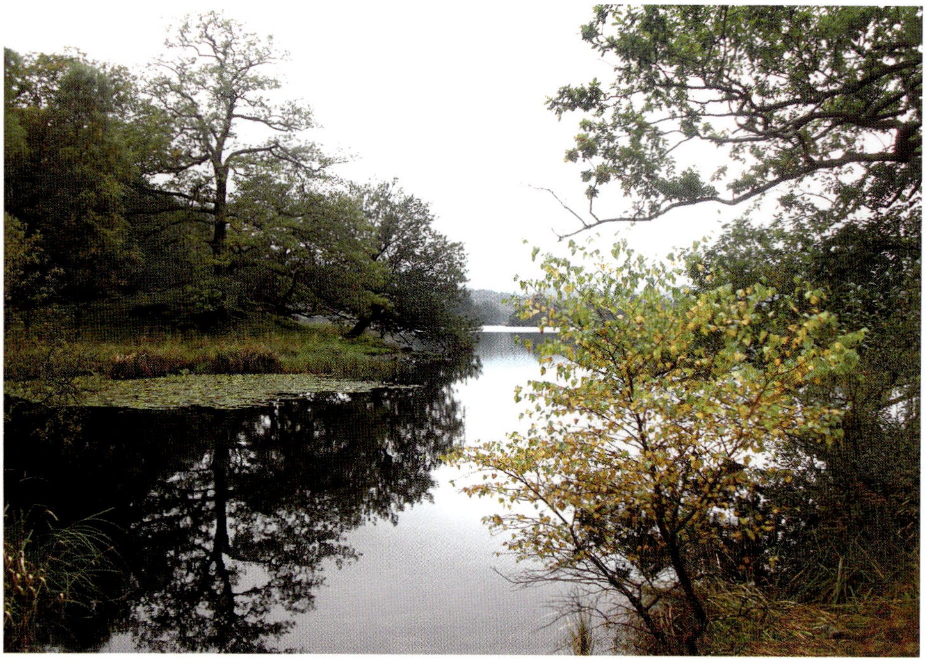

Capturing the mood. This photograph of the approach to Rydal Water was taken on an autumn morning and evokes the mood of the season. We can almost smell the chill air and the dank vegetation. What are the visual aspects that contribute to this sensation, and how would you convey them in your image?

Roadside sketch. A spontaneous ink and watercolour sketch done on site along the coast. The land is marshy and flat, with just a few points of interest. Areas of paint were applied first and ink added later. Although not in coloured pencil, this sort of sketch captures the mood and the palette, so is a useful exercise.

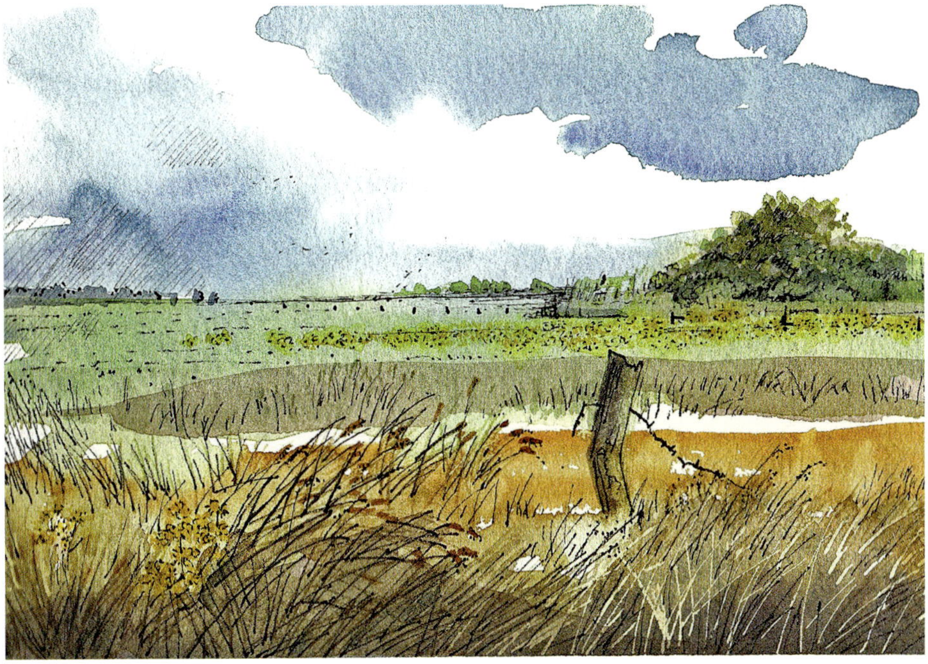

Local Colour

Accurate colour is one of the most effective ways of creating a sense of place. Each habitat has its local colour, determined by the geology, soil, vegetation, season and prevailing weather. A hillside covered with bracken will look quite different from one covered with scrubby grassland. In our native landscape, greens and browns predominate, and coloured pencils offer a plentiful choice. No one wants to carry boxes of colours into the wild, but a good selection of greens, a few blues, greys and earth colours in a pencil roll will allow you to record the local colour. Coloured pencils are designed to blend and will create all the shades you need. Just record little samples in your sketchbook – and don't forget to label the colours! You can use watercolour mixes instead, but aim to build your own local colour chart for reference.

Once back in the studio, any local colour you have noted in your sketchbook or observed in your photos can be accurately matched against the appropriate coloured pencil shades. This cannot be done successfully from the box, by looking at the colour of the core or the casing: the colour of the pigment needs to be seen on the paper you intend to use. I always use a colour chart that I make myself for each set of coloured pencils I buy. The colouring in is a moderately time-consuming task, but once you have the chart available for use, it will prove invaluable every time you embark on a project. It can be made by hand on Bristol board (or your chosen paper), or printed on the computer and then coloured in. To make a colour chart proceed as follows:

- Trim a piece of smooth Bristol board to the exact size of A4 paper you use in your printer.
- Create an A4 document consisting of four columns. Columns one and three should be blank and columns two and four lined. In columns two and four, type the names of all the colours in the manufacturer's set, following their shade order. Remove the line borders if you wish.
- Print the document on Bristol board.
- In each space, draw a long, slim rectangle in the colour named opposite. This rectangle will eventually be divided into three equal parts.
- Fill in the whole rectangle with a layer of the named colour, using either small ellipses or single direction cross-hatching.
- Repeat the process with a second layer (going in the opposite direction if you are using cross-hatching) but stop after the first two-thirds.
- Do the same again, covering only the first third. You should now have a rectangle showing three different levels of layering with the corresponding strength of colour.
- Do the same thing with all the remaining colours.

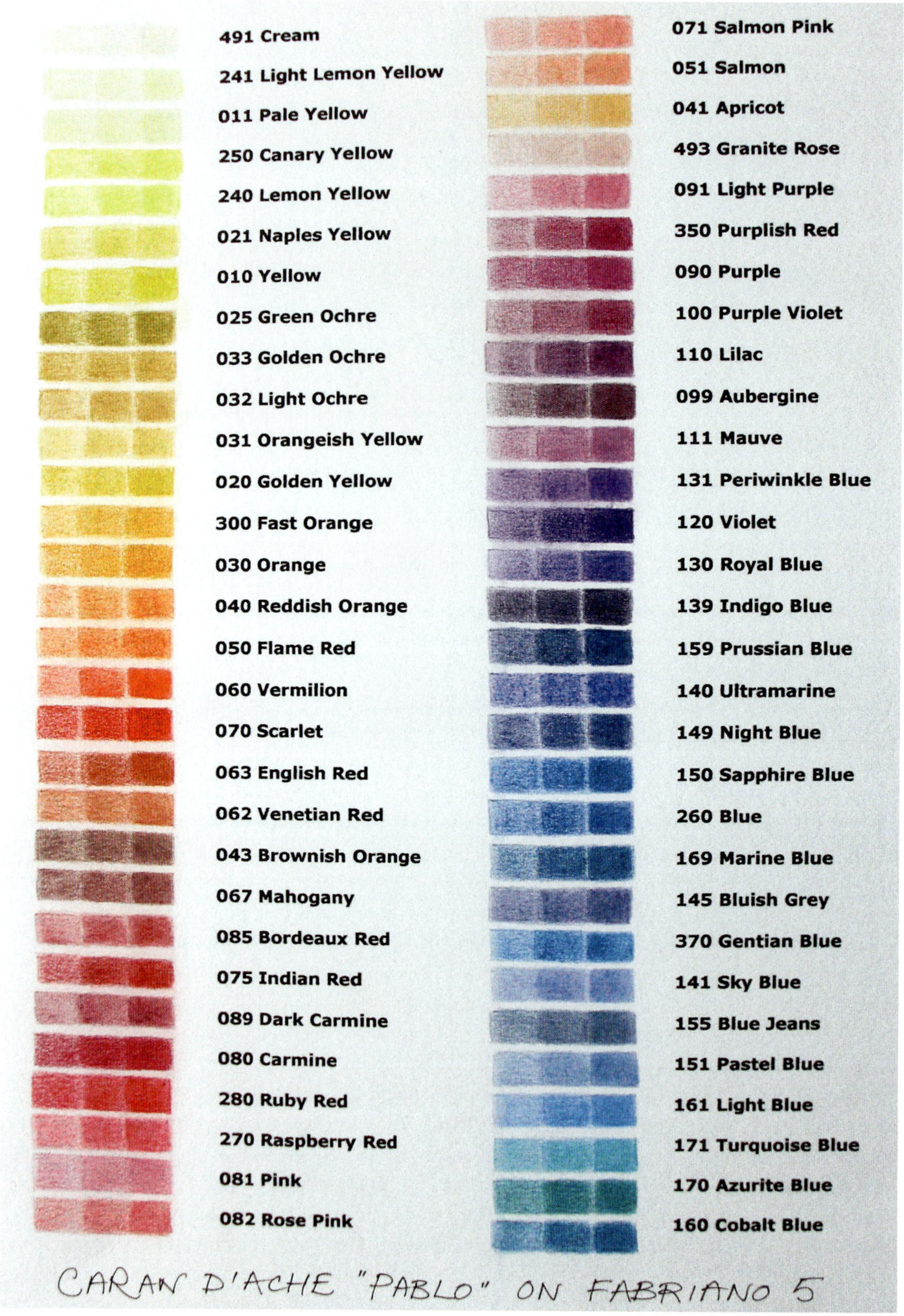

Caran D'Ache 'Pablo' chart. Making a three-tone chart for each set of coloured pencils is well worth the effort, and will help you enormously with any decision making about colour. Choosing from the pencils in the box will not! Always test on paper first, especially when blending, but a chart will make the initial choice much easier.

This chart should give you a good idea of what a particular pigment will look like with up to three layers of colour. It makes colour matching much more accurate, and will help you to find the right shade for a given subject. If you acquire more coloured pencil sets and repeat the process, you will have even more choice and more likelihood of finding the perfect colour(s). It is worth noting that manufacturers of art materials have their own versions of shades for coloured pencils as well as watercolours, acrylics, pastels, and so on; therefore one make of Indigo or Lemon Yellow will differ from another. The components vary and have a bearing on the finished shade: Sap Green, for example, differs considerably from brand to brand.

If you prefer to collect pencils from several manufacturers rather than buy sets, a similar chart can be made based on colour or hardness/softness. Even if you have every available collection, the chance of encountering two identical colours is slim; the choice is immense and may feel overwhelming at first, but you will soon settle for some favourites and get to know when to use them.

Habitat

I have always chosen to work on several images from one type of habitat, then move on to another. This started when I was printmaking, and arose naturally from my trips to specific sites and holidays in particular locations. I found that the many photographs I took and the sketches I made would inspire me to produce a series of images for different-sized etching plates. Smaller images were usually more commercial, but were also a way of trying out techniques and colours that would then appear throughout the series. They were a good preparation for a much larger work, and a way of solving potential problems without experiencing disaster on a grand scale. The more images I made, the more I became absorbed in a specific habitat, with its plants, geology and local colour. I much preferred this to the selection of one image because it happened to appeal at the time.

It was also a barrier to boredom: I never thought 'What shall I do next?' because I was so absorbed in the current environment. Moving on to somewhere completely different always felt like a fresh start, with new plants, new features and a new locality. Everything would change: the geology, the colours, the flowers, the season. The light was invariably different, and consequently, so was the mood. I continued this when I moved to ink and coloured pencil, and it is a method of working that I still find sustains my interest. Every area has its own ecology and its own atmosphere. By studying and observing what creates this, we can get close to that elusive artistic goal: a genuine sense of place.

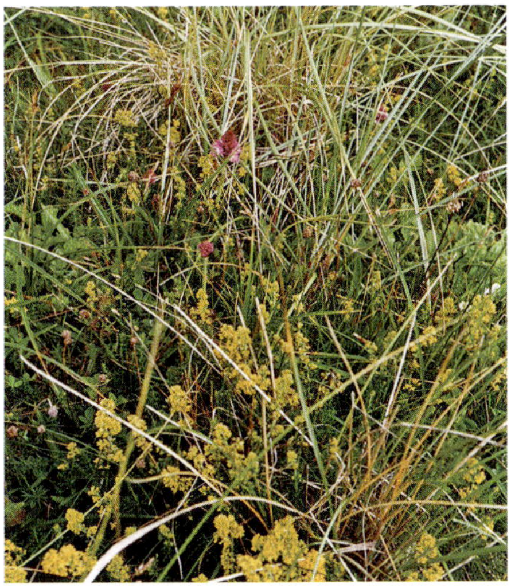

Machair on Machrihanish. I always take photographs of the plants that grow together in my chosen location. They are a record of the ecology and can be used in context if I need them for an image. This collection shows some of the characteristic machair plants at Machrihanish Bay on Kintyre, and has been a reference for several images.

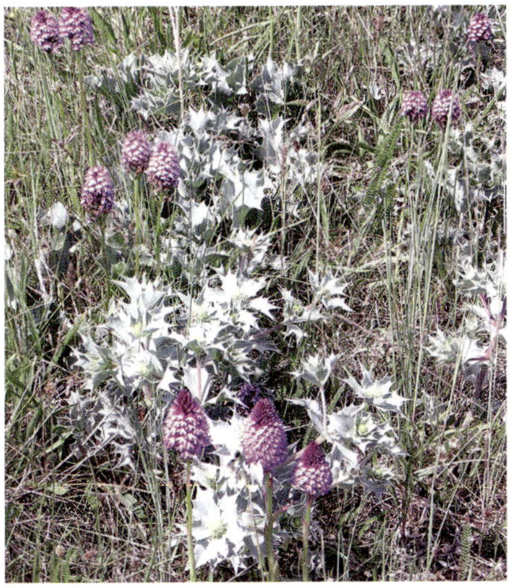

Chalk coast dunes. Far from Kintyre, this arresting combination of pyramidal orchids and sea holly is typical of the dunes at Sandwich. I have a collection of photographs of the flora of my local area and use them regularly in my compositions.

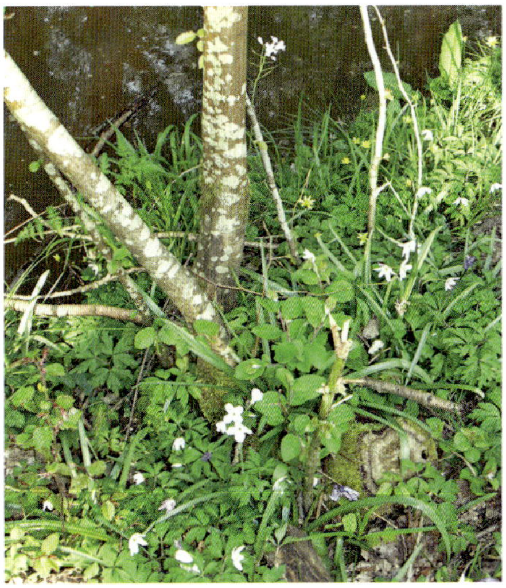

Kent woodland. This collection from my favourite woodland includes lady's smock, wood anemones, celandines and bluebells. All through the spring, until the tree canopy thickens, the wood has a fine display of flowers, including several species of orchid.

Plant Solutions

Ever since my childhood trips to Ainsdale, wild plants in their habitat have always been a feature of my work. As well as being an area of interest for me personally, they remind me to steer clear of landscape clichés and easy solutions. The recognizable shapes and colours of native plants tap into our visual memory, and we find them instantly evocative. A half-glimpsed, impressionistic look may have even more impact than a detailed one. Knowing about plant habitats and likely species can help make sense of clumps of foreground and tangled undergrowth, fill empty spaces and add interest. I always have my flower and tree guides beside me in the studio to check plant features and growth patterns. I also check flowering times to avoid having unlikely plants in bloom together. They are rarely the stars of the show; I simply incorporate them as I work.

I should mention grasses, too, at this point. Throughout my years as an etcher, I used a decades-old copy of C.E. Hubbard's *Grasses* to give me the delicate grass forms I needed in my work. Its expert line drawings inform more than any photograph, and I still use it today.

Using Photography and the Computer

When I am exploring new territory, I take lots of photographs. Landscape in ink and coloured pencil requires a steady hand and a studio environment, so my reference photographs are my starting point. Sketches and local colour samples contribute information, but I usually make my choice from this image bank. Sometimes when I am photographing outdoors, I feel that a particular shot will be perfect; often it disappoints and some less spectacular one really captures the light, mood and place. Whenever I work on a series, I select a batch of images that complement each other but have variety. I am then ready to try out different formats and crops on the computer and to present each image in a way that suits the subject and fits the group.

I take a long time over the decision-making process, particularly if I am embarking on a large work. Whether you do the same depends on your temperament and your level of tolerance of disasters! Some artists believe in meticulous preparation, so that they are free from the subsequent irritation of trying to put things right; others like to work things out as they go along and believe that there is no such thing as a disaster. A few are just supremely confident after years of experience. I concede that starting my artistic endeavours on copper plate may have had some influence on my approach: there are no simple alterations when metal and acid are involved. Nevertheless, I believe that preparation actually frees you and encourages spontaneity when you do start work, secure in the knowledge that you have set down good foundations.

Composition is crucial, and one of the most difficult things to alter once you have started. The next chapter will look more closely at aspects of composition, and your freedom as an artist to take charge of what you see.

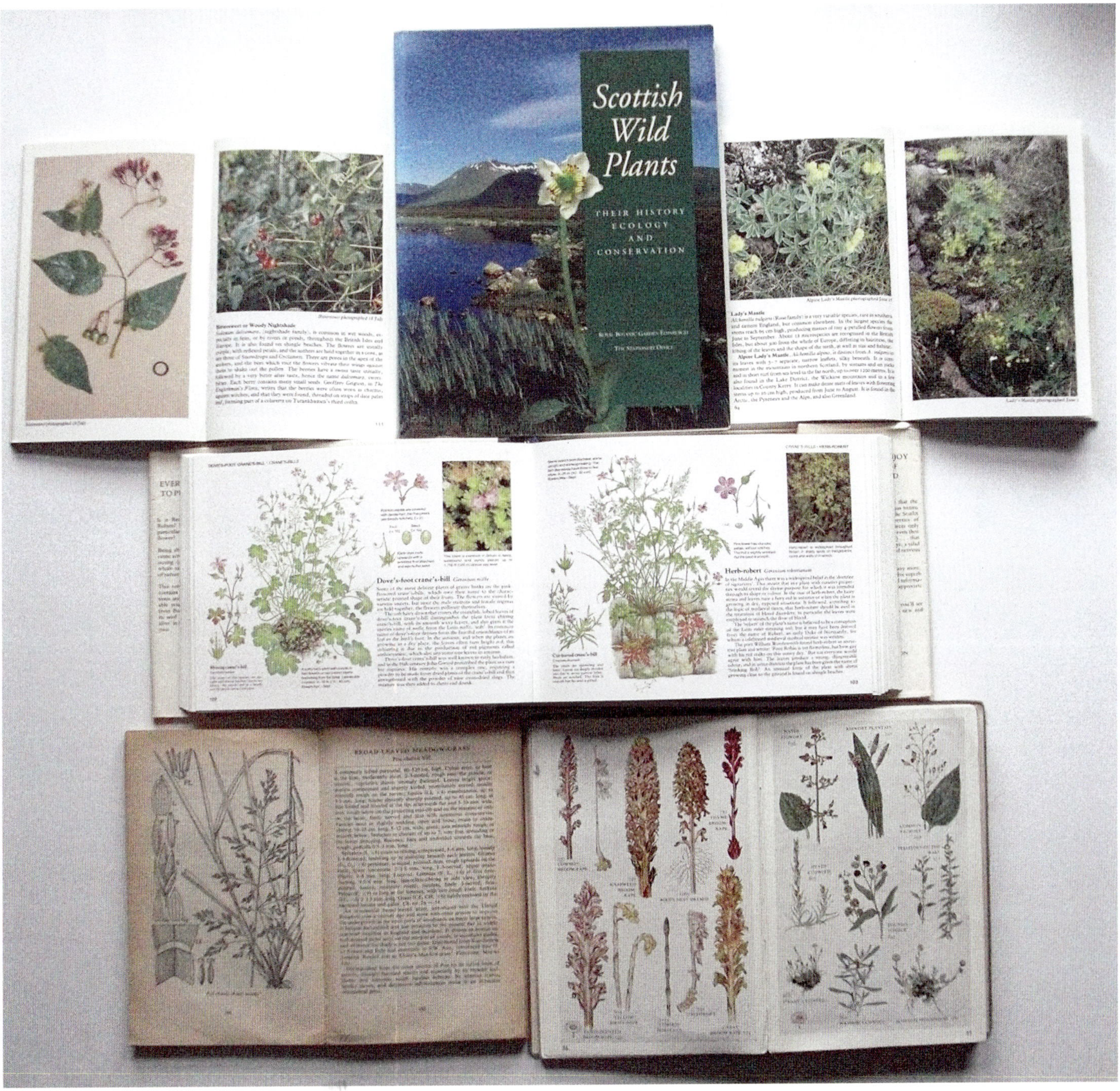

Trusty books. Some of the well-worn but invaluable guides that have been my constant companions, in and out of the field. The more you recognize plant forms, the more confident you will feel about depicting them in their natural habitat; and the more successful your attempts, the more you will enjoy the process.

CHAPTER 3

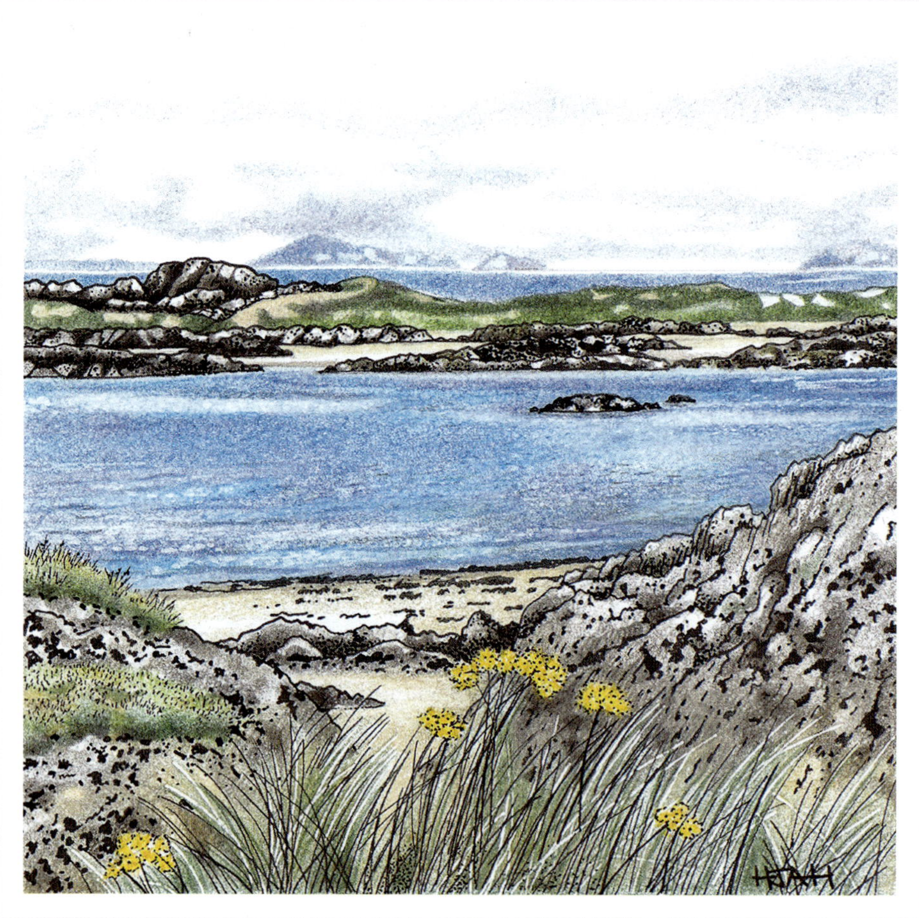

Singing Sands.

Composition Matters

Whatever your method of working as an artist, thinking ahead is part of the process. Put aside the myth that the artist works in a frenzy of creativity and produces an instant masterpiece. It is true that we tend to get absorbed in the process and put in long hours, but even those working in a very expressive style usually have carefully mixed colours ready at the outset and an idea of where to put them. Experience counts, too. Most working artists spend a lot of time planning, experimenting and rethinking, often in their sketchbooks. Composition is an important part of this process, and well worth a bit of extra effort at the beginning. I have always found that far from being boring, it is encouraging to see how you can breathe new life into an image simply by making a few adjustments to nature's original.

CHOOSING A VIEWPOINT

Image Size and Shape

We are familiar with landscape and portrait modes, named after the most common painting formats. We have them on our cameras, computers and printers, and they are the most widely used for artworks. Standard landscape and portrait proportions may suit your image, but do consider other options, particularly if you are planning a pair or a series. Fashions in framing change regularly, and favoured formats also come and go; sometimes a particular artist will start a trend.

A square format is neat and appealing, and will give focus to a busy landscape. If a lot is going on in a picture both horizontally and vertically, choosing an off-centre focal point and enclosing it in a square will make better sense of all the visual information.

You can also take standard landscape and portrait modes and exaggerate them. A tall, slim format works for landscapes with several layered sections such as grasses, pebbles, sand and sea. Panoramic landscapes with few foreground features suit a wide format without too much depth.

Have a good look at the whole picture and its content. Does it suggest a particular format? If you focus on a smaller area, will this change the format? If you are planning two images, which shapes will work best as a pair? How will you place them together? Will they have the same eye-level line or a contrasting one? Would one long image be better as a triptych? Once you start experimenting with different formats you will see new possibilities; when you find a version that really enhances your image, choose it.

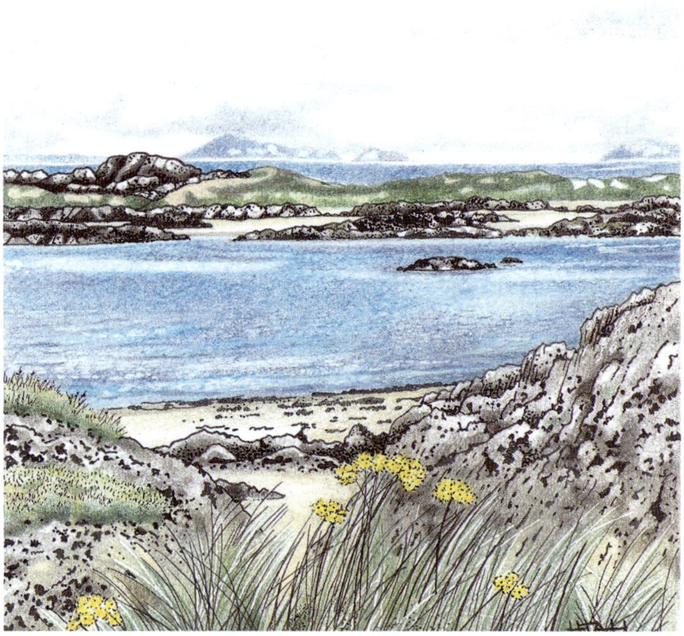

Singing Sands: square format. This was part of a panoramic stretch of coastline with many rock formations in the foreground, a series of bays and several islands. I chose a square format to enclose it and make a definite decision about content. There is a bit of everything, but it is not too busy.

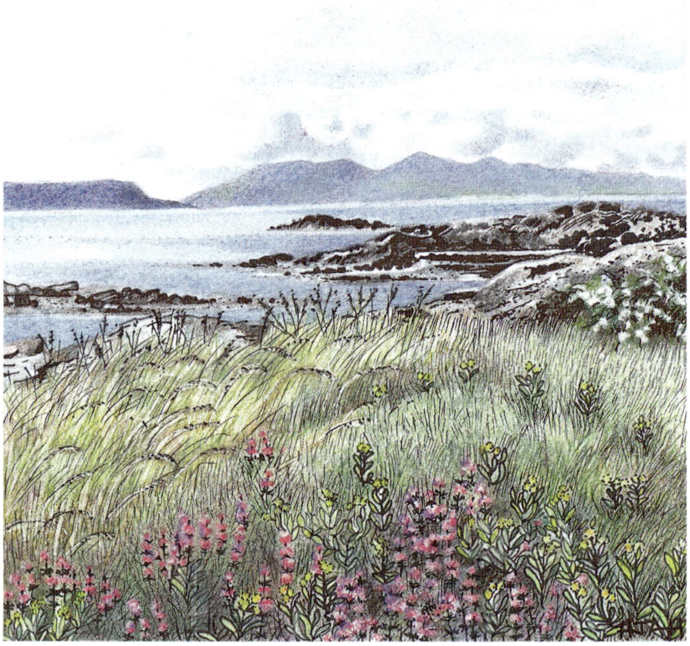

Western Isles: square format. This was a similarly wide vista with islands, outcrops and locally abundant flora. I decided to simplify it within a square format, focusing on the wildflowers to give a sense of the terrain, backed by curving rock formations and two distinctive island masses.

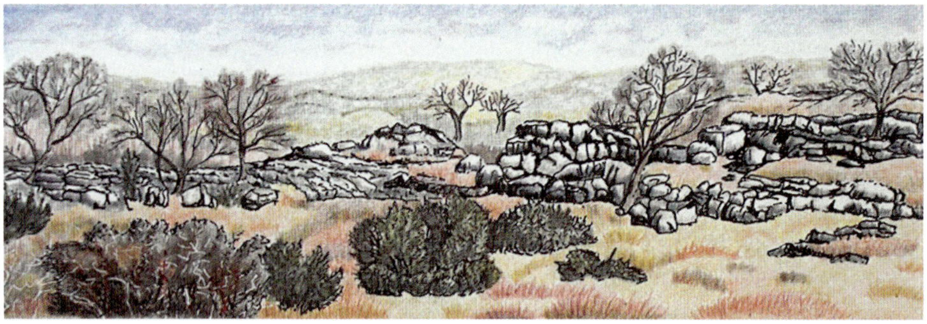

Farleton Knott: panoramic format. The interest in Lynne Farrell's depiction of Farleton Knott lies in the breadth of the landscape rather than its height. This suits the panoramic format, and throws into focus the repetitive shapes and textures of the drystone walls and the terrain that Lynne captures so well.

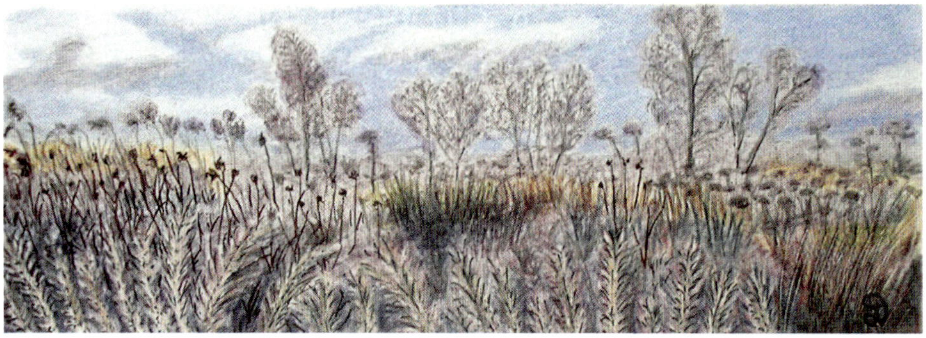

Winter Reedbeds: panoramic format. Lesley Treanor chose a simple image of reedbeds, but has made them more interesting by cropping the shape to give a wide but shallow format. She has mixed ink and coloured pencil throughout and, working in a relaxed style, has allowed the understated colours and shadows to tell the story.

Winter Grasses: slim format. Aileen Clarke's choice of this format on the 'Winter Contrasts' course suits the layered nature of the image. She has integrated ink and coloured pencil well, and has used a subtle colour palette, keeping the foreground stronger in contrast to the distant tree forms.

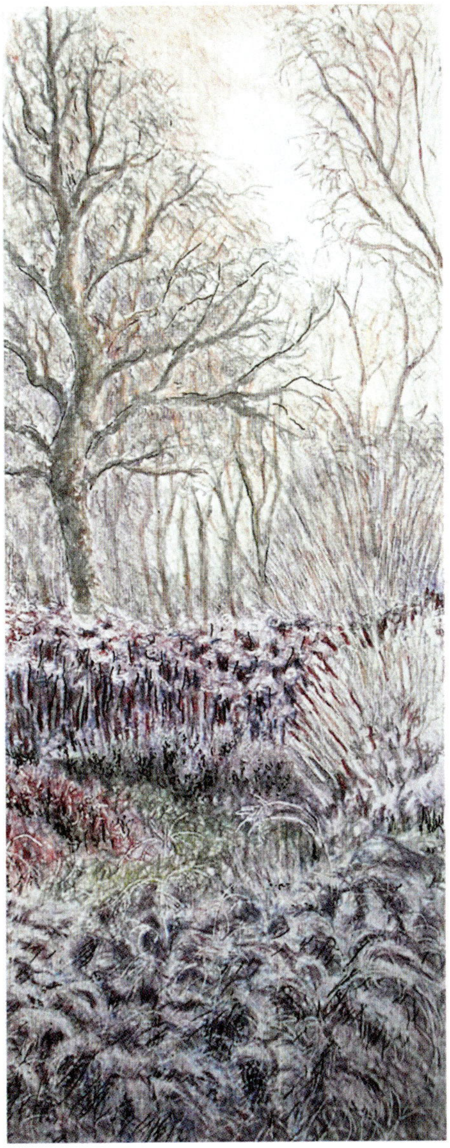

Snowdrop Woods: slim format. Jan Leeder particularly likes this format and has used it effectively for her view through the snowdrop woods. She has made a feature of the tree trunks, varying their colour, texture and tone as they move into the distance. The snowdrops are beautifully observed, with a careful balance of ink and coloured pencil.

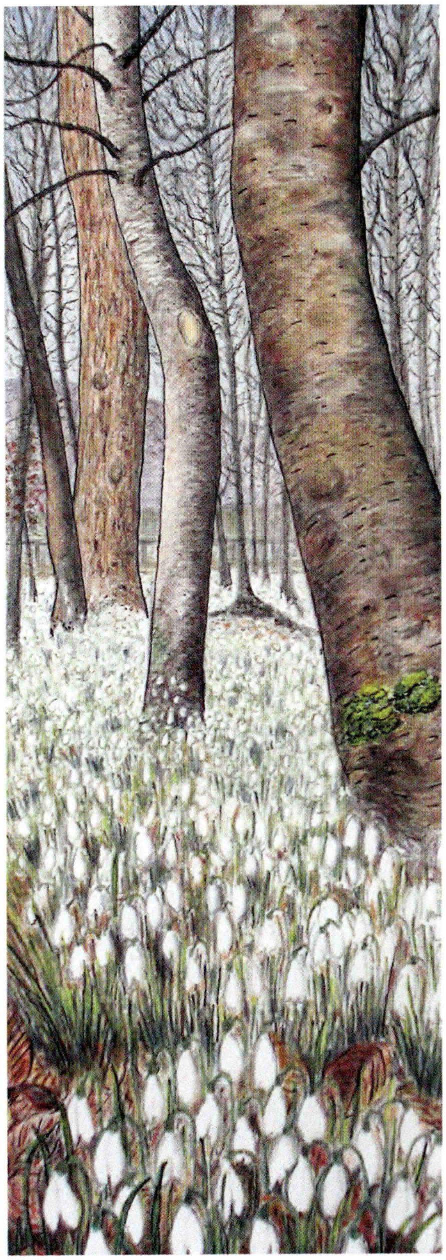

How Much To Use?

In the old days of photography, most of the work for the amateur photographer went into composing a shot before taking it. Once taken, we tended to see it as done, and only serious enthusiasts and professionals had the luxury of editing the result. Today it is the norm for digital photographs to be edited afterwards, so we don't need to spend as much time composing a picture on site. Nevertheless, the temptation to see a printed photograph as fixed is still quite strong. You may feel that the image you have selected speaks for itself. I have noticed that when students bring in a landscape or portrait image that they have chosen as their subject, most expect to work on it exactly as it is.

If you are working from a photograph taken by a professional and published in a magazine, it will already have been subjected to artistic scrutiny. It will probably be well balanced and pleasing to the eye, but may not be as close to nature as you imagine. Special lenses may have been used, and the image manipulated. Your own amateur photograph may be more of

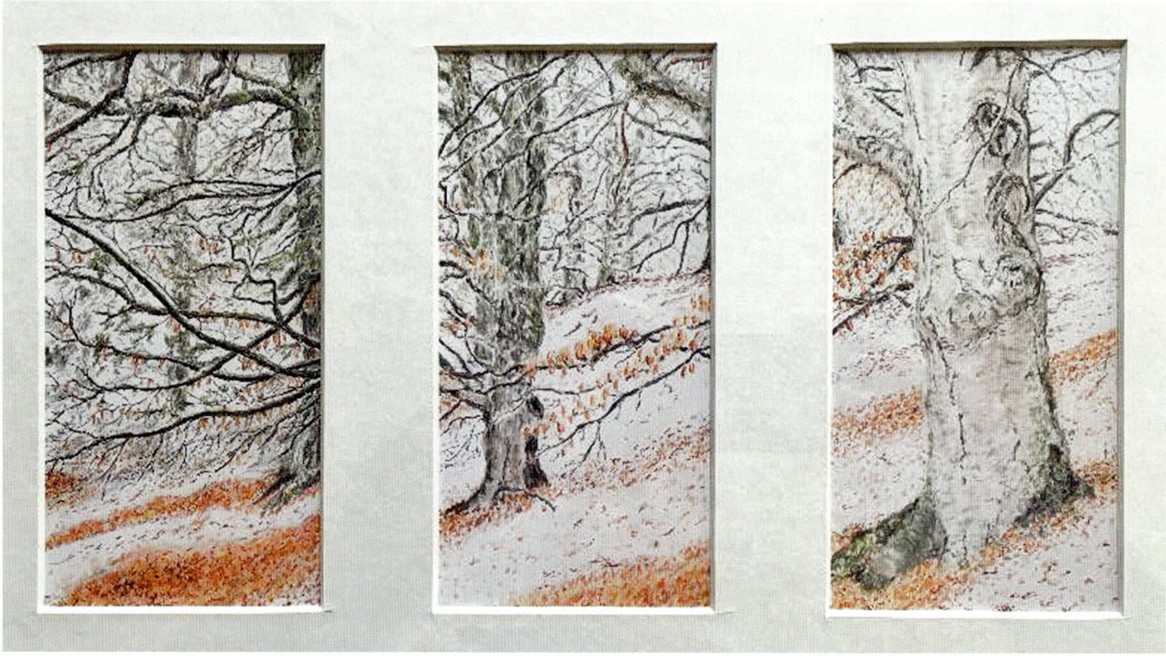

Woodland Triptych. Ann McCrea began this triptych on the 'Winter Contrasts' course, completing one section and half of the second. Later I was delighted to receive an email attaching the complete work. She used a limited colour palette, experimenting with Faber-Castell 'Sanguine' ink amidst the coloured pencil. The breaks in the triptych contribute to the sense of a downward trajectory.

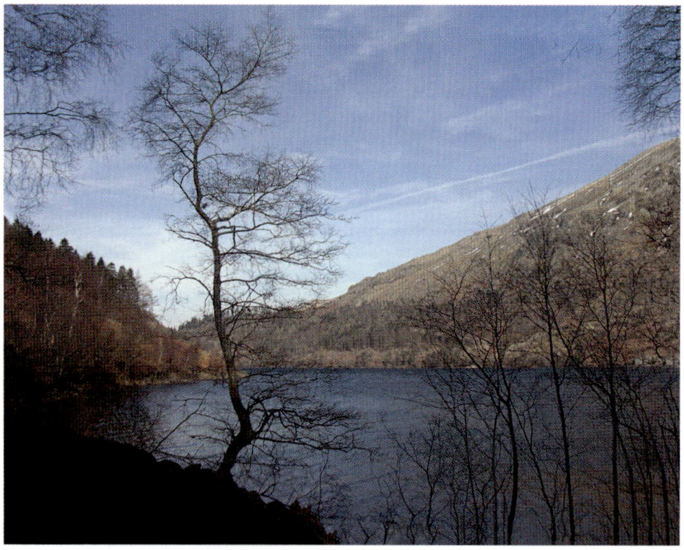

Thirlmere: the full photograph. This picture of Thirlmere in February is the sort that amateurs like me take; there is plenty of scenery, but the expert touch is lacking. I now take them as raw material, expecting to work on them later if I want to coax them into becoming art. Usually a photograph is just a starting point.

a snapshot, capturing the scene but not necessarily showing it to best advantage. Photography and art are friends, but they are not the same thing; it is worth having a good look at your chosen image and considering what will translate effectively and what will not.

It is quite likely that your image will include too much information – or not enough. It may be too busy, with too many different sorts of foliage and competing layers. Alternatively, if you have thought carefully about the focal point but not noticed the dull surroundings, it may have stretches of uninteresting field or foreground that will present a problem. Do not despair! The solution could be to move in closer, choose a good focal point, find (or import) some interesting textures, and have a rethink. Photographs are a good reference tool, but they are not your picture; they should be a starting point and an aide-memoire. You are the artist, and it is your job to extract from them what you need in order to create your own fresh interpretation.

Using Masks and Mountboard

If my students have chosen to work from a printed image or have brought their own photographs, I always suggest experimenting with mounts in different formats. By masking out most of the image they can concentrate on one framed section. It is usually quite a revelation to them when they see what striking images they can create with different windows. I use standard sizes and shapes, but also juggle two separate halves of mountboard to give even more permutations. Most people end up with an exciting composition that they had not previously envisaged. I have noticed that this really inspires them and

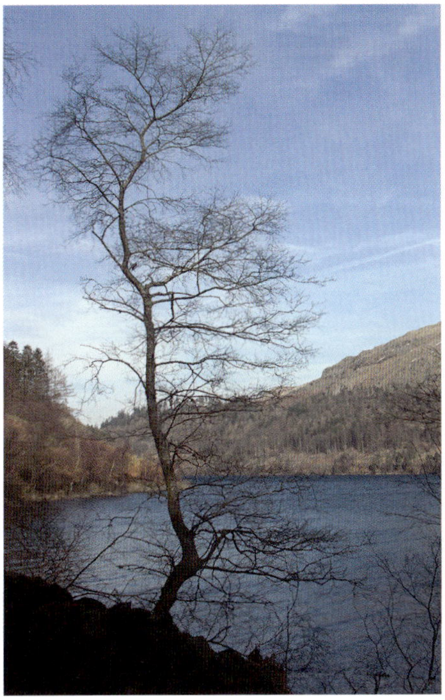

Thirlmere: the cropped version. I decided that the tree was the best feature, and chose a slimmer format to include its entire length, plus a section of the richly coloured bank behind. I placed the tree off-centre, allowing its shape to twist backwards to occupy the left-hand side of the picture.

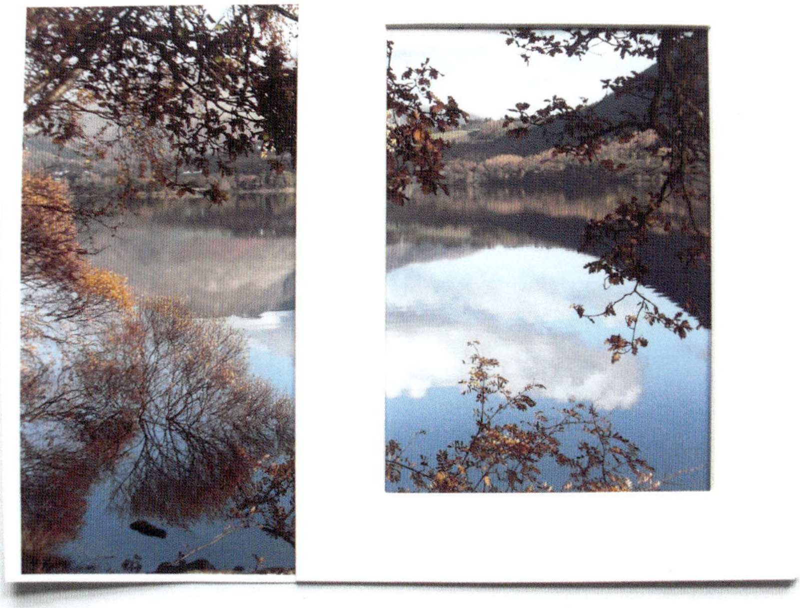

Masking a large image. This autumnal view over Derwentwater has enough material for several smaller images. This is just one possible crop using a ready-made mount. You can also slide two halves of a mount up and down for more flexible options such as a long narrow format.

makes them extra keen to start work. I like this very 'hands on' approach because it really engages people; the alternative is to manipulate your own images using computer software. This works perfectly well, but does not deliver quite the same 'Eureka!' experience.

Cropping and Enlarging

Computer software allows us to do anything we want with our photographs. Some artists use it as their sketchbook for trying out possible compositions, saving different versions before making a final decision. I spend a long time on the viewing and cropping process when I am preparing a new work or series. If I am embarking on a large piece that will take weeks, I do not want to invest all my energies in the wrong choice.

From my image bank I choose likely photographs, based on their visual appeal and whether they convey the all-important sense of place. I bear in mind how they will work as pairs or fit into a series. I look for images that echo each other, mirror each other compositionally, or have a similar feel but different areas of interest. I try out different proportions and formats, as described above. Sometimes I need to zoom in and increase the size, enlarging a section to create a less busy composition. This latter process is one of the most valuable aspects of digital manipulation because it is a problem solver, necessitating a complete rethink. I don't always end up with what I had imagined; the important thing is to feel full of enthusiasm and eager to start on what you finally choose.

Specific Features and Geometrical Shapes

To work, your picture should include something of interest. Even a flat fenland landscape or a stretch of beach should have good proportions, a focal point and some variety. In a minimal or semi-abstract landscape, the focal point does not have to be an object; it can be a simple change of technique, direction or concentration of colour. If a landscape has several horizontal lines separating beach, sea and sky, introducing a vertical at some point will break the monotony. If you have chosen something more complex, decide which areas of interest you want to include, so that the image does not become too confusing. You may even decide not to use so much of the image and to concentrate more closely on one section.

When we look at a landscape outdoors with the naked eye, we tend to focus on individual things one at a time, such as a dominant tree or a river. It helps if you can take a step back and see the ensemble: notice how its features fit together, and what geometrical shapes link them. Well-constructed pictures have always contained simple shapes and may follow circles, semi-circles, ovals, triangles and so on. Photography helps us to see this, as it provides a frame and a setting within which we can see the relationships more clearly. Notice how the areas relate to each other, what sort of shapes they make, and how you can use these shapes to lead the eye round the picture. Provided you keep to the same perspective, you can exaggerate the angles if you wish. If your image contains a focal point and not much else, it will make for a dull picture.

Interesting Angles

When choosing an image, remember that those offering a different angle on the subject often produce a better picture.

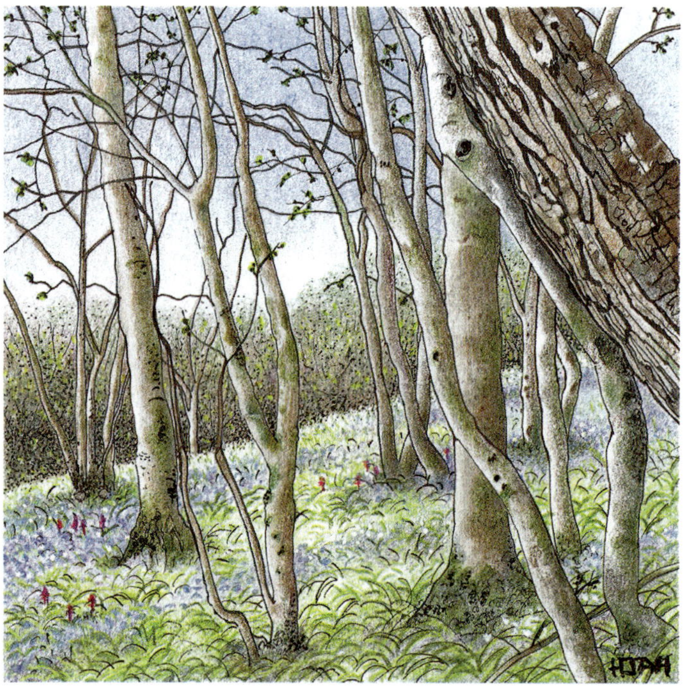

Bluebell Slope. I resolved the bluebell wood dilemma by choosing a slope with a shadowy copse behind it. I also used a slanting tree trunk to add a diagonal and some textural detail in the foreground. Steer clear of flat expanses of bluebells with identical, vertical trees: just enjoy them in nature.

Viewing the subject head-on can give our eyes an uninspiring journey with nowhere interesting to settle. I am a great fan of diagonals, as they add movement, drama and even a bit of mystery. Features that lead our gaze around or across the picture, or hint at what might be beyond, all sustain our interest. Where is that path going? What is behind the trees? Where have the overhanging branches come from? I used to fall into the trap of fading a picture out towards the edges: I covered the area, but in a half-hearted way. This was simply because I lost motivation once I had moved away from the main area of interest. Try to resist this temptation to abdicate responsibility: you may have lost interest, but you should still retain the viewer's. Feeble edges make your image seem incomplete, and there is no sense that it is part of a real landscape that continues off stage.

Some popular landscape subjects regularly present problems with composition; my pet hate is the bluebell wood dilemma, which can also include all those delightful drifts of snowdrops, wood anemones and wild garlic. How many of us have enjoyed walks in spring woodland and eagerly taken photographs? How often do they look dull in comparison with the real experience? The flowers carpet the ground, the trees rise upwards, and there is often not much in the middle. I have seen many images like this – the internet is full of flat bluebell woods – and have spent hours myself scrambling about at ground level in the hope of getting an interesting angle.

I usually resolve the problem by trying to find a slope, which will introduce some diagonals and a little hinterland. In *Bluebell Slope* I chose a curved descent with a copse in the background, introducing a new angle, a shadowy dip and a change of foliage. I also framed the composition behind a sharply diagonal, textured section of tree bark. It may take some time and ingenuity to do justice to spring woodlands; some uneven or hilly ground or a meandering path will help, but creative cropping and artistic licence back in the studio can take you a long way.

A horizontally layered, flat shoreline also presents problems. I live very close to one that has interesting skies, an ever-changing sea, pebbles, seaweeds and a mass of locally abundant foreshore plants. There are plenty of attractive features and a rich botanical diversity, but it lacks verticals: everything is horizontal, there are no bays in sight, and the same vista stretches for miles. Landscapes such as this need a change of angle to introduce diagonals or verticals to create balance. Alternatively, overhanging branches, tall plants and clumps of bushes are all devices that will break the monotony.

OBSERVING AND BREAKING RULES

Keep Things in Perspective

This much-used expression advises us to look at the whole picture and to see things in relation to everything else. Keeping a sense of proportion is also implied. Perspective, or the perception of distance, is an illusion that artists use to give the impression of a three-dimensional scene on a flat surface. It is not essential to picture creation, but some knowledge of the rules will help if you are trying to make a landscape look real and it doesn't seem to be working. Perspective can be used to create extra dynamics; it also helps to move the viewer's eye over a scene. If you want to alter the angle of a path, field or other feature to make a composition more interesting, perspective will help you to do it successfully. Architects and artists depicting urban scenes use quite complicated perspective, but a few basic guidelines will suffice for simple landscapes. Once you have understood a few principles, you can make better sense of where things should be.

Eye Levels and Vanishing Points

Whenever we create a picture, we take up a position that determines what we can see. Depending on our viewpoint, some things will appear above (for example the sky, treetops) and some below (flowers, grasses and suchlike). Choose a comfortable *eye-level* line for viewing your subject; this will be the level of the artist's (and viewer's) eyes in relation to the scene. You can change your eye level by changing your position: if you are at the top of a cliff your eye-level line will be high and most of the picture content will be below this (beach, water, some sky); but if you are crouching amongst the wayside flowers, your eye-level line will be low and the content will mostly appear above you.

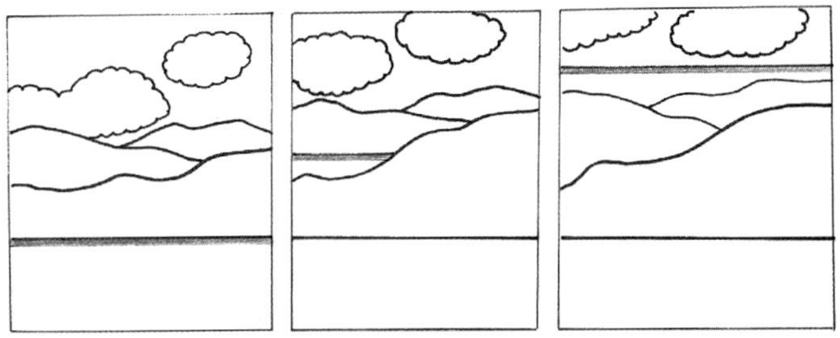

Eye levels. Low: the eye rests at water level and much of what we see is *above*. Medium: the eye rests on the second shoreline, revealing features *above* and *below*. High (as from a cliff top): we now see an expanse of water and features *below*. Here the eye level and the horizon line coincide, where water meets sky.

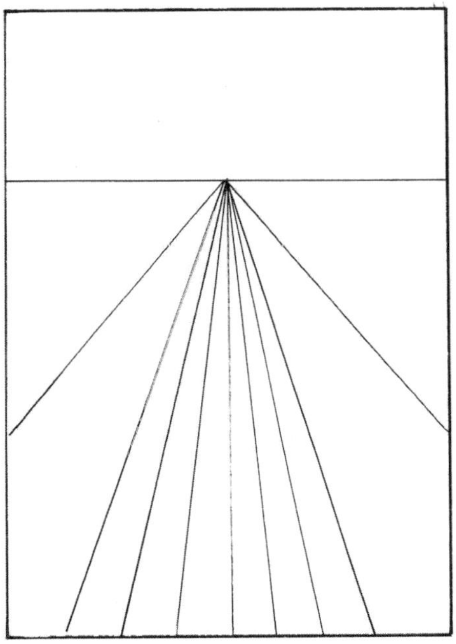

One-point perspective. In this basic version straight lines going back into the picture converge at a vanishing point set on eye level. This would apply to railway lines, roads and so on as they recede.

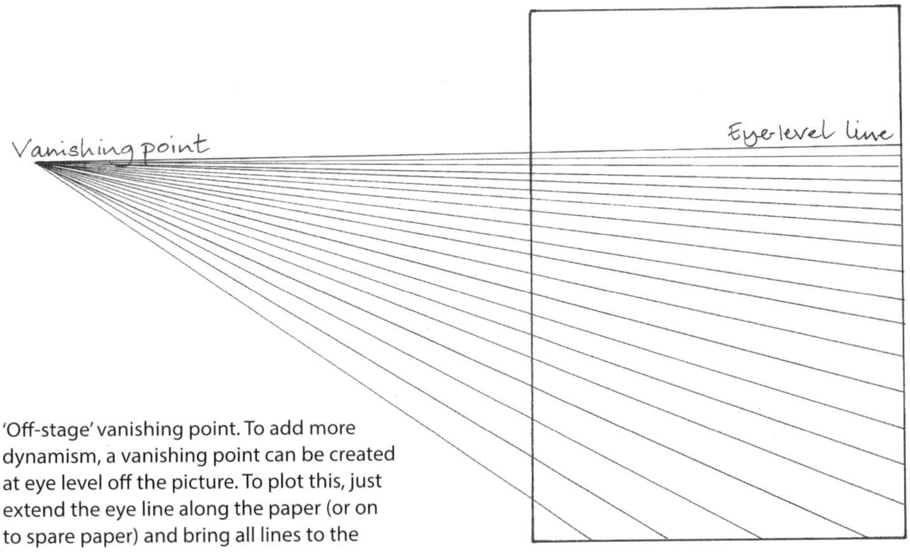

'Off-stage' vanishing point. To add more dynamism, a vanishing point can be created at eye level off the picture. To plot this, just extend the eye line along the paper (or on to spare paper) and bring all lines to the chosen point. This creates more interesting angles and can be used for paths, fields, flowing water and suchlike.

If you feel you want a different eye level for your picture, do it before you start. Never change your viewpoint when you are mid-way through a sketch or a painting; this would be like a life model changing position mid-pose. If you are working outdoors, making an initial sketch and then photographing the same scene for reference, take this into consideration and keep the viewpoint and eye level the same for both. You will then be able to take information from either, without any conflict of perspective.

If you are working at home from your own photograph or from a printed image, you will need to locate the eye level; in fact your eye will probably gravitate naturally towards this level and all you need do is recall or notice it. Practise finding the eye level on other images, and notice what you see above and below to familiarize yourself with the idea.

The *eye-level line* is important because at some point on it, receding parallel lines in the picture will appear to converge. This spot is known as the *vanishing point.* The parallel lines in your picture – formed by retreating paths, furrows, hedges – will create an illusion of distance if you show them in perspective. We know that the eye perceives objects as smaller the closer they get to the vanishing point, and that the nearer they are to us, the larger they appear. Perspective gives us a way of showing objects and features to scale and in relationship to each other. The trick cleverly creates the illusion of distance on a flat surface.

One-point perspective is the simplest form to manage: the image has one vanishing point on the eye-level line within the picture frame. If the vanishing point is central, the eye will zoom straight backwards; a vanishing point that is off stage, but on an extension of the eye-level line, will produce more interesting angles for paths, fields and so on. Perspective can get as complicated as you like, and you can, like Paolo Uccello, make it your mistress. Alternatively, you can absorb a few basics and use them to keep your pictures on track.

The Golden Mean

Sometimes known as the *golden section* or *the rule of thirds*, this concept was devised by the Greeks and based on the proportions deemed most satisfying to the human eye. Later studies supported the idea that designs set out using the golden ratio of 1 to 1.618 are aesthetically pleasing. It is very important in mathematics, and occurs everywhere in the natural world in structures and growth patterns. For our purposes, the rule of

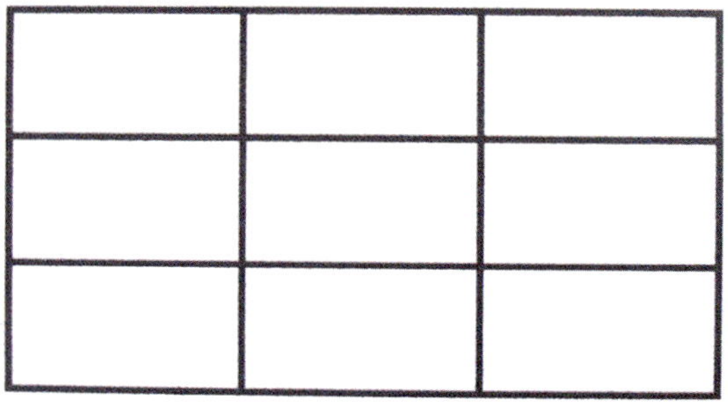

The importance of thirds. As a general guideline for creating a pleasingly proportioned picture, keep in mind this simple, classical division into thirds in both directions, with the main point of interest placed at one of the intersections.

thirds assists composition and the placing of focal points. A focal point on one of the intersections, which leads the eye around the picture, will have better visual appeal than one placed centrally. Sometimes the focal point and the vanishing point will coincide, but you can place a focal point anywhere that works aesthetically. From abstract to botanical art, you will see evidence of artists using this ancient ratio.

Rebellion is Best Left to the Experts

Some artists like to disregard or subvert aesthetic norms. This is usually because they know these norms extremely well and are playing with them and with us. Colour and composition can certainly make the viewer feel unsettled if that is the aim. Works that do not observe perspective may emphasize other aspects, or may disorientate us; if you choose to do this, be aware that your work may be making a statement but will not appear realistic. My feeling is that this is an area best left to the experts; there is a fine line between knowing subversion and not knowing good practice. A few basic rules, devised long ago, have helped generations of artists to make better pictures and feel a sense of achievement. However, landscape is rarely rebel territory, and even the wildest applications tend to nod towards good composition.

TAKING CHARGE

Artistic Decisions

Some decisions are best made using time-honoured guidelines such as the rule of thirds; others are much more within your own artistic control. It is important to get a good composition, but once that is established, you can adapt the elements of the landscape to suit your image. What you include, the colours you select and the atmosphere you create, are all within your control. If you are working to a commission or on a well-known subject, there are limits on your freedom to make changes. Otherwise, you are in charge and can be director once you have set the stage. Nature may be all-powerful, but do not be intimidated: you have the last word in the creation of your own picture.

Moving, Adding and Simplifying Objects

Nature has a tendency to be over-abundant and is rather haphazard about placing things. It may not be wise to move mountains, but as artistic director, feel free to adjust other features. You can shift a tree that is too central, or alter a patch of forest that needs thinning. Just moving an object slightly can make a big difference aesthetically. Vegetation can be pruned, and unwanted objects such as telegraph poles taken out completely. If there are too many trees, bushes or clumps of foliage, do a little gardening and create shapes that work within the frame. Providing you keep the vanishing point, you can bring more dynamism into your image by deepening angles, widening rivers and paths, and adding height or width to foreground features.

You may have concentrated on the focal point, and have an image that is devoid of foreground features; if this happens, you can easily introduce more material to add interest and local colour. I often integrate new flowers or grasses that I know belong to the specific habitat and season. Think about how you will incorporate them in a way that makes the foreground more interesting: for example, taller clumps of vegetation and shady hollows will create more variety and tone, as will rocks and stones. Most plants are more likely to cluster and mingle with other species than be scattered everywhere uniformly. Even if you are filling up space, think about the results beforehand – don't go to the opposite extreme and overcrowd the image. A wise artist friend used to say that the eye needs somewhere to rest, and I always follow her advice.

Depending on the landscape and the season it is possible that you may instead want to simplify things. I often find that summer foliage appears too profuse, and confuses rather than enhances the picture. If you have a partially obscured focal point that you want to show, clear away some of the surrounding material. Too much busy detail in the foreground or to the side will detract from it; it is quite permissible to decrease the number of rocks, bushes and trees on the route towards your point of interest. Even if the theme of your work is nature's profusion, it should still have direction, focus and salient features. You may aim to show a slice of nature, but inevitably we choreograph what we see; it may be chaos, but it's my chaos!

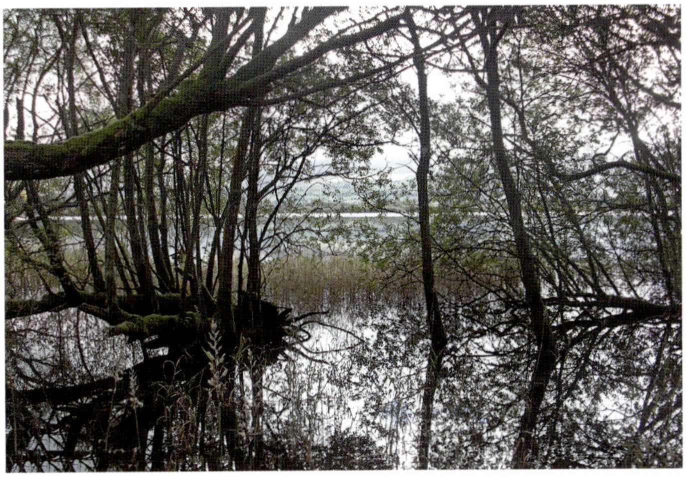

Clearing clutter. This image shows what nature can often be like without artistic intervention. The edge of the lake splits the image in half. Some of the foreground features have potential; however, there is far too much to take in, and nowhere for the eye to rest. Pruning, cropping and dredging are urgently required!

Using Information from More Than One Image

This can be done easily unless the view is very well known. I often find that I like one photograph for its composition, but would prefer to use the overhanging tree from another. I regularly change features such as waterside plants because I prefer the ones in another image. Borrowed elements may give you the image you want, but check whether there is a difference in scale, and adjust if necessary. Sometimes the experiment fails, so try a quick sketch to make sure that the idea will work without disturbing the balance.

If you have an image that inspires you, a good composition with interesting features and perspective that works, you are now ready to try out some techniques. I should point out at this early stage that there is no need for an elaborate drawing. All you will need is a very light sketch placing the main features in the landscape. No outlines, shading or detail are needed. All the mark-making will be done in ink and coloured pencil and built up gradually. Time for the drawing pens!

CHAPTER 4

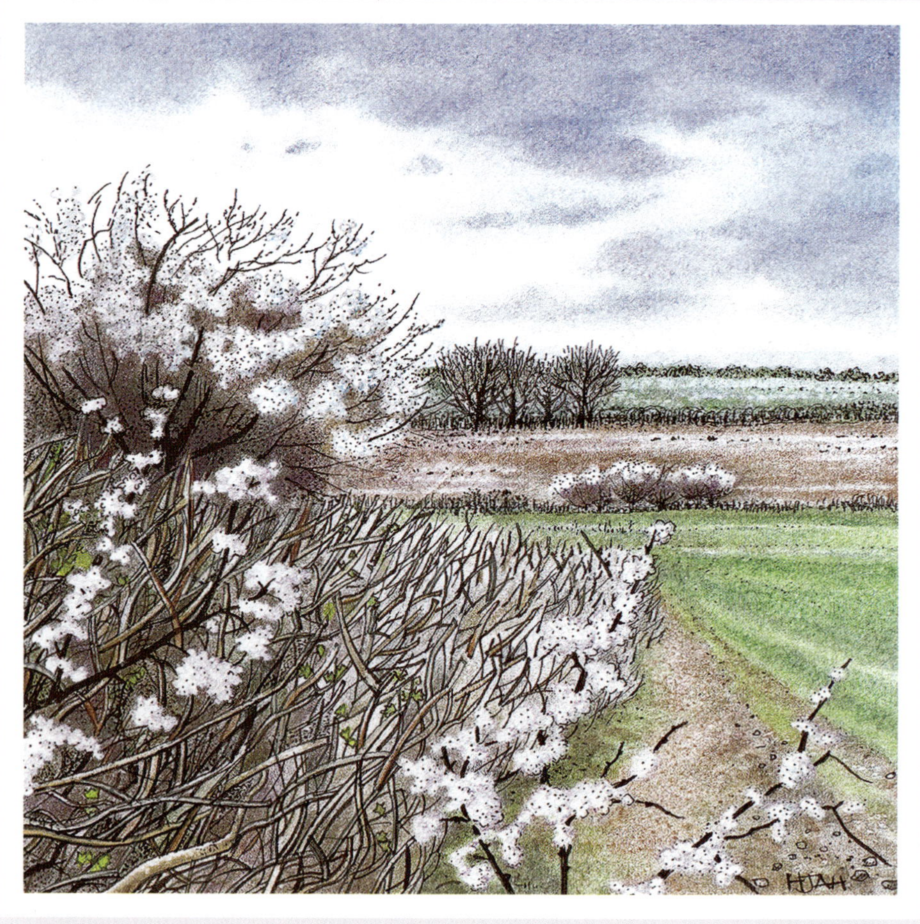

Blackthorn Spring.

Basic Techniques

This chapter will guide you through the simplest techniques needed for working in ink and coloured pencil. I shall present them separately for the sake of clarity, but they will be integrated when you use them in your image. In both cases, the techniques are easy to learn and do not require years of practice to achieve an encouraging result.

MARK-MAKING IN INK

Lines are Not the Only Marks

Pen and ink sketches are often referred to as line drawings, and line will certainly form a large part of your work. However, this is not the only method of mark-making in ink. Dots of different sizes, irregular markings, small blobs and shapes made with tools and 'found' objects can all be used for different effects. When you are working out how to interpret landscape features, do consider options other than lines. For example, to create very dark areas I occasionally use cross-hatching, a common technique in line drawing and printmaking. However, it is not necessarily the best treatment for shade in every context, and can look too linear and heavy for the rest of the picture. Once you start thinking in an integrated way, a blend of dense ink dots combined with deep shadow colours may present itself as a better solution.

Creative Use of Mark-Making

To get a better idea of creative mark-making, I find it helpful to study the work of artists who have excelled in its practice. They do not necessarily need to have worked in ink: it is their use of marks, rather than the medium, that can be of interest to us. Some have worked in pen and ink, others in graphite, paint or printmaking. They all share an ability to make interesting marks of varied strength and density. There are examples from Rembrandt to Ravilious: some of my personal favourites are Claude Lorrain, Corot, Van Gogh, Piper and Hockney. If you move away from the coloured plates in art books and browse the drawing sections, there are some wonderful examples of mark-making, from medieval to modern. In Van Gogh's landscape drawings, some of which are in ink, you will see varied marks, which succeed in conveying direction, density, light, shadow and perspective. Some areas have lines, others dots and squiggles, but they work together to create a lively, integrated image.

Experiment with different sorts of mark-making yourself: use ink strokes to create direction, incorporate dots of varying sizes, and try out irregular shapes. When I started printmaking, I kept a little sketchbook with interesting examples of mark-making that I had seen on my travels. Everything gets added to your visual memory and can be dusted down and used later in your work.

Using Ink Marks to Establish Perspective

When working in ink and coloured pencil, you can use both to establish perspective. We know that the size, strength and direction of the marks you make in ink determine the distances in the picture; this can be supported by your use of softer, bluer colour to create aerial perspective. Stronger features in the foreground dominate, and the size and strength of features in

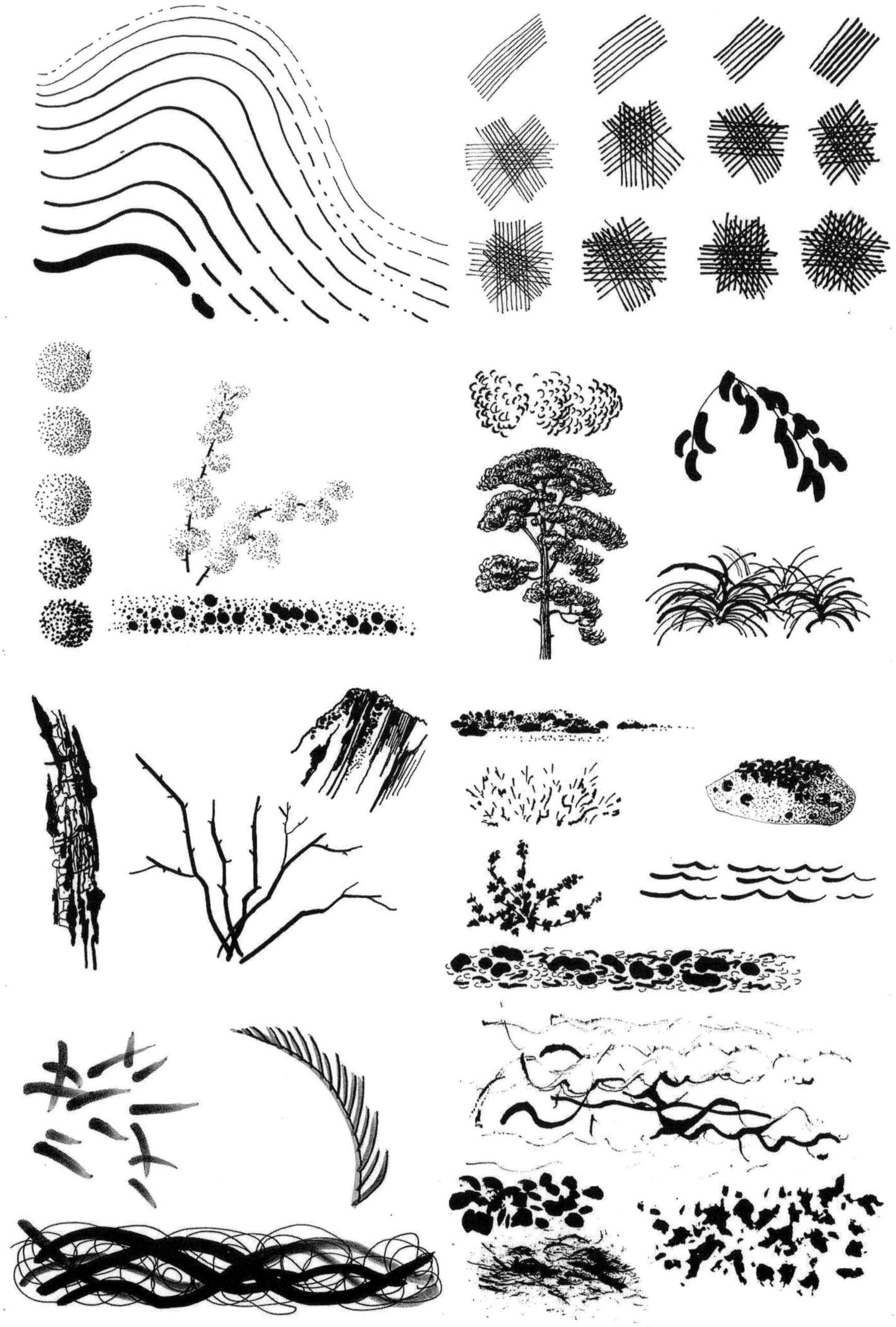

Mark-making in ink. **Row 1:** Different thicknesses of line, broken lines, hatching and cross-hatching. **Row 2:** Dots of all sorts, curves and half-circles. **Line 3:** Broken and jagged lines and irregular shapes. **Line 4:** Brush-stroke shapes, and shapes made with objects dipped in ink (clockwise): twigs, crumpled silver foil, old toothbrush and lollipop stick.

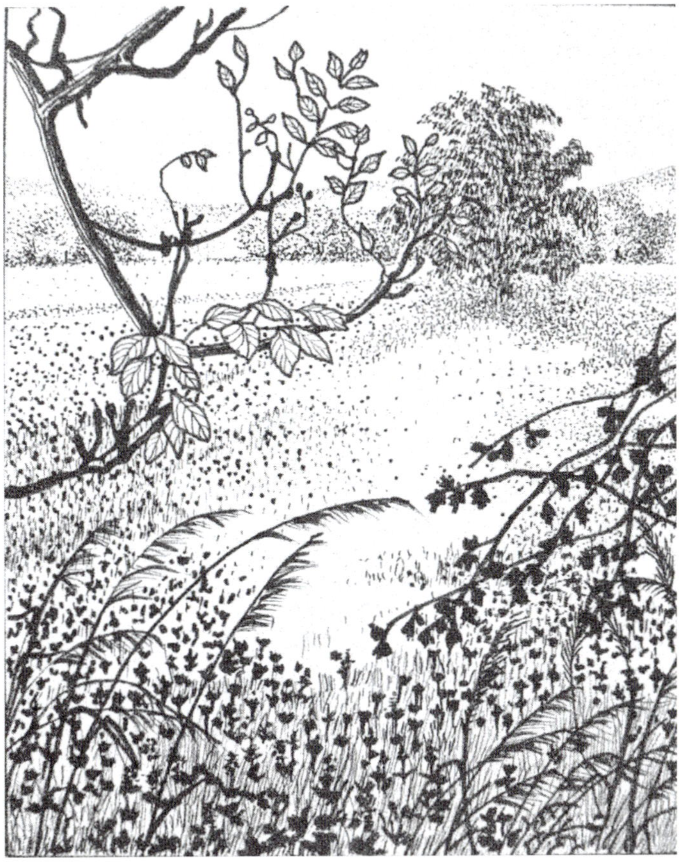

Mark-making for perspective. The size and strength of ink marks can be used to show distance. In this sketch the foreground branches are strong, with outlined leaves. We know that the tree is in the middle distance and that the distant bushes and hills have the smallest markings. The grasses in the field also diminish in size and strength.

the middle ground indicate their relative distance. The size of the smallest markings shows us the fullest extent of the landscape. Use this knowledge when you are composing a picture so that it makes sense visually. Bear it in mind if you add more marks and dots at a later stage, and make sure that they are an appropriate size for their distance.

Using Marks to Establish Texture

You can use marks in different ways to convey a variety of textures. Fine, directional strokes topped with dots will create silky grasses; jagged lines and mottled markings can be used for tree bark. Smooth textures call for a relative absence of markings or small, regular strokes. Pebbles and rough ground give plenty of scope for creativity. Providing the size and strength of the markings are in keeping with the surrounding area, you can enjoy combining ink and colour in inventive ways. I am

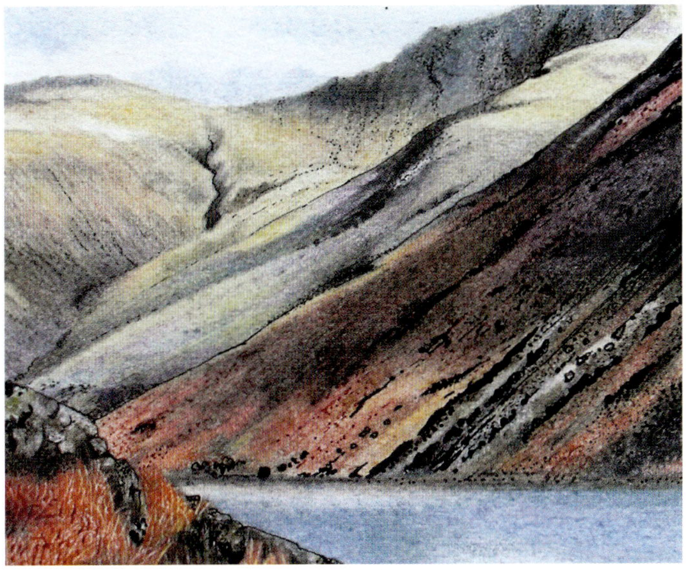

Wild Wastwater (detail): an integrated approach. This image shows how small ink details on a hillside amidst the coloured pencil will show direction and add texture. Gullies and paths help to explain the lie of the land, but must be an appropriate size to suit the distance. Markings that are too bold will leap forwards.

still experimenting and finding new ways of depicting texture, from seaweed to seed heads. Ways of achieving this for specific subjects will be explored in full in later chapters.

Using Marks for an Integrated Look

I often find that my students are irresistibly drawn to ink outlines, in the hope of colouring them in. Many of us enjoyed this process in childhood, so it is probably second nature. Add to this the trend for adult colouring books as relaxation, and we have a powerful pull. However, it will not give the results we are hoping for and should be resisted! One of the disadvantages is that we tend to ignore areas that do not obviously need ink. It is easy to run out of imagination for fields and hillsides and leave them blank.

For a genuinely integrated look, ink and coloured pencil need to work together throughout the image. This means deciding how to combine the two in every part of the picture. I am not advocating clutter: there should always be some ink-free spaces where the eye can rest, but avoid leaving large expanses without any markings at all. Try adding tiny ink marks to distant fields and mountains so they mingle with the colour. This will add texture, but also perspective and something of interest for the eye. The finished image will be a well-balanced mix of media that could never be mistaken for an exercise in 'colouring in'!

BASIC COLOURED PENCIL TECHNIQUES

Much of the success of coloured pencil work depends on the interaction of the three Ps: paper, pigment and pressure. Artist-quality coloured pencils contain a much higher proportion of pure pigment, and this makes a big difference on the page. Some papers are more suited to coloured pencil than others, and the surface texture affects the smoothness of the finish. Try a few brands to find out which paper best suits your method of working and your make of pencils. The amount of pressure you apply with the pencil will also affect the look you achieve; you will soon learn to vary this according to the softness of the pencil and the number of layers.

Stay Sharp!

One rule applies to all your coloured pencils, whatever the make: they must be sharp! Invest in a good quality, pocket pencil sharpener and some spare blades. Coloured pencils need to be resharpened frequently as you work, and blades will eventually need renewal.

Why such a fine point? The paper has fibres, and a sharp point will get between them and deposit pigment evenly. A blunt pencil does not give such good coverage and may skim the surface, particularly if the paper has a slight texture. There is a temptation to press too hard if the pencil is blunt, just to get more colour; this flattens the fibres of the paper, preventing successful application of more layers. Finally, working with a blunt instrument deprives you of control; it is difficult to handle detail, edges become clumsy, and corners are difficult to access.

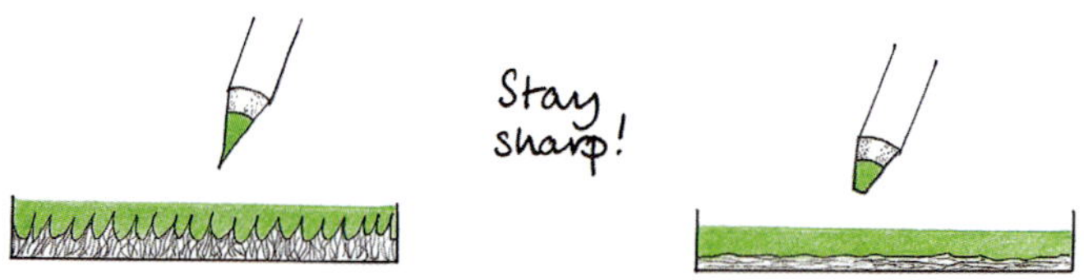

Stay sharp! Paper contains fibres, and a well-sharpened pencil point can get between these and deposit plenty of pigment. The fibres are undamaged, and will take more layers once the first one has been put down. A blunt pencil will squash the fibres, creating a shiny surface that will be reluctant to take more colour.

Small Ellipses and Cross-Hatching

Unlike painting, which involves mastering many types of brushwork, coloured pencil has just two main methods of application if you want a smooth surface: small ellipses and linear cross-hatching. These are the two that I use in my work, and I alternate them depending on the requirements of the piece.

To build up ellipses, hold the pencil just below vertical and work in small circles, keeping the strokes very close to each other to ensure total coverage. Maintain a light to medium touch and aim for a smooth finish. Do not press too hard as this will flatten the surface. Keep the ellipses tight and avoid loosening them and increasing their size; I refer to this affectionately as 'knitting' – and it makes too many holes!

You may be familiar with cross-hatching in drawing as a method of creating tones, from light grey to deepest black. To apply a first layer in coloured pencil, start with fine parallel lines, set close together. Repeat the process from the opposite angle, going over the previous lines. This should produce a smooth coverage, but you can add a third layer in a diagonal direction if you wish. Alternatively, swap to small ellipses for the final layer to give a refined finish.

Try to remember that coloured pencil work is, by its very nature, slow art. Rather than hoping to speed things up, it helps if you can accept this, and enjoy the proven therapeutic aspects of the process. We know that the combination of concentration and repetition keeps us in the moment and takes us into the near-meditative state known as flow – until we suddenly realize that hours have passed! Fortunately, the image grows steadily at the same time, so patience is rewarded. If you are not naturally inclined to be meticulous and prefer quick results, you have a few choices: appreciate that coloured pencil work is different and learn to love it, concentrate on its therapeutic properties and think of your well-being, or choose a medium that better chimes with your temperament.

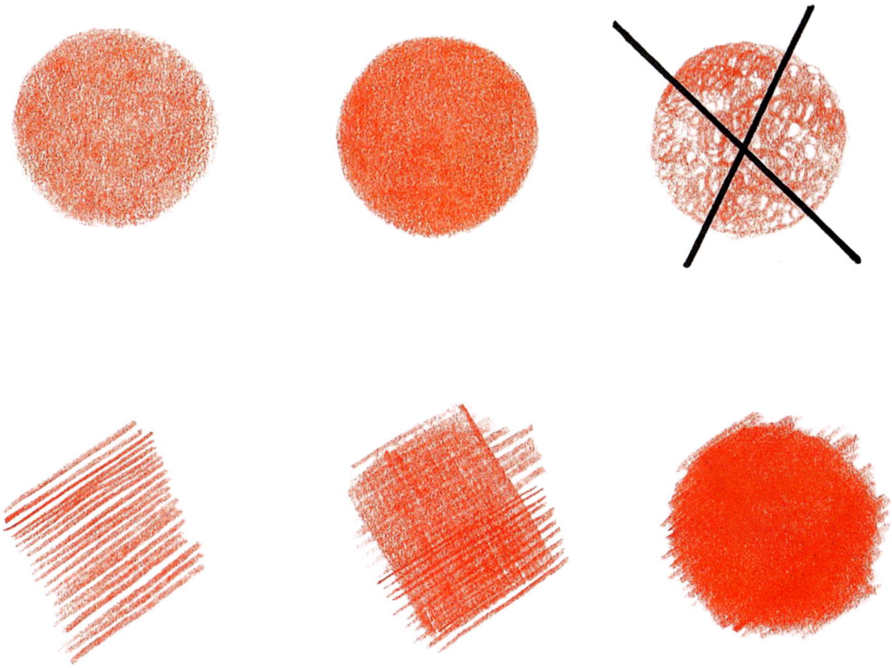

Ellipses and cross-hatching. **Row 1:** One layer of Faber-Castell 'Light Cadmium Red' applied using the ellipse method, building up to three layers (the paper will take more) and 'knitting' – letting the ellipses become too large and loopy. **Row 2:** Single hatching, cross-hatching and cross-hatching with one layer of ellipses on top.

Blending

All good artists' coloured pencil ranges are designed to blend smoothly. One layer of a single colour will give a light coverage; three or four layers of the same colour will give a much deeper tone. Depending on the type of pencil, even more layers can be built up. However, a truly rich and interesting finish comes not from one colour, but from the blending of several shades. The eye may read it as one deep colour, but closer inspection will reveal all the different components. A plum may look reddish purple; however, its colour is best conveyed not by a single reddish-purple shade, but by a mix of the purples, reds, blues and greens that can be seen on its surface. This applies equally to landscape: use a subtle combination of different colours for a mountain or stretch of water rather than one colour that appears at first glance to be an exact match.

If you purchase sets, some of the colours in your selection may look perfect for landscape and others too lurid. If the greens seem rather bright and unnatural, try blending them with more subtle earth colours and discover how they mix and match. Using a blending colour that contains some element of the complementary (red into green, for example) will neutralize anything too vivid and unnatural-looking. Practise using different combinations of colour, and be experimental. Eventually

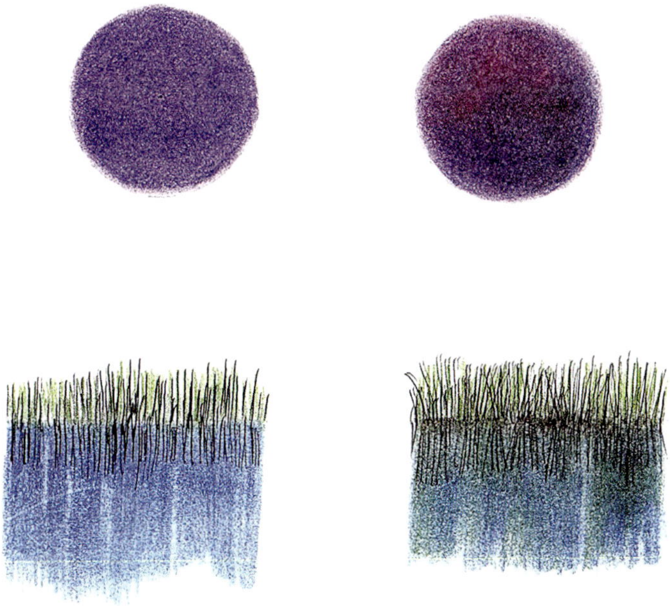

Single colours and blends. **Row 1:** The first circle has three layers of Faber-Castell Mauve. The second has a more interesting blend of Mauve, Red-Violet and Dark Indigo. **Row 2:** For the water's edge on the left, I used Faber-Castell Helio Blue-Reddish. The second version has a base of Helio Blue-Reddish mixed with Chrome Oxide Green and Dark Sepia.

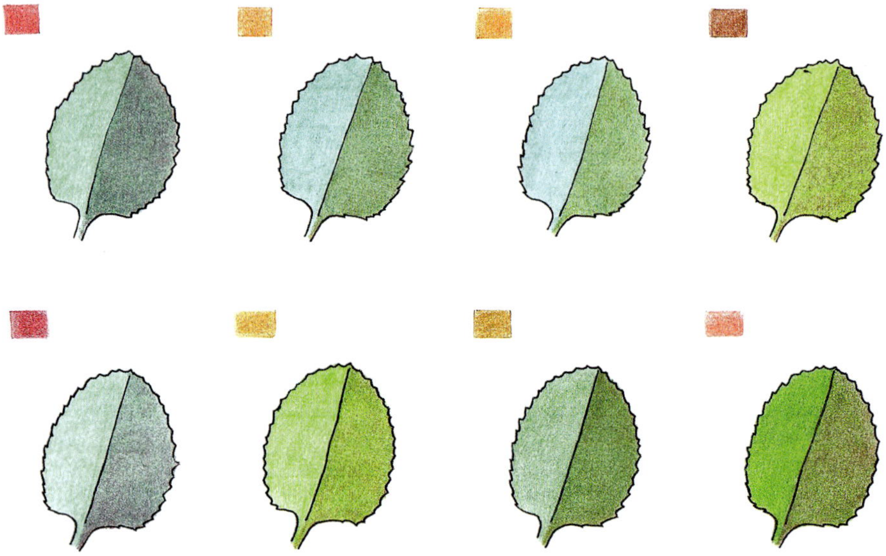

Modifying colours. Examples of some brighter Faber-Castell 'Polychromos' greens blended with earthier pigments. **Row 1:** Emerald Green and Burnt Carmine, Chrome Oxide Green and Burnt Ochre, Phthalo Green and Terracotta, Grass Green and Burnt Sienna. **Row 2:** Light Phthalo Green and Red-Violet, Leaf Green and Brown Ochre, Hooker's Green and Raw Umber, Permanent Green and Venetian Red.

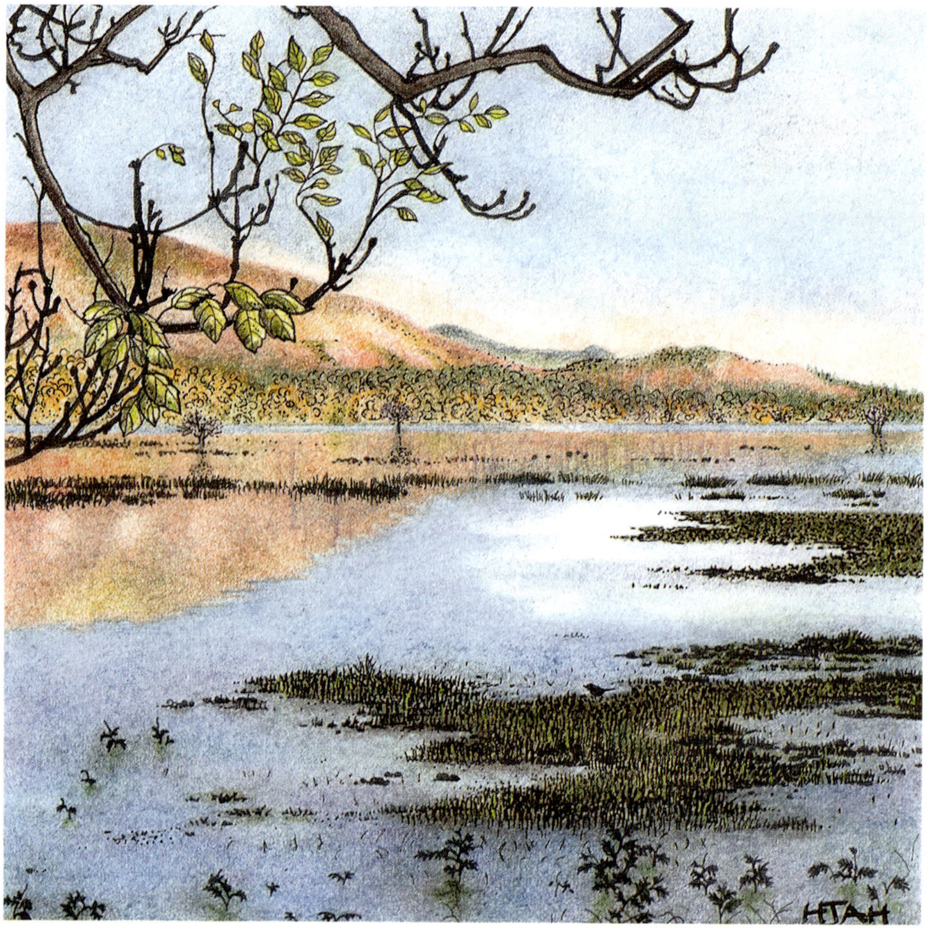

Unusual colour choices. Faber-Castell's Dark, Medium and Light Flesh were surprising choices for the autumnal fells above Derwentwater, but fitted the mood. Be flexible in your selection of colours and try unusual blends as well as your favourites.

you will get to know your pencils and be able to identify which colour is needed in a particular situation, and which you can use to 'knock back' any that are excessively lurid.

Branded sets may contain colours that you think you are unlikely to use, but sometimes an unexpected colour will prove to be just right, despite the label. I was surprised to find myself using Faber-Castell's Flesh colours for an autumn mountainside above Derwentwater, so it is best to keep an open mind.

Building Up Layers

Layering is the best method of achieving rich, deep colour. Sometimes I see coloured pencil work that looks pale and insipid, simply because the artist has stopped after one layer and a bit of blending. Coloured pencils have plenty of pigment and will produce great depth of colour. Skilled botanical coloured pencil artists, for example, can create the deepest hues of a black tulip simply by gentle layering.

Beginners tend to make two basic errors when building up colour: too few layers or too much pressure. The first comes from being too tentative and the second from being too hasty. It may seem tedious to keep applying layers, but the rewards make it well worth the effort as your work takes on a convincing depth. Remind yourself to enjoy the process, stay in the moment, and watch the richness as it develops.

Secondly, keep a light touch always. You may be tempted to apply pressure in the hope of getting more colour on to the paper quickly. This also happens if you are unhappy with the performance of less highly pigmented pencils and try to increase their vibrancy. Pressing too hard from the outset is no solution and will crush the fibres of the paper, causing it to become shiny and reject further pigment. Doing so using just one colour will result in a doubly disappointing finish. Keep to ellipses or gentle cross-hatching, and blend subtle colours as you build up the picture. You will be amazed at the depth of colour you can achieve by this simple method.

If you want to layer effectively, it is a good idea to work with the properties of your pencils. Hard pencils such as Derwent 'Artists' and medium-hard Faber-Castell 'Polychromos', Derwent 'Procolour' and Caran D'Ache 'Pablo' are better for first layers. They can be applied to most paper surfaces suitable for coloured pencil, and never leave a waxy deposit. You can build up multiple layers if you keep a light touch. I use softer, waxier pencils such as Derwent 'Coloursoft' and Prismacolor 'Premier' to add a final layer of powerful pigment or a vivid pop of colour where needed.

However, if you use very soft pencils as a first layer on a shiny Bristol board, their higher wax content may cause them to slide or gather on the surface. This is a mismatch between paper and pencils, so it is worth trying out various combinations and considering your subject before you commit to a great work. Any of the hard to medium ranges will be fine for all the stages of your work, so there is no need to invest in several different makes unless you want to.

Adding a Pop of Colour

Some of the waxier coloured pencils are excellent at delivering a strong pop of colour when required. I use these to bring out brightly coloured flower heads, dominant foreground leaves, dappled sunlight, and any parts of the image that need a distinctive shot of colour. They are useful when you do not need layers, but just want a powerful single application of colour. Little touches such as berries and lichen all benefit from the rich, waxy texture and strong pigment. I also use them for perking up parts of an image that have started to look tired. When you work at length on an area, some of the original features may get a bit lost; a dash of concentrated pigment will revitalize them, and softer pencils do this very efficiently.

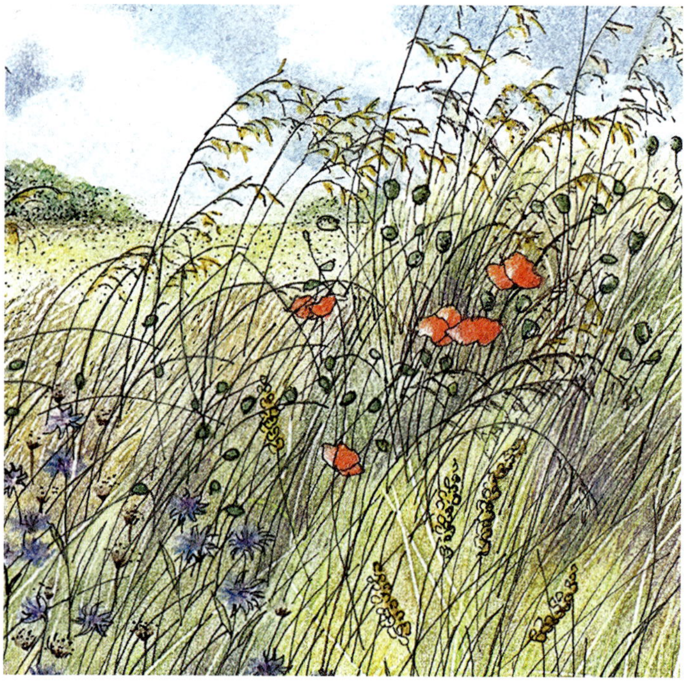

A pop of colour: *Wild Meadow* (detail). The poppy and cornflower flower heads were reinforced in the final stages with an extra layer of rich colour. I used Prismacolor Poppy Red and Blue Violet Lake, with a dash of Faber-Castell Ultramarine to help them stand out.

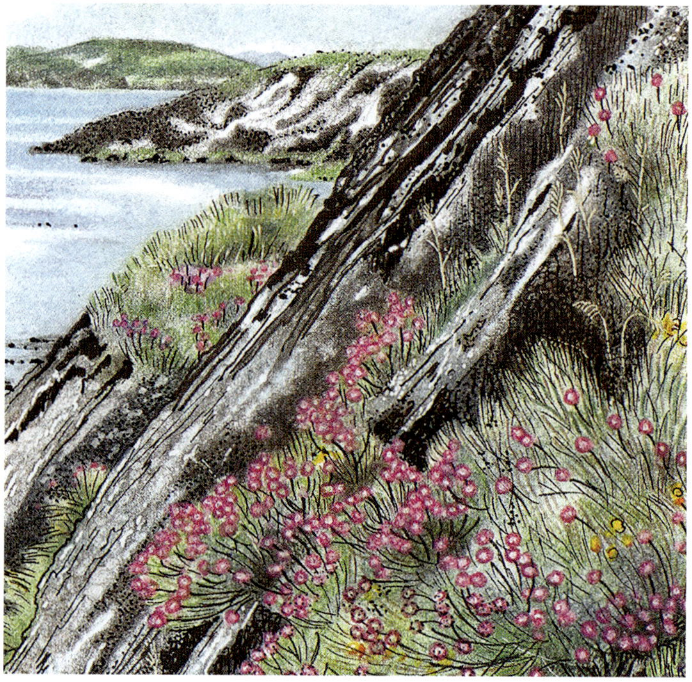

A pop of colour: *Gigha Shore* (detail). Flower heads set against a dark background, as in this picture, need plenty of contrast to stop them being overwhelmed. I used a final layer of Prismacolor Magenta and Deco Pink for the clumps of thrift.

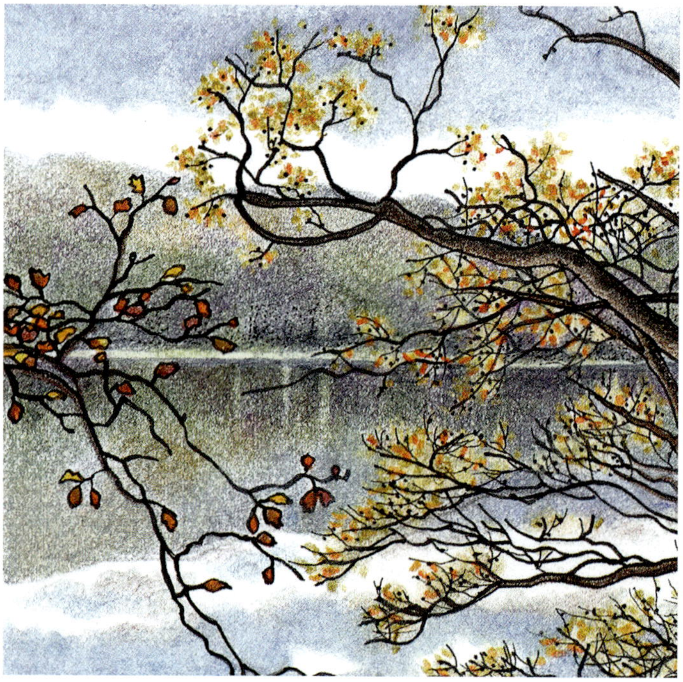

A pop of colour: *Curving towards Derwentwater* (detail). The foreground leaves were outlined in ink for emphasis, filled in with Prismacolor Orange and Pumpkin Orange and highlighted. I also used these strong autumnal shades for the bright leaves on the other trees, adding Yellow Ochre and Spanish Orange.

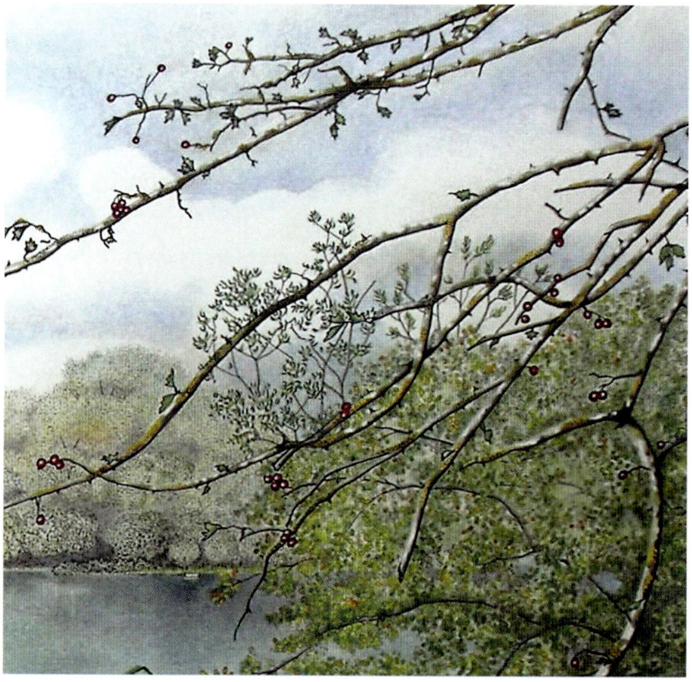

A pop of colour: *Summer into Autumn* (detail). I applied a second layer of Prismacolor Crimson Lake to these hawthorn berries as a finishing touch, keeping clear highlights to make them shine. Adding this extra touch of colour once the surrounding foliage is complete makes them really stand out.

Burnishing

Burnishing differs from blending, as it involves flattening rather than mixing colours. It is a final stage, to be done when you are certain that no more layers of pigment are required. You will need either a burnishing pencil or one of the waxier ranges of pencils. Here you can apply some pressure, as the purpose of burnishing is to flatten the surface, smooth the pigment and impart some shine. It is used sometimes in botanical work for berries, fruits and evergreen leaves. I find that it has a limited use in landscape, with one or two exceptions. If a mix of blue shades for sky or water looks too mottled, burnishing will smooth it effectively. Prismacolor Cloud Blue and Powder Blue are soft and waxy and work well as coloured pencil burnishers for uneven skies. Several of Prismacolor's pale shades, including White, make good burnishers and will soften colours that are too dominant. They will also partially obscure any ink mistakes, but will not cover them completely.

Specialist burnishers are colourless, but may cause a slight alteration to very pale pigments, so practise on a test piece first. Remember that burnishers are for the last layer: once you have used them, the paper fibres will be flattened and unreceptive to further pigment.

Finer Points

At the opposite end of the scale, hard, fine pencils such as Prismacolor Verithin can be used to sharpen edges and add last minute detail. Always have a look at the final picture and decide whether it needs any more soft or hard colour to bring it into balance.

Once you have practised mark-making in pen and mastered the art of ellipses and cross-hatching, there are no more ink or coloured pencil techniques to learn. However, there are a few alternative ways of working on the image, and these need to be added to your repertoire. The next chapter covers three exciting new skills – embossing, lifting out and sgraffito – after which you will be confident and more than ready to branch out on your own!

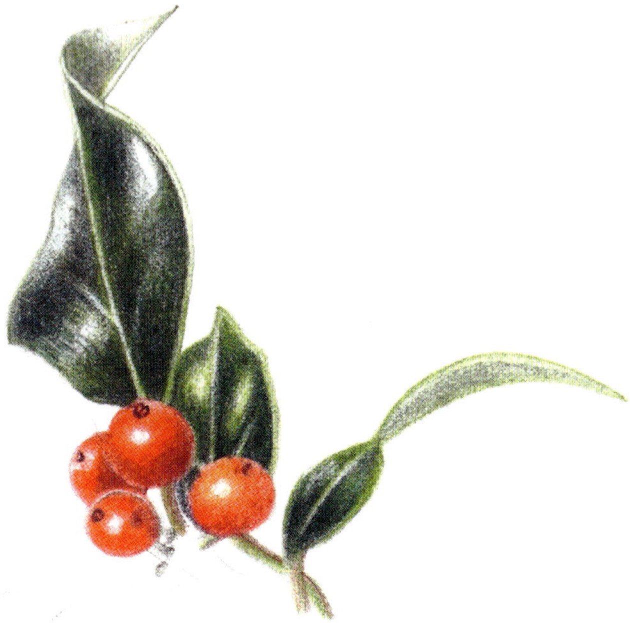

Burnishing: sprig of holly. Burnishing creates a smooth, shiny surface suitable for a final layer. It is used by some botanical artists working in coloured pencil for subjects with a silky finish such as tulips, berries and evergreen leaves. It can be done with a colourless burnisher or a coloured pencil with a very waxy consistency.

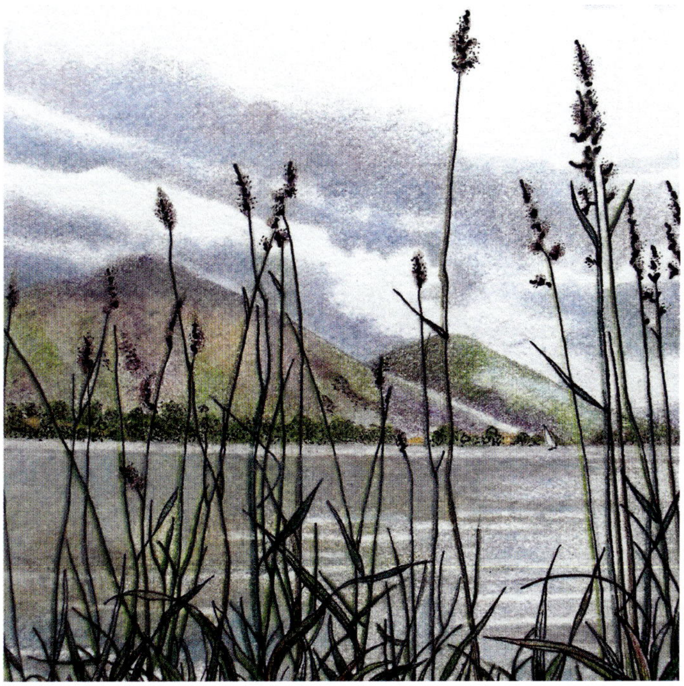

Burnishing: *Summer Calm by Bassenthwaite* (detail). Water, fells and sky were all carefully burnished in this image to create the pearly afternoon light over the lake. Burnishing does not suit every aspect of landscape, but water and skies can benefit from its smoothing effect. Burnished and non-burnished areas within the image can be used to create contrast.

CHAPTER 5

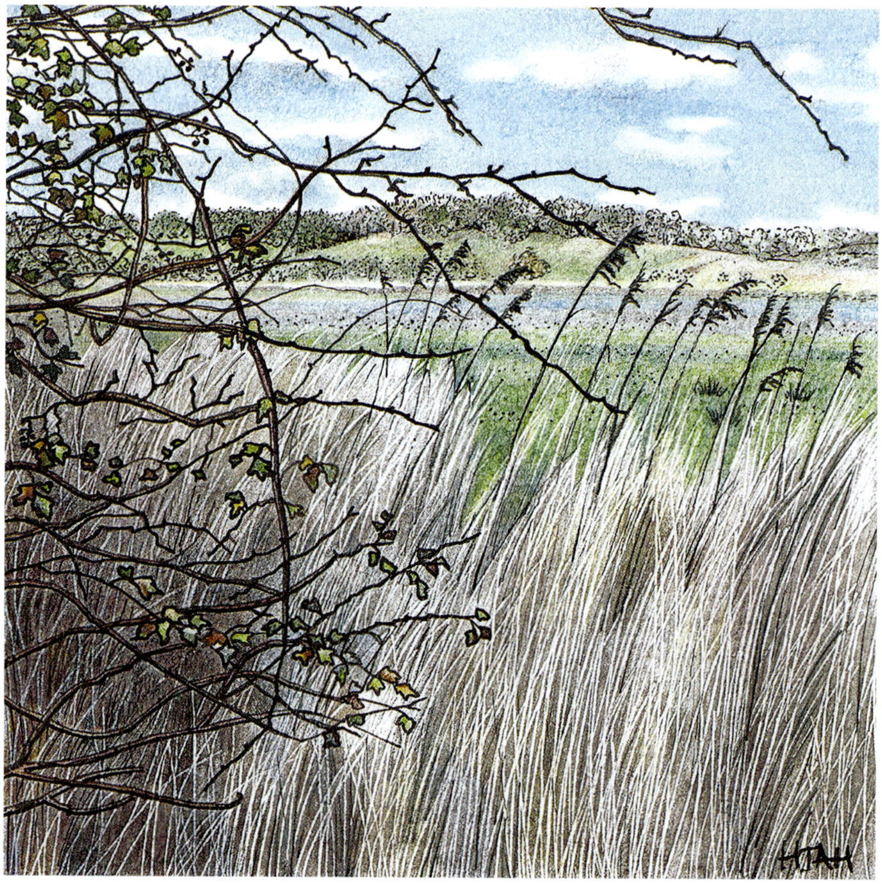

Last Autumn's Brambles.

Embossing, Lifting Out and Sgraffito

I am sure that by now you are keen to get started, so you will be glad to know that this is the final preparation chapter, and possibly the most enjoyable. When I am teaching a course, I am very aware that students need to take in a lot of information before they can start on their own work, and I often find myself apologizing for this. In a medium such as watercolour, a beginner can make step-by-step progress from washes to final details, following specific stages and instructions. Working in ink and coloured pencil in an integrated way produces a different puzzle each time.

Once you have established the basic outlines, images require different techniques and starting points, and each one is a separate voyage of discovery. You can only begin to assemble the picture when you have gathered all available resources. However, you will soon have all the techniques at your fingertips and be able to chart your own path. The additional techniques described in this chapter are fun, and will add interest. I shall outline them briefly here, and give more detailed examples of their use in context in the next.

EMBOSSING

Most of my students love embossing. The simple process of pressing something into paper then running colour over the top always produces expressions of surprise and delight. The results are very appealing and can be used to interpret many aspects of the natural world.

Embossing Tools

Embossing tools can be bought or made and will produce different results, depending on the paper and the instrument. Embossers are usually metal and double-ended, with a tiny circular ball at each end, or a single pen-like shape with a smooth metal tip. The circular tips press firmly into the fibres of the paper without any sharp edges, indenting but not breaking the surface. Sizes vary, from quite large tips for making round marks to fine pens for delicate, feathery lines. Papers with looser fibres are easier to emboss, and you may need to use fine tips for smooth, shiny papers. Always try out an embosser on test paper first, as the indentations are difficult to estimate and may not be the size you need. You can experiment with other embossing tools, including home-made ones, to achieve whatever sort of marks you require.

Embossing On Paper

Embossing directly on to paper will produce white markings that stand out distinctly against the surrounding colour. This is because the embossed areas have been pushed to a level lower than the surface of the paper, and have consequently escaped the pigment. Hold the pencil almost horizontally, so that it skims over the embossed sections and settles only on the surrounding areas. Once you have established these coloured areas and can see the adjacent indentations clearly, return the pencil to a more upright position and deepen the surrounding colour using ellipses. You can add ink marks to the colour if you wish, leaving just the white embossed lines exposed.

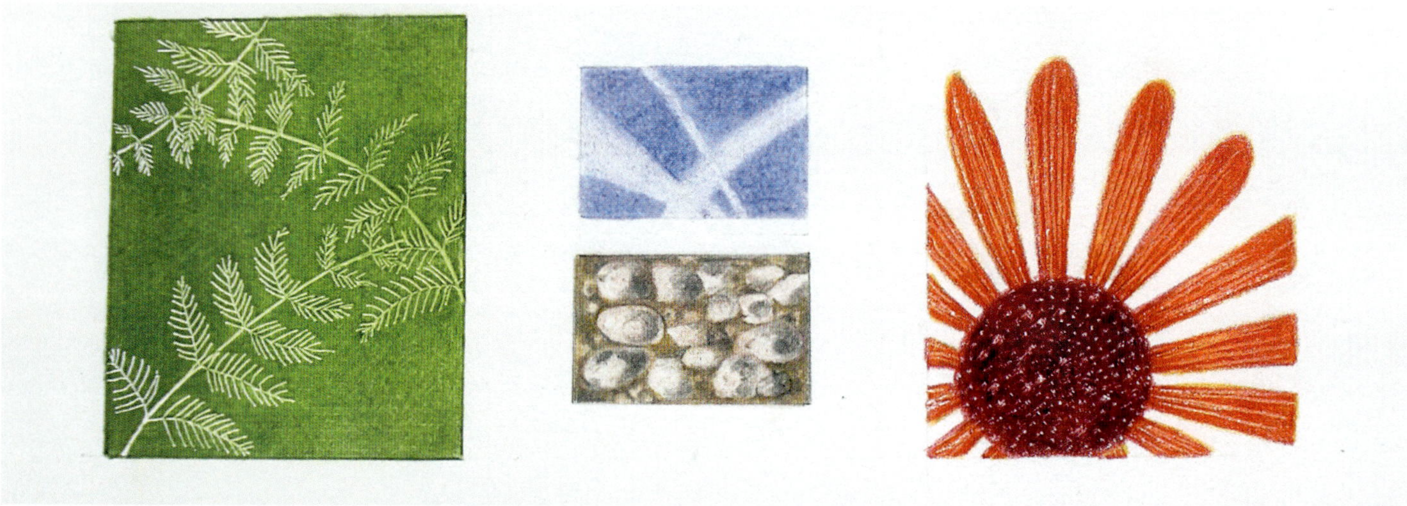

Embossing, lifting out and sgraffito. *Left*: Leaf pattern using embossing tools, with Permanent Green Olive coverage. *Centre*: Sections lifted out of Ultramarine and irregular shapes in a wall, both created using Frisket. Additional highlights were lifted with a battery eraser. *Right*: Veins and markings using sgraffito – Prismacolor Crimson Red over Spanish Orange (rays) and Black Raspberry over Crimson Red (centre).

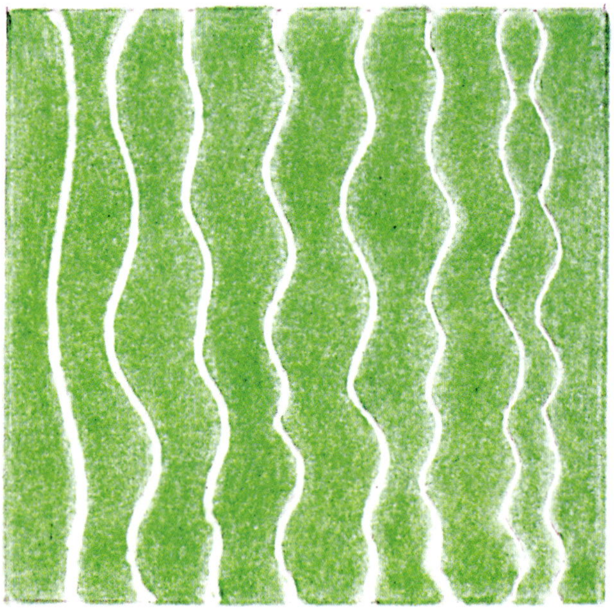

Different embossing tools on white paper. I used varying sizes of embossing tool, pressing directly on to the paper. I then coloured over the lines, holding the pencil at a low angle so that it skimmed over the indentations. More layers of pencil can be added between, with the pencil at the usual, higher angle.

The effect of white embossing is quite stark, but it can also look decorative. It is popular in card-making and stylized design, but the strong contrast may appear too artificial for the natural world. I usually emboss on a base of pale, blended colour in my landscape work. It is also possible to inject some broken colour into embossed white lines by using very hard coloured pencil in the grooves.

Embossing on Colour

Embossing over colour gives a more natural look, and is a good technique for subjects such as grasses and reeds. As the eye naturally distinguishes a range of colours, white embossing would look artificial and one-dimensional. Choose shades that form good base colours for the features you want to emboss, then apply them using ellipses or cross-hatching. The colour distribution can be planned or random, but remember that the colours you are using should be those of the reeds or grasses, not the background. Keep the colours light or bright, as they will need to stand out when embossed. The spaces *between* the grasses will eventually provide the background and shadow areas; these can be darkened as you wish, but the embossed grasses should remain clearly visible.

Once you have put down a coloured base, emboss the grasses or reeds using your chosen tools. The indentations will then contain the base colours, and these will be revealed as you work around them. You can add deeper shadows between and at the base, creating vegetation that has both tonal range and realistic colouring. To achieve an even more integrated look, add some very fine ink markings in between with a 0.03 pen.

Embossing over colour: base colours. Stage 1: For these winter grasses I used Faber-Castell 'Polychromos' Sky Blue, Yellow Ochre, Brown Ochre and Cold Grey II, keeping the colours separate to avoid a greenish mix. I used a mainly linear stroke, softening the effect with a paper stump before starting to emboss.

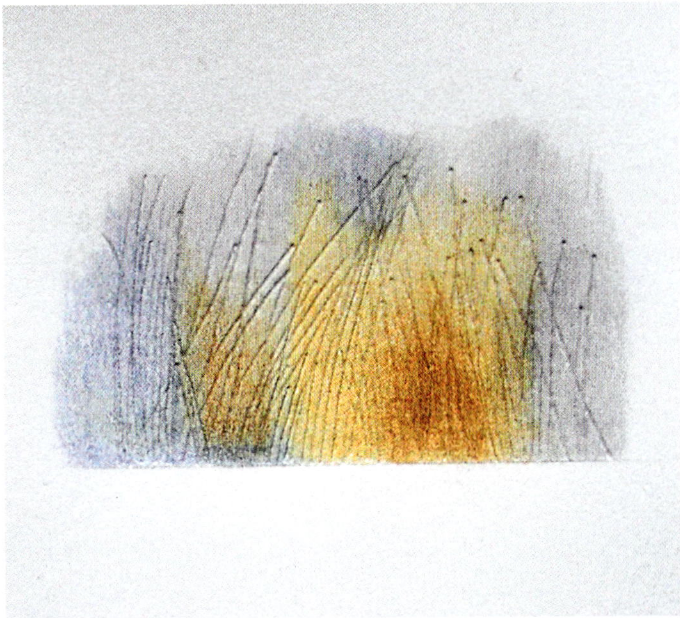

Embossing over colour: using the embossing tools. Stage 2: I tested these on spare paper first, choosing one of the smaller circular-ended ones and a stylus-type for fine lines. It is easy to get a wider line than intended as they look deceptively small. I ran both sizes firmly across the base colours, following the grass shapes.

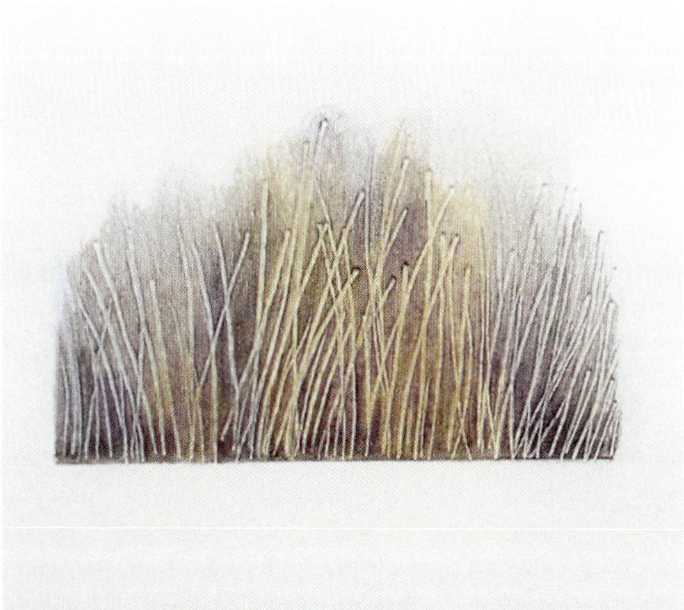

Embossing over colour: adding surrounding colours. Stage 3: These needed to be darker to reveal the grasses. I started with Nougat, holding the pencil at a slant so that it skimmed the embossed lines, depositing colour on the background. I then returned it to an upright position, working the sharp point between the lines using Dark Sepia and Violet.

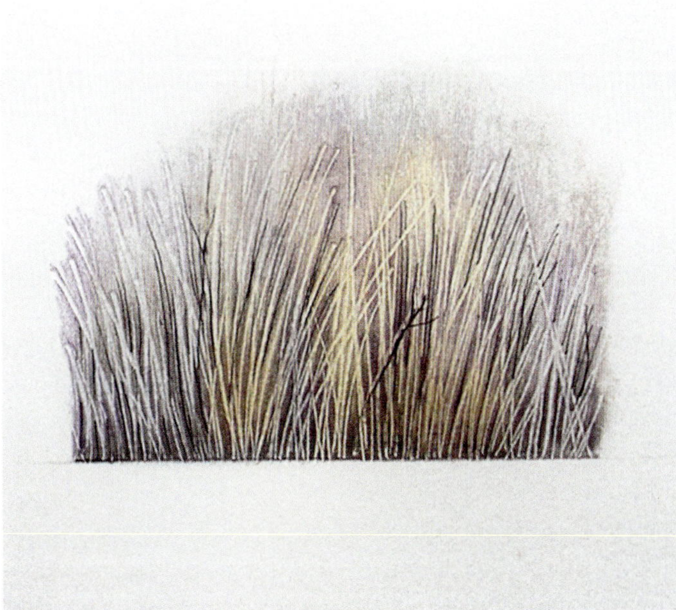

Embossing over colour: shadows and pen work. Stage 4: I continued to add shadows, starting at the base and lightening nearer the tops. Using a very fine (0.03) pen, I inked in some additional grasses, weaving them between the embossed lines, passing under rather than over any junctions. Feathered tops can be added in ink if you wish.

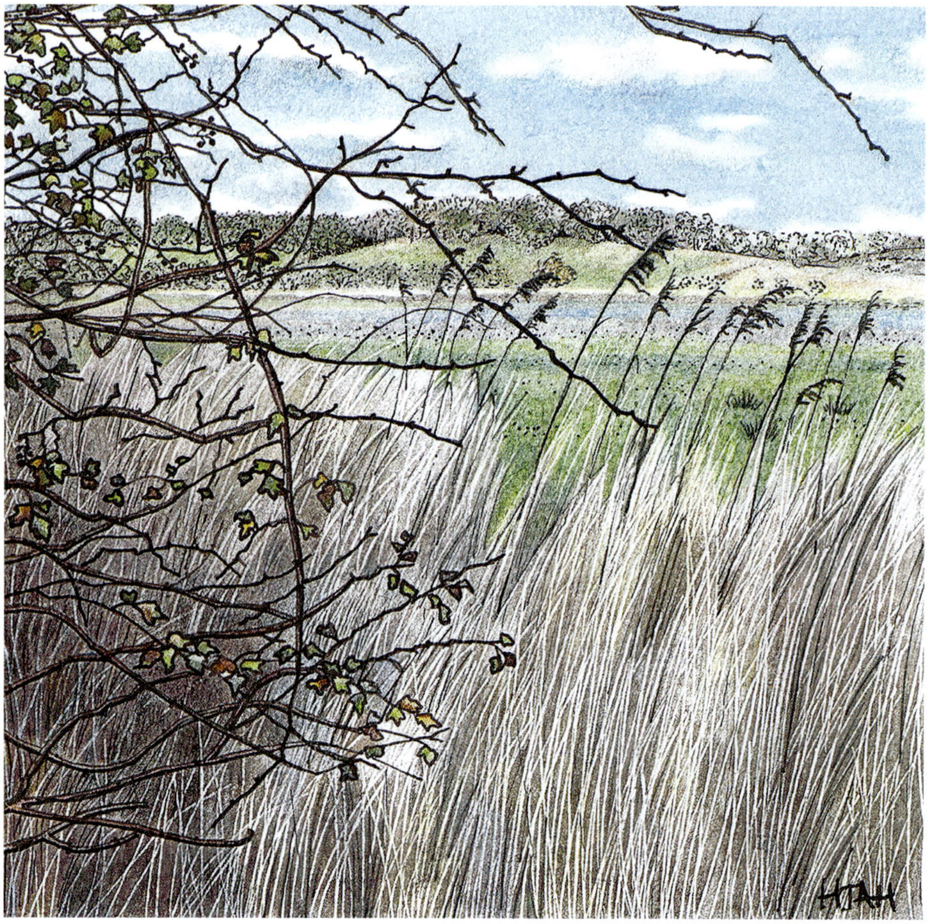

Last Autumn's Brambles. The reeds in this image were thoroughly bleached after the winter. I used embossing over a base of soft colours, introducing deep shadow colours in between for the muddy ground. I deepened the tone on the left by darkening the patch under the brambles and using strong inking and outlining for the overhanging branches.

Using Embossing to Enhance Your Work

I like to use embossing in combination with ink and coloured pencil for a range of textures found in the natural world. I keep a collection of examples and add to them whenever I have a new idea. I try to be inventive and to make use of the different sizes, shapes and colours. This is fun, but it is also a way of letting the medium interpret what we see. What emerges is a *style* rather than just a copy of reality in coloured pencil.

I use the method described above for grasses and reeds and other clusters of foliage. Embossing is also useful for winter undergrowth with dead climbing plants. For a more natural look, I draw a fine line in a light colour and carefully emboss over it, so that the result is not pure white. I use embossing for seed heads, fluffy grasses, tree roots and bark; it can also be used in snow for soft imprints and frozen foliage. The seashore provides plenty of suitable subjects: stones, shells, limpets on a rock, seaweed, choppy waves and pebble beaches are just some of the features I have depicted using a combination of embossing, ink and colour.

Less is More?

As embossing is a noticeable and rather decorative process, it tends to draw the eye. In botanical coloured pencil work I was always advised to use it sparingly; you could spot when someone had just discovered it and gone a bit mad. Landscape is not subject to such eagle-eyed scrutiny; if you like embossing and want to make it a real feature in your work, go ahead. It can be carefully integrated and play an important part in the creation of the image. You can use any of the techniques in your own way; there are no rules.

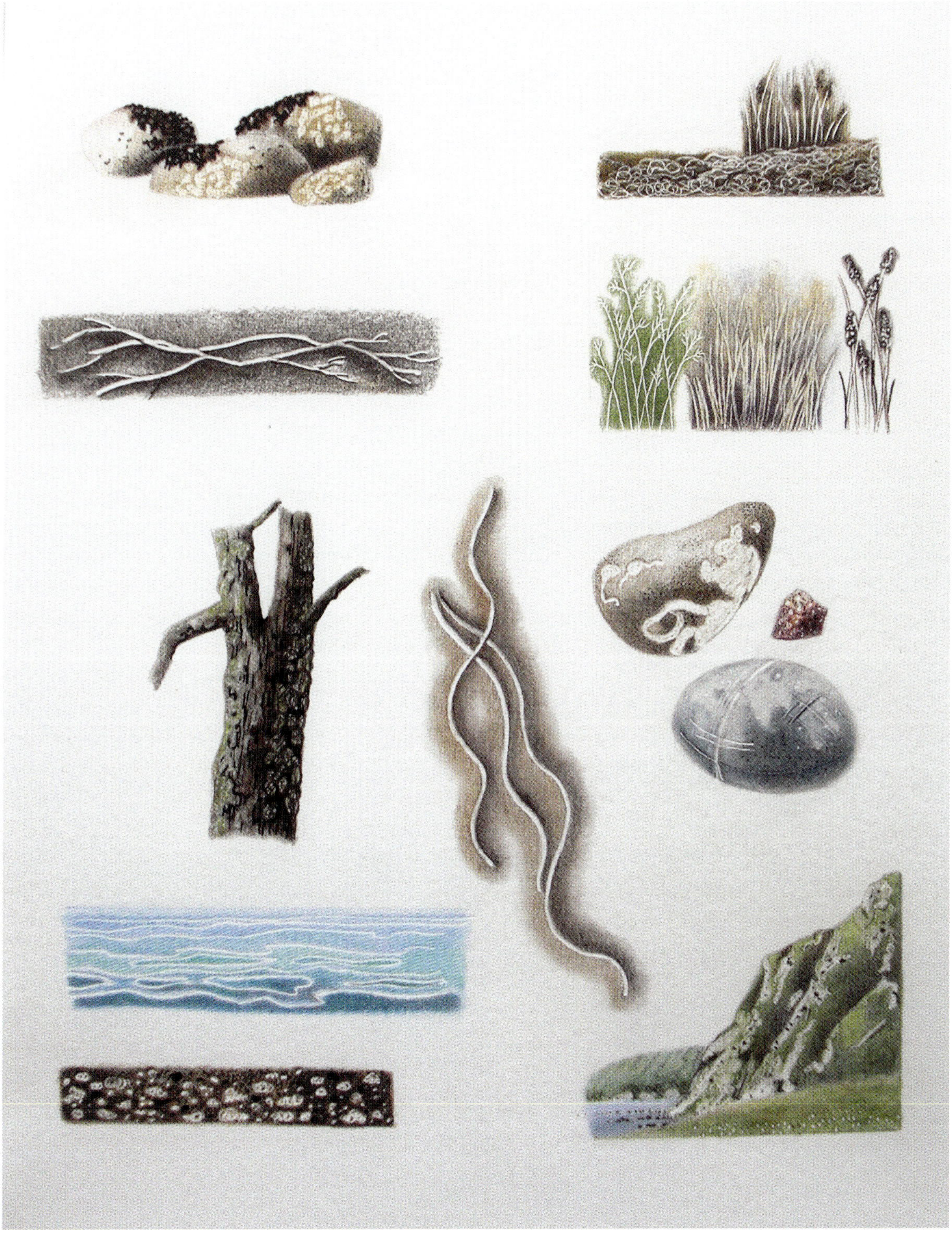

Embossing nature. This page shows how embossing can be used to depict many aspects of the landscape, from larger features such as water, rocks, cliffs and rough terrain to detailed observations of pebbles, bark, tree roots, grasses and flower heads. Here I have enjoyed experimenting, adding ink and coloured pencil to suit the subject. Try some ideas of your own.

LIFTING OUT

Coloured pencil can be lifted out easily, either to correct mistakes or to introduce paler shapes and markings that add to the image. This is a useful procedure that can be used at any stage, and offers more scope for creativity.

Removing Colour Creatively with Frisket Film

Frisket film is double-sided, with an adhesive side that can be peeled away and placed directly over coloured pencil. When you draw on the reverse (non-sticky) side with an HB pencil, using fairly strong pressure, the coloured pencil underneath lifts off, leaving a band of clean paper. Frisket is designed to remove colour without damaging the paper, so do not be tempted to try book covering or other types of adhesive, which may be much fiercer.

You can use Frisket to remove lines, blobs and shapes at any stage. You could, for example, put down a base colour, take out some shapes, then add a different coloured pencil layer on top. The result would be a blend of two colours, with the Frisket shapes in the second colour only. If you want the shapes to be white, they should be taken out once you have applied both colours.

Frisket works best on light to medium coverage; a heavy layering of colour may leave some residue, especially if the pigment tends towards staining. Be as inventive as you like; I once used it to create a very convincing row of cabbages! I regularly use Frisket to take out cloud shapes. It does give a hard outline, but this can be softened by working back from the edges with a very light application of colour. It is also helpful in the last stages of a work if you need to inject more light. Frisket will lift out shafts of light or highlights, which you can then leave or colour lightly.

Lifting Out with Erasers of Various Types

A putty rubber, plastic rubber, battery eraser and eraser shield can all be used to lift out creatively, as well as for correcting mistakes. Malleable putty rubbers will squeeze to a point for use on small areas, or roll into a sausage shape to remove colour from a larger area. They can be stroked across the paper to suggest light, rain or mist.

Plastic erasers will remove highlights and more precise shapes. They will take out wide lines or pale blocks, as when they are used with charcoal; unlike a putty rubber, a plastic eraser will leave hard edges. They can also be cut up into smaller, sharp-edged pieces for managing features such as the feathery edge of a meadow or forest.

Battery erasers are powerful and need a light touch; however, they have a small surface area, making them ideal for taking out dots of strong light. They are perfect for dappled effects

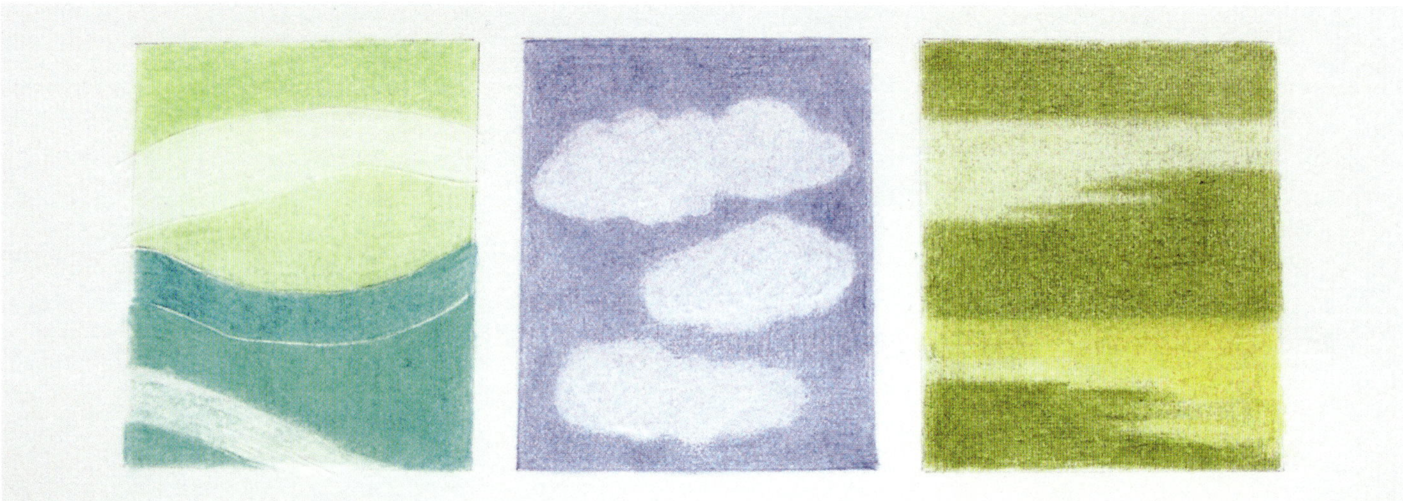

Lifting out using Frisket. *Left*: From the top, one strip of Grass Green was removed, revealing the paper underneath. A second strip was taken out and Cobalt Green applied. The two colours were then blended and lifted together to reveal white. *Centre*: Cloud shapes lifted from Mid-Ultramarine. *Right*: Two sections were removed to add light, one being replaced with yellow.

Putty rubber for light, rain and mist in *Brotherswater*. When applying ink and coloured pencil, I deliberately left the tops of the mountains without any definition, concentrating on the lower slopes. I was then able to use putty rubber to suggest mist meeting snow at the summit. Different strokes will give different weather conditions, or lift patches of light.

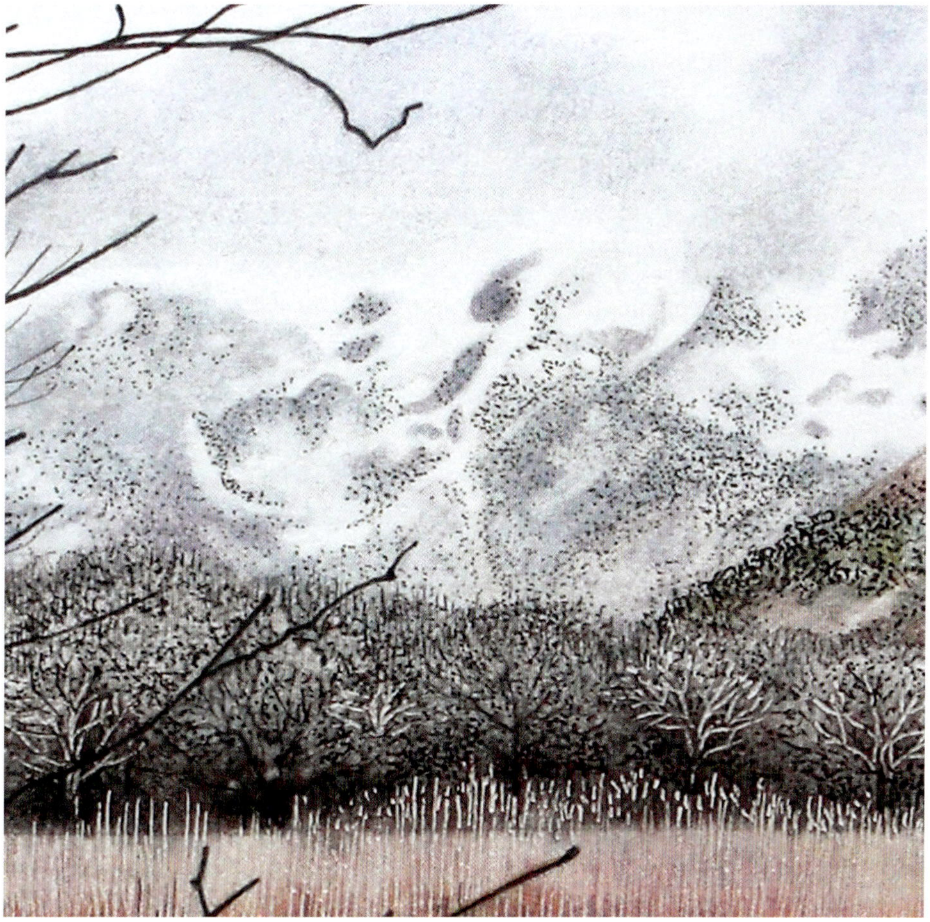

Battery erasers for highlights. In this detail from *Flood by Wastwater* I have used Derwent's battery eraser to 'draw' in some light patches on the fells and to pick up highlights on the foreground bushes. I find this a very useful and versatile tool for last-minute lightening up.

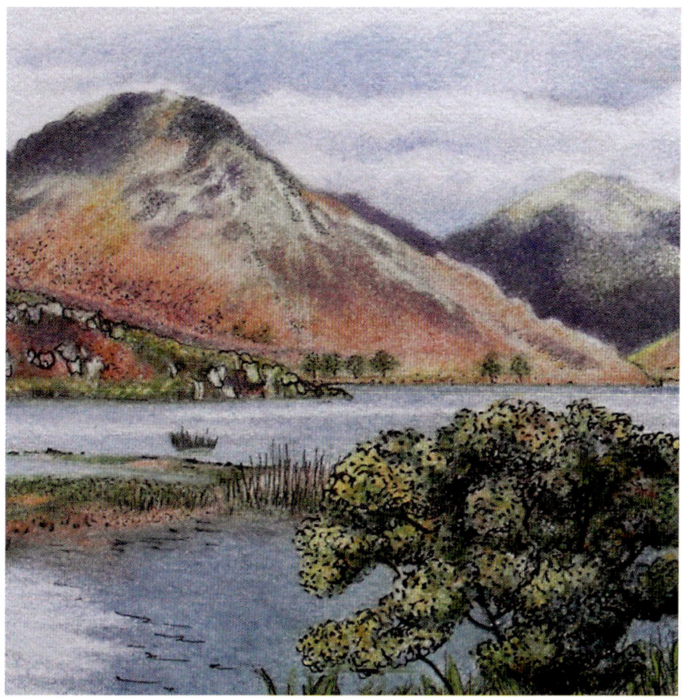

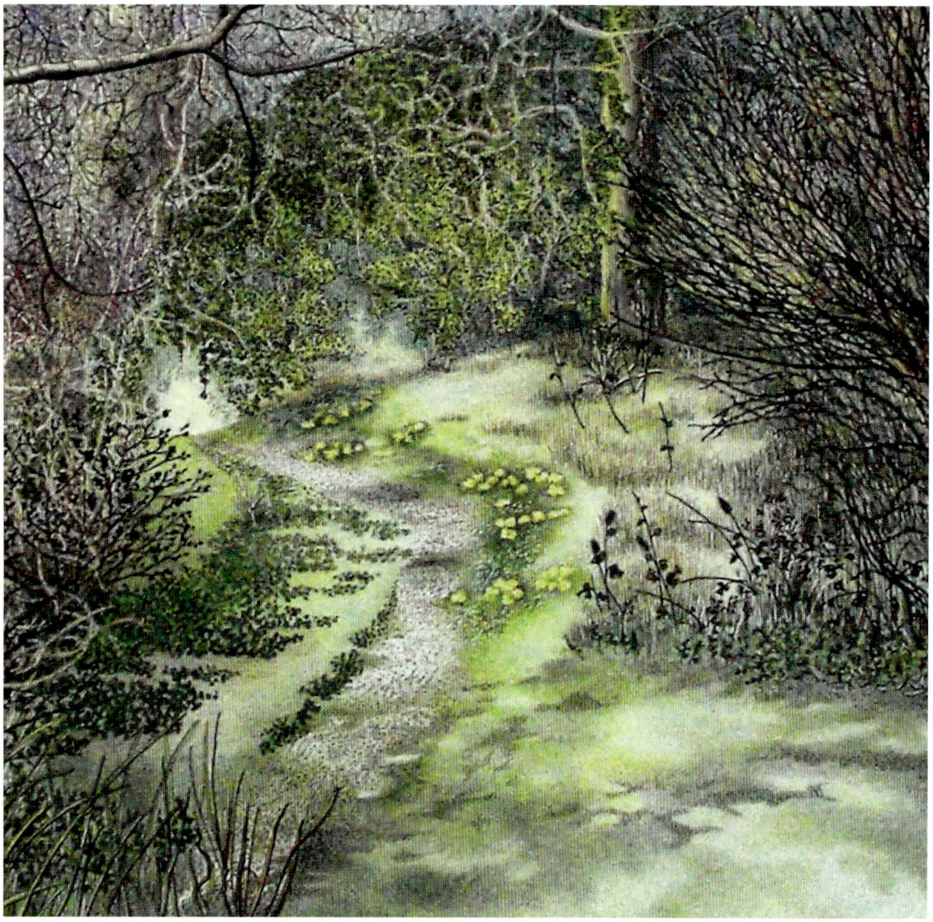

Putty rubber, Frisket and battery eraser for highlights. In this detail from the foreground of *Winter into Spring* I used Frisket, battery eraser and putty rubber to create the patches of dappled sunlight on the ground and the foliage elsewhere. Frisket takes out larger areas, putty rubber softens edges, and the battery eraser lifts out smaller, more concentrated highlights.

and last-minute highlights such as on leaves and water. The tips pick up pigment, but can be easily cleaned by allowing them to run over fine sandpaper.

Eraser shields have a range of small shapes cut out of the metal. These are geometric rather than organic, but will limit the area erased, as the metal protects any surrounding colour. They are also useful for tidying up edges where the colour has spilled out of the frame.

Lifting Out to Correct Mistakes

Frisket will erase coloured pencil mistakes and take out whole areas – just pencil over the back as far as you need. It works if you have used the wrong colour, or if the colour is too strong and needs to be pushed back. Sadly, it will not take out ink marks! Putty rubber is good for lightening an area if you have put on too much pigment, but is unlikely to erase completely.

SGRAFFITO

From the Italian verb *sgraffire* meaning 'to scratch', sgraffito describes a method of removing a surface layer of colour to reveal another colour underneath. Although it works better on softer surfaces such as oil pastel, it can be used on coloured pencil if it is sufficiently compacted. Waxier pencils are more likely to respond. Put down one layer of colour, then add another to increase the density and intensity. Use a sharp craft knife (on its side rather than the point) and gently scrape away fine lines or patches of colour. As with embossing, a single colour will give white markings, whereas two colours will, if done carefully, reveal the colour of the first.

Sgraffito can be used for tiny flecks of light and patches of broken colour, as well as for waves, complex textures and leaf veins. It is not an easy method and will take a little practice – and maybe a few holes in the paper – but if you can make it work it will add another technique to your repertoire.

Plastic eraser for shapes and feathering. Standard plastic erasers can be sliced into pieces with a blade and used to take out hard-edged shapes and sections. Fine strips of eraser can also be cut diagonally, or to a point at one end, and used to create feathered edges – useful for grassland, slanting rain and linear highlighting.

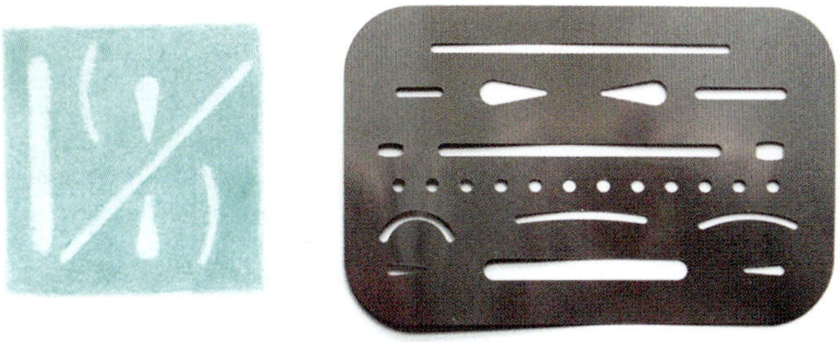

Eraser shields for shapes and highlights. Eraser shields mostly have geometric shapes, but these can be modified; they are useful for taking out dots, curves and linear features such as gateposts. The circular shapes will create small highlights if used with a battery eraser. Try adding colour shapes as well as removing them.

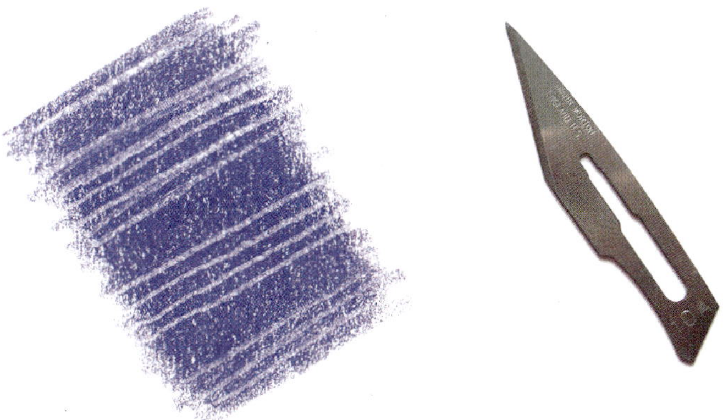

Sgraffito with white paper. With a sharp blade and medium pressure, I scratched lines into two layers of blue coloured pencil, revealing the white paper. You may prefer to remove the blade from the handle; this keeps it flatter and in better contact with the surface. The point can easily cut into the paper, damaging rather than scraping it.

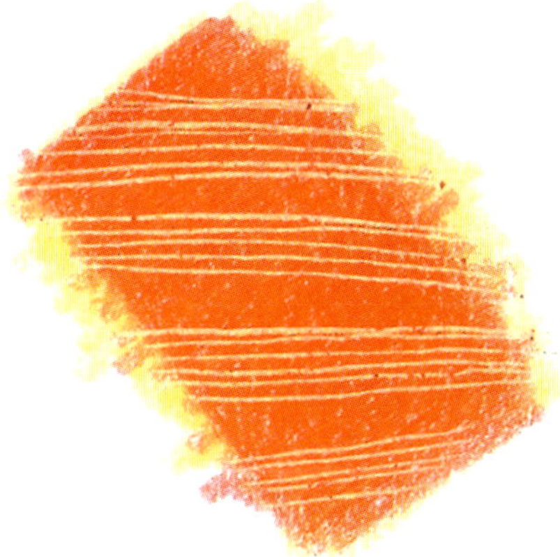

Sgraffito with two colours. This method is more successful with waxier pencils as the pigment lifts more readily. I put down a layer of yellow coloured pencil and added a layer of red on top. Using the side of the blade and a light pressure, I scraped off the red layer to reveal the yellow layer beneath.

PUTTING EVERYTHING INTO PRACTICE

Now that you have experimented with the use of pen and coloured pencil and added some extra techniques, it is time to put everything into practice. You are ready to look at a fresh sheet of Bristol board and your chosen image and really start to exercise your creativity.

CHAPTER 6

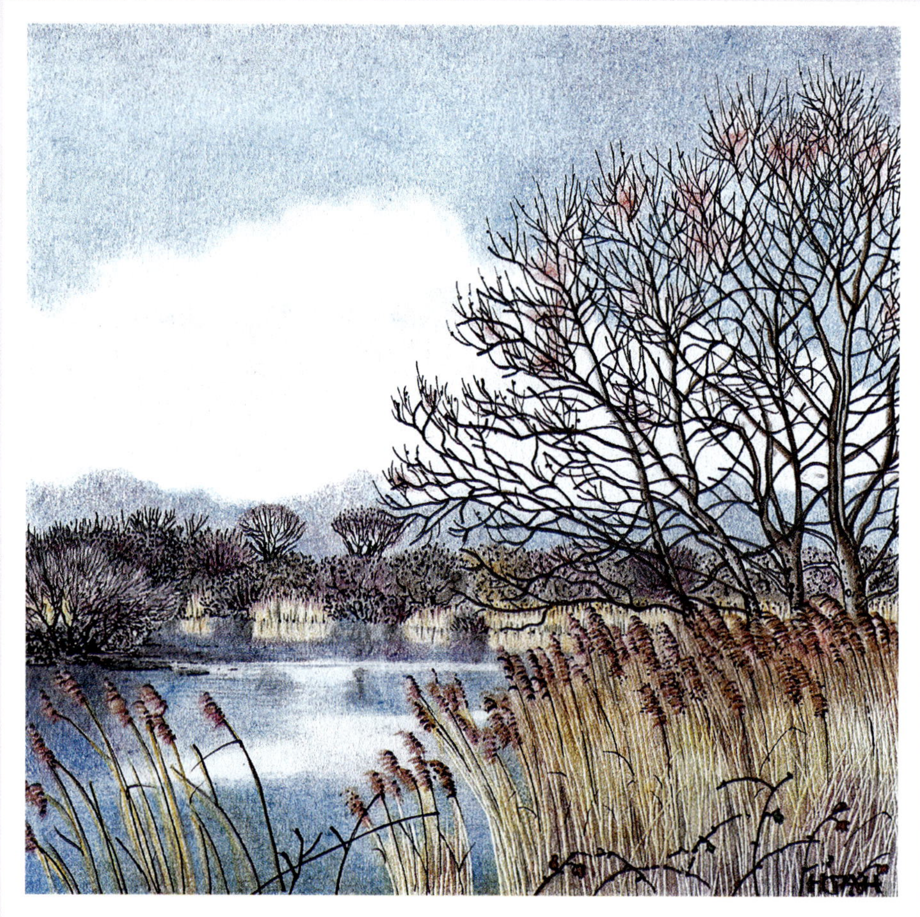

Spring on the River.

Pen to Paper

This chapter explains in detail how to approach your subject and what to put down first. By now your brain must be full of information and ideas, but you may still feel a bit anxious about starting. I always do. It is what artists call white paper syndrome: fear of making the first mark. Distance yourself from the feeling by returning to the image you have chosen, and take a closer look. Where you start and which methods you use will depend on your image, so study the different features and work out how you could 'translate' them into ink and coloured pencil.

PRELIMINARY SKETCHES

The Bare Minimum

The initial drawing needs to be minimal and very faint. The pencil marks are just guidelines to ensure that the features of the landscape are in the right place and that everything works compositionally. Pencil detail is superfluous and will get in the way; the image will be created by working directly on the paper with ink and coloured pencil. Before you begin, remove most of the graphite with a putty rubber, as it will show and persist under pale-coloured pencil. If you feel uncertain, try out a new idea on a spare piece of your chosen paper; I always keep some at my side for testing colours, blends and techniques. Do not use a different make or thickness (or cartridge paper) as the effect will not be the same. Once you have seen that a technique will work in practice on the same paper, you can go ahead and apply it with more confidence.

Why Complex Drawings Don't Work

The more you draw and shade in pencil at the preparation stage, the more likely you are to be lured into outlining and filling in. A highly detailed drawing will encourage you to repeat the process in ink – and start off on the wrong foot. Once you have embarked on a drawing using lines and shading in ink, you will be tempted to fill in with colour, forfeiting the chance to apply all the exciting, integrated approaches offered by this combination of media. I really do start with a skeleton sketch: I merely dot in the border of a forest, the edge of a path or a line of mountains using pencil. I only draw in one side of a tree (the shadow side) because I know that I will use colour and texture rather than an outline to define the sunny side. Always be aware that an ink line, once drawn, is there to stay!

ASSESSING THE SUBJECT – VITAL QUESTIONS

What's In Front?

When I start to tutor a course, I pin a large notice to the wall asking this simple question. It is the first and most important consideration, and the answer should provide you with your starting point. Are there obvious features in the foreground that need to be established first? How will you work round them? How much pen work can you do at this stage? Even more importantly, does anything need to be white embossed before you start? I find that some students are very tentative about mark-making in ink and veer towards an almost entirely coloured pencil approach; others feel so comfortable sketching

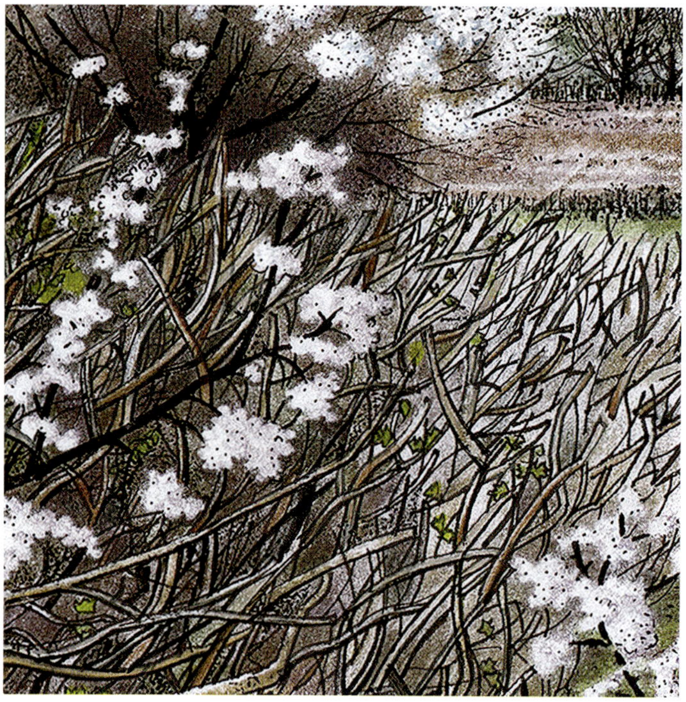

Building the blossoms in *Blackthorn Spring* (detail). Starting with tiny dots using a 0.03 pen and avoiding an outline, I created some shapes in the foreground. The branches were drawn in around these, adding structure and intersections. The blossom was given shadow and variation using pale tones in coloured pencil and a few more dots.

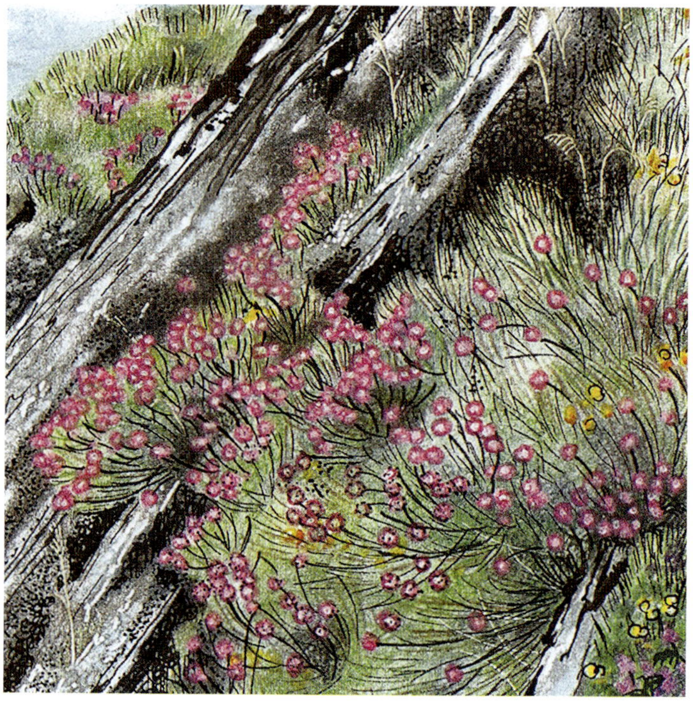

Foreground thrift in *Gigha Shore* (detail). I put the flower heads in first, observing the plant and positioning them where the ends of the stems would be. I then added curving stems below and between them in ink. Using embossing, fine pen work and several shades of green, I was then able to introduce grass and more small flowers.

in pen that they do too much initially and get themselves into a 'colour tinting' trap. The answer lies in how you choose to interpret the different features of the landscape; assess the tools you have at your disposal and use them to devise a creative solution.

To look at a few examples, in *Blackthorn Spring, Gigha Shore* and *Winter in the Gravel Garden* I had to begin with the dominant flowers and grasses that occupied the foreground. In *Blackthorn Spring,* the clumps of blossom in the foreground needed to be established first. Being in front, they could not be added after the branches; to have an inked branch intersecting them would immediately destroy the illusion. I began by lightly marking their extent with tiny ink dots, then fitted in the branches behind and around them, but did not cross them. I used random dots to indicate the spread of the blossom, to avoid creating an artificial-looking outer ring. I then developed the surrounding area, leaving each cluster as a fluffy white shape, adding more ink dots and pale shadow colours at a later stage to give more definition.

The drifts of thrift in *Gigha Shore* were dominant foreground features, and wherever they appeared, the slanting rocks had to be fitted in around them. I started with the flower heads, using a light application of Faber-Castell Magenta and Light Magenta, and scattered them in groups, following the spread of the plant. They grew in colourful drifts towards the tops, so I added curving pen lines to give the plants some structure and show how they fanned out from the base. The ink lines were done in a free, sketchy style to suggest movement and even a hint of sea breeze. I used finely embossed lines to add lighter touches to the grass, and filled in the remainder with shades of green, changing to dark shadow colours at the base. Once the clumps of thrift were in place, I was able to assess the angle of the rocks and could start to include some background texture and detail. I did this gradually, adding any other flowers or grasses that were growing in front of the rocks. Once their relative distances were established, it was possible to build up the area surrounding the plants.

Winter in the Gravel Garden was a composition made up of overlapping pampas grasses and allium seed heads, rising in front of a background of silver birch. I began by establishing which plants were dominant and which were partly obscured, including the trees. The large grasses formed a pattern across the foreground and needed to be placed first; I used the same method of tiny dots to indicate their shape, including the drooping fronds. Where the grass heads overlapped, I adjusted the dots accordingly, so that one dropped behind the other. I kept to a subtle colour combination, using mainly Derwent Slate Violet for the shadows, with warmer Light Sienna and Light Ochre for the mid-tones. I retained quite strong highlights, using the putty rubber to shape these as a finishing touch.

Once the grass heads were in place, I could see where the stalks overlapped and how any surrounding plants fitted in. For these, I embossed over pale colour, adding background colour and pen strokes to achieve a mixed texture, always working round the pampas heads. By progressing from the foreground to the background, adding more plants, I arrived at the top of the border and could see how much of the treeline would be obscured by the taller grasses.

It is quite normal to work from front to back when using this method. As you progress towards the back of the image you have control over what you can see and how much. It is a good idea to run your eye over the whole picture just to check what is in front at every stage. There is nothing more disappointing than diving in enthusiastically with ink and intersecting part of the delicate foreground you were hoping to retain.

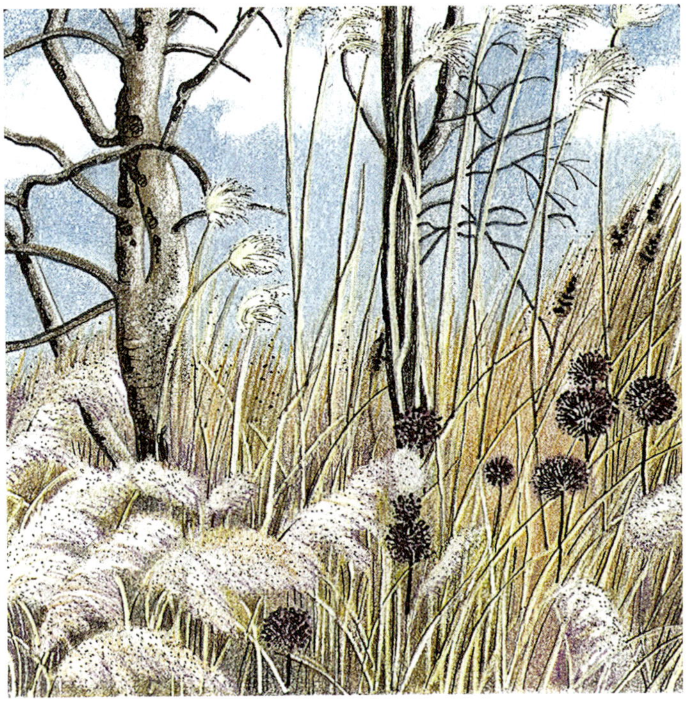

Grasses in *Winter in the Gravel Garden* (detail). The shapes of the pampas grasses were dotted in using a 0.03 pen, noting where they overlapped or obscured parts of the tree bark. I then used colours to give warmth and shadow to create form, softening the pure white highlights with a putty rubber.

What Needs Coloured Pencil First?

One solution to white paper syndrome is to approach some areas quite tentatively, using coloured pencil but no ink. I often do this if an image has clumps of foliage in the foreground or the middle distance, and I am unsure what species they are, or how to treat them. In my original photograph of *Marden Morning* the trees in the distance appeared as an indistinct mass, with very little variation of colour. This often happens when you are working from a photograph, and as the artist, you are usually free to make decisions.

If you are working on a commission, or if all the features need to be exactly represented, follow what you see as closely as you can. If not, use some artistic licence and solve the problem creatively, in a way that will work best for your picture. A row of bushes may need some definition to distinguish different species and make it interesting; an application of soft colour in several shades will allow you to try out shapes and see how they work. I would advise a light touch, as this is simply to establish the form, and it will be much easier to erase. If you are not happy with the result, Frisket film will come to the rescue and you can start again. This is not possible if you launch straight into mark-making in ink.

For the trees in *Marden Meadow*, I decided to try out some shapes using blue-green and grey-green shades to give a better sense of distance. I used a blend of colours, putting in shadows at the base and keeping some highlights to show the direction of the light. I decided to add an even more distant row, using a much bluer colour mix. Once I had established the tree shapes and their relative distances, I was able to add a few branches in ink, keeping the marks light and subtle. The dominant tree on the left then appeared much nearer, being less blue, more strongly coloured and with clearer markings. So, if you are feeling uncertain, experiment with colour first. When you are happy with how things look, ink marks can be added of a size and shape appropriate to the distance and subject. You can follow up with more layers of colour and add light and shade at a later stage.

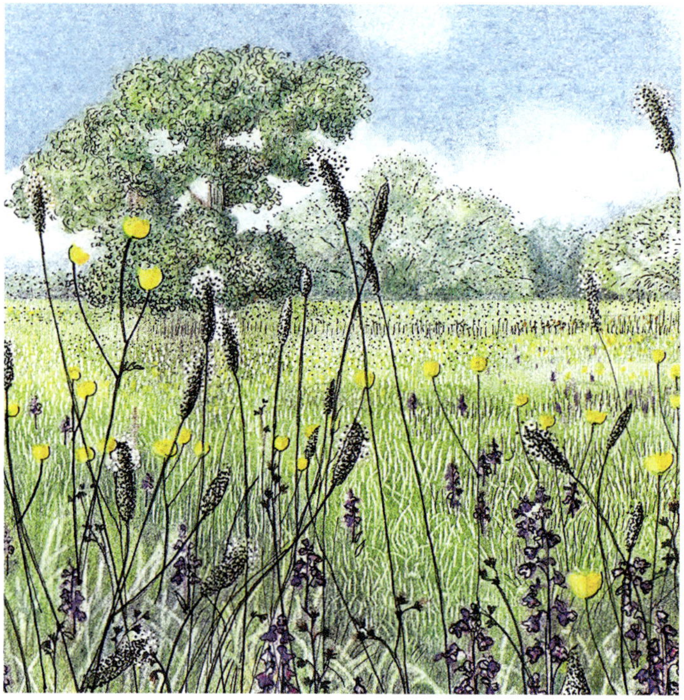

Creating shapes in coloured pencil in *Marden Morning* (detail). Using coloured pencil first to develop the shapes of the background trees allowed me some margin for error. I used paler and bluer greens to create distance and to bring the stronger, darker green tree forwards. Once I was happy with the colours and shapes, I added some ink markings.

I always start with coloured pencil whenever I am depicting a mountain range. Using subtly blended colours, it is possible to achieve all the varied shades we see in nature. I use coloured pencil to create the shape of the mountain and its summit and never outline in ink, although I may do this later for rock formations. Outlining is much too definitive and looks artificial; it also removes any possibility of alteration. When the mountain top is in coloured pencil, a putty rubber can be used to erase areas of cloud or mist and to create a variety of weather and light effects.

Skies usually call for coloured pencil only, with little or no ink. I nearly always leave them until last, when all the background markings have been established. This helps me to choose the sky the picture requires; I don't necessarily limit myself to the one that appears in my photograph, or in nature. Skies in amateur photographs are often underwhelming, so this is an area where artistic licence can be freely exercised. You are the artist and can use the sky to complete your picture in

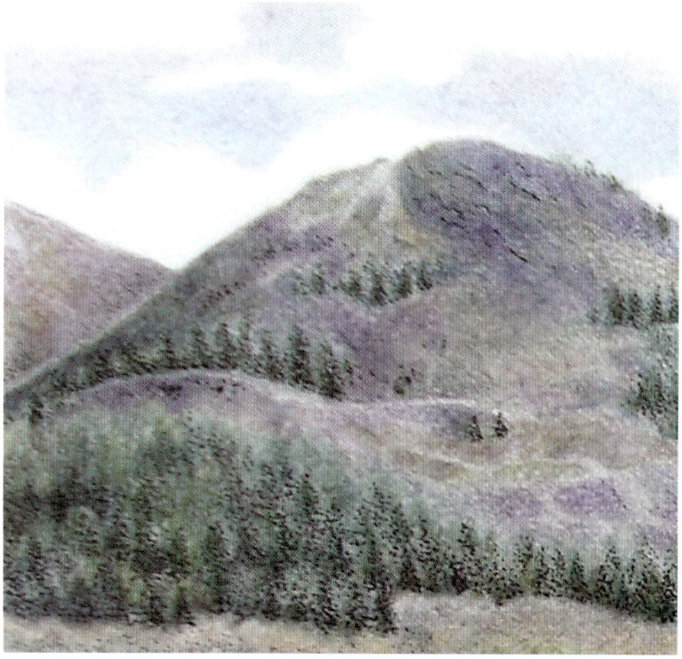

Shaping the fells: *Catkins by Bassenthwaite* (detail). I put down blended colours first to recreate this winter mountainside, varying the shades according to the terrain and adding the tree shapes as I progressed. I lifted out small areas of colour and deepened shadows and gullies, adding detail and direction using small ink markings only as a final stage.

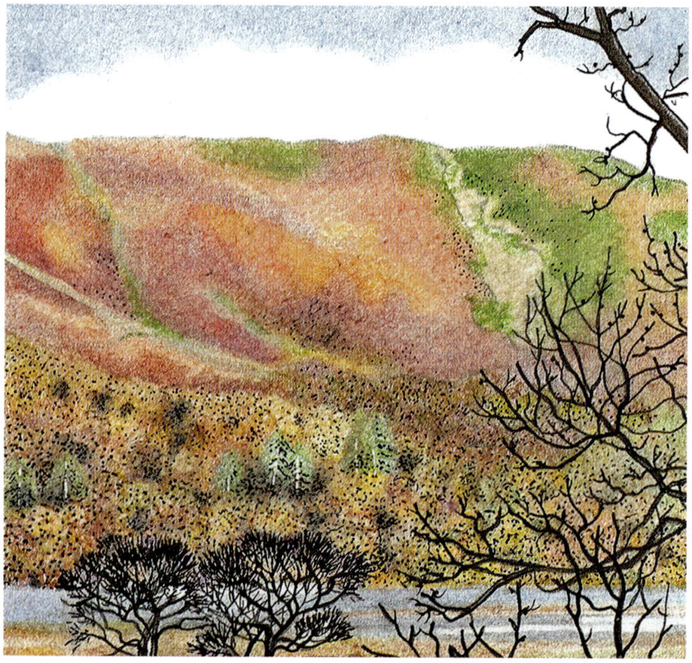

Shaping the fells: *Derwentwater Morning* (detail). Using only coloured pencil and avoiding any outline, I built up the shape of the mountainside, following its contours and colour shifts. I lifted out tracks and bare sections, using tiny ink dots to define the gullies and shadow areas. I increased their size to define the tree shapes in the forest below.

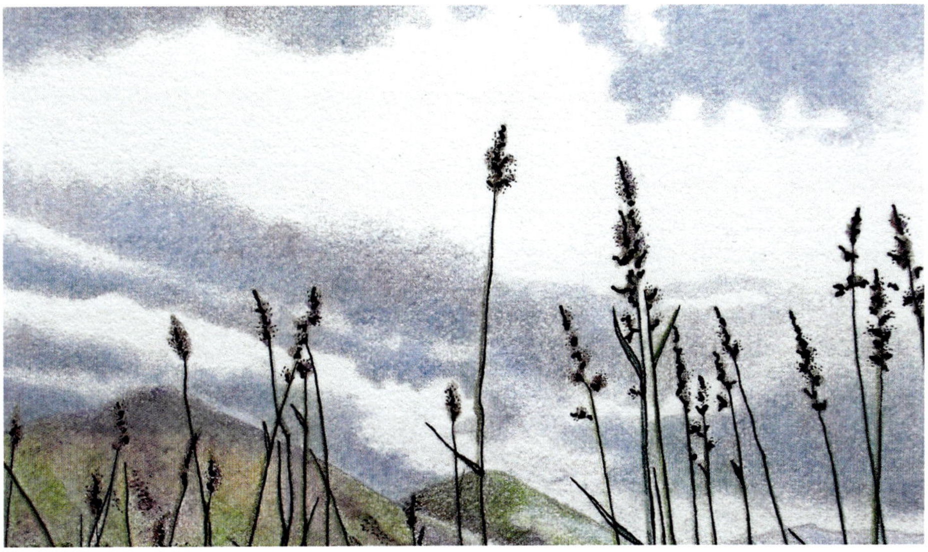

Adding the sky: *Summer Calm on Bassenthwaite* (detail). The late afternoon was luminous, but there was a hint of something building up over the fells. I gave the clouds a diagonal slant and weighed them down with grey and mauve to give an unsettled look.

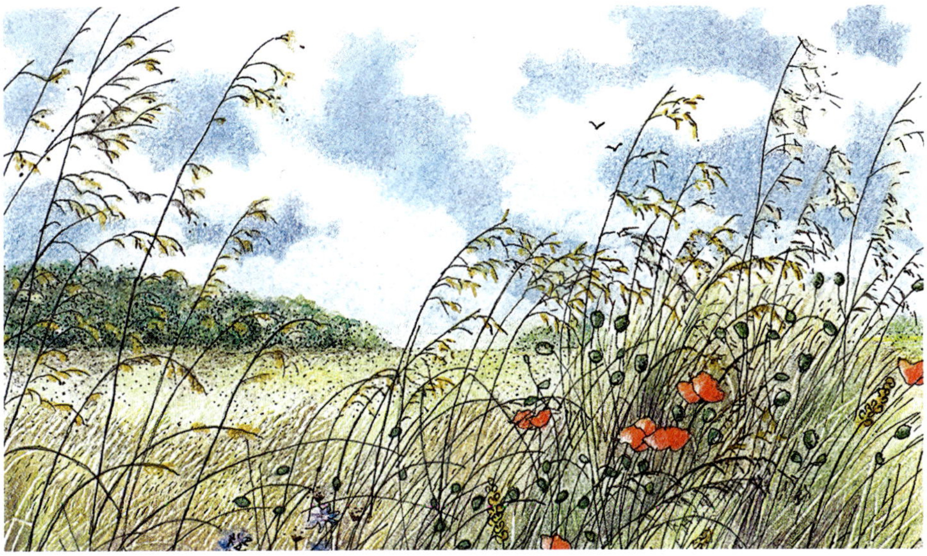

Adding the sky: *Wild Meadow* (detail). In contrast, this bright, sunny day demanded a lively sky to keep it looking fresh. I chose very clear colours – Ultramarine, Sky Blue and Cobalt Blue – and added pure white patches of fluffy cloud. The simple foreground was enlivened by an energetic sky, and the mood remained upbeat.

the best way possible for the image. An interestingly moody one will add drama if you feel that your landscape is rather flat and low key. If the landscape is quite complex with lots of busy features, a more peaceful sky can provide a restful contrast. It goes without saying that whatever clouds, drifts or colours the sky possesses, the light over sky and land should have the same direction and quality and give a sense of unity.

Start with coloured pencil whenever you feel unsure about your interpretation as it can always be erased with Frisket. Coloured pencil, unlike ink, is not a commitment. When you like an effect, bring in some smaller marks in ink and build up gradually, developing the two media in tandem.

Where Can I Safely Put Ink?

Using my minimal sketch as a guide, I like to give some structure to the image by putting down a few ink markings that I know I will need. In some pieces, such as the ones I have just described, it may not be possible to start with this. Nevertheless, you should be able to introduce some preliminary work in ink at an early stage.

First make sure of the direction of light, whatever your subject matter. If you are starting with trees, for example, note where the light falls and keep the shadow side consistent throughout your work. You can certainly ink in the shadowed parts of the trunk and branches as these will be very dark. I

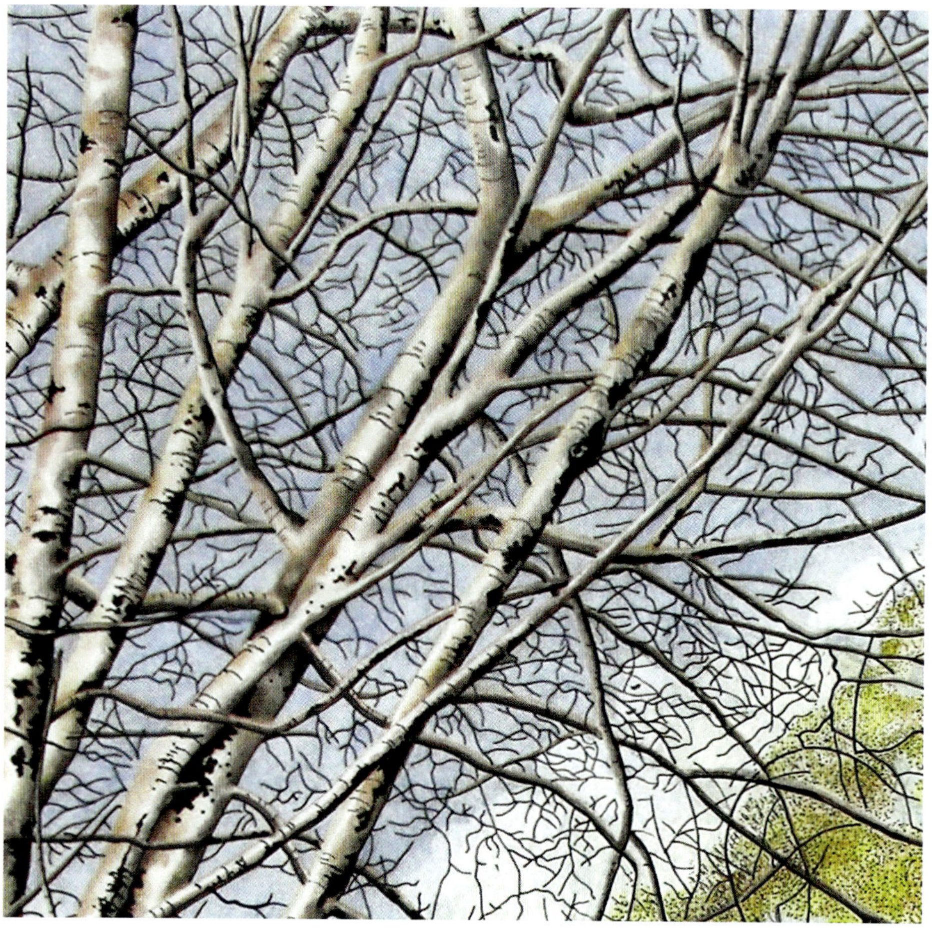

Building up bark and branches. I started with ink on the shadow side of the trunk and branches, leaving the opposite side 'open'. I added a dark shadow colour alongside, fading it gradually into a lighter and warmer brown towards the middle. On the lighter side, I used paler colours, adding ink markings on the bark to denote texture.

usually follow this up with very dark-coloured pencil ellipses immediately alongside, to remove any obvious outline and to create the darkest tone. In the example I used Faber-Castell Dark Sepia, but Walnut Brown and Caran D'Ache Raw Umber are also good colour choices; do experiment and discover the right colours for your own image. I then introduced paler tones and patches of light as I worked towards the sunnier side, adding some creative ink markings at this point to give detail and texture to the bark.

As you include more branches, take note of where they cross each other, which ones are uppermost, and which surfaces catch the light. Stop as you approach a junction; be careful to drop one branch under the other rather than making a 'noughts and crosses' intersection. If you observe all the light and shade – and bear in mind that a lower branch will have shadow under the passing point – you should be able to achieve a convincing tangle.

Ink does feel rather final, but there is no need to be afraid of it if you have a plan. If you are used to sketching very freely with pen, you may need to rein yourself in to take into consideration the coloured pencil component, not to mention embossing and other techniques. However, if you think first, apply the translation process and ask 'How can I best convey the impression of…' you may well be surprised at your own inventiveness!

Does Anything Need to be Embossed in White First?

Depending on the requirements of your image, embossing a feature in white first might need to be your very first consideration. Embossing directly into paper gives a startlingly white effect once a colour has been applied over the top. The darker the colour, the more startling it becomes. It also appears uniform, without any nuances of colour, and can, as a result, look decorative but rather flat and artificial. I find that I rarely use it, preferring to lay down some colour first before embossing.

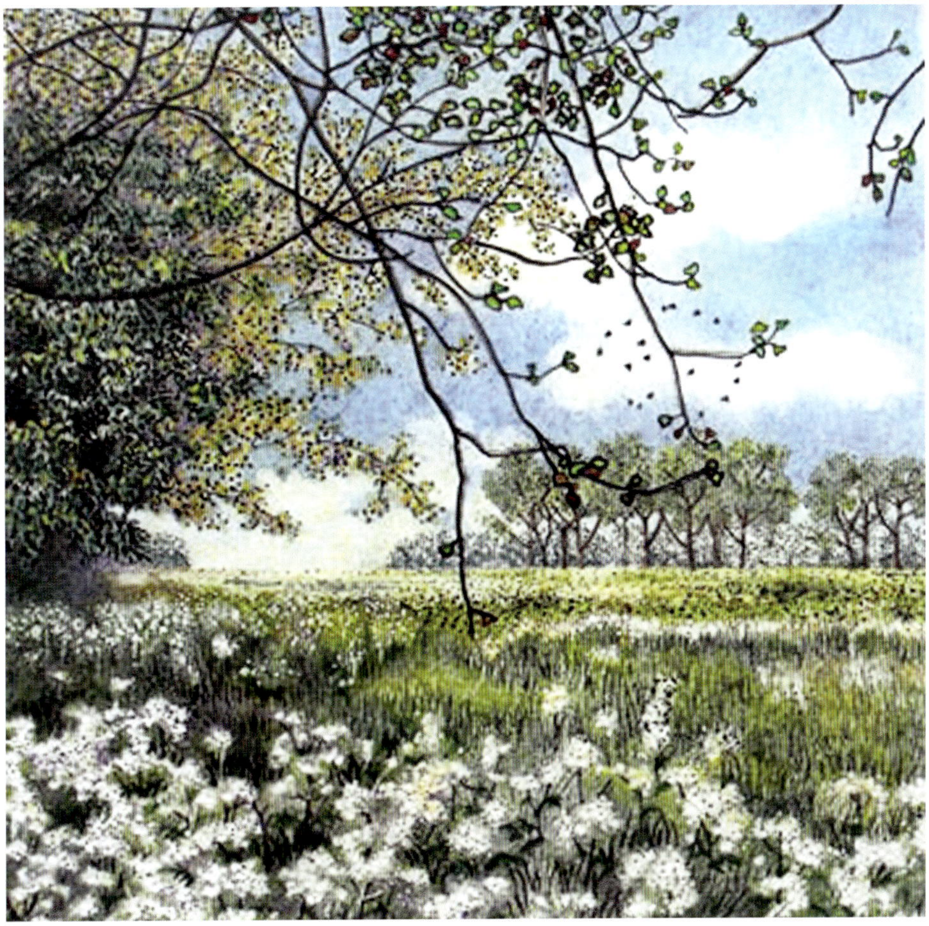

White embossing: *Spring into Summer*. The white cow parsley heads were embossed at the start, before applying any ink or coloured pencil. Umbel-like flower shapes were then created by working round white areas with colour, deepening from mid-green to a more shadowy mix where necessary. Tiny 0.03 ink dots were added later to give more texture.

However, it does have some useful applications: for rocks and pebbles, small white flower heads (in a meadow, for example) and heavily textured surfaces where it can be used in combination with other techniques. If you do have any pure white features that you have chosen to emboss, be sure to put these in before you apply ink or coloured pencil. For example, a clump of snowdrop heads, seen against the base of a tree trunk, would need to be embossed before starting any work on the tree itself.

Once you have decided where to start and which areas need to be embossed, inked or approached more cautiously with coloured pencil, you will be ready to build up your image. Keep looking at your source image, test out new ideas and colours before committing yourself, and if they work, proceed with confidence!

THE NEXT STEP

The next chapter will explore common features of landscape and how to depict them using all the techniques at your disposal. You can then put them to immediate use and also contribute some of your own inventions.

CHAPTER 7

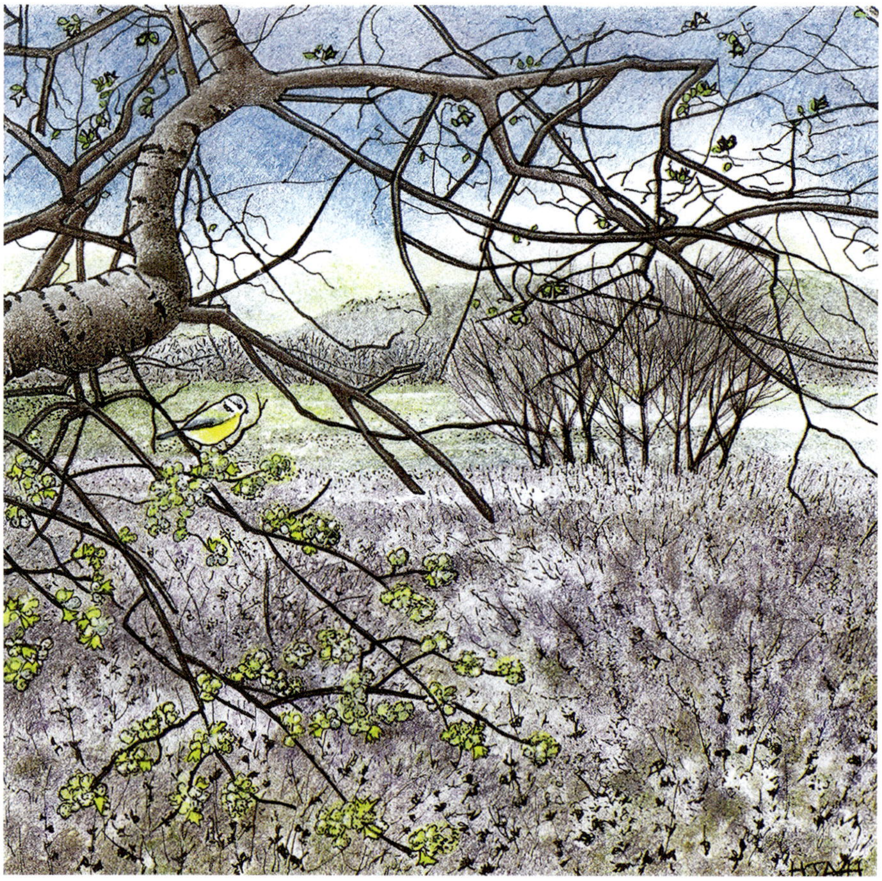

Transition to Spring.

The Importance of Integration

Using ink and coloured pencil together creatively is the essence of this method of working. When I started tutoring, I often went into detail about this at a later stage, as a check on how my students were getting on with their work. Now I prefer to stress its importance at the outset. It is very easy to slip into focusing on one medium (usually the one you find more comfortable), with just the hint of the other; the results may be fine, but I regard it as a missed opportunity, given all the inventive and beautiful ways they can be made to work together. In this section we shall look more closely at some practical examples of this integrated approach and how to achieve it.

THINKING IN TWO MEDIA

No Baggage Required

If I think back to my days as an etcher, I used to walk the countryside and plan how to express what I saw using the tools I would have at my disposal in the studio. These included techniques such as open bite, coarse aquatint and sugar lift; each one had its own fascinating character, and, I always felt, did most of the work for me. I didn't feel that I had to be a brilliant artist, and there was no need to be highly skilled with pencil or paint. I learned to let the techniques speak for themselves and concentrated on making them work as an ensemble. Coming from a completely different discipline, I did not have the expectations accumulated from years of drawing and painting. I simply engaged with the techniques and tried to make them express what I saw in their own unique way.

We bring a lot of baggage with us into the art room. I am often approached by people who have admired work done by my students; when I ask if they would like to join us, they back off and tell me that they have no artistic ability whatsoever. At some stage in their education, they were told that they could not draw and have taken that as a definitive assessment. Others turn up but judge their own work much too harshly, even assuring me when we meet that they will be useless. (They are usually agreeably surprised!) Drawing and painting are not the only things on offer: printmaking, collage and mixed media are just three alternatives that may be more forgiving and rewarding for the amateur. I certainly came to art via printmaking and have moved in different directions ever since.

In addition, we now have in our minds the television artist, who is often seen in a race against time, competing to become the 'winner'. This is as far removed from the way most artists work as is possible; it is simply a tried and tested entertainment format that gets ratings. However, for the viewer, it gives rise to unreasonable expectations and a desire for instant success. We would not expect this in other walks of life, and would assume that we had to put in some serious work and practice first. It is precisely the fact that most artists have already done this that makes them so adept.

Fortunately, it is possible to clear away all this baggage and still work successfully in ink and coloured pencil; drawing and painting are not directly involved and you can use specific techniques to build up an image. Go back, if you can, to a time when you enjoyed coloured pencils as a child. (I still remember my Christmas tin of thirty-six Derwent pencils as one of the presents that made me most happy.) You can take control again and choose to express aspects of nature in your own way, by employing the basic techniques you have practised. You are free to be inventive, decorative if you wish, and to enjoy the process.

How to Avoid the 'Colouring In' Trap

The illustrations in this chapter all show how creative you can be, and how you can use the techniques you know to represent elements of the natural world. I find that it helps to build up a library of examples that you have used successfully and to keep them for future reference. You will soon start to see things differently and be able to translate what you see directly into the techniques you know. If you can think in the medium you are using, rather than referring to drawing or painting, you will feel more confident. Once you feel comfortable doing this, you will be less inclined to outline everything in ink or work mostly in coloured pencil for fear of taking the plunge.

Now that you have a good composition, know where to start and have devised ways of depicting different features, you should be able to build up your image. Keep in mind that you will be using layers of colour to create depth, and resist the temptation to press too hard with the coloured pencil for the first application: this will make mistakes harder to correct and may distort the balance of distance and proximity, the subject of our next chapter.

WORKING IN AN INTEGRATED WAY: SOME PRACTICAL EXAMPLES

The following descriptions and illustrations demonstrate how I have resolved a few aspects of the landscape; in each case I used a combination of ink, coloured pencil and their associated techniques. It is not a definitive catalogue of everything you might want to include, but more an encouragement to think in a certain way when you are interpreting your own landscapes. They all feature in my work and result simply from observation and the methods at my disposal. Sometimes I just try out what I think might work, and so can you.

Trees and Bushes

Trees are a mainstay of landscape work and can be approached in a variety of ways. If they are very distant – a forest on a hillside, for example – they can be fed into the landscape with just a change of colour, shape and the addition of a few ink markings. In the last chapter we looked at the use of coloured pencil as a tentative starting point for trees in the middle distance, with the addition of ink and more colour once they look right. Trees or branches in the foreground can create a framework, controlling how we see the image. They can also provide interest, drama, complexity and an opportunity to show interesting texture and detail. Leaves on overhanging branches are one of the few occasions when I allow myself some outlining and colouring in; it introduces a different technique, and a sharpness that can change the focus dramatically.

Creative use of trees can inject life into a dreary composition; remember that you can add them, take them out, move them, prune them and slant them – all in the interests of a better picture.

Nature's Tangles

I find negotiating the tangles made by nature one of the most enjoyable aspects of my work. I love the way branches, leaves, undergrowth and roots criss-cross and intermingle. I could (and do) spend hours following them through, bringing some forwards and dropping back others to create an organic-looking profusion. It is not as difficult as it seems if you keep an eye on the direction of the light and follow the golden rule: what's in front? I use this technique for everything from roots to topmost branches, combining ink, colour and embossing to achieve a convincing tangle.

To build up a tangle, always keep an eye on what is in front. Overhanging branches that dominate the foreground need to be strong; you may need to exaggerate their form by reinforcing the shadows and highlights to make them stand out against the background. Branches passing underneath will recede if given a small amount of shadow under the junction. The size and strength of branches or foliage in a tangle will help to define their distance, with those that are nearest appearing dominant. I use a combination of ink, colour, embossing and lifting out to create my tangles; because I continue to experiment and get deeper into the thicket, I freely admit to overdoing it on occasions!

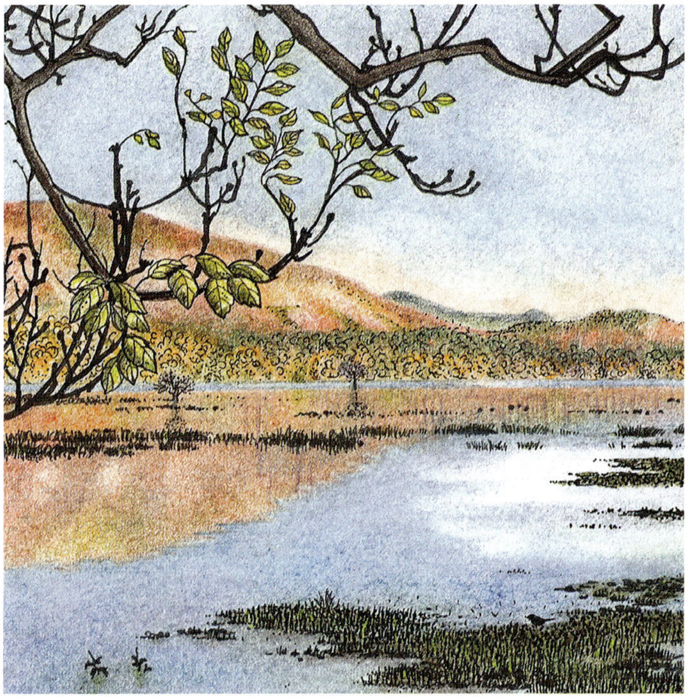

Overhanging tree in *Bird in the Flood*. In this image, the overhanging tree brings some necessary interest to an image that relies on colour rather than content. Its closeness also gives us a better impression of the relative distances. The leaves were outlined, coloured in and highlighted and the buds made into a feature using ink.

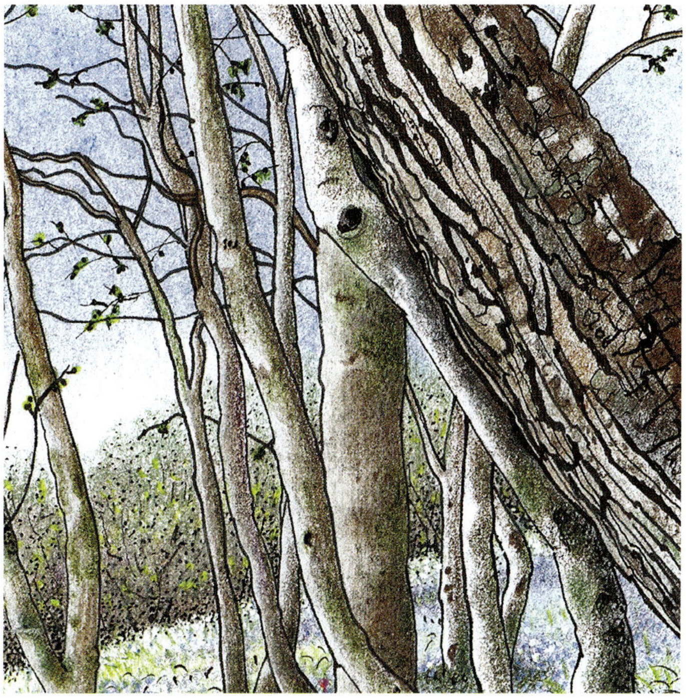

Tree bark in *Bluebell Slope*. Here I have used a slanting tree trunk to frame the picture and introduce diagonals into the composition. Bluebell woods are appealing, but often present a rather rigid vertical composition with the interest at ground level. A diagonal with interesting textures in ink and coloured pencil offers a different outlook.

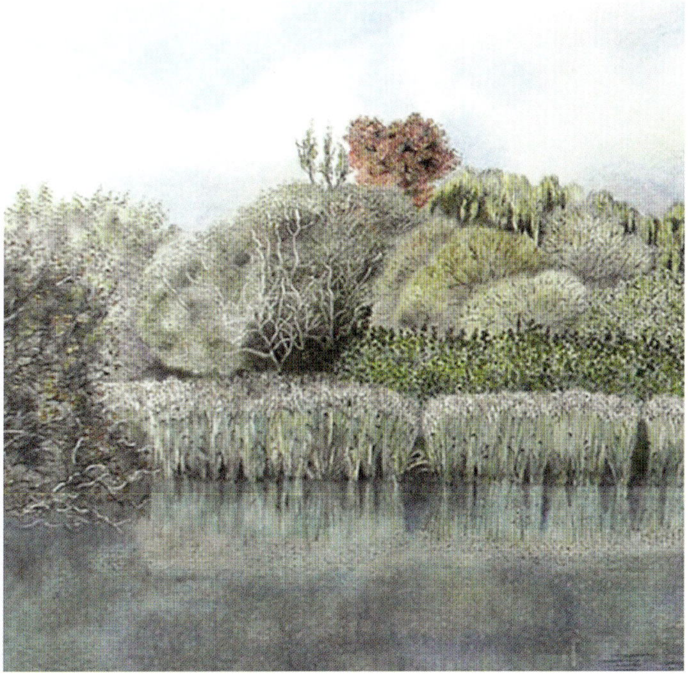

Middle-distance trees in *Summer into Autumn*. These trees were created using coloured pencil initially to establish their shapes and relative positions. Distant trees often appear as a mass in both photographs and in nature, so you may need to decipher their individual forms before committing to ink markings. I introduced them gradually where I could distinguish branches and leaf clusters.

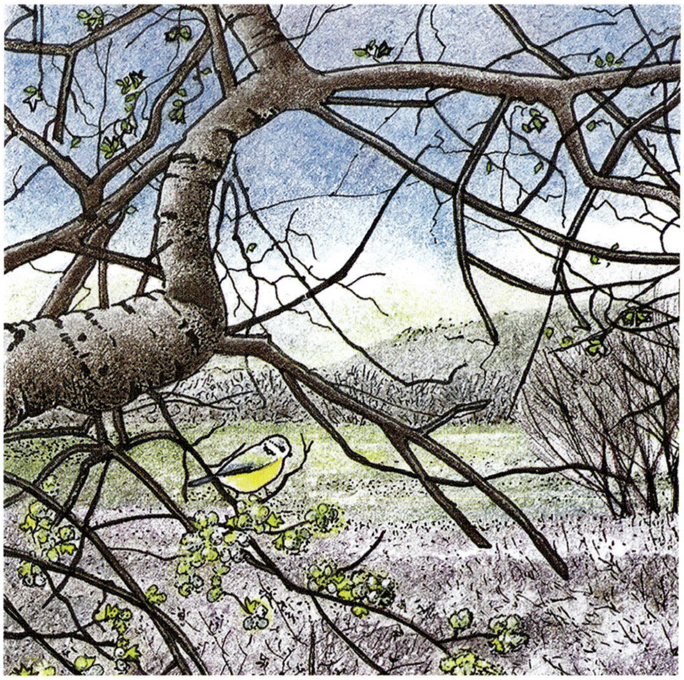

Trees as framework in *Transition to Spring*. Here I used the unusual shape of the tree as a setting for the whole picture, building the rest of the image within its curve. I used quite strong ink markings with light, shade and texture to make it a dominant feature.

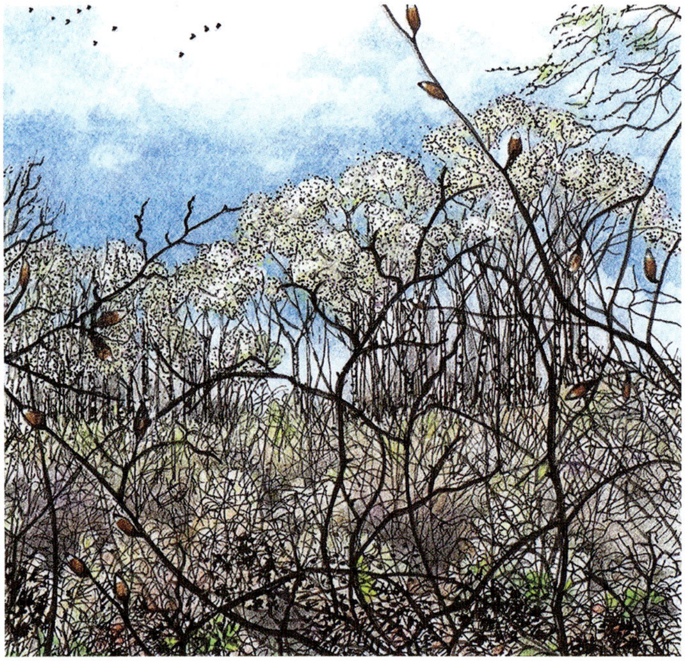

Tangled undergrowth in *First Signs of Spring*. This early piece is probably my first attempt at a tangle. The budding branches dominate the foreground, but behind them the undergrowth is a mass of dead leaves and twigs, punctuated by patches of local colour. I created these in an almost abstract way, taming them into clumps by using shadow and highlights.

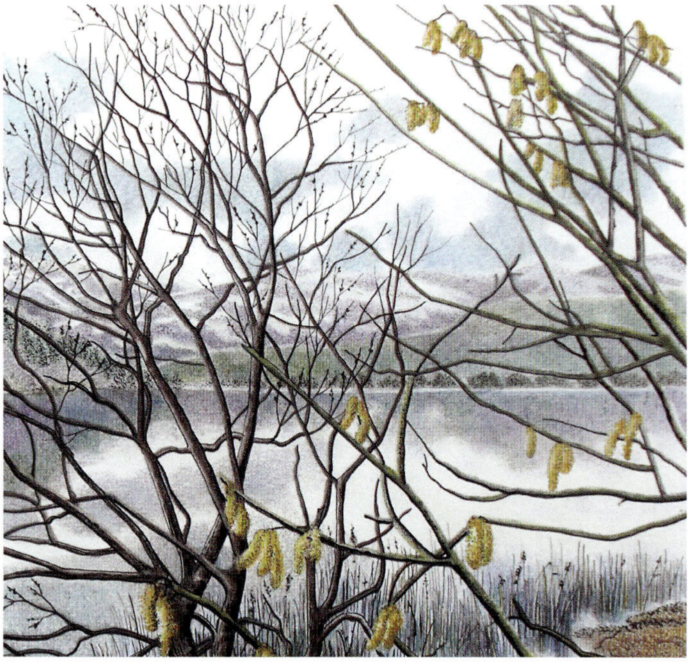

Foreground trees in *Catkins by Bassenthwaite*. In this detail from a large work, two trees overlap on the shoreline. The closer of the two was tackled first, from the spread of its branches to the position of the catkins; the second one was constructed so that its branches passed underneath. I also emphasized their differing colour and bark texture.

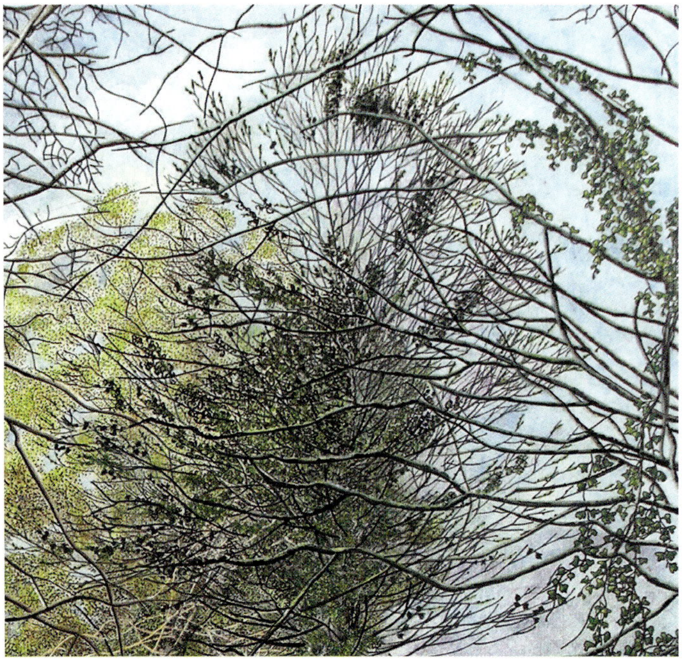

Tangled trees in *Winter into Spring*. This detail shows three overlapping trees and a cascade of ivy; I used colour and strength to distinguish them, working from front to back. Emphasizing the underside and bluish-green of the closest branches, I introduced the bare branches and ivy on the second tree, and contrasting colour and more delicate markings on the third.

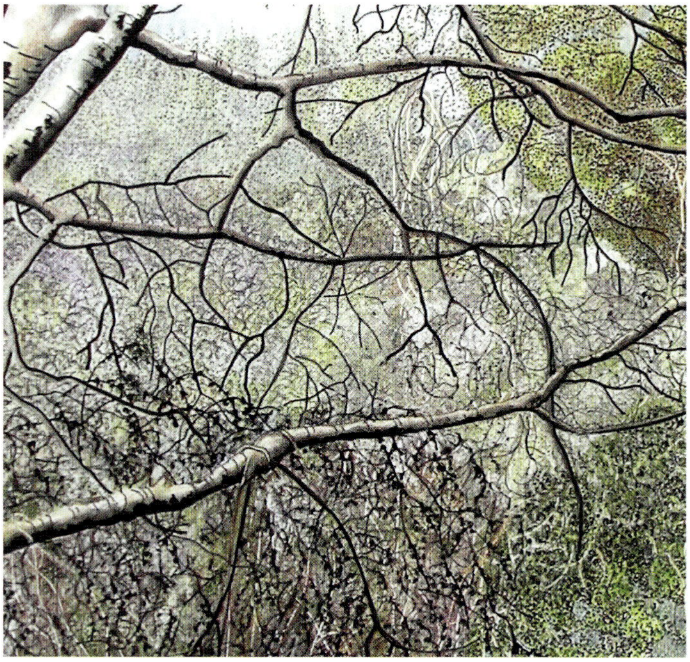

Foliage tangles in *Winter into Spring*. The stretches of old, dried foliage and bright new growth made for a perfect tangle. I used a combination of pale, wintry colours and bright spring greens to convey the contrast. The detailed tree bark dominates the view, and the receding drifts of undergrowth are distinguished by strength of colour and size of markings.

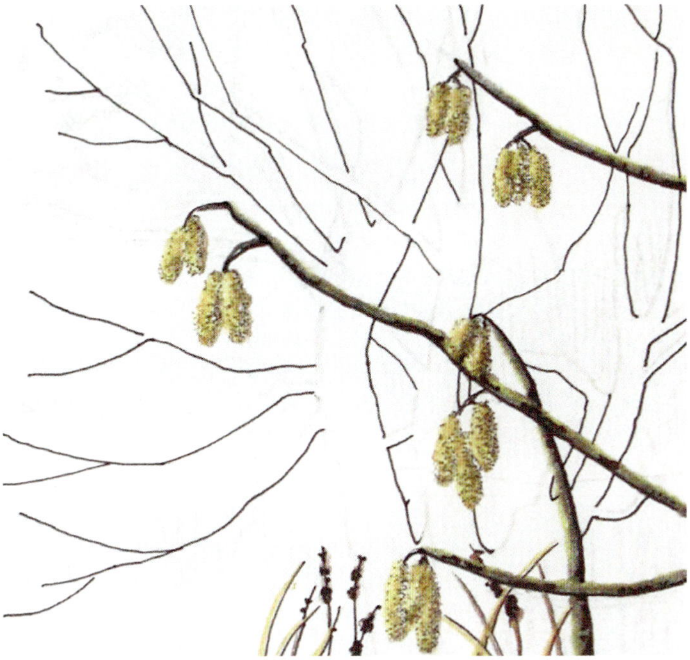

Creating a tangle: stage 1. I placed the catkins first, using tiny ink dots (more on the shadow side), strong colours and highlights to make them stand out. I then added the branches and markings, using ink on the shadow side, Dark Sepia and Derwent's Lichen Green. Note that the tree branches behind also have ink only on one side.

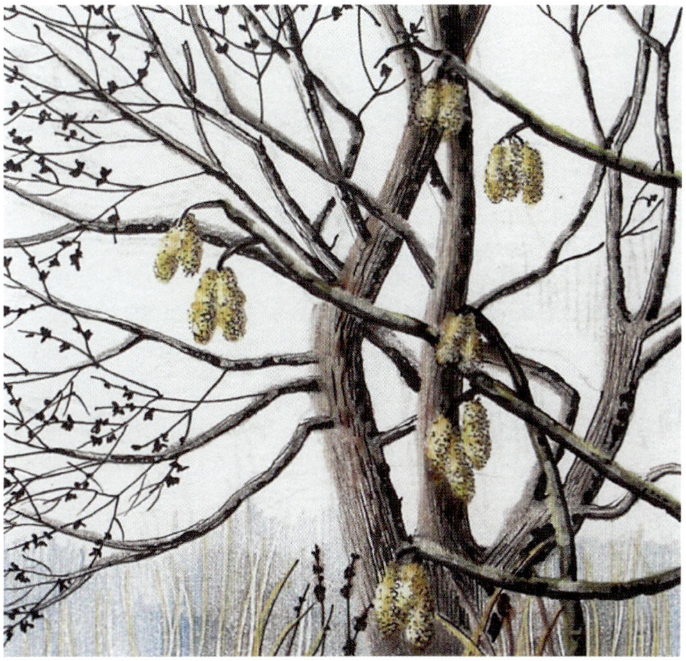

Creating a tangle: stage 2. Once the catkins and foreground branches were established, I sketched in the grasses in front of the tree trunk. I built up the tree behind, inking the shadow side of the bark and branches, adding texture and dried leaves. Using coloured pencil, I worked from Dark Sepia to warmer browns and neutrals, following the form.

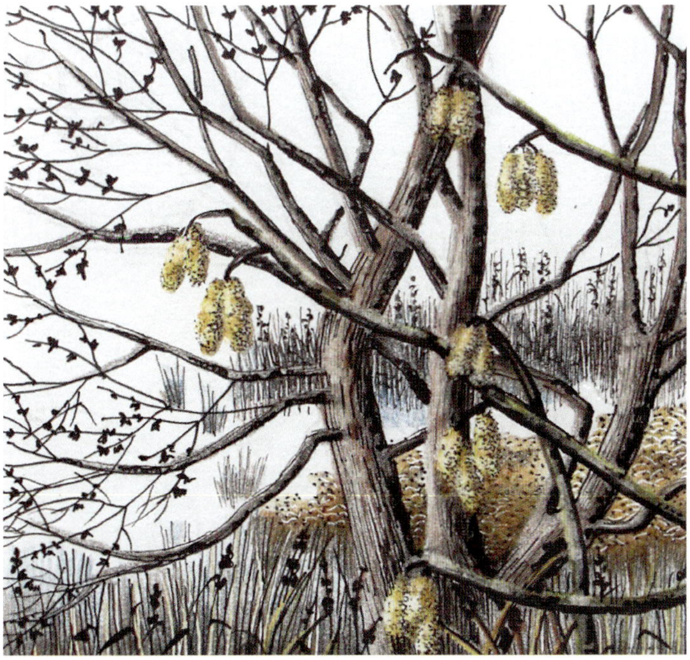

Creating a tangle: stage 3. I could now add grasses and reeds and a patch of bank; I used a mixture of mark-making in ink, embossing over colour and blended coloured pencil, always keeping behind or in front of the trees as appropriate and decreasing the size with the distance.

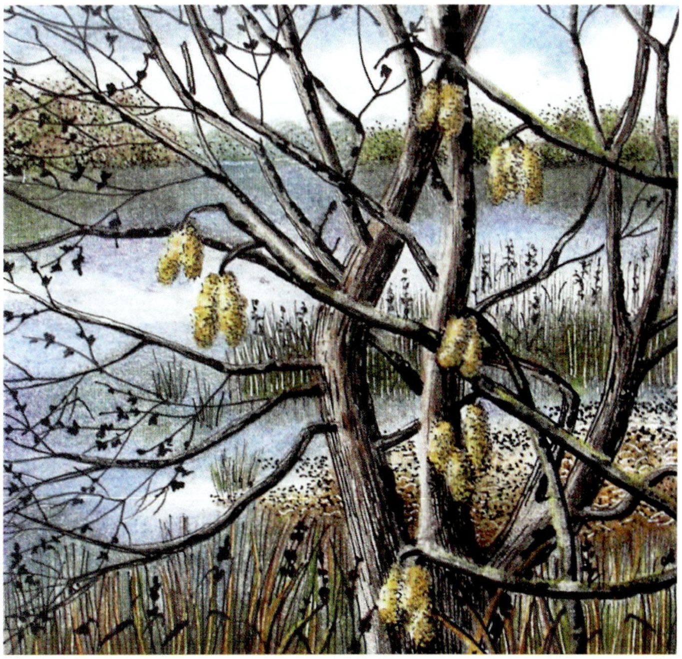

Creating a tangle: stage 4. With the foreground in place, I worked on the distance, introducing clusters of bushes in coloured pencil and ink. The size of the ink markings fixed the distance, and I used progressively more blue. I then added the water, working between the reeds, adding shadowy reflections and lifting out light with Frisket and putty rubber.

Mountains, Slopes, Tracks and Gullies

In the last chapter I explained that it is preferable to approach mountains in coloured pencil without any outlining. Although this is the first step, I always add some ink markings to keep an integrated look. They are needed for dominant features such as rock formations, but are also useful for clumps of trees, paths, sheep tracks, streams and gullies. On a bare hillside these ink markings may be subtle, but they are crucial in establishing the shape and perspective of the mountain. Topographical features all need to be an appropriate size and to follow the lines of the mountain. Always observe their direction and angle as these may change across the picture, depending on the position of each section of a range. The direction of any coloured pencil shading should also follow the form, so that the fells fold into each other but retain their own individual structure.

Highlights and shadows are important as they show the rise and fall of the terrain; dips and gullies can be made even darker by the addition of tiny 0.03 dots at the base of the coloured pencil. Further highlights and patches can be lifted out with Frisket, putty rubber or battery eraser depending on the desired effect. You may choose to fill these with a different, lighter colour and more ink markings to represent bare, stony ground or screes. Details from my Wastwater trio show all these techniques in use, from tiny sheep tracks dotted in pen to deep gullies.

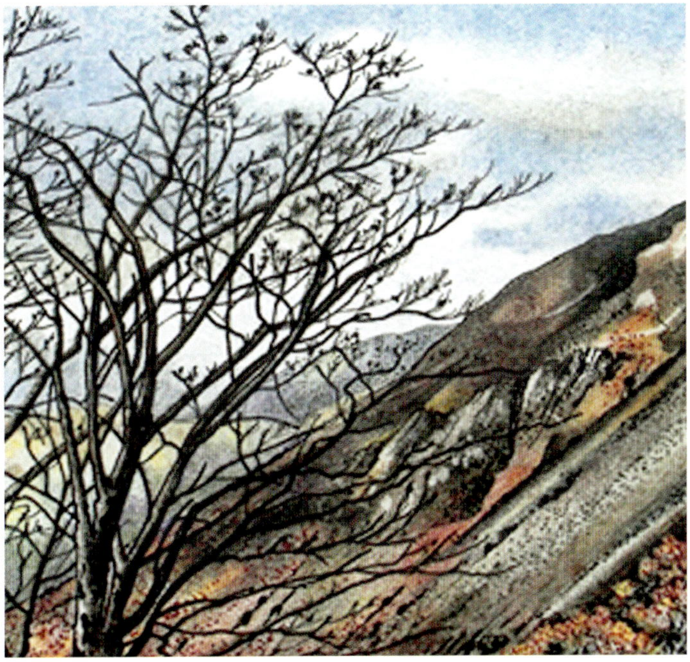

Mountains: rocks and screes. The first of the Wastwater series, *Tree by Wastwater*, shows the screes in autumn. I used strong lines and marks in ink, following the slope of the fells and adding blends of Faber-Castell Dark Sepia, Walnut Brown, Burnt Sienna and Indian Red. I created texture, and on all three images I used 'Irojiten' Fluorescents for highlights.

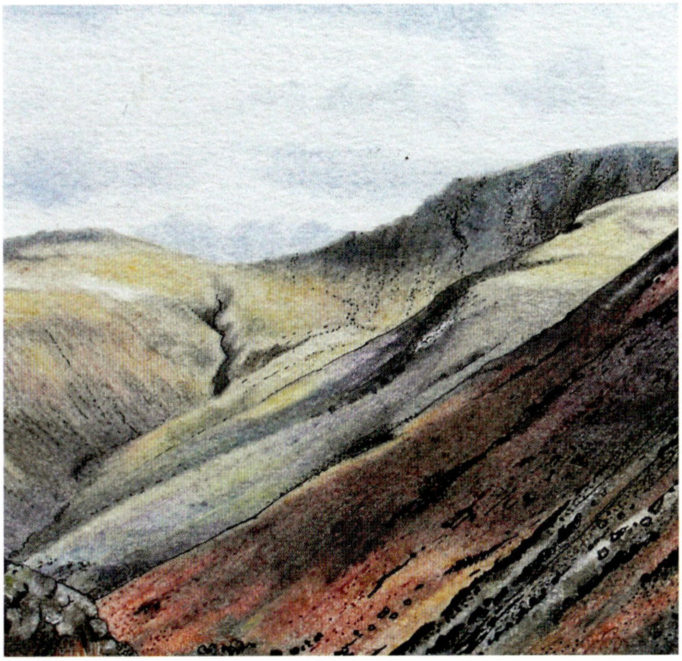

Mountains: tracks and gullies. Beyond the screes the colours changed and the fells became bare. Deep gullies created form and shadow, and small tracks gave a sense of distance. I used ink sparingly just to indicate the terrain. Shadow colours were Faber-Castell Dark Indigo and Prismacolor Parma Violet, with a hint of Pompeian Red for warmth.

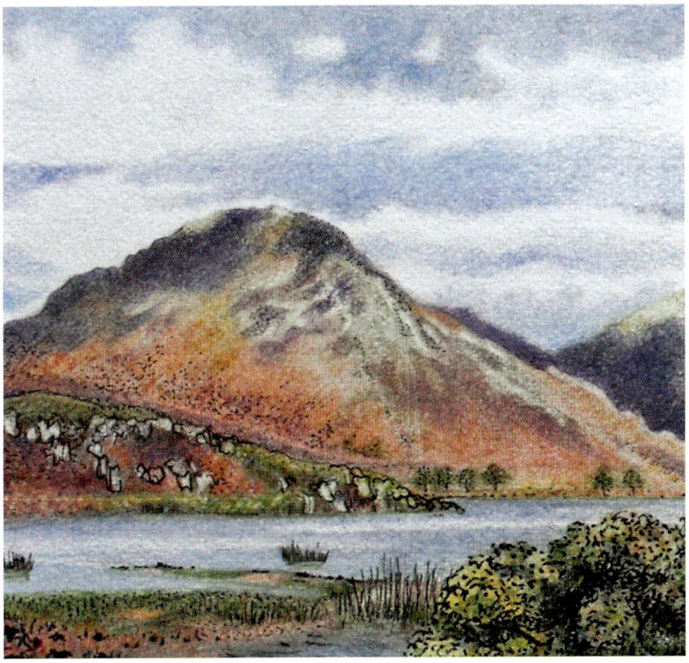

Mountains: light and shade. The structure of a mountain is revealed by the fall of light and shade, as in this image. I used fine ink dots to create a path and steep sides, then added the ridge and slopes using directional strokes in shadow colours. I used a battery eraser to take out highlights and patches of lighter ground.

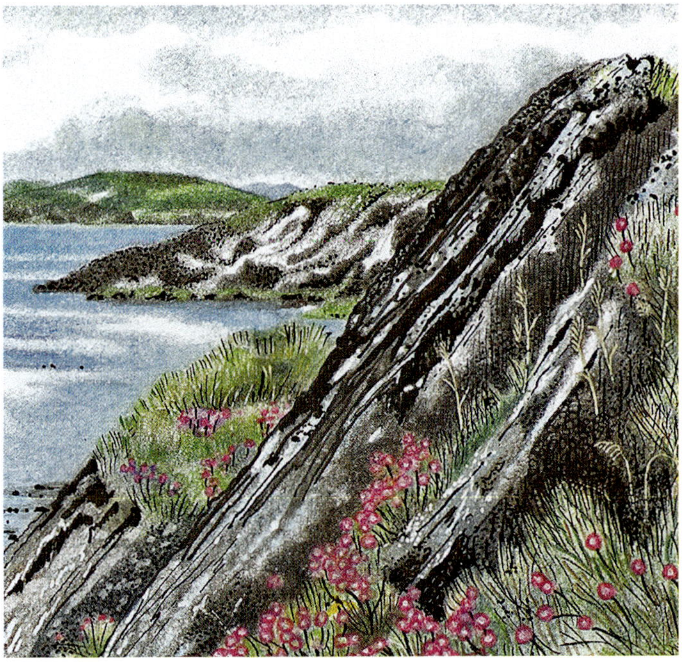

Mountains: coasts and cliffs. For these two sections of rocky coastline I used everything: strong and fine ink lines, random marks, dots, embossing, lifting out and layers of colour – whatever would convey the striking rock formations that made up Gigha's shore. Once the flowers were in place, I simply observed, and let ink and coloured pencil create the rest.

Water

Water is a compelling subject in any medium. At first glance it seems well suited to coloured pencil and the technique of blending without the addition of ink. I don't use very much pen work, even for reflections, as I prefer the more blurred effect of coloured pencil lines. Sometimes I use harder markings in pen above the water and pencil lines below, a technique taken directly from my etching, in which I contrasted hard and soft ground lines. This helps to distinguish above water from below water, and introduces a look of fluidity. Disturbed surfaces such as rough seas and rushing streams can take more ink markings, backed up by deeper tones in the water. On calmer waters I make use of 0.03 dots to mark out the extent of reflections and shadows. These act as guidelines while I work and will eventually be covered with quite dark-coloured pencil. They also show the flow of the water and help to keep it going in the right direction.

Lifting out plays a much more important part, and can be done in the usual ways with Frisket, putty rubber and battery eraser, depending on the requirements of the image. Use it to introduce large areas of light, reflections of clouds, gleaming highlights, cresting waves and points of light from the shore reflected in the water. Lifting out, or leaving out, will bring water to life: you can soften the edges, work back into the space with a lighter colour, or just leave it to sparkle.

The secret of success with water is the same as with plums. It may look like one colour, but it acquires so much more life if you blend it with harmonious associates – and maybe something a bit more surprising. Even if you have a wide area of water, don't rush to cover it, or think that pressing harder will speed things up. Get yourself into meditational mode and go with the flow! It is the slow, methodical application of different layers that creates the impression of shifting colour and greater depths below.

Blue is the colour – up to a point. A well-chosen blue may be the base colour, but once you have put down a first layer (or as you are doing so), think about lifting out or leaving some light. Sometimes you may prefer a 'lifted out' look with a trace of colour; at other times, only white paper will do. After that, harmonious colours from the same part of the spectrum (more blues, greens and a hint of purple) can be introduced as appropriate. Different colours will be required if the water goes into deep shadow or gets muddy; you may need darker greens, browns and indigo. The range of colours should suit the subject, weather and time of day. Some stretches of water are Mediterranean blue, but don't take this as your default colour palette. It is easy to fall back on our received ideas, established in childhood, of what things – such as water and sky – look like. Sky and water are always closely linked and dependent on the weather, so all three should speak to each other in your picture.

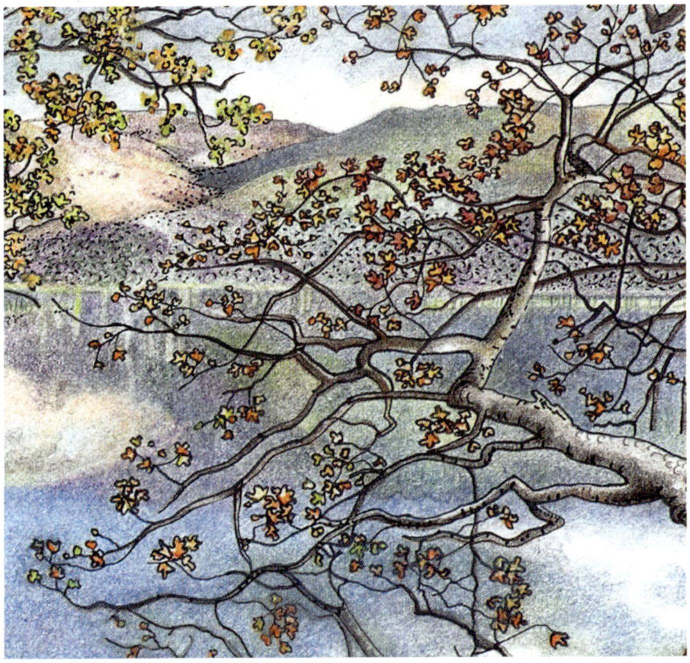

Water: blending and lifting. This section of water has a rich blend of colours, including those created by the reflections and shadow areas on the opposite bank. Cloud reflections were lifted out with Frisket, and the edges softened with a putty rubber. Fine vertical lines of light were also taken out at the water's edge.

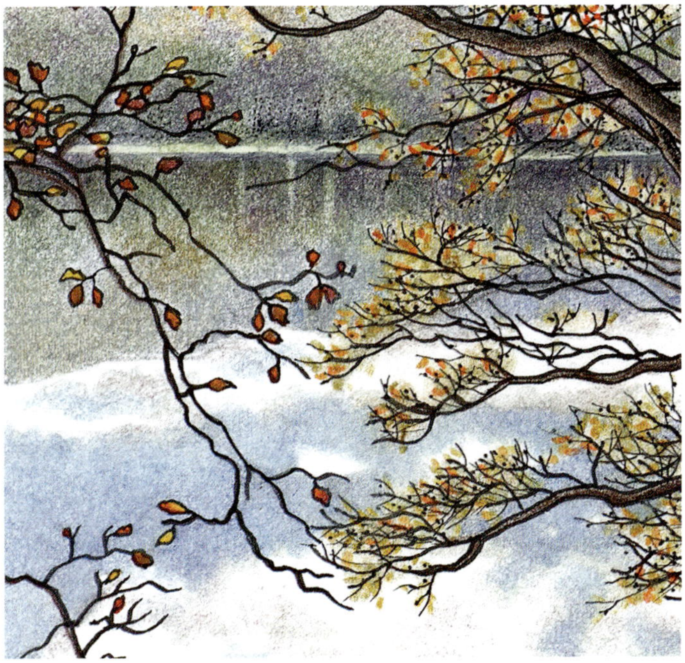

Water: reflections and clouds. This image shows more clearly how reflected clouds are lifted out with Frisket and putty rubber. More colours can be added to give a stormier look. These clouds exist only in the water, as we do not see the sky immediately above. The greens, browns and purples from the opposite bank create depth and shade.

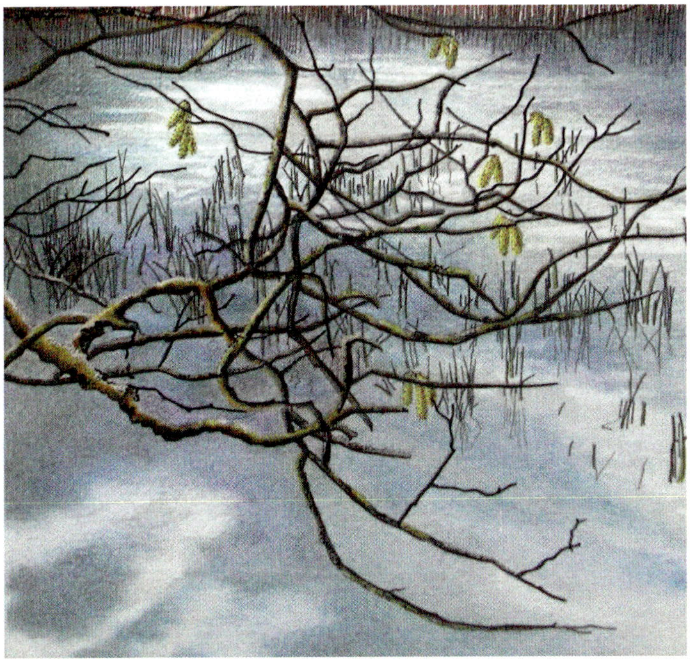

Water: flow and direction. Sometimes currents meet in water, making more interesting patterns that will add interest to your image. Here, a few waves are joining the main body of water and I have used them to lead the eye up the picture to the tangle of branches.

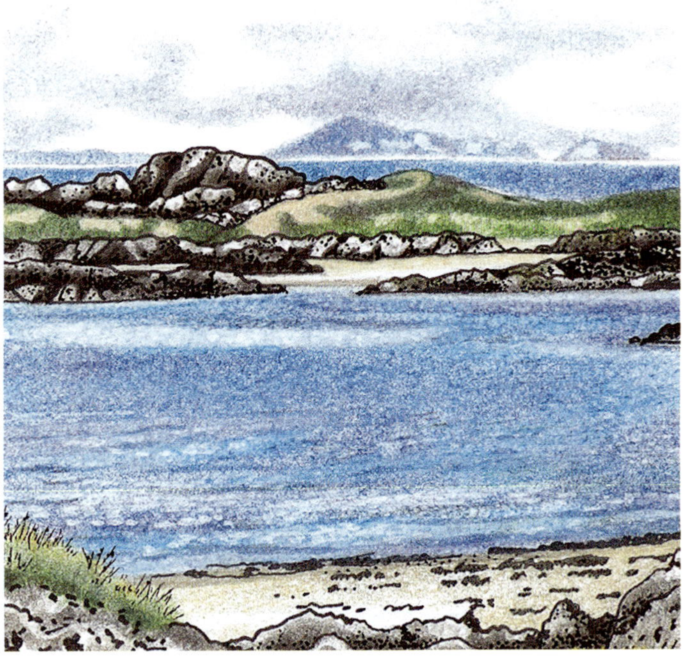

Water: movement and speed. Calm water needs good blending and a smooth surface; swift-moving stretches of water can be more broken in texture. Waves can be lifted out with Frisket, battery eraser or sgraffito, and ink marks added to give a more ruffled look. I used several colours, lifting out and ink dots for the current in *Singing Sands*.

Skies

I generally use just two or three colours, then smooth them with a burnisher or a light blue from one of the waxier pencil ranges. Derwent Coloursoft Cloud Blue or Prismacolor Powder Blue and Cloud Blue are ideal for this purpose. They will remove any roughness, as skies often require an even texture. White clouds can be lifted out with Frisket after a first layer of colour, or left white as you work. Frisket does produce hard edges, but these can be softened by an application of light colour, fading gradually. Always take out slightly more cloud than is necessary to allow for this soft colour transition. Clouds can be given a stormier appearance by the addition of more shadow and appropriate colours. Experiment with putty rubber brushed across the surface of the sky to create paler drifts or low-lying mists. The resulting effects can be modified further by the addition of a different colour.

BE CREATIVE!

Wherever you start and whatever techniques you use, remember to do the translation process first. Consider how to interpret what you see, try things out, and don't be afraid to take the plunge. Be as creative and inventive as you wish and enjoy the process. In the next chapter we shall take a closer look at some of the details that will give your landscape even more atmosphere and authenticity.

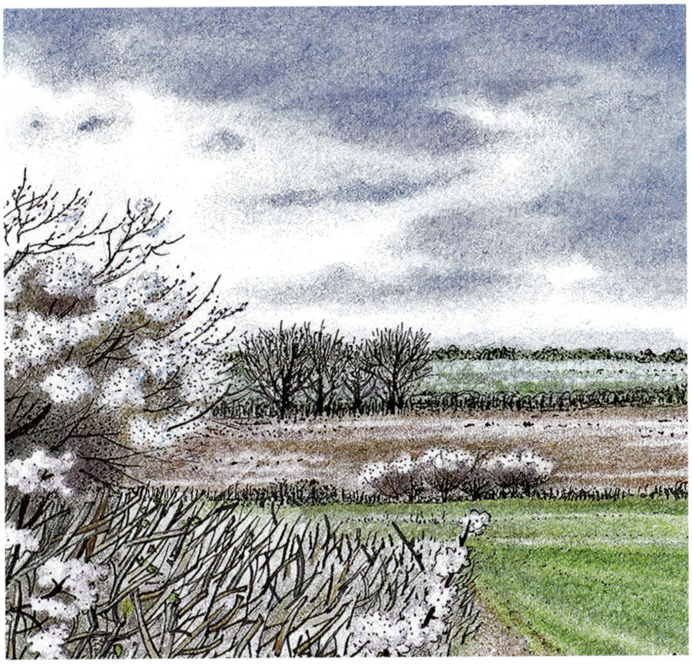

Skies: gentle drifts. For this early spring sky I used cool Ultramarine blues and lifted out drifts rather than cloud shapes with Frisket. I softened the edges by stroking putty rubber across the pigment, keeping the movement linear rather than circular. This is a simple but effective method and looks good with additional paler streaks of colour.

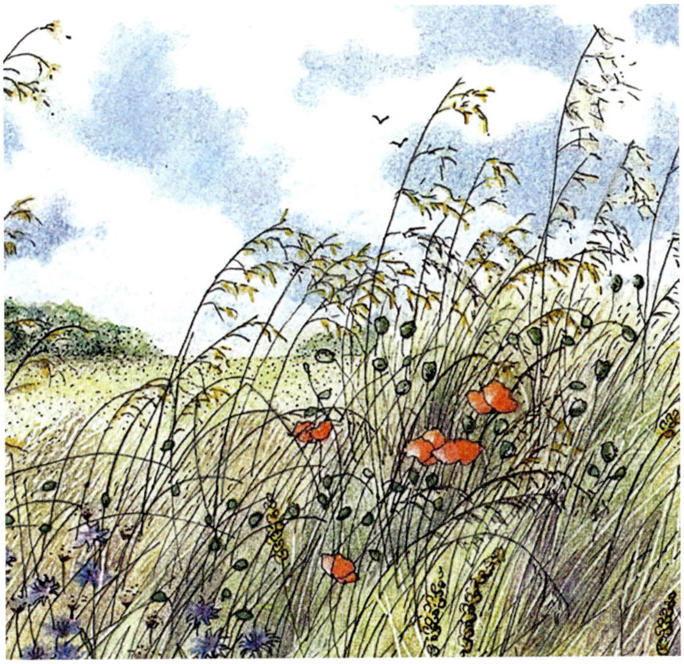

Skies: bright and crisp. Sometimes the day and the subject call for traditional storybook clouds, and this image has all the clichés! I used a blend of Faber-Castell Light Ultramarine and Sky Blue, lifted out with Frisket and putty rubber. I then used Prismacolor Powder Blue as a burnisher for a smooth effect.

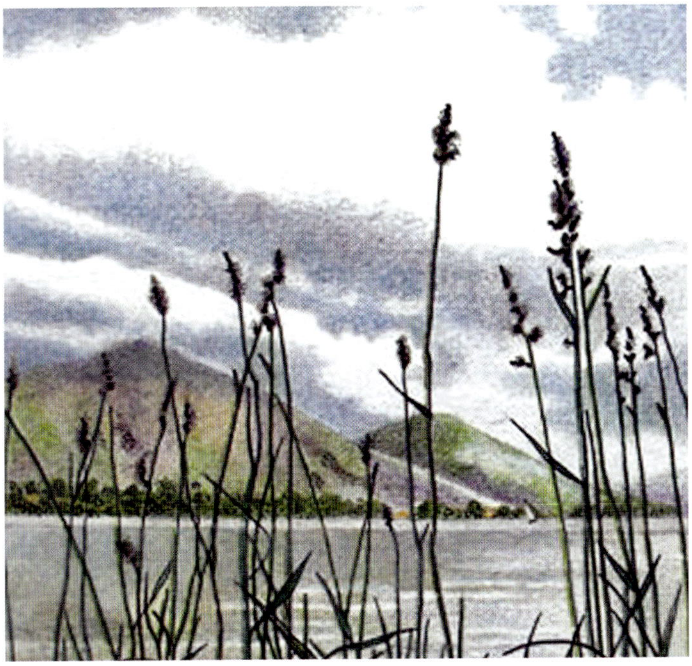

Skies: heavy and sultry. For this mid-afternoon image I wanted to suggest a change in the weather. I gave the cloud formation a diagonal slant and added Faber-Castell Cold Grey III to the edges of Light Ultramarine and Sky Blue. I lifted out clouds with Frisket and putty rubber, adding more grey and some Prismacolor Parma Violet to the undersides.

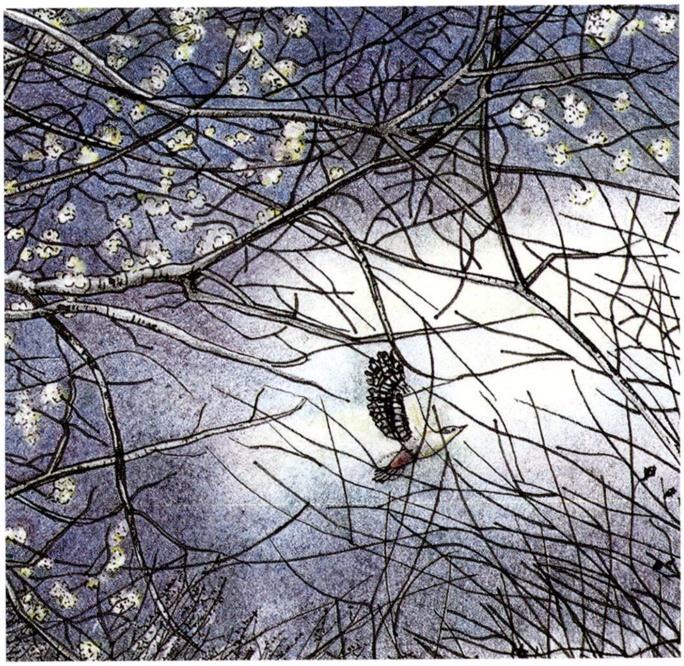

Skies: night and dawn. I chose Faber-Castell Dark Indigo, Indanthrene Blue and Cobalt Blue for the night sky, blending them to different degrees, then fading them out with the help of a putty rubber. I added some very light touches of Manganese Violet and a barely perceptible Light Yellow Glaze to create the dawn light.

CHAPTER 8

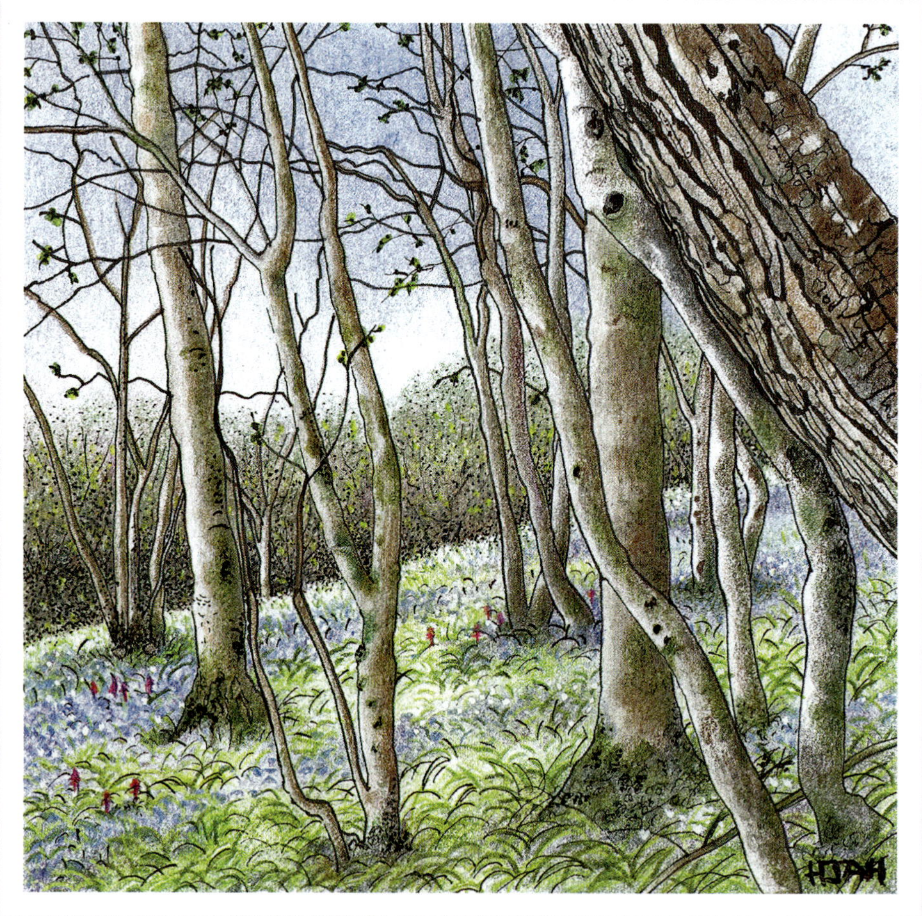

Bluebell Slope.

A Closer Look

Having looked at some general aspects of landscape in the last chapter, we shall now home in on some of the features you might use in the foreground, or in close-up in larger works. These will include tree bark, rocks and pebbles and a selection of flowers and grasses, all of which will add interest and a sense of place to your picture. My approach to these features continues to be one of interpretation rather than naturalistic representation: despite enjoying botanical work, my focus here is on using the combination of ink and coloured pencil to suggest a particular plant. We shall not be counting stamens; however, the form and colour of a plant, and its ability to denote a particular environment, will be important in setting the scene.

USING DETAIL EFFECTIVELY

Tree Bark

I love using ink and coloured pencil for features such as tree bark; the combination seems made for it. I always start by checking the direction of the light, and concentrate any initial ink marks on the shadow side. I begin with quite a strong line in a 0.5 or 0.7 pen, making sure that I do not cross over any incoming branches. I add any obvious markings such as breaks in the bark surface, hollows and so on that would be best conveyed in ink.

I then return to the shadow side and apply coloured pencil ellipses, starting immediately alongside the inked line and using a deep brown such as Faber-Castell's Dark Sepia or Derwent's Burnt Umber. This removes the appearance of a pen outline and gives a seamless look, at the same time deepening the shadow. Lifting the pencil pressure slightly to soften the edges of the colour, gradually introduce a warmer mid-brown (or whatever colour your tree requires) as you move towards the middle. Any patches of lichen or similar details can be added at this stage, as well as more ink detail (smaller lines, knots, texture etc.)

As you reach the lighter side of the bark, add some patches in warm or cool neutrals such as Faber-Castell's excellent grey range, Caran D'Ache's Beige or Brownish Beige or Prismacolor's Putty Beige. You can use a battery eraser to lift out random patches of peeled bark or highlights.

The colours you choose and the texture of the bark will depend on your subject, but there are plenty of options available. Some of the waxier pencil ranges have perfect colours for lichen and moss: Derwent 'Coloursoft's Yellow Green and Lichen Green and Prismacolor's Yellow Ochre, Grey Green Light and Limepeel are some of my favourites, and their texture makes them particularly suitable for a final layer bursting with colour.

Rocks and Pebbles

Rocks offer a lot of scope for creativity. Wherever you go, the rocks and pebbles are different, depending on the geology of the area. If you follow the coastline, rock formations and colours are constantly changing and they all lend themselves to interpretation in ink and coloured pencil. The few examples of rocks and pebbles that I have shown here just hint at the range of possibilities for creativity. I have used a mixture of embossing, mark-making in ink, blended coloured pencil and lifting out using various methods.

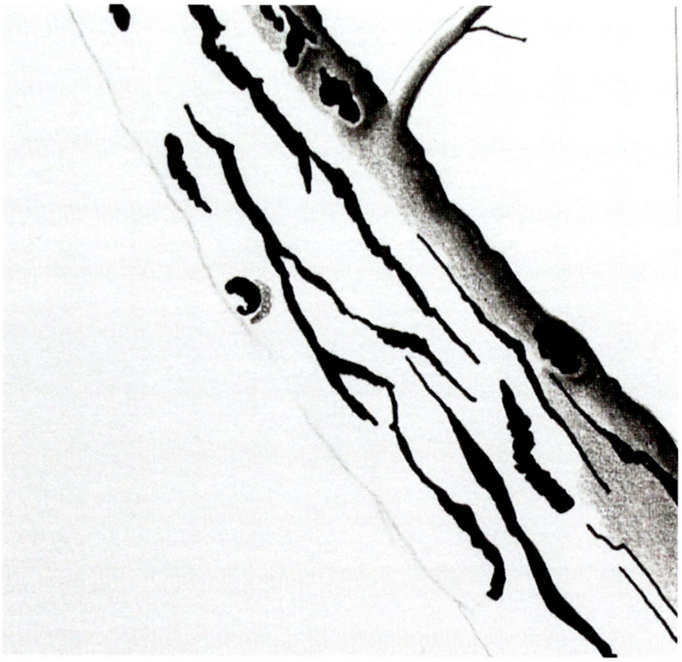

Tree trunk in ink and coloured pencil: stage 1. I began on the shadow side, with a strong ink outline in 0.5 pen, leaving the opposite side of the trunk in pencil. I blended fine ellipses in Faber-Castell Dark Sepia immediately alongside to deepen the shade, gradually fading it out. I then added irregular gashes in ink along the bark.

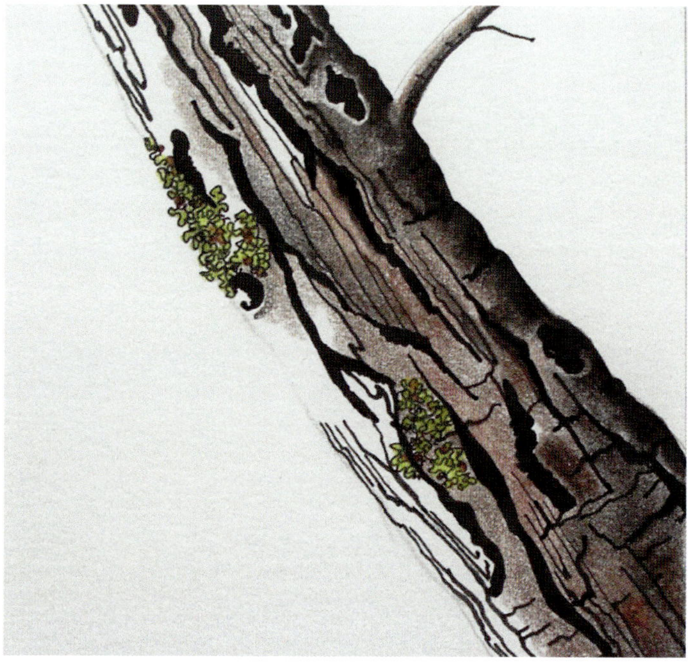

Tree trunk in ink and coloured pencil: stage 2. Towards the centre of the bark I introduced Faber-Castell warmer browns – Walnut Brown and Burnt Sienna – and blended them into the Dark Sepia. I inked in some lichen patches, colouring them with Derwent's Lichen Green, Prismacolor's Limepeel, and more Burnt Sienna. Finer ink lines were also added to the bark.

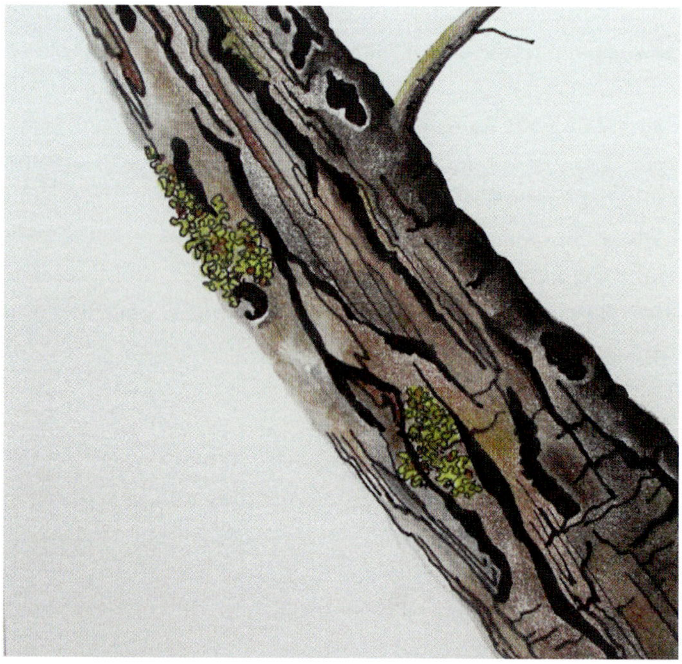

Tree trunk in ink and coloured pencil: stage 3. The lighter edge of the trunk was completed using a mix of paler neutrals including Faber-Castell's Warm Grey II and Prismacolor's rich Putty Beige (very useful in landscape for a blob of rich but neutral pigment). More ink lines were added, this time following the curve of the bark.

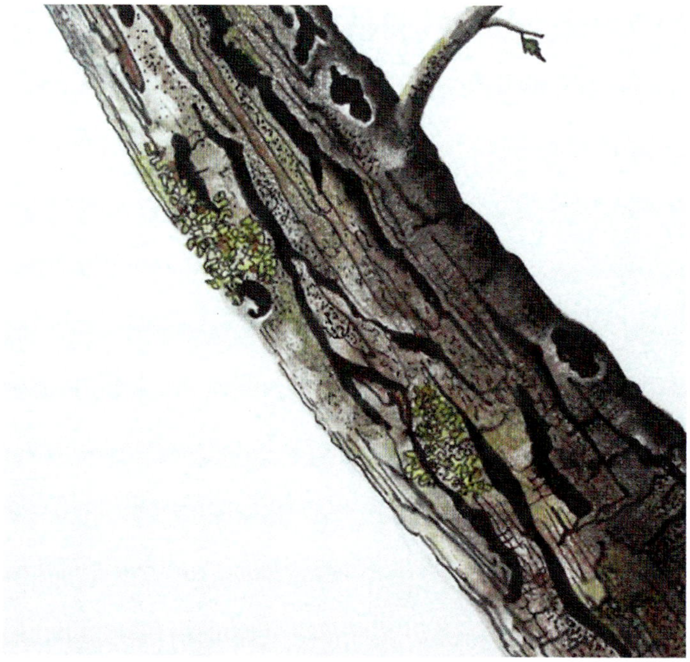

Tree trunk in ink and coloured pencil: stage 4. After assessing stage three, I added more layers of colour to the bark, decreasing the warmth of the browns and adding more Lichen Green. As a finishing touch, I took out some irregularly shaped highlights with a battery eraser, and introduced more textural markings on the surface.

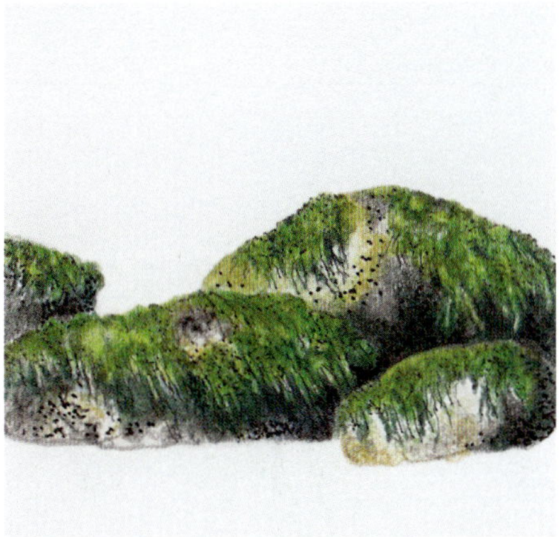

Seaweed rocks. I pencilled in the rock shapes and draped seaweed over them, using Prismacolor Kelp Green and Chartreuse, with Faber-Castell Pine Green at the base. For the deep shadow I used Dark Sepia and Prussian Blue, adding ink dots and fine seaweed strands with a 0.03 pen. Lighter areas were in Faber-Castell Warm Grey I and Green Gold.

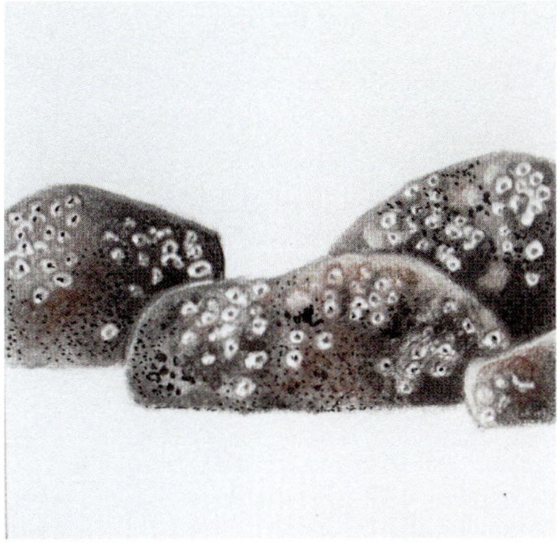

Barnacle rocks. I created the barnacles using a circular embosser, working around them with a blend of Faber-Castell Warm Grey III, Burnt Sienna and Caran D'Ache Brownish Beige. For the areas of deep shadow, I added Dark Sepia and 0.03 ink dots. Lighter patches were then lifted out with a battery eraser and holes were added to the barnacles.

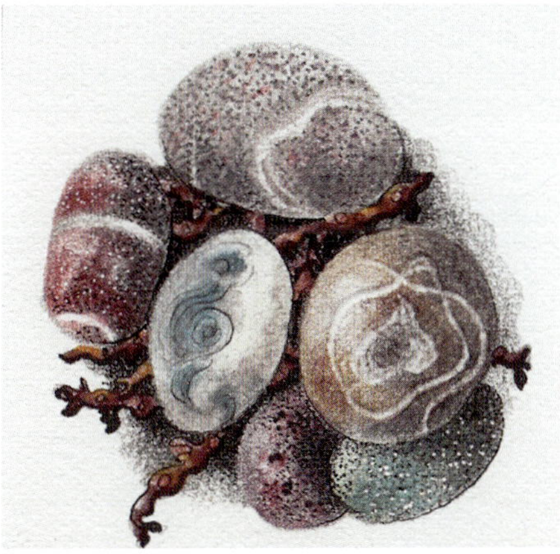

Pebbles on seaweed. I used 0.03, 0.1 and 0.5 pens for this collection of stones and seaweed, seen from above. I used embossing for dots and the incised markings on their surface, and a limited palette of Caran D'Ache and Faber-Castell pencils for the colouring. Light and shade were important in establishing the form of the pebbles and the background.

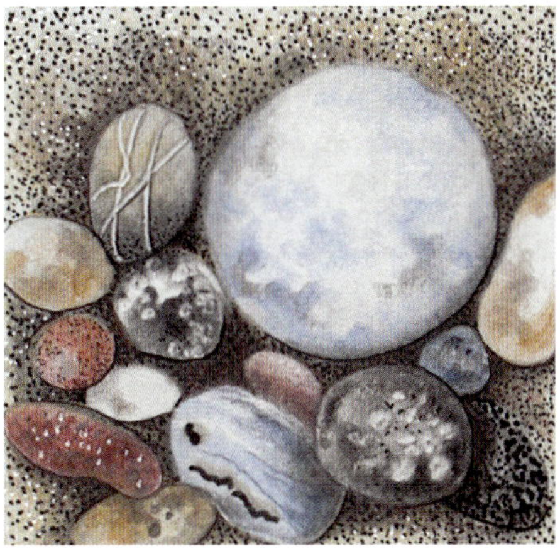

Pebbles on wet sand. I used the same combination of a limited palette, ink markings and embossing for this selection of pebbles. Light, shade and highlights established their relative positions. The background was done with a 0.03 pen, embossed dots and a blend of Caran D'Ache Cream, Light Ochre, Sepia and (the perfect colour for wet sand) Brownish Beige.

When tackling rock and stone, it is important to work out the direction of the light and which parts will be in shadow; shading and highlighting accordingly will give the rock form and substance. Coloured pencil can be lifted out with Frisket to create interesting marks, to increase or restore highlights, and modify the colour. Use your ingenuity to create shells, lichen, seaweeds and so on. Pebbles can be treated in a similar way, varying the markings, colours and highlights. To form the base for a stony beach, use tiny ink dots, with or without coloured pencil; these will read as sand or soil beneath the stones.

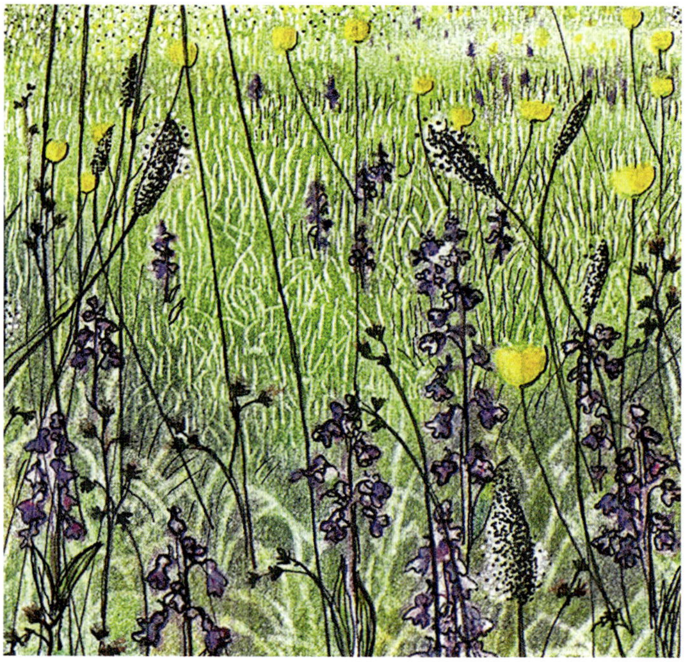

Green-winged orchids in *Marden Morning*. I created a frame of orchids, buttercups and plantains in the foreground, inking a fine outline to indicate the orchid shape and to give them prominence. Their recognizable colours also served as distance markers across the meadow, leading the eye towards the trees. The buttercups are half outlined to help them stand out without looking too heavy.

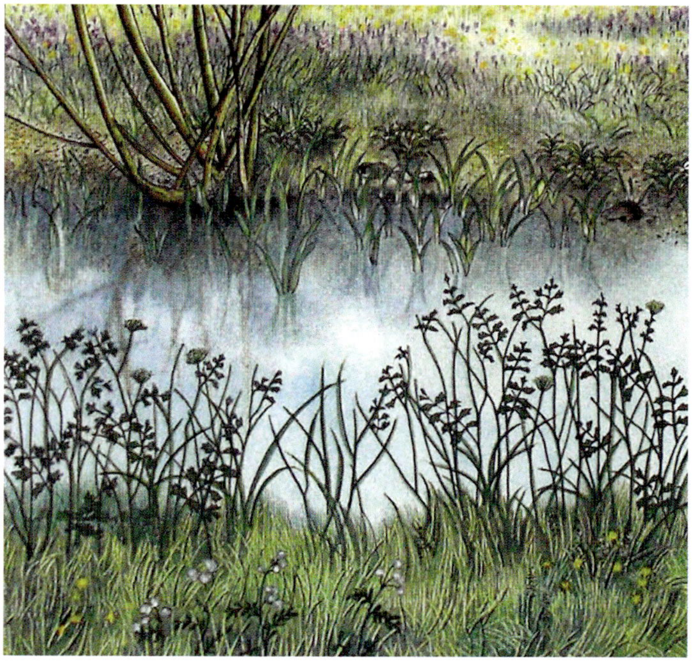

Hemlock water dropwort in *Marden Meadow Pond*. Although the characteristic umbels are still quite small, I used the triangular shape of the leaflets on these young plants to add interest to the foliage on the bank. Lady's smock can be seen in the grass, and the purple heads of the green-winged orchids in the meadow opposite.

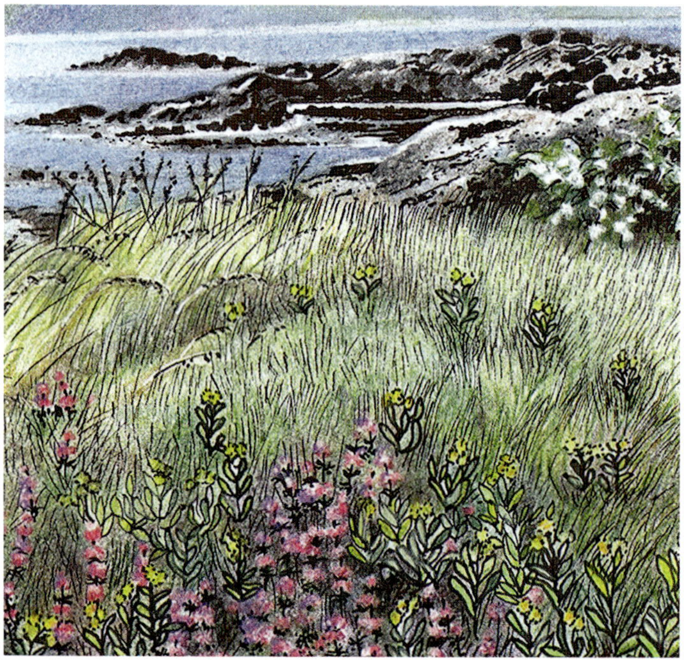

Coastal flora in *Western Isles*. Roseroot and bell heather formed just some of the clusters of July flowers along this stretch of Scottish shoreline. I let them dominate the foreground, using a mixture of outlining and coloured pencil to create a mass of colour. In the middle distance, a burnet rose spreads across the rocks.

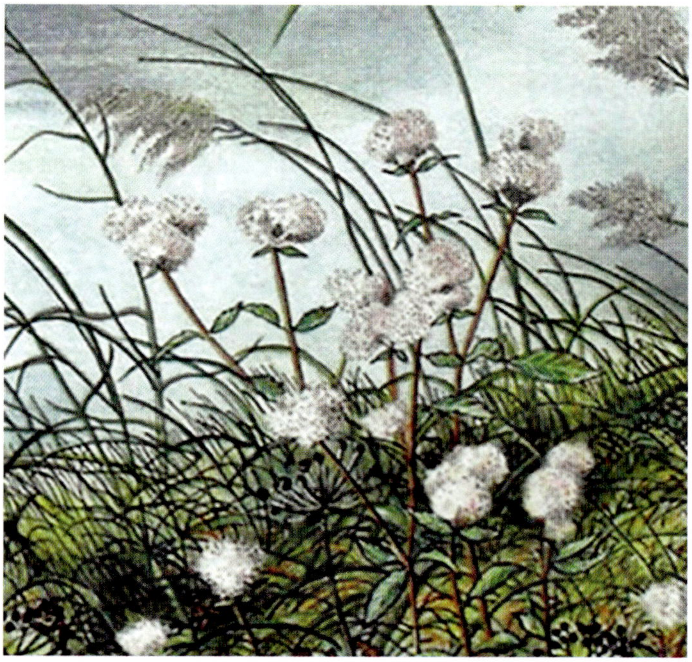

Hemp agrimony in *Summer into Autumn*. These lakeside plants were all turning towards autumn, and the reddish flowers of hemp agrimony had developed pale, downy seeds. Even in their dry state, they are handsome plants with clearly defined leaves. I set them against reed heads, with the spreading leaves and brownish-purple seeds of fool's watercress below.

Flowers

Community Thinking

Plants make a recognizable statement about the sort of environment you are depicting, and evoke a response in the viewer. This may be a specific, nostalgic memory of hedgerows from childhood, or just the sense that things look right. Identifiable flowers and grasses are always preferable to multi-purpose green strokes that give us no information. Remember that it is your right to move, substitute or remove anything in your picture, so assemble a collection that belongs to a plant community and says something about your chosen landscape. These days I try to be authentic in my choices, and resist the temptation to settle for obvious crowd-pleasers such as the ubiquitous poppy! Some plants are powerful symbols, and (through no fault of their own) have become artistic clichés simply through overuse.

Decide which plants are in front, and always check whether anything needs white embossing before you add ink or colour. Work from front to back, weaving in leaves, grasses and whatever can be seen behind, remembering to decrease their size as they recede. Many plants lend themselves to interpretation in ink and coloured pencil; some can be shown as a distant pop of colour, others can be used as close foreground interest, finely outlined and coloured. You can choose exactly how you want to represent each species in the context of your image. The images opposite show communities of plants in context from a selection of works; they are all species that were growing close together in the very different environments I chose.

Single Examples

I have chosen four favourite examples of plants that can be interpreted creatively using ink and coloured pencil. An exhaustive catalogue would be the subject of another book, so this is just a small selection to show you the sort of effects you can create yourself. You don't always need the showiest or the most colourful plants; I often use common varieties such as sorrel, ragwort, thistles or meadowsweet, partly because their familiar shapes strike a chord. Before starting, I always check the direction and fall of the light to see which part of each flower should be highlighted.

Cow parsley (*Anthriscus sylvestris*): I often use plants from the *Apiaceae* family (previously *Umbelliferae*), whose white or yellow flower heads can be created using a few simple techniques. They are attractive in all seasons, with frothy blossoms in spring and summer, followed by a distinctive shape and conspicuous seeds in autumn, perfect for ink with just a hint of neutral colour. In winter, snow and frost transform them into striking foreground features. To create the cow parsley heads in the example, I followed their shape and with a couple of embossers I made small, white clusters of dots, increasing the number towards the light. I added tiny ink marks amongst the embossed dots to help define the shapes of the flower heads and establish their extent. Adding touches of green and some soft shadow gave them form. When set in context against a darker background and green foliage, the umbels will stand out noticeably, and pure white highlights will sparkle.

Ribwort plantain (*Plantago lanceolata*): Ribwort plantain, seen with green-winged orchids in *Marden Morning*, is another plant that lends itself to an ink and coloured pencil interpretation and is useful as foreground foliage. In this case, I embossed the long stamens around the flower head and softened them with Faber-Castell Warm Grey II to create a halo effect, completing the rest of the flower using ink dots and shades of brown.

Teasel (*Dipsacus fullonum*): Teasel is another striking plant that looks good in every season. In summer it has pinkish-mauve florets that form a belt round the flower head, and in winter its dark, spiny silhouette will draw the eye if you are short of a focal point.

Sheep's sorrel (*Rumex acetosella*): Sheep's sorrel, common sorrel, and broad-leaved dock, all from the *Polygonaceae* family, will bring patches of warm colour to grass and moorland. Their rusty red hues are attractive and instantly recognizable.

Grasses

Familiar grasses make fields, hedgerows and foregrounds much more interesting and will complement the flora when used in the right habitat. Rather than falling back on single stroke ink or pencil lines to cover an area of long grass, look at the habitat and choose two or three different varieties appropriate to the environment. (You can always add shorter, single-stroke blades of grass in between to fill in.) I make frequent use of my

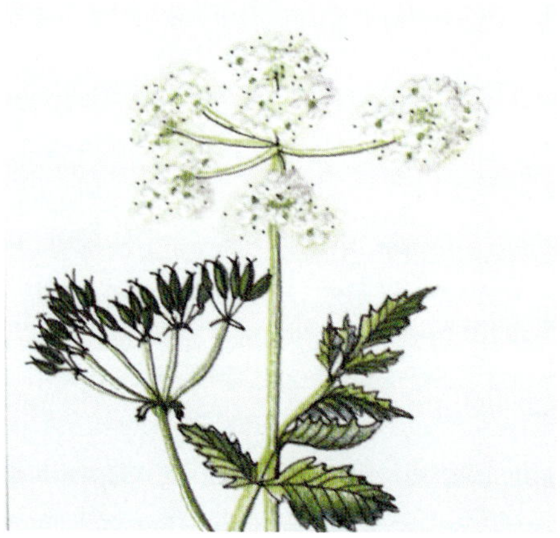

Flowers: cow parsley. I embossed flower shapes and added tiny ink dots. Using a 0.03 pen, I inked one side of the stalks, the leaf outlines and the seed heads. I used Faber-Castell May Green, Permanent Green Olive and Dark Indigo on the leaves and seeds, and brushed the flowers lightly with May Green, adding Prismacolor Greyed Lavender for shadow.

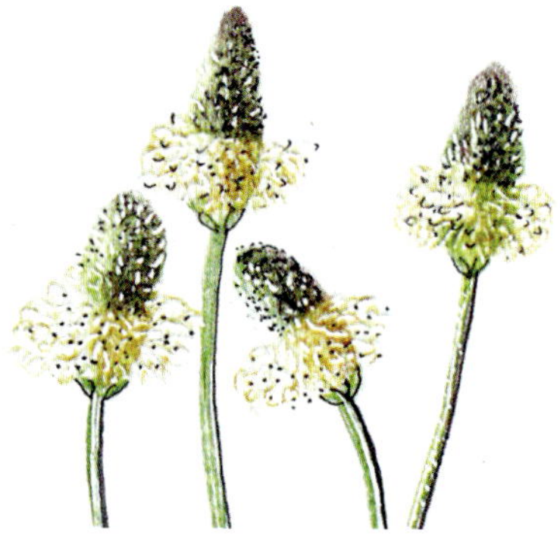

Flowers: ribwort plantain. After lightly pencilling the shape, I embossed stamens around the flower head and created a halo of Faber-Castell Warm Grey II, Green Gold, and Raw Umber. I used Burnt Umber, Permanent Green Olive, Olive Green Yellowish and May Green for the stalks and heads, adding small ink dots for texture and shadow and tiny embossed hairs.

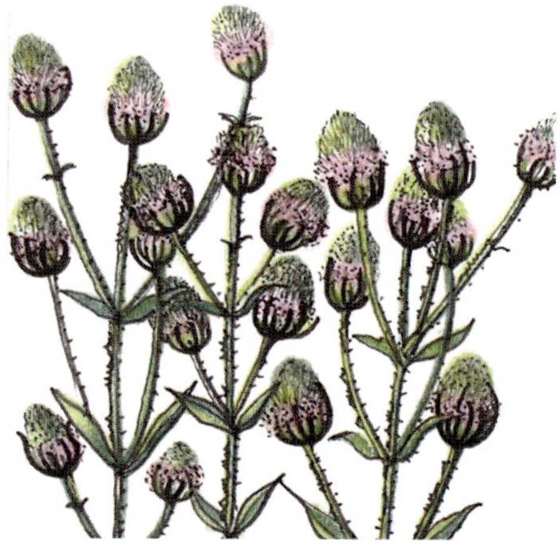

Flowers: teasel. I started with the characteristic, curved bracts, spiny stems and pointed leaves, using fine ink lines throughout to convey the upright profile of the plant. For the pinkish-mauve belt of flowers I chose Faber-Castell Light Magenta and Violet, completing the spines above and all the foliage in May Green, Permanent Green Olive and Juniper Green.

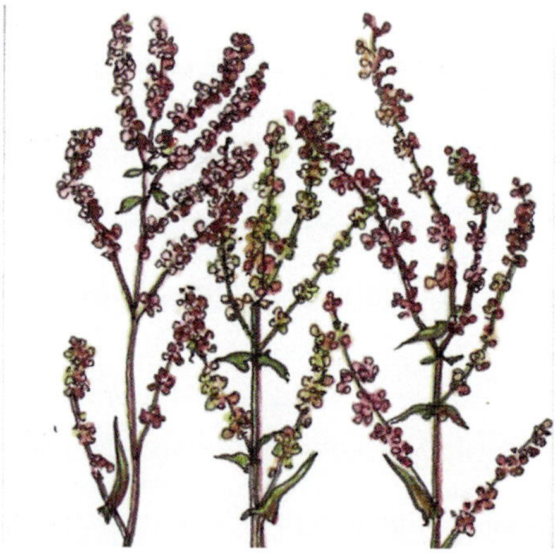

Flowers: sheep's sorrel. Starting with the lower stems and arrow-shaped leaves, I outlined in ink. For the flower stalks, I followed my pencil lines, creating small ellipses in ink, clustering them right round the stem. I used a combination of Faber-Castell Burnt Carmine, Indian Red, Burnt Sienna and Earth Green Yellowish throughout, adding Permanent Green Olive to the leaves.

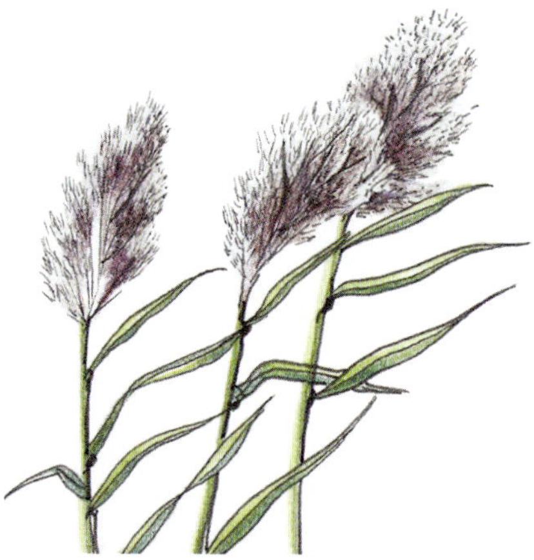

Grasses: common reed. I inked one side of the stems and outlined the leaves, adding May Green, Permanent Green Olive and Juniper Green. For the spikelets I used a 0.03 pen and a light touch, then introduced patches of soft colour using Caran D'Ache Brownish Beige and Prismacolor Parma Violet. The tips were highlighted with Caran D'Ache Silver Grey.

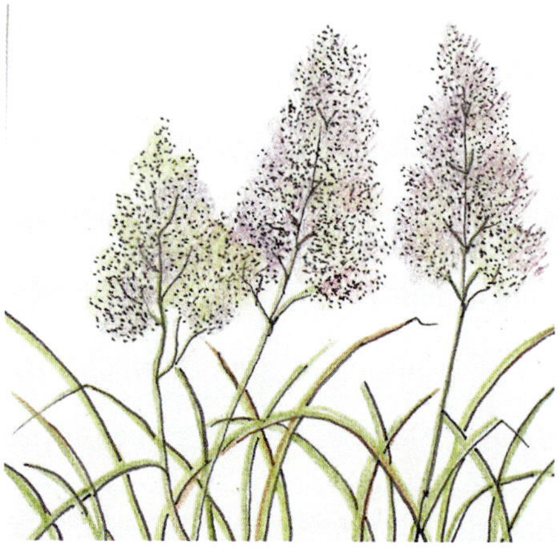

Grasses: Yorkshire fog. I followed the pointed shape of these delicate heads of *Holus lanatus* using tiny ink dots and a few fine stalks. I wanted to show its range of delicate colours when open, so chose Prismacolor Parma Violet and Limepeel with Faber-Castell Manganese Violet and May Green, adding Burnt Ochre on the leaves.

well-thumbed copy of *Grasses* by C.E. Hubbard, as the line drawings show their structures very clearly. Some species such as Yorkshire Fog (*Holcus lanatus*) create drifts of subtle colour that will add life and interest.

Grasses can embellish your work in any season; they fade to attractive neutrals in autumn, sometimes bleaching out completely, and are transformed again by frost and snow. I have chosen four different examples, concentrating on their

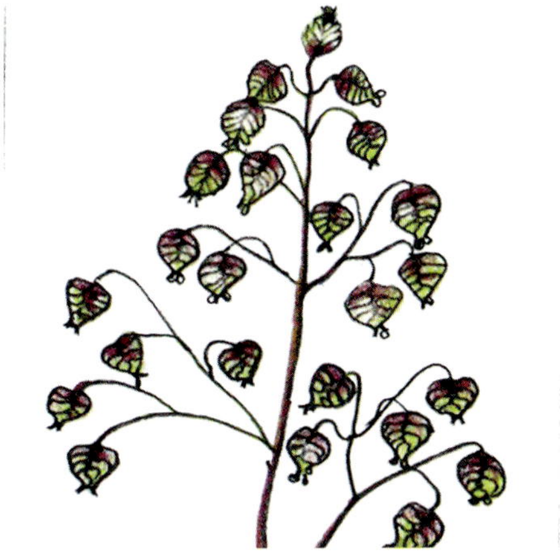

Grasses: quaking grass. The structure of this plant causes it to 'quake', so the stems and flower heads must look fragile and wobbly. I started with a very fine ink lines, attaching the hanging spikelets and outlining their pattern. I then used a combination of Faber-Castell Red Violet, Mauve and May Green, lifting out highlights with a battery eraser.

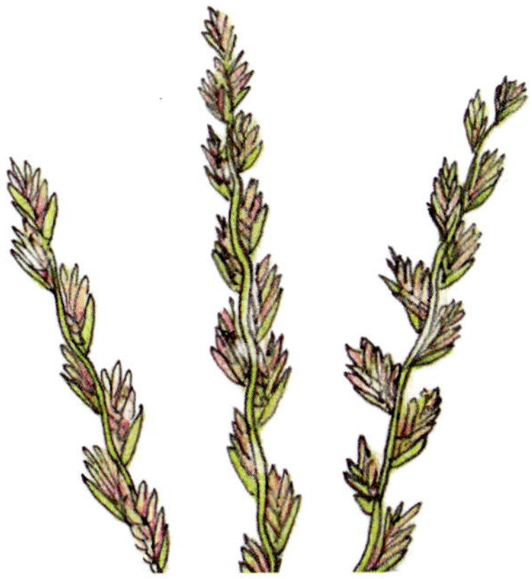

Grasses: perennial rye grass. The wavy stem of this grass is the best starting point and an attractive feature. The spikelets are stalkless and are set neatly on alternate sides of the stem. I followed their pattern using fine 0.03 ink lines, and coloured them individually using Faber-Castell Permanent Carmine, Burnt Ochre and May Green.

interesting shapes; some are close-up and would benefit from being outlined and coloured in, others can be depicted in the usual integrated fashion.

Common reed (*Phragmites australis*): This tall and elegant grass has been part of my artwork since I began printmaking, and developed into my signature plant. For me, it epitomizes the lakesides and wetlands that I love to explore and feature in my work. It seemed perfect for etching, but also translates very well into ink and coloured pencil. It has strong stems, tough but graceful leaves, and huge flower heads that start upright but bend as the seeds ripen. The combination of purplish-brown spikelets and soft white hairs surrounding each floret makes it ideal for fine ink and coloured pencil.

Yorkshire fog (*Holcus lanatus*): This is a very decorative grass, from when it is greenish-pink and tightly furled to when it reveals its feathery mauve flowers. Drifts of Yorkshire fog in a meadow add pastel pinks, greys and mauves before fading to silver in the autumn.

Quaking grass (*Briza media*): Some grasses can be used more for their attractive overall shape than for their flower heads, although quaking grass qualifies on both counts. The triangular, greenish-purple spikelets on fragile stems create good foreground interest; they dry as they age, appearing almost transparent if set against a darker background.

Perennial rye grass (*Lolium perenne*): I chose this common grazing and hay grass for its characteristic structure of spikelets alternating on opposite sides of the stem. Shown here in relative close-up, even when used at a much smaller size, perennial rye grass will add an authentic touch to meadows and grassland.

TIME TO STEP BACK

We have now worked through all the ways of using ink and coloured pencil together, from the general features of the landscape to the more detailed ones that reflect its ecology. It is now time to step back and consider how your picture works in its entirety; in the next chapter we shall make any necessary adjustments, inject whatever is lacking, and admire the results!

CHAPTER 9

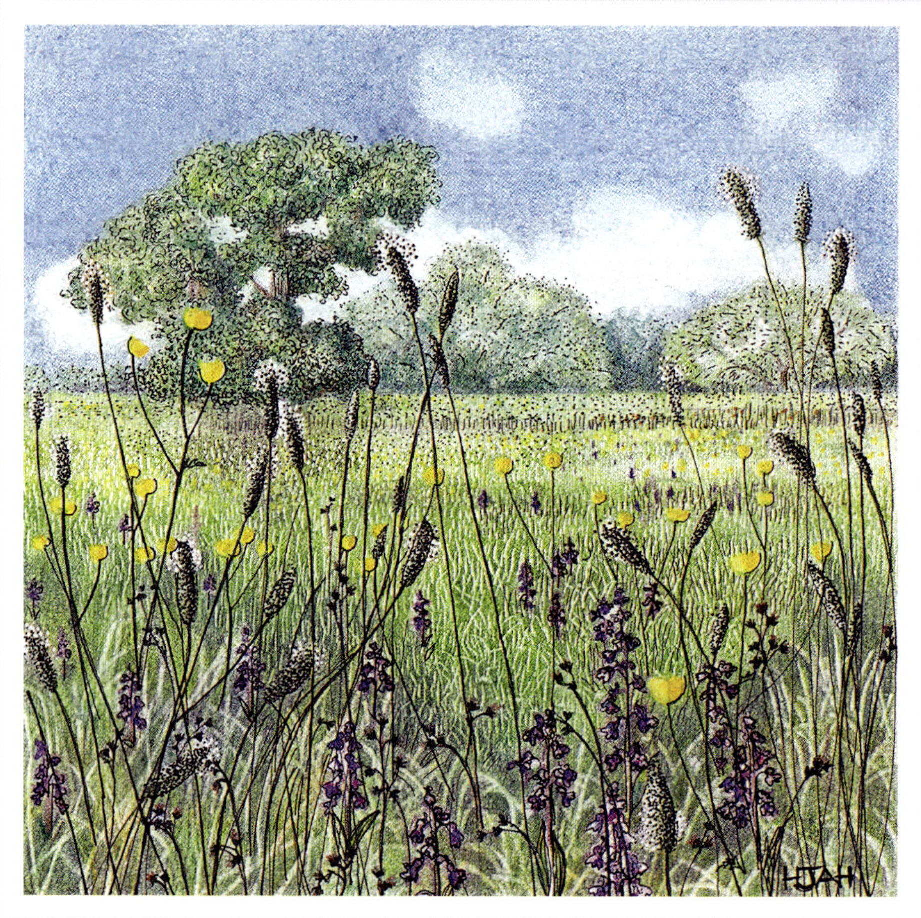

Marden Morning.

Seeing the Whole Picture

Once you have built up much of your image in an integrated way, using both ink and coloured pencil, it is time to shift your focus to consideration of the whole. Up to this point it has been important to identify what is in front and to concentrate on specific areas, adding the surroundings and background once you know what is visible. From now on, everything you do should be designed to pull the image together and to ensure that it works in its entirety. The elements in this chapter – tonal balance, light, shade, delicacy and strength – are all inextricably linked and can be addressed in any order, but should all be included in the appraisal of your work as you reach the next stage.

TONAL BALANCE

You may have paid close attention to perspective and composition, but still feel that your picture seems somehow flat and uniform. When you are concentrating on form, colour and detail, it is easy to overlook one of the most useful ways of injecting life into your image. Variety of tone is something we absorb automatically when we see it in a picture or in the wild: it looks natural, adding interest and sometimes drama. However, when we are creating our own artwork, we need to remind ourselves that it is there and has an important function. Once we can *see* tones and appreciate their purpose, we can recreate them in our own pictures. Uniformity of tone is a classic beginner's mistake; this is hardly surprising as we try to remember all the other instructions and mix the right colours. I also suspect that when we see tone in nature, it is so much part of our understanding of a scene that we take it for granted. Now is the time to look at your work and see whether more tonal variety would make it come alive.

What Do We Understand by Tone?

Unless you are taught about tone at school or at college, you will probably have just a passing acquaintance with the idea. The word *tone* simply describes the lightness or darkness of any colour, regardless of its hue. If we lived in an entirely monochrome world, we would be more familiar with tone: colour complicates the issue because it tends to steal all the attention. However, tone matters as well, because works with little or no tonal contrast look dull and bland. Whatever your medium, if you have a reference photograph, a black and white copy will show you the different tonal values. I always print one when I start a new piece of work, so that I can refer to it and not lose sight of this important component.

As an etcher, tones were of vital importance in deciding how long an aquatinted plate should stay in the acid – the longer the dip, the deeper the tone. I always took proofs in black in the initial stages, introducing colour only when I had established the different tonal values. My early practice as an artist happened to involve thinking tonally, but I know that this is not the case for most of my students. The simple strip illustrated shows a tonal range in greyscale, but the same range applies to any other colour, as shown on page 97.

The range of tones in a landscape does not have to be extensive; once too many are introduced, or if they are too similar, the eye fails to distinguish between them and their impact is

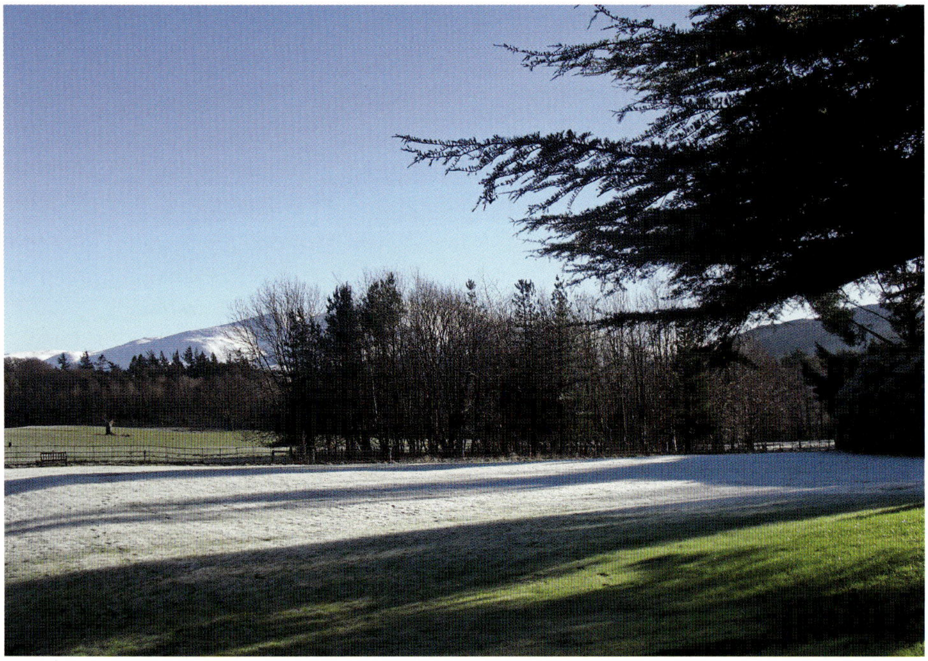

Tonal awareness: image in colour. This view from Higham Hall on a frosty February morning has a good tonal range; the trees appear lighter with distance, and there is interesting contrast between the bright snow and the cast shadows in the foreground. However, the colours still attract the eye, as in the green patch of lawn.

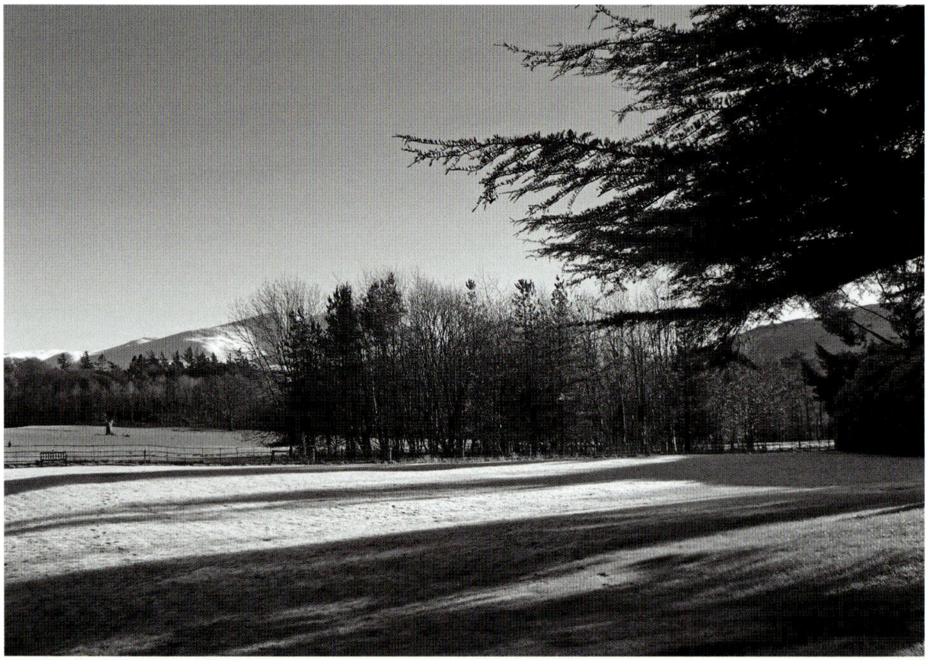

Tonal awareness: image in black and white. The same scene, viewed here in monochrome, allows us to distinguish tones without the distraction of colour. Half-close your eyes to see which areas have strong white highlights and which are in deepest shadow. Notice the relative tones of the groups of trees as they lighten with distance.

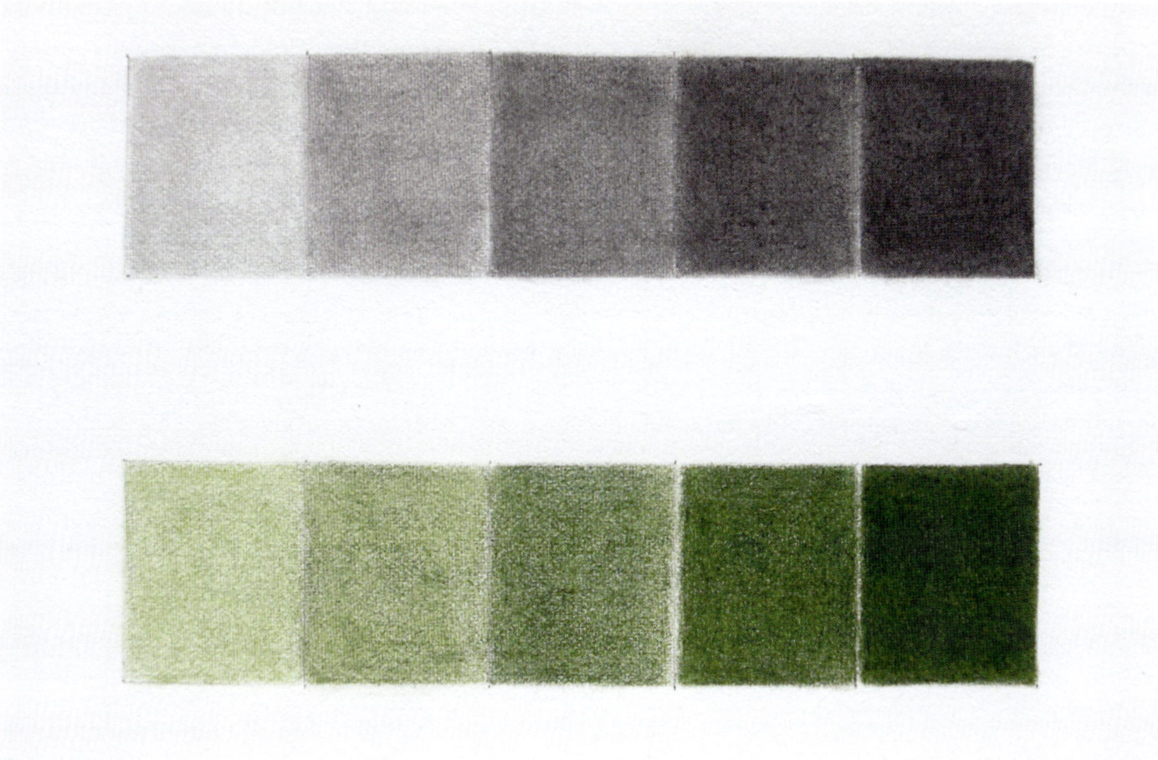

Tonal strips in greyscale and colour. The first strip, done in Faber-Castell 9000 2B pencil, shows five tones (excluding black and white). The eye can comfortably distinguish these, and they would have an impact when used together in a landscape. The second strip demonstrates the same progression in one of my foliage favourites, Faber-Castell Permanent Green Olive.

lost. About five will suffice to appreciate their difference; it is precisely when this transition between tones is clearly visible that the picture will spring into life.

Tone and Perspective

Tone is, of course, tied to perspective, and is also used to express distance. We can manipulate this according to the requirements of the landscape; for a dark green pine wood in the far distance, you could still use dark green shades, but a lighter *tone* of dark greens than one seen in the middle distance. When you are combining ink and coloured pencil, the ink component should be in keeping with the tone you need. If you are heavy-handed with the ink, a feature or an area may appear closer than it should; keep the ink markings in tune with the strength of the coloured pencil, and both should be tonally appropriate for their distance.

LIGHT AND SHADE

It is inevitable that the play of light and shade over a landscape will be closely related to its tonal values. From the start, even as we observed or photographed our chosen subject, the light source was part of the picture. Sometimes it is striking, and may even have influenced your choice of viewpoint; at other times it is subtle and casts a gentle glow. Even on a dull, wintry day, the light still has a source, although we may need to track it down. Light and shade give form to the things we see in nature; the parts that catch the light and the parts that disappear into shadow tell us a lot about shape and volume. When a feature is highlighted, the tone is necessarily lighter, sometimes almost white; areas that are in deep shadow will therefore be much darker in tone. Mid-tones are often where our eyes can discern the most detail, as they are not dazzled by the light or confused by the darkness. This is worth remembering when you are depicting bushes and trees, in case you feel obliged to show the form of every leaf – you don't!

Letting in the Light

Light can be useful in leading the eye through a picture, and you may find it easier to add it as your image develops. It is conveyed by colour, or a lack of it, and an absence of ink, so it can be adjusted whenever you feel the need. As an etcher I became used to creating different tonal areas in aquatint, then burnishing them to introduce more light. As a result, I still tend to assess an image after I have worked for some time; I then choose to lift out the light, using a putty rubber or battery eraser. Some artists are good at spotting and retaining light areas from the beginning, usually because they have had some tonal training; this is ideal – but if, like me, you find it easier to work backwards, please do.

Light and shade need to be part of the entire landscape, from distant mountains to foreground grasses. The colours that we use to express light can range from white, and the colours associated with sunshine and sunset from the yellow part of the spectrum, through to the more unusual shades that precede a storm or penetrate a pearly mist. Sometimes just a paler tone of the original colour will be enough to suggest the passage of light across a field, for example. At the other extreme, this is one of the occasions when I might use one of 'Irojiten's Fluorescents, aptly named Sunset Orange or Dazzling Sun. The choice is yours, but the addition of the tiniest hint of another colour can often make a big difference. As always, less is more, so don't get carried away!

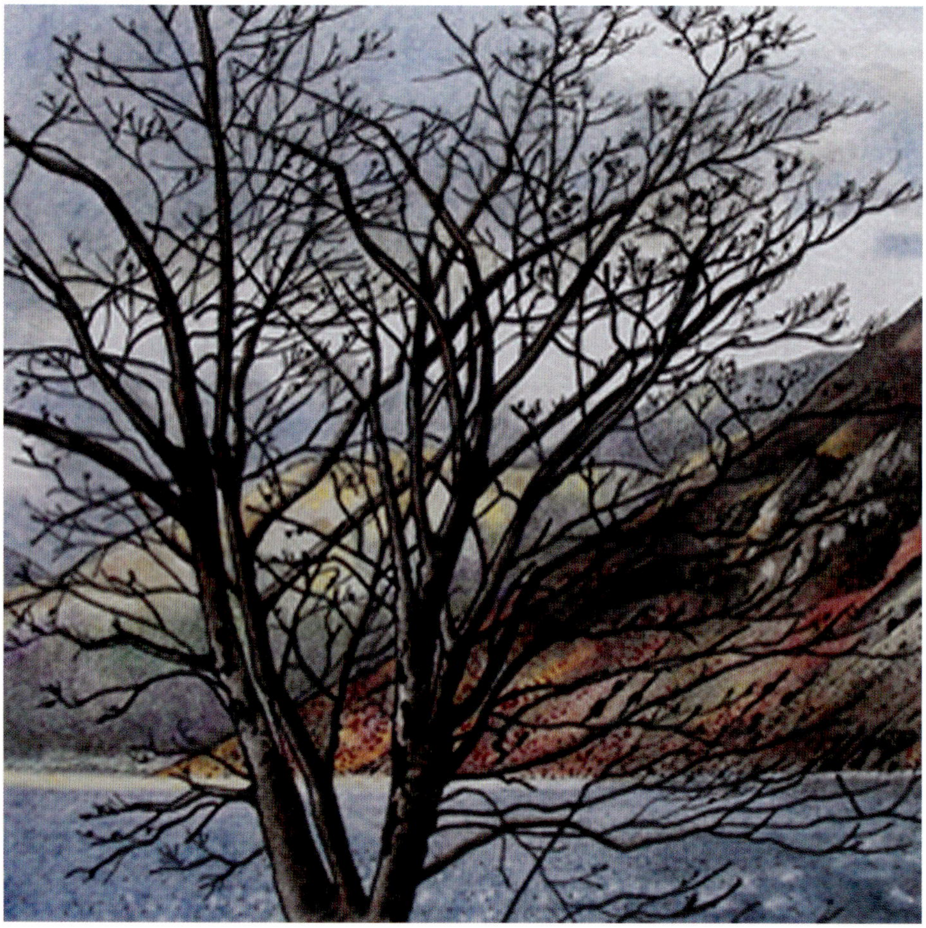

Fluorescent fix: *Tree by Wastwater*. The light on this autumn afternoon in the aftermath of the floods was so unusual that it seemed to ask for a bit extra. I used Irojiten Fluorescent Sunset Orange and Dazzling Sun to give an extra gleam on the screes, distant fells and the water's edge.

Recipes for Deep Shade

Shadows occur away from the light, and present a new challenge; finding colour combinations that will convey their mysterious darkness is one of my favourite coloured pencil pursuits. I will state at the outset that black hardly ever comes into the equation, and never on its own. Whereas the black inked line has its own dramatic appeal, black coloured pencil always looks dead to me. Instead, I make use of the excellent dark shades available from all good manufacturers, blending them into whatever combination suits the work. As with a limited painting palette, I often use dark blends mixed from colours that are already part of the image, to give a more unified look. Take a break from your work once you have assessed what it needs, and practise blending shadow colours that will really complement your image.

For very dark, shady areas such as heavy undergrowth or deep woodland, I tend to choose a mix of dark brown, dark green, very dark blue and dark purple. Try varying the balance of your colours, their order of application and the depth of tone. If you keep the same colour combination, but shift the balance slightly as you work on the shadowed area, you can create patches of colour that appear more green, purple or brown. All this will create rich shadows that hint at colour rather than kill it. The chart shows just a few examples of interesting dark blends made with colours from Faber-Castell 'Polychromos', Derwent 'Procolour' and Caran D'Ache 'Pablo'. The permutations are endless, so try some out using your own collection of colours.

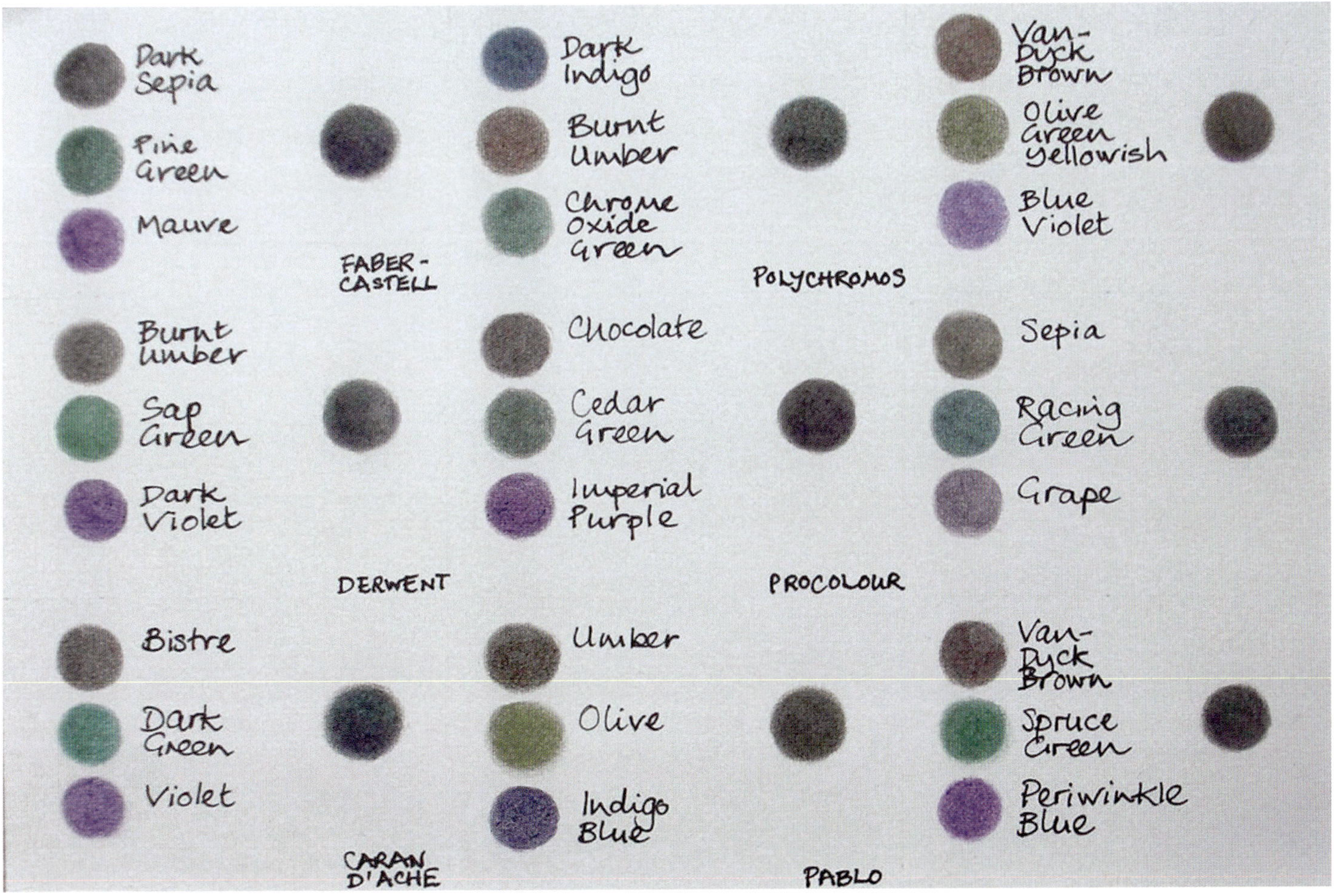

Deep shadow mixes. The top row shows three separate colour blends using dark browns, greens, blues and purples from the Faber-Castell 'Polychromos' range. The middle row adds similar deep shadow mixes using Derwent 'Procolour'. The bottom row features Caran D'Ache 'Pablo' colours. Seen in its natural element on paper, each mix demonstrates a subtly different blend of deep colours.

Note that colours with the same name from different companies are not identical. Burnt Umber is not a standard description, and one brand's Burnt Umber may resemble another's Van-Dyck Brown. Each company has a recipe for a colour that is unique. This gives you a fantastic choice to enjoy, and every reason not to use black!

Making Use of Ink

To achieve an even darker look, I often add tiny ink dots amidst the blended colour, particularly at the base. I often need to encourage students to be brave, as the natural tendency is to be tentative with shadow. If the subject requires it, take the plunge; but remember to darken the shadow gradually using small ellipses, not by pressing too hard. If you overdo it, but have used a light touch, Frisket can come to your rescue! Once you have brought real darkness to, for example, the interior of a wood, the trees will emerge and there will be a real sense that something unseen lies behind.

Moderate Shade

Not all shadow is deep and dark: a little moderate shade will add more mid-tones to your image. It is useful for adding form to hillsides, casting a soft shadow over fields and bringing variety and interest to foreground grassland. I have favourite colours that I use for this purpose, and find that the waxier pencil ranges are particularly useful, as this is a late-stage process unlikely to require further layers. A layer of soft mauve or purple will neutralize yellow or orange and give a shadowy haze to foliage.

My preferred choice is Prismacolor's Parma Violet: it is creamy and easily applied as a top layer, leaving a soft film of colour – perfect for that time on a late summer's day when shadows deepen. Prismacolor's Greyed Lavender and Rosy Beige are paler, but will also help to create mid-toned rather than deep shadow. Derwent's Slate Violet and Mars Violet in the 'Artists' series, and Grey Lavender and Pale Lavender

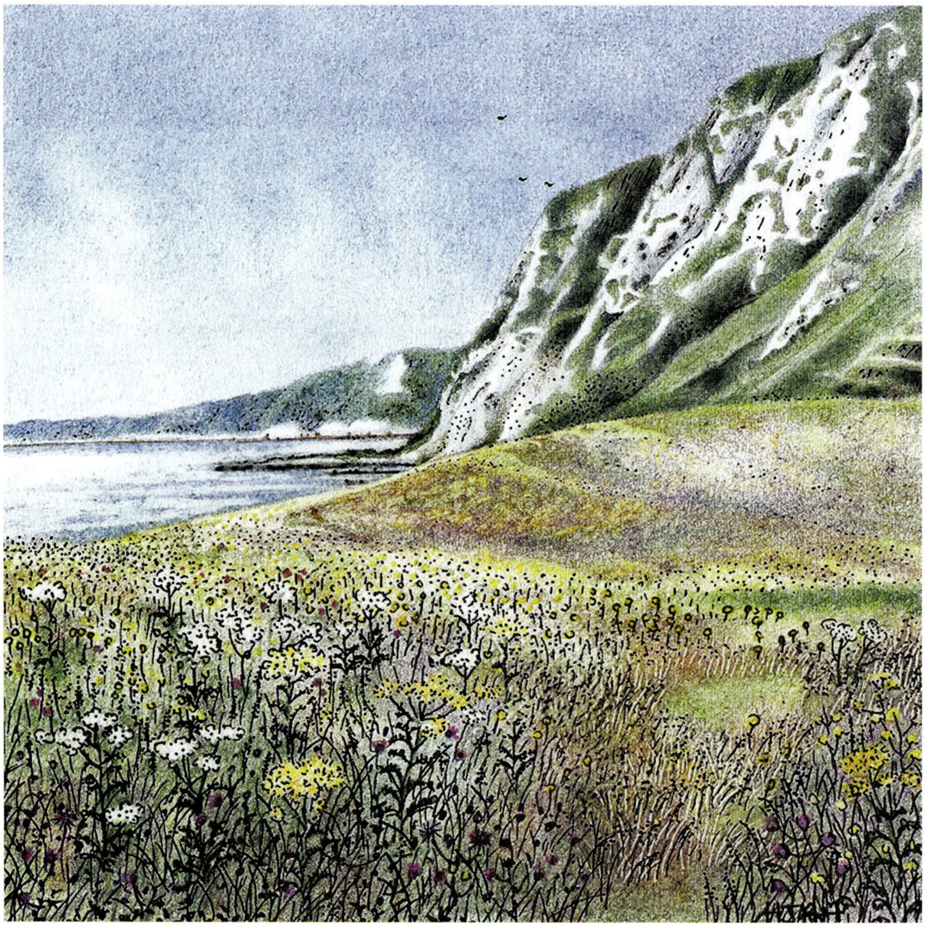

Soft shadows: *Flowers at Samphire Hoe*. Soft shadow was used on the cliffs but also on the expanse of field full of yarrow, ragwort and knapweed. I used Prismacolor Parma Violet and Celadon Green to neutralize the yellow, creating pathways and patches of shadow in the foreground and across the fields.

in 'Coloursoft', can all be used to add neutralizing shades. Caran D'Ache's subtle 'in-between' shades have beautiful soft browns; my favourite is Cocoa, almost the colour of shadow itself, and an excellent neutralizer that I use together with Brownish Beige and Beige. Faber-Castell have fewer muted colours, but Blue Violet, Mauve, Nougat and Warm Grey II, III and IV are all useful.

These images both have foregrounds in which flowers and grasses are abundant; they would appear flat and undifferentiated without the use of soft shadow to create clusters of plants and dips in the terrain. If foreground flowers, fields and meadows appeal to you as an artist, get to know some soft shadow colours and experiment with them.

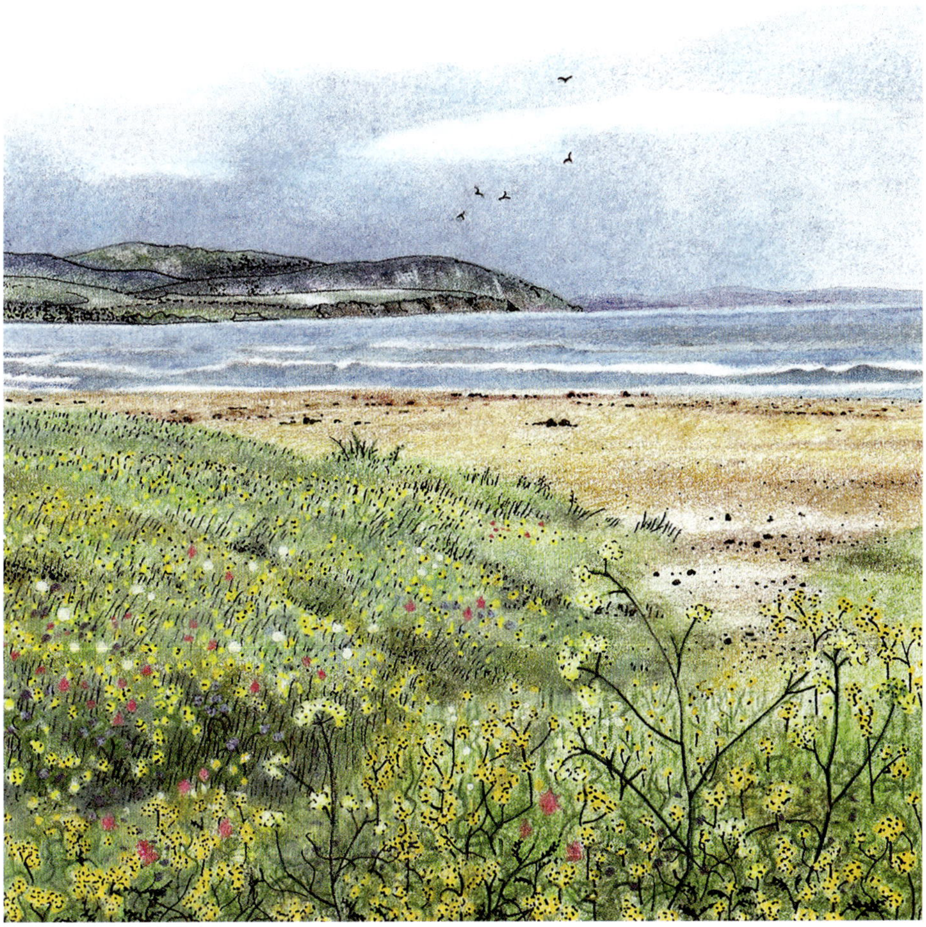

Soft shadows: *Machair at Machrihanish*. The foreground in this image consisted of machair – the richly flowered grassland found along the Scottish coast. Using soft shadow, I created gullies and pathways to describe the terrain, as well as clumps of lady's bedstraw, charlock and a scattering of pyramidal orchids. Management of light and shade was essential in this very simple image.

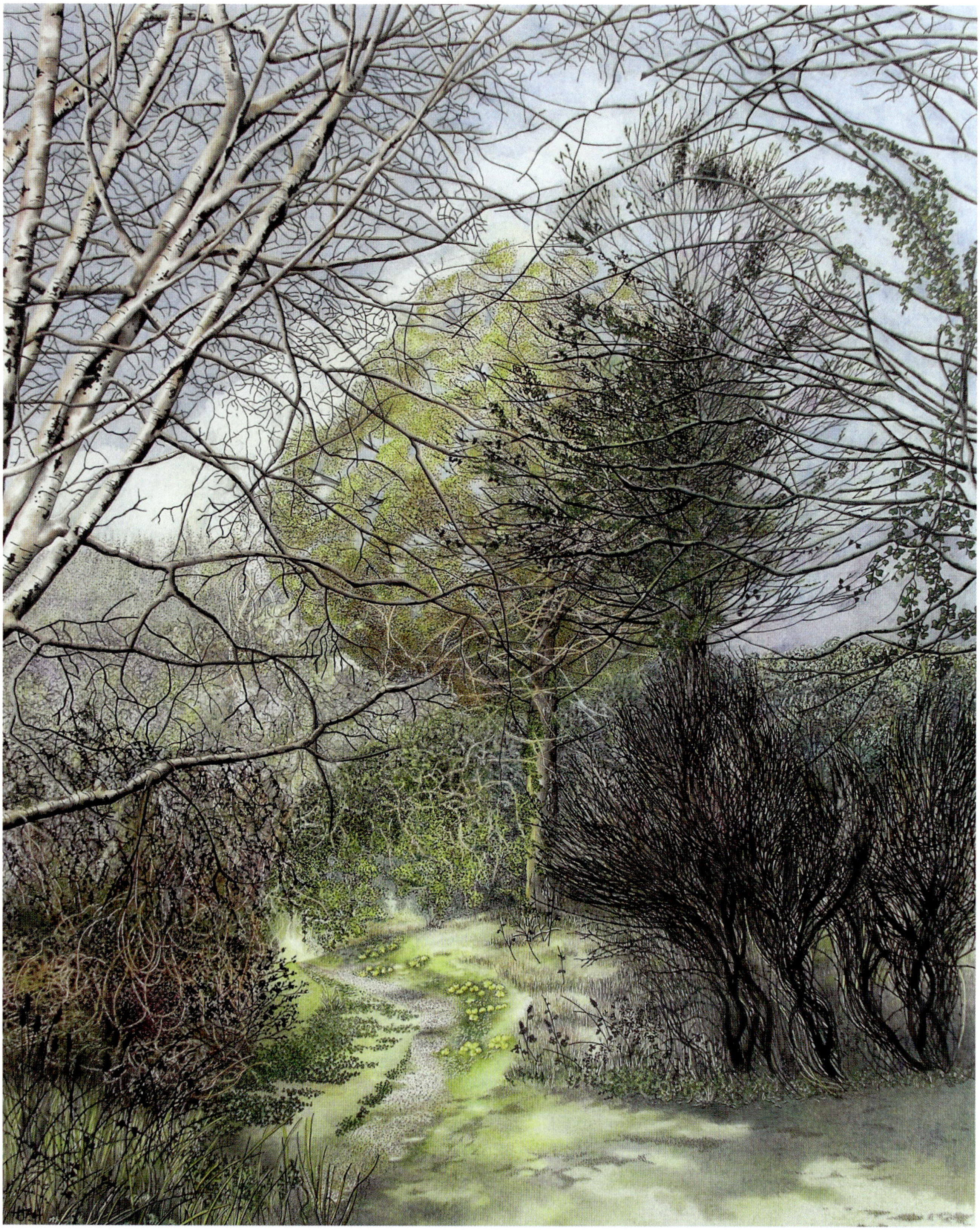

STRENGTH AND DELICACY

When your work is nearly finished, you will probably need to do a few last minute adjustments. Check that you have the right balance between strong markings and softer ones throughout the image. This is closely linked to perspective, so look at the whole picture and identify any distant marks or areas that leap forwards uncomfortably, as well as foreground features that may need strengthening.

Lifting Out or Deepening Colour

There may be a tonal problem that can be easily resolved by lifting out or softening colour with a putty rubber, battery eraser or Frisket. The area can then be carefully reworked with a lighter colour or paler tone of the same colour. If an area of colour seems rather feeble, more layers can be added, either using the same colour or a darker one; tiny ink dots can also be used where appropriate to add more depth or texture.

Damage Limitation for Ink

If you have over-inked, softening the effect may be more problematic. Try a mist of white or pale blue pigment over the top to soften the impact, but resist the temptation to obliterate

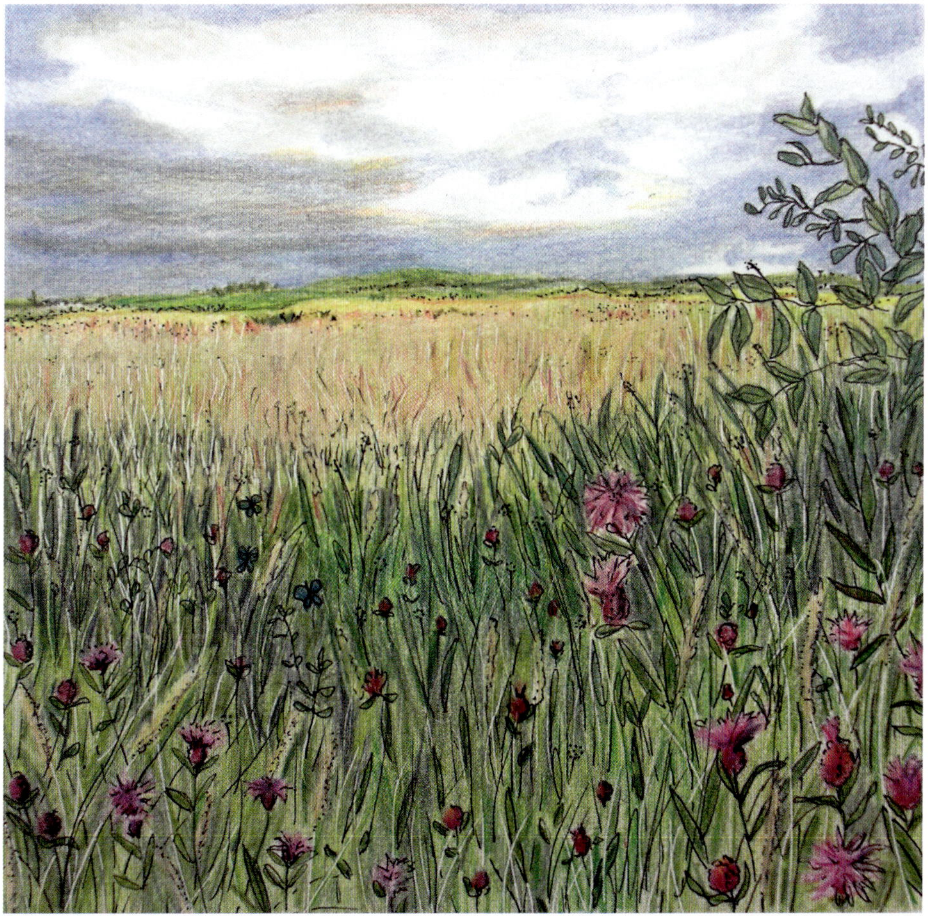

Summer Meadow by Rachael Wood: before the finishing touches. This is an image of local meadowland produced by one of my students on a one-day workshop. The foreground foliage is well observed and the colours accurate; however, at this stage some features need strengthening and the grassland needs more tonal contrast.

◀ Light and shade: *Winter into Spring*. I have included this work, even though I consider it a learning piece (I think I got carried away with the tangles!) Nevertheless, it does have light and shade and an abundance of shadow mixes. I used Caran D'Ache Brownish Beige and Prismacolor Parma Violet for the patches of shade in the foreground.

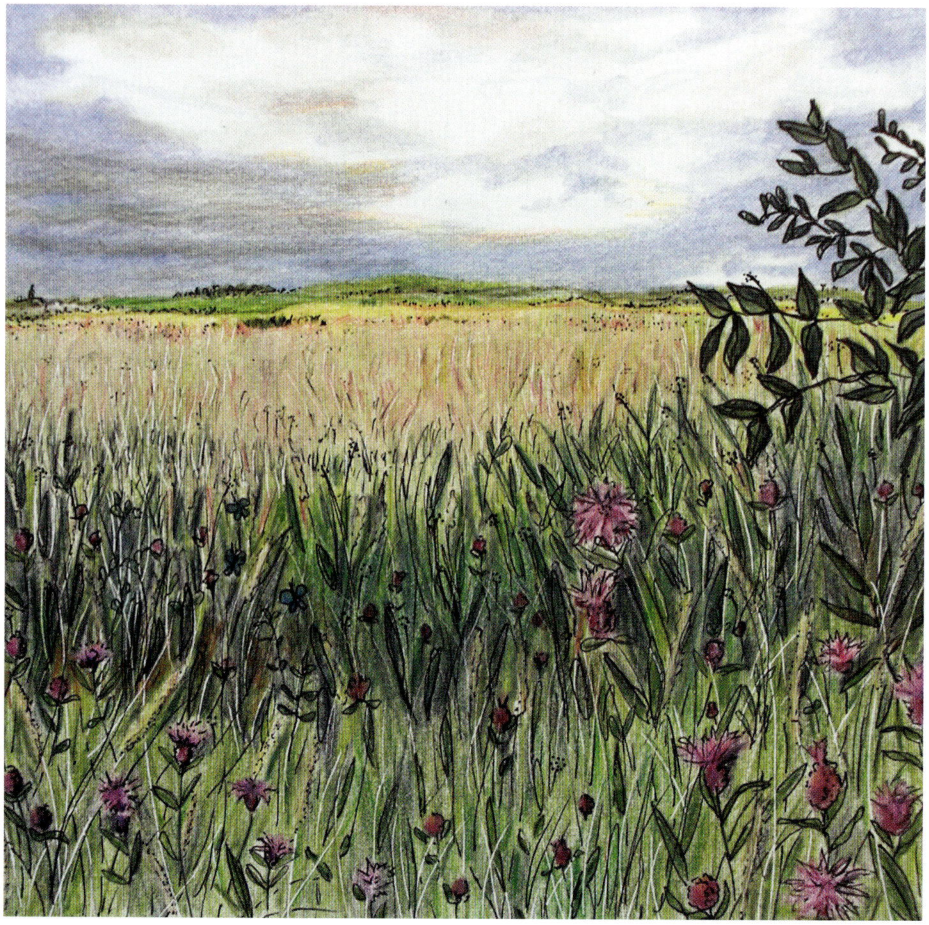

Summer Meadow by Rachael Wood: the finished image. Rachael has strengthened the overhanging branches with more ink and colour, and created a shadowy ditch in the foreground to break up the block of grassland. The image now has a greater variety of tone and looks more three-dimensional.

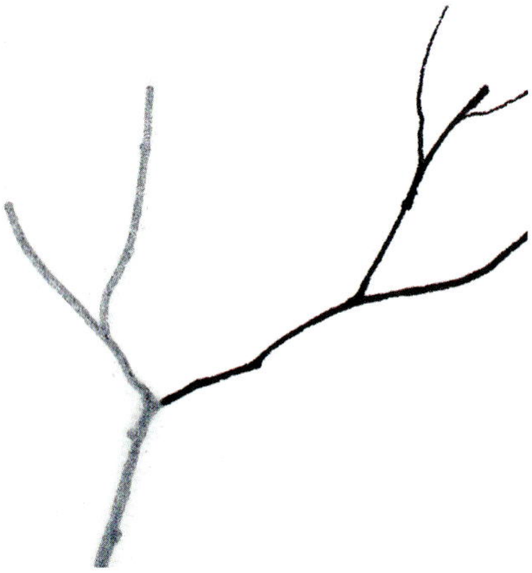

Damage limitation: softening ink marks. The branch on the left and the trunk have been toned down by a gentle application of Prismacolor White and appear much less prominent than the branch on the right. This will work if you have used too strong a tone and need to knock back the ink. Sadly it cannot be made to disappear.

the ink by pressing too hard. This will just create a hard, shiny surface that will look even more noticeable, as it will also differ in texture. Take advantage of the fact that we perceive distance as having a bluer haze, and use one of the waxier, soft pencils by Prismacolor (Sky or Powder Blue) or Derwent 'Coloursoft' Cloud Blue to knock things back a bit. This will only be damage limitation, but may just make a difference.

Refreshing Dominant Features

Even if you have protected your work by resting your hand on a sheet of acetate, as suggested, some coloured pencil pigment may have blurred the ink lines in the foreground. You may also find that adding a lot of background colour has lessened their impact. I nearly always need to apply more ink, and sometimes more colour, to close foreground features such as overhanging branches. This is well worth the effort, as once it is done, they will appear far more prominent and three-dimensional.

FINISHING TOUCHES

You have now looked at the whole picture from the point of view of tone, light and shade, and strength and delicacy. You should be able to see a range of tones, a light source with highlights and shadows, and markings in ink and coloured pencil should be of a size and strength appropriate to their distance. There are a few final questions that you might like to ask:

- Does the picture work as an integrated image?
- Do I have any 'bald patches' that need more ink?
- How do I know when to stop?

The first two questions are connected, and are a gentle reminder that whole areas of coloured pencil without any ink at all might look as though the two do not belong together. The eye does need some restful areas, but this does not necessarily mean the complete absence of one medium. Ask yourself whether it really looks like a landscape in ink and coloured pencil?

Knowing When to Stop

Knowing when to stop is a very subjective feeling. It depends on your vision of how the picture should look, what you think you can achieve, and even whether you are enjoying the process. Some people are happy with 'good enough' and others are exacting perfectionists. It is possible to take adjustments too far, and I still do this sometimes. In art, as in most areas of creativity, you win some and you lose some. If you know that part of your image has not worked well, but that to alter it could be disastrous, you can accept it as it is and move on. I have a long and successful history of starting again and find that it works wonders, but you may feel less enthusiastic.

On a good day, I reach a point at which the image drops comfortably into focus, and I can view it with a sense of achievement. Until then, I usually keep going and try to adjust the things that look in need of attention. When I was printmaking I found this 'almost there' stage agonizing; then suddenly I would take a proof that just seemed to settle down happily. My advice is to do the best that you can, then take a cool look at your picture, preferably from a distance. It helps if you step away from it for a while and do something else – maybe a day or two if you are not working to a deadline. If you are happy that the right features have prominence, and that the rest of the landscape has fallen neatly into place without any jarring elements, you have probably achieved a well-balanced picture and can congratulate yourself.

Tidying Up

Like so many other things, art always involves a bit of tidying up once you have finished. I often frame my smaller works leaving a border of paper inside the mount, so that they resemble etchings. If you do this, or float the picture on mountboard inside the frame, your image will need very clean, sharp edges. An eraser shield placed along the edge will help you to remove any bits of coloured pencil that have crept out on to the paper. Use a putty rubber rather than a plastic one and take care not to disturb the fibres of the paper. Any dirty marks around the image can also be removed with a putty rubber, so that your picture looks clean and well presented.

Signing Off

Your signature is the last step, so don't add it in a way that will encroach too much on the picture space or draw attention away from the image. You may be proud of your work, but flourishes, curly bits and large letters will distract; be aware of the size and nature of your work, and present your signature in a similar way, preferably at the bottom right or left. I just use my initials – all four of them – to identify it clearly as my work.

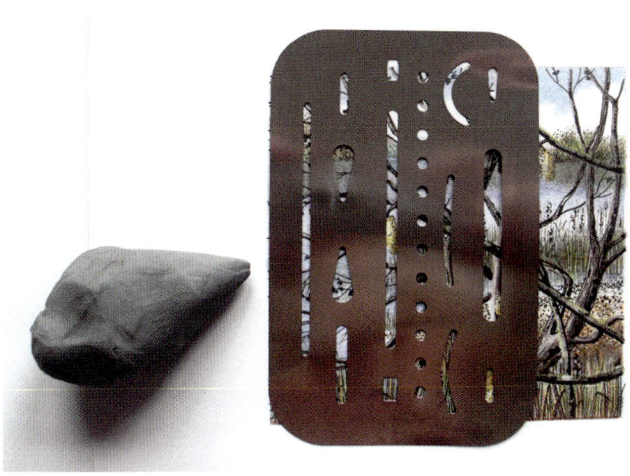

Tidying the edges. The edge of an eraser shield is very useful for tidying up any stray bits of pencil, especially on a small work. This will give a clean, sharp edge if you wish to leave a space between paper and mount, or frame without a mount. Always use a putty rubber to avoid damaging or smudging the paper.

CHAPTER 10

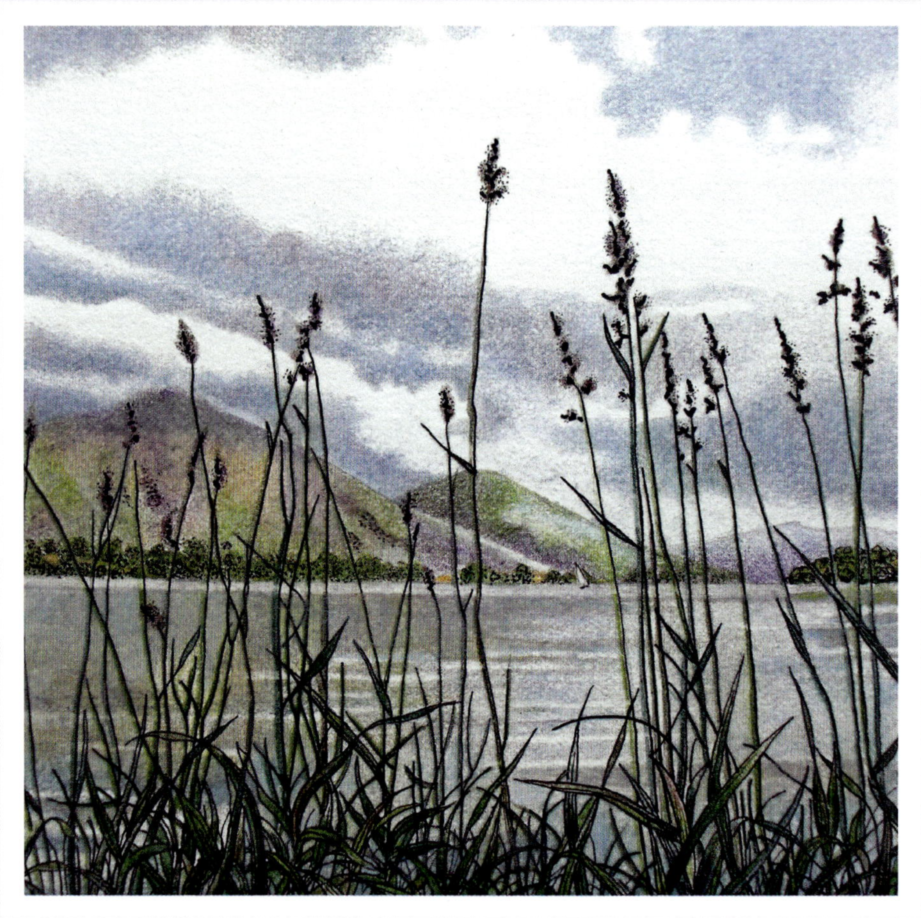

Summer Calm on Bassenthwaite.

Working on a Series

I have always chosen to work on a series of images at the same time; I like working to a theme, developing a shared colour palette, and creating a sense of place through more than one image. Depending on the subject, it is also a good way of exploring new materials and surfaces, as different themes suit different makes of coloured pencil and paper. For those who prefer to learn in a step-by-step way, I have included two related fenland images as a starting point and will approach them gradually, suggesting techniques and using suitable colours from the Faber-Castell 'Polychromos' range. If you do not possess a particular colour, remember that there are very near equivalents in other makes that you can substitute. Bear in mind that there is rarely an exact colour for something; it is more likely to be a combination of several, giving a much richer, realistic look.

I shall then take the process further, showing three very different series and demonstrating how the images echo each other in theme, techniques and palette. Rather than describing each image separately, I shall present them as a group, highlighting their similarities.

FENLAND SCENES

These two small images were inspired by a working visit to Flatford Mill, Suffolk, in high summer. In both instances I chose a square format 12×12cm, cropping my original photographs. For *Quiet Backwater* I simplified the image and concentrated on the reflections of the trees and plants that we can see; this has created a less fussy water surface and a mood of calm. I borrowed meadowsweet from another image, using it to create a semi-circular composition. In *Summer Waterside* I pruned some of the background to avoid too much competing foliage. Both have a high eye level and foreground interest in the form of plants: abundant reeds, grasses, purple loosestrife, arrowhead leaves and meadowsweet. The temperature is hot and everything is very still, making water and reflections an important feature. These images are a good exercise in tonal values: the shadows are very deep and the highlights bright, so don't be afraid of showing the contrast.

Use these as step-by-step practice pieces if you would like to be guided through the process of building up an image. Once you have done this, you will start to envisage your own ways of interpreting what you see and can experiment with your own versions.

STEP-BY-STEP EXERCISE

Summer Waterside

COLOURED PENCILS FOR *SUMMER WATERSIDE*

For *Summer Waterside* you will need the following Faber-Castell 'Polychromos' coloured pencils:

- Cadmium Yellow Lemon
- Magenta
- Light Magenta
- Middle Purple Pink
- Mauve
- Light Ultramarine
- Ultramarine
- Dark Indigo
- Permanent Green Olive
- Juniper Green
- Pine Green
- May Green
- Earth Green Yellowish
- Olive Green Yellowish
- Chrome Oxide Green
- Earth Green
- Brown Ochre
- Burnt Umber
- Dark Sepia
- Warm Grey II
- Prismacolor 'Premier' (optional):
  - Grey Green Light
  - Cloud Blue

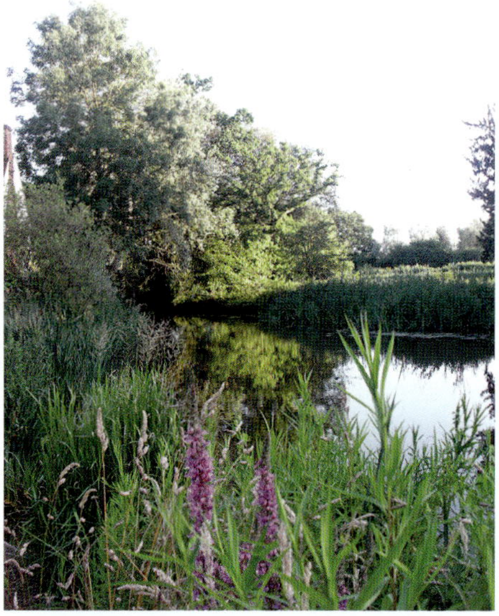

Summer Waterside source photograph. The image I chose was a portrait format snapshot, cut in half by the waterline. To create a better composition for my work, I used a square format instead, cropping the taller tree and altering some aspects of the foreground. I included three spikes of purple loosestrife and took out the large reed on the right.

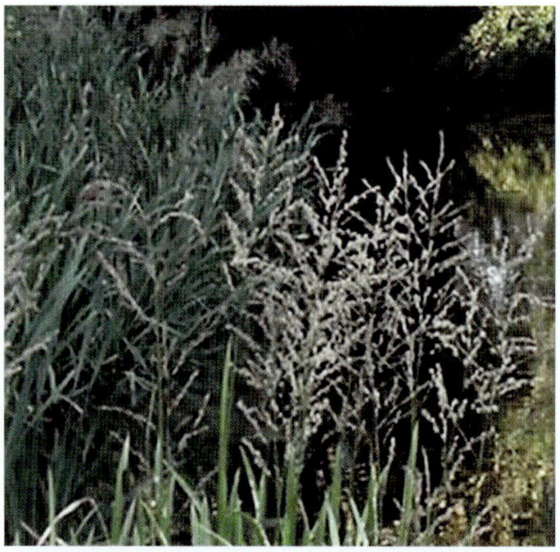

Waterside Grasses. These grasses, just visible on the left-hand side, looked silvery in the light. I used lines of finely embossed dots for the heads to express their pale colour and structure.

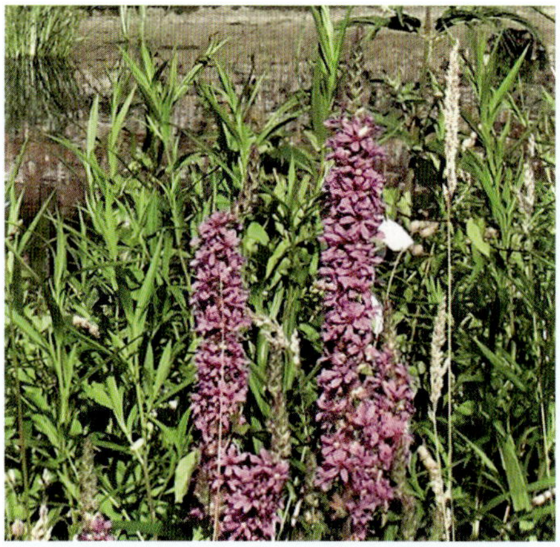

Purple loosestrife. One of the best known and striking waterside plants. Its deep pinkish-purple flowers are six-petalled and arranged in whorls around the tall spike.

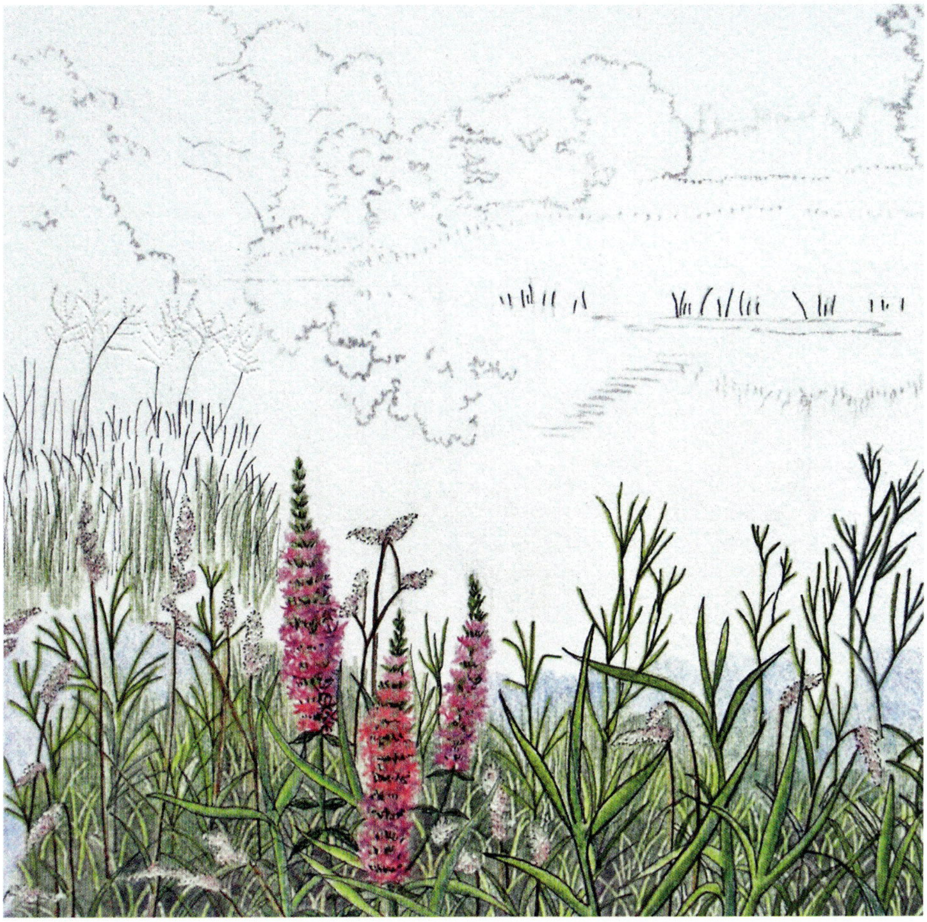

Summer Waterside: stage one. I concentrated on the foreground using a mix of ink and coloured pencil to establish the main shapes and features. More grasses were added in the background by embossing over an Earth Green Yellowish base, then introducing darker greens and shadow colours. The pale grass heads were also embossed and coloured lightly.

STAGE ONE: FOREGROUND

- Using a 0.03 or 0.05 pen, ink the outlines of some foreground leaves and reeds.
- Use dots to indicate the shapes of the grass heads, then fill in with Warm Grey II, leaving a few highlights and adding Brown Ochre for the stems.
- Emboss the foreground grasses using fine lines, and the middle distance grasses (left) with small dots.
- Build up the shape of the purple loosestrife in whorls using Magenta, Light Magenta and Middle Purple Pink. Note that the flowers have six petals and pairs of opposite, pointed leaves.
- Fill in the larger grasses and reeds using May Green and Permanent Green Olive. Use these two colours to add a green line alongside the ink in smaller versions.
- Keeping a feathered edge at the top, fill in the rest of the foreground area using Earth Green Yellowish, working behind the leaves, flowers and stems.
- Use a medium embossing tool to create more blades of grass throughout. This will later appear pale green.
- Deepen the background with Permanent Green Olive and Chrome Oxide Green to reveal the embossed lines, using Burnt Umber and Mauve to create some deeper shadows.
- Blend in some Pale Ultramarine to show areas of water in the foreground.
- Add a hint of Light Magenta to the grasses, lifting out a few highlights with a battery eraser.

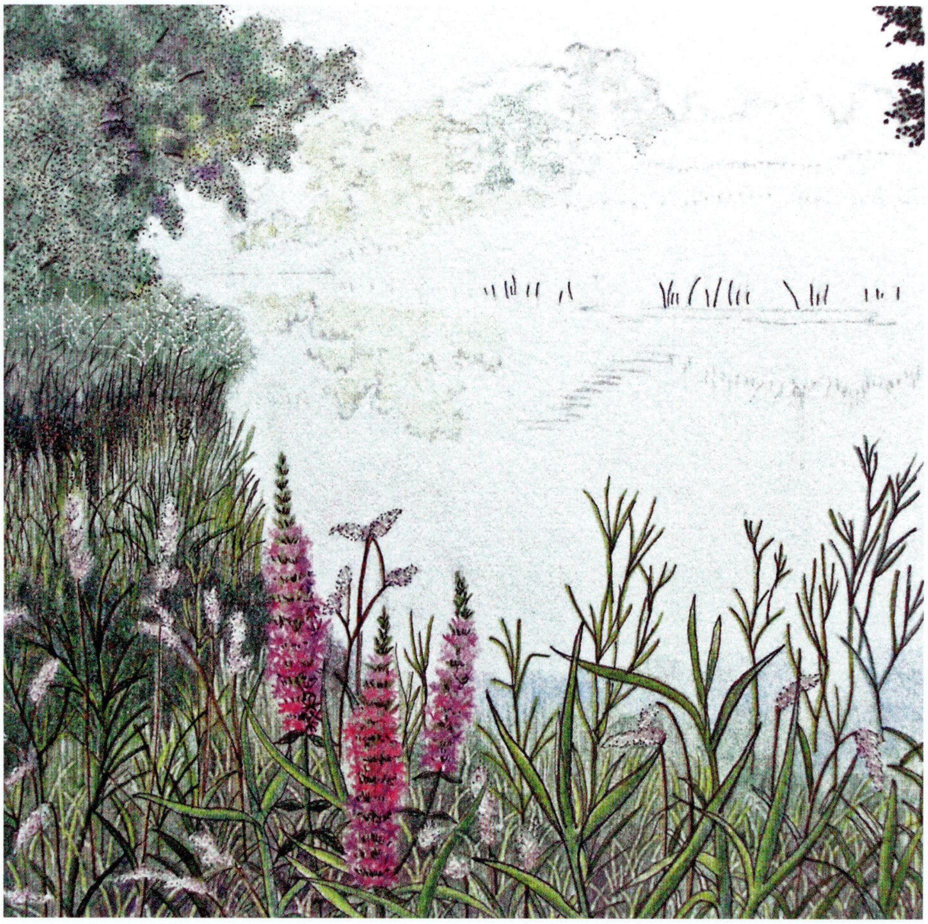

Summer Waterside: stage two. I built up the left-hand side using bluer greens to create distance. Shadow colours were added to the mix wherever I needed shade, such as below the reeds and to separate the two trees. I used dots to create the foliage shapes of the trees and lines for the visible branches.

STAGE TWO: LEFT-HAND SIDE

- Working on the left-hand side of the image, build up the second clump of reeds using fine ink lines, Earth Green and Juniper Green to give a slightly more distant look.
- Keep the tree behind relatively light; the foliage is greenish-grey, helping it to stand out against the larger tree. Use 0.03 dots with a blend of Earth Green and Juniper Green, highlighting with Prismacolor Grey Green Light.
- The distant, taller tree hangs over the water, creating deep shadows underneath. Use small dots to place the foliage, then a blend of Pine Green, May Green and Juniper Green.
- For the shadow areas, use Pine Green, Dark Indigo, Dark Sepia and Mauve in varying combinations, using tiny ink dots to darken more if necessary.
- Indicate some branches with an ink line and lighter Warm Grey II highlights alongside.
- Return to the foreground and use the same shadow combination below both clumps of reeds, working carefully between to keep a feathery edge at the top.
- Work round the grass heads smoothly so that they stand out against the darker background.

Summer Waterside: stage three. I used different shapes and colours to distinguish the trees on the opposite bank, keeping plenty of highlights wherever they were in full or partial sunlight. The reeds at the water's edge were built up in clumps, heavily shadowed at the base with lightly embossed heads to catch the light.

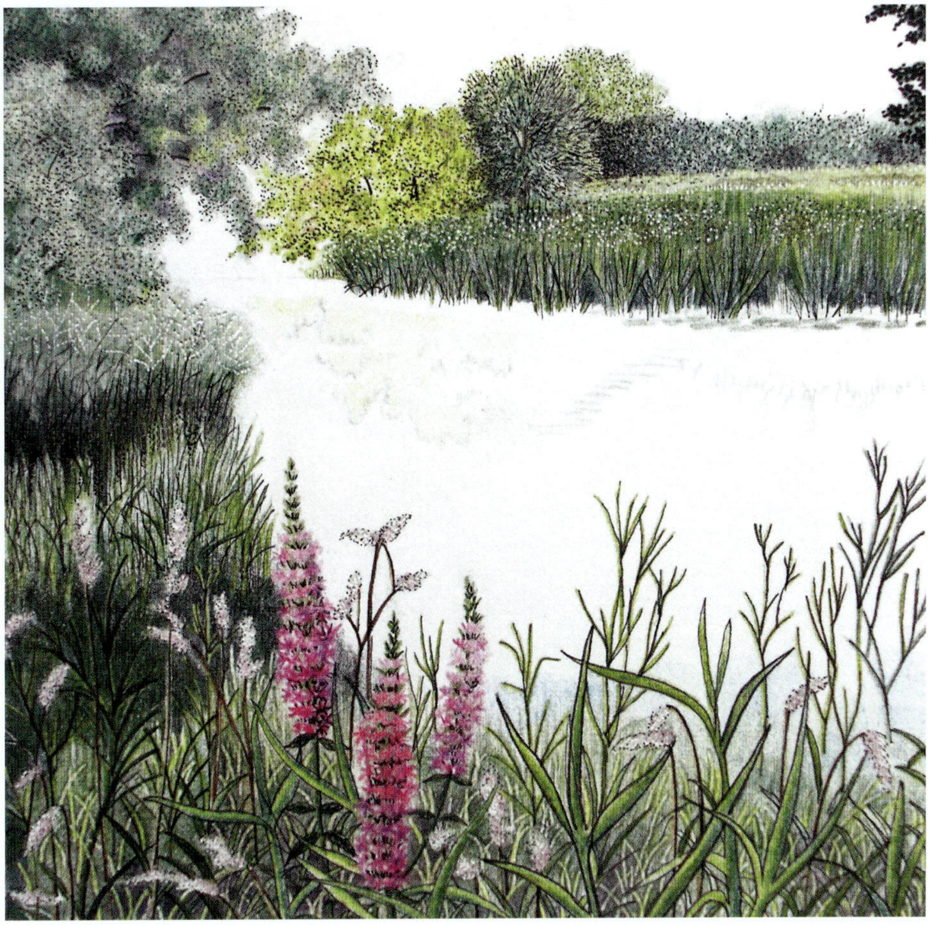

STAGE THREE: BACKGROUND

- The lime green tree and its reflections form the focal point where the light falls. Keep it well lit, and in a different colour. Build up the foliage with 0.03 dots and Cadmium Yellow Lemon, May Green and a touch of Brown Ochre.
- The tree behind is a different shape and colour; use linear ink marks, Juniper Green and Permanent Green Olive, with Cadmium Yellow Lemon for the highlights. Blend in some Dark Indigo on the left-hand side to help locate it behind the first tree.
- The most distant tree is behind the row of bushes; keep the tone light and use Permanent Green Olive with a hint of Pale Ultramarine and some Cadmium Yellow Lemon where the light falls.
- The line of bushes is soft-edged and should look distant. Use Juniper Green with a soft application of Dark Indigo as it disappears between the two trees.
- Introducing a few leaves from a nearer, very dark tree on the right adds a new, deep tone and hints at something beyond.
- Sketch in some of the reeds at the water's edge, observing their form and V shape at the base. Introduce dots and circular embossing along the tops and along the lines of the field.
- Add a mixture of greens: Juniper Green, Permanent Green Olive and May Green, adding Dark Indigo and Burnt Umber at the base.

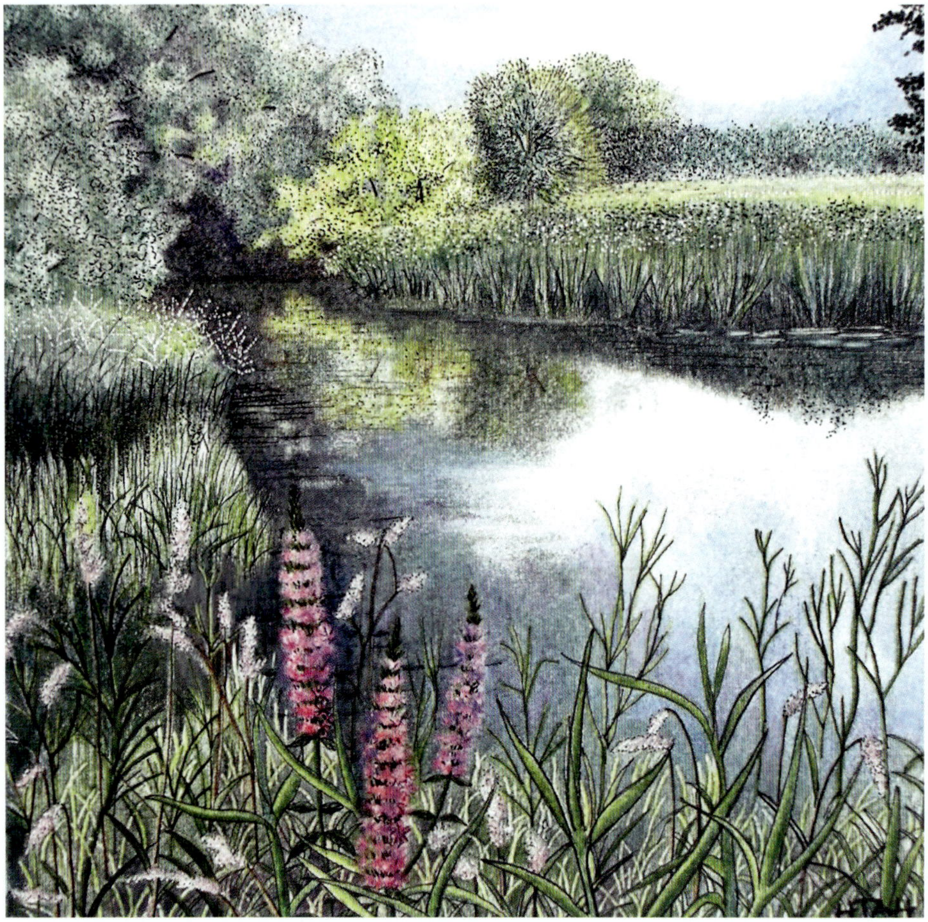

Summer Waterside: stage four. The stretch of water showed the full tonal range, from patches of white to the deepest shadows under the tree. I built it up from a highlighted base colour (Light Ultramarine), adding more shadowy colours in a varied mix according to the surroundings: greener amongst the reeds, browner under the trees.

STAGE FOUR: WATER AND SKY

- Build up the reflections of the trees and bank using the same colours but a very light touch, leaving a few highlights on the water.
- Taking Light Ultramarine as a base colour, work round the areas of light, softening the edges and covering the rest of the water.
- Add more colours to the blend on the left hand side: choose from Ultramarine, Chrome Oxide Green, Mauve, Dark Indigo and Burnt Umber, varying the mix and spreading it very lightly across some of the reflections. Be sure to keep the small highlights and a large, soft-edged area of light.
- Introduce a few ink markings to create ripples along the water's edge.
- Use Prismacolor Cloud Blue as a burnisher if you want a smooth, glassy surface.
- Keep the slim strip of sky simple with Light Ultramarine, deepening towards the right. The cloud shape should echo the area of the light on the water.

STEP-BY-STEP EXERCISE

Quiet Backwater

COLOURED PENCILS FOR *QUIET BACKWATER*

For *Quiet Backwater* you will need the following Faber-Castell 'Polychromos' coloured pencils:

- Ivory
- Light Yellow Glaze
- Cadmium Yellow Lemon
- Magenta
- Mauve
- Light Ultramarine
- Ultramarine
- Dark Indigo
- Permanent Green Olive
- Juniper Green
- Pine Green
- May Green
- Chromium Green Opaque
- Burnt Carmine
- Raw Umber
- Burnt Umber
- Dark Sepia
- Warm Grey II
- Warm Grey V
- Prismacolor 'Premier' (optional):
  - Cloud Blue

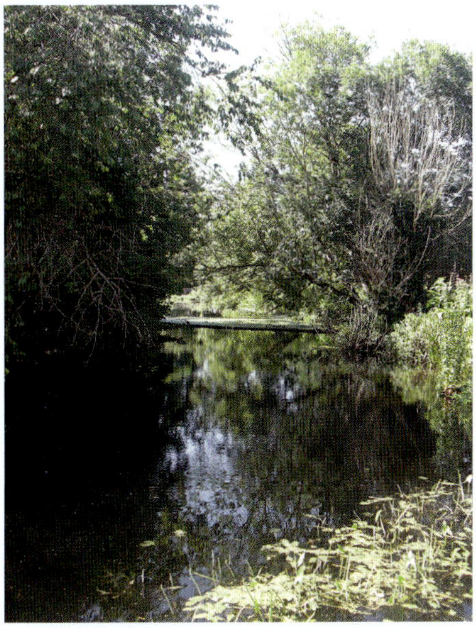

Quiet Backwater source photograph. This image originated from the back of the mill, where the water gathered above a small weir, spanned by a large branch. Once again, the tonal range went from very light to deep shadow. The foreground was mainly water with a few arrowhead leaves, so I borrowed some meadowsweet to help the composition and add interest.

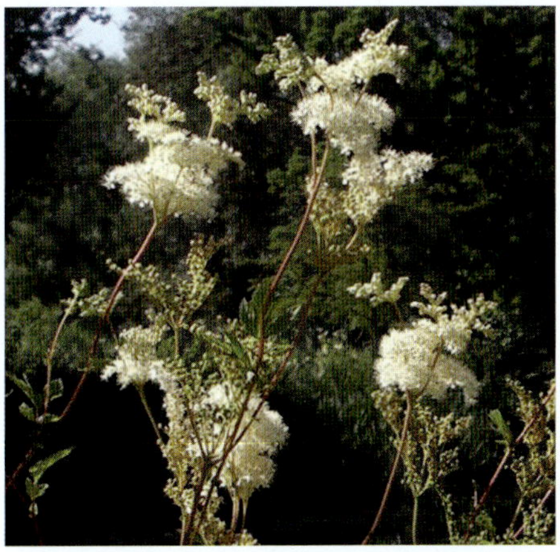

Meadowsweet flowers. These aromatic plants with fluffy flower heads were everywhere. I often use them in my work: they are a wonderful subject for embossing enthusiasts, and emerge very well against a darker background.

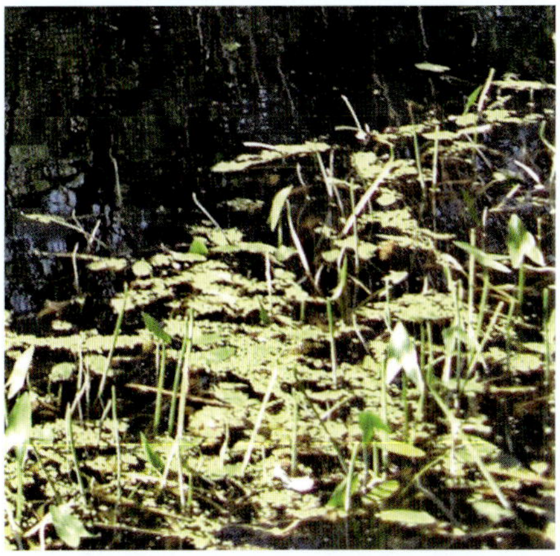

Arrowhead leaves. The arrowhead flowers were finished, but their characteristic leaves added interest to the foreground and suited the waterside environment. Their bright green colour worked well against the muddy water.

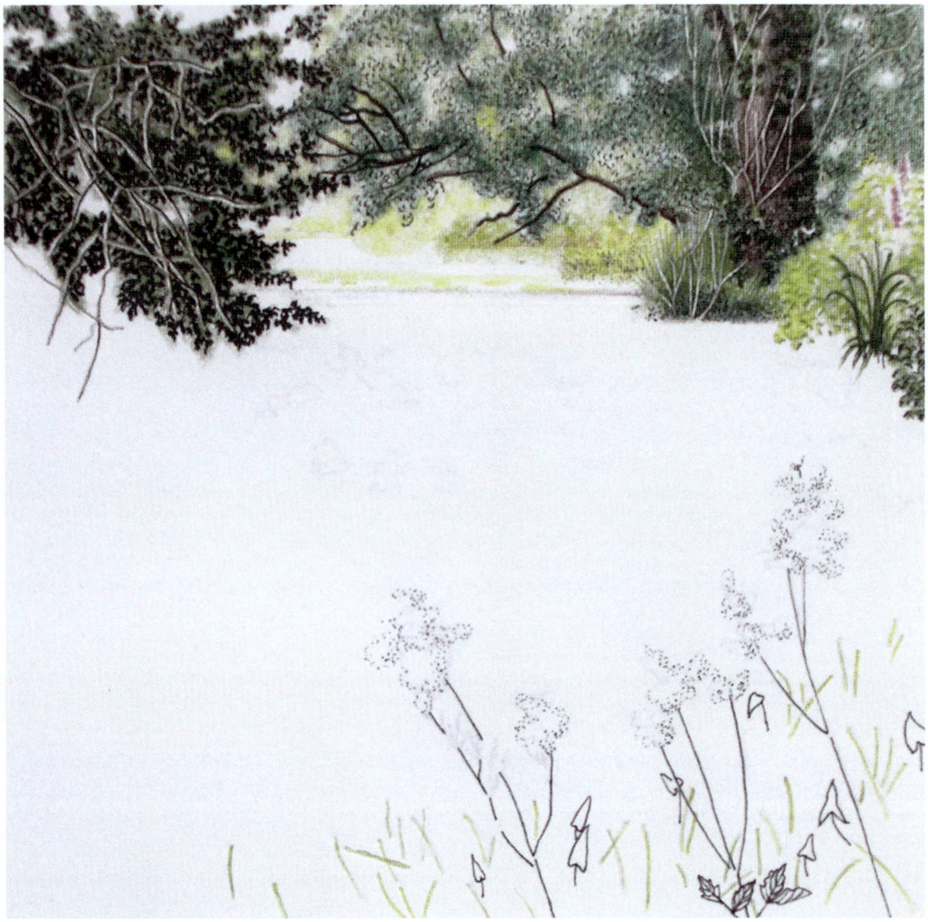

Quiet Backwater: stage one. I began with some embossing, starting with the old tree branches in the background and the stalks and meadowsweet in the foreground. I then built up strong ink markings and colours on the darkest tree and softer ones on the overhanging tree. The line of the weir was marked lightly in Dark Sepia, but not inked.

STAGE ONE: BACKGROUND

- Using Warm Grey II, draw in the branches of old wood visible on trees to both left and right. Emboss firmly over the colour.
- Alternating Cadmium Yellow Lemon and May Green, repeat the process for the stems of arrowhead in the foreground, using a medium embossing tool.
- Sketch in one side of the long, overhanging branch using a 0.05 pen and soften the line with Burnt Umber.
- Add some foliage to the dark tree in ink, following the shape and clusters and leaving some background spaces.
- Using a fine pen, ink the stems and leaves of meadowsweet, arrowhead leaves and some of the right-hand foliage.
- Introduce colour to the trees: Chromium Green Opaque, Permanent Green Olive and Pine Green on the left and blends of Juniper Green, May Green and Cadmium Yellow Lemon in the centre.
- Mark out the line of the weir lightly in Dark Sepia, but do not commit to ink at this stage.

Quiet Backwater: stage two. The foliage on the right-hand side was added in ink and coloured pencil, paying attention to light and shade. I deepened the shadows behind the overhanging tree and established the position of the weir, using ink for the stones at the base. More foreground details were added with a hint of colour.

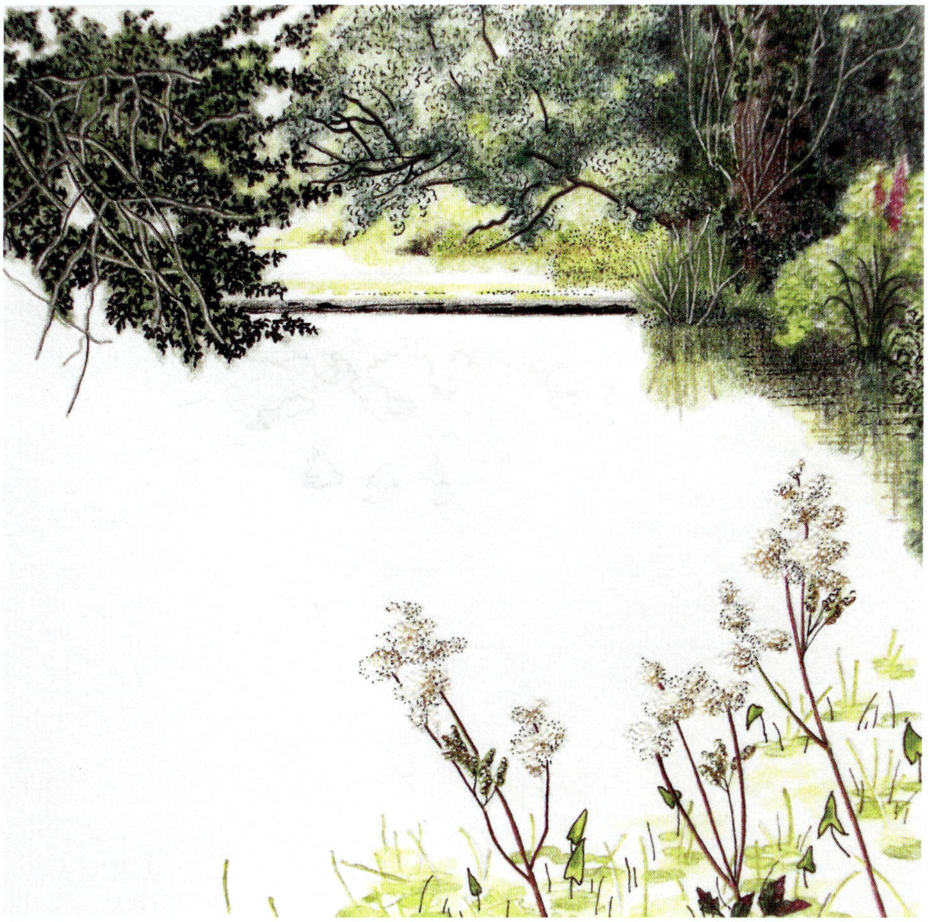

STAGE TWO: RIGHT-HAND SIDE AND FOREGROUND

- Using Cadmium Yellow Lemon, May Green and Permanent Green Olive, with Magenta for the purple loosestrife, build up some of the foliage on the right-hand bank, observing what is in front. Chromium Green Opaque and Dark Indigo will provide some darker areas, but be aware that this section is receiving a lot of light.
- The weir passes behind the reeds and ends by the tree. It is straight, but not a line. Use Dark Sepia and Warm Grey V to create the structure, adding irregular ink marks at the base to create stones.
- Add shadow and reflections below the foliage on the right bank, introducing some ink markings near the water's edge. Use Burnt Umber or Dark Sepia and echo the green colours you have used above.
- Work out the layers of waterside foliage in the far distance, keeping to Cadmium Yellow Lemon, Light Yellow Glaze and May Green; this area is very bright, so when you use ink dots, keep them light and tiny. A very soft application of Dark Indigo will create some shadow at the water's edge.
- When the foliage on the bank is in place, add more shadow to the tree behind, particularly on the right. Burnt Umber, Dark Indigo, Mauve and Pine Green will all produce deep shade, so vary the mix as you work.
- Holding the pencil at a low angle, brush a hint of Raw Umber and Ivory across the shadow side of the meadowsweet flowers in the foreground. Keep some pure white highlights but allow the colour to pick up the embossing. Add some Burnt Carmine and Permanent Green Olive to the stems, close to the ink line.
- The arrowhead flowers are over, but some leaves and stalks remain. Cadmium Yellow Lemon and Permanent Green Olive will give them some shine and can also be used for the green algae on the surface of the water.

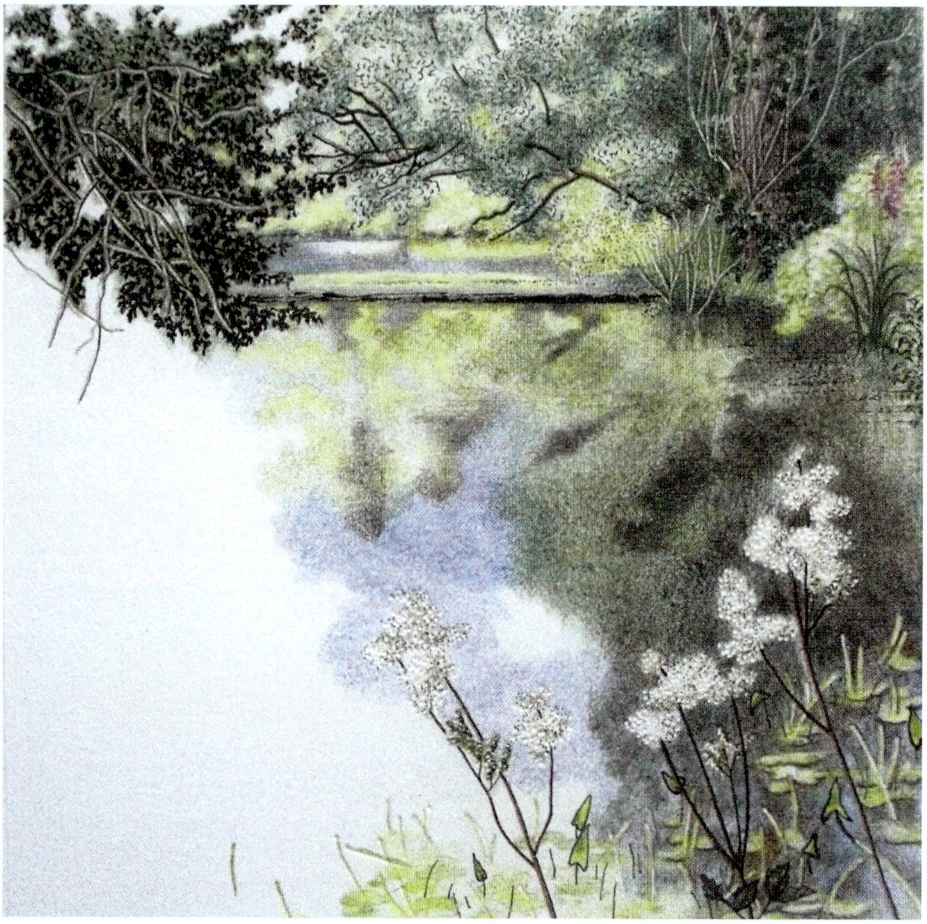

Quiet Backwater: stage three. I concentrated on the water and the reflections, observing where the light and shadows fell, and the mix of colours required to convey this. I worked darker colour round the meadowsweet flowers and developed the leaves and stems in the foreground.

STAGE THREE: WATER AND REFLECTIONS

- Start to build up a base for the water, bearing in mind the colours of the reflections. Keep to the same palette, with Cadmium Yellow Lemon, Chromium Green Opaque, Burnt Umber or Dark Sepia and Ultramarine. Blend colours into each other with a tortillion for a smoother, misty look.
- In the foreground, break up the colours around the plants to achieve a more dappled effect.
- Above the weir there is more green algae; the water is catching the light, becoming darker towards the bank on both sides. Try Ultramarine with a burnishing layer of Prismacolor Cloud Blue.
- Work carefully round the flower heads to reveal their embossed shape. Setting them against darker colours will make them stand out.

Quiet Backwater: stage four. At the final stage I deepened the tones underneath both trees and the weir, keeping the background bright and in full sun. Further patches of light were lifted out on the overhanging tree, in the water and on the meadowsweet flowers. The tonal balance of the whole image was checked and adjusted.

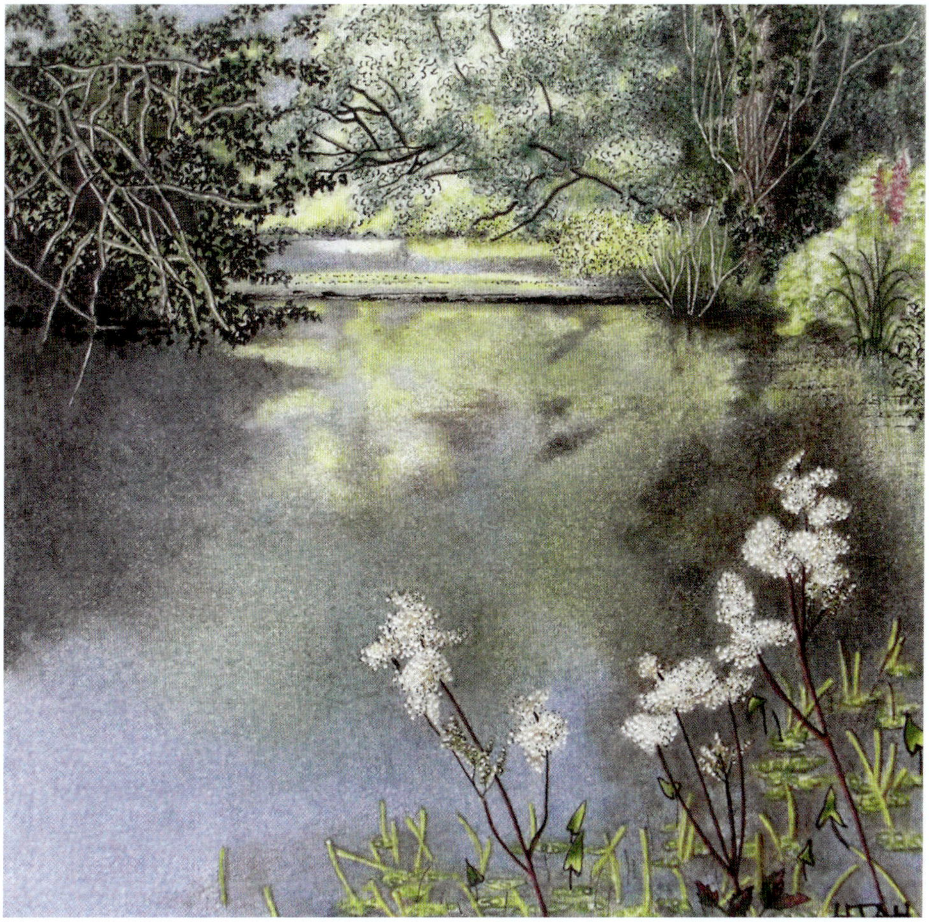

STAGE FOUR: WATER, SHADOWS AND LIGHT

- Complete the coverage of the water using Ultramarine, moving towards stronger shadow colours under the tree. Use the mixture as before: Burnt Umber, Dark Indigo, Mauve and Pine Green.
- Increase the layering to create the deepest shade where the tree meets the water, strengthening this with ink dots. Add some larger stones in ink at the edge of the bank. This should be the darkest point of the picture tonally.
- Keep the distant bank very sunlit in comparison, lifting out more colour with a putty rubber if necessary.
- If you want a smooth, burnished surface to the water, apply Prismacolor Cloud Blue as a final layer. Keep it very light over the yellow areas, applying more pressure over the darker patches.
- Use Light Ultramarine for small patches of sky where visible.

Finishing Touches

Even if you follow step-by-step instructions, your versions will differ from mine. (If I did mine again, it would also look different.) When you think you may have finished, take another look at the whole picture, preferably after a break, and assess what it may need.

- Half close your eyes and check the tonal range. Can you see where the light falls? Are the shadows deep enough?
- Do you need to lift out any more light?
- Does anything need strengthening or knocking back?
- Do any of the trees need separating from each other using light against shade?
- Do the foreground flowers and grasses need more colour or definition?
- Does the image feel harmonious and complete?

My final versions have a few minor changes. In *Summer Waterside* I deepened the colour of the water in the foreground, redefined the purple loosestrife flowers and grass heads, and lifted out more light at the focal point. In *Quiet Backwater* I lifted out more highlights on the meadowsweet and added a coot on the water.

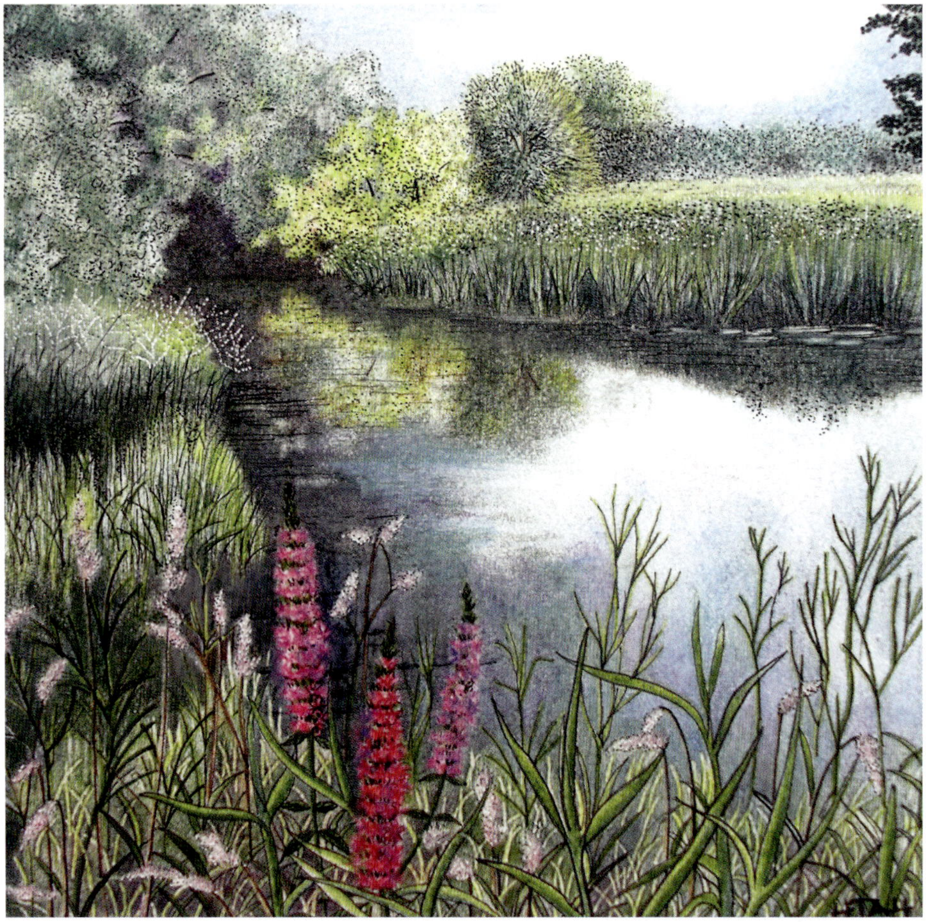

Summer Waterside: finished image. A few changes were made for this final version: the water in the foreground was darkened, and the purple loosestrife flowers were sharpened and tidied up. Additional light was stroked over the tops of the reeds, the field and the trees on the right using a putty rubber.

Quiet Backwater: finished image. I liked the semi-circular composition, but felt that the eye needed somewhere to land on the expanse of water. I kept the smooth surface, but added a coot in the shadows at the base of the tree to draw the eye.

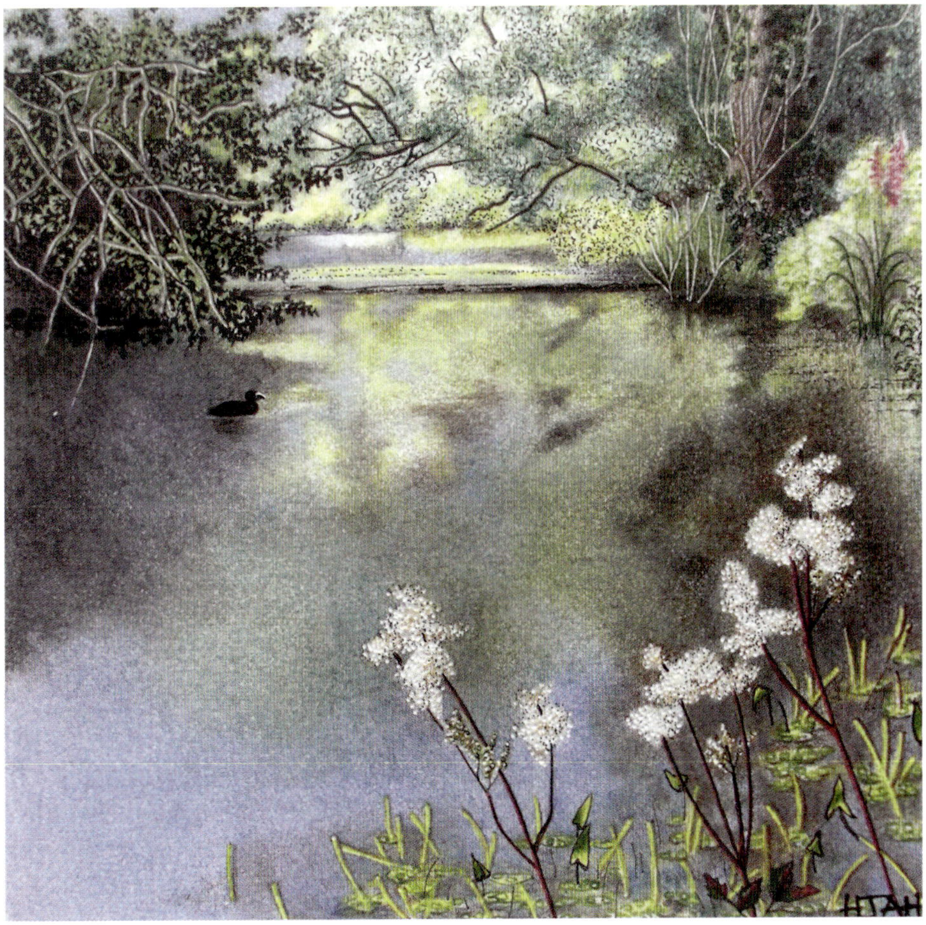

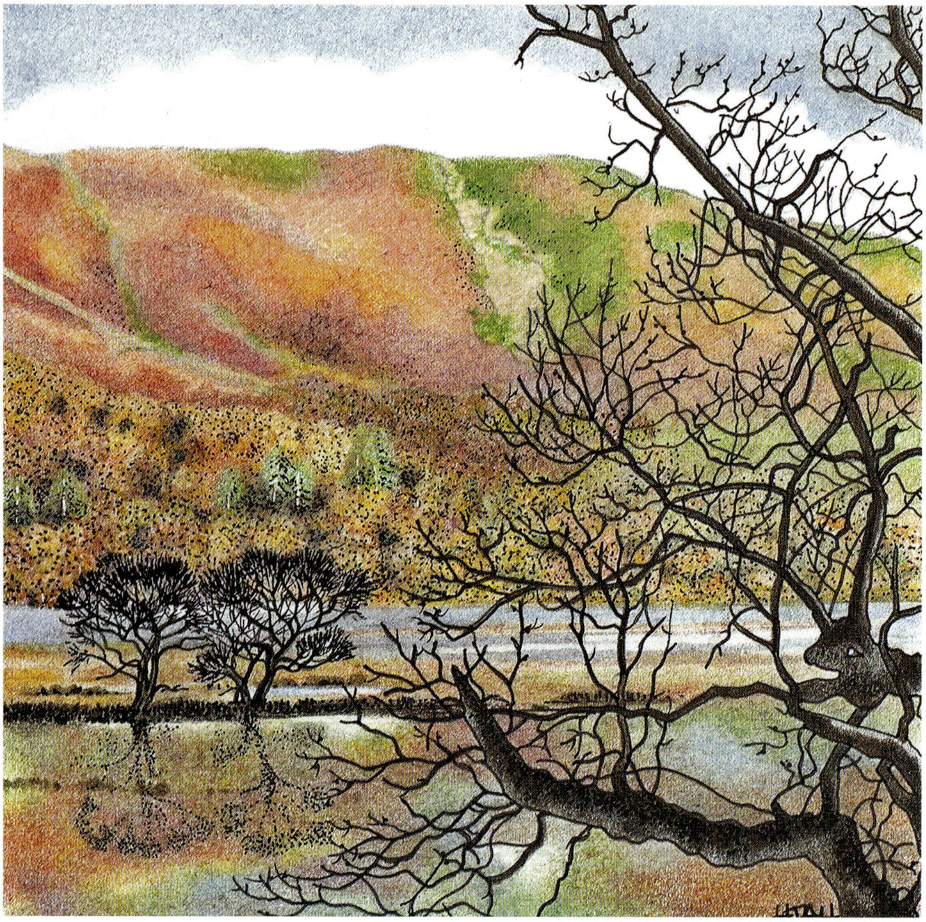

Derwentwater Morning. This image has a low eye level, with Catbells rising behind. The tree shapes are stark and ink dominates; the colour palette is an unusual mix, even for autumn, as most of the surrounding terrain is underwater.

DERWENTWATER QUARTET

I happened to be staying by Derwentwater at the time of an autumn flood some years ago. I had arrived in torrential rain as water levels were rising; later I was called out from my evening meal to rescue my car as the lake invaded the car park. The following morning was one of the most beautiful I had ever seen in the Lakes; the fells were reflected in huge expanses of water and the sun shone through wisps of mist. I spent the day walking round the lake, sketching and photographing, eventually deciding on a quartet of images to record the day. I chose two from each side of the lake, and a small, square format using the original Fabriano 5 hot-pressed watercolour paper and Faber-Castell 'Polychromos' pencils in a bright autumn palette. *Derwentwater Morning* and *Bird in the Flood* were looking towards Catbells, and much of the terrain covered by water was usually accessible marshland or fields. *Curving towards Derwentwater* and *Quiet by Derwentwater* were on the path that skirts the opposite edge of the lake.

In all four images, the trees in the foreground were dominant and could be put in first; I used a range of Faber-Castell Indian ink pens from SX to M, which gave a very rich line. Switching to coloured pencil, I added Faber-Castell Dark Sepia next to the ink for deep shadows, and a range of their browns or greys as appropriate, lifting out a few lighter patches with a battery eraser. As the autumn leaves were a feature, I outlined them in an SX pen, on this occasion planning to use some colouring in at a later stage. I introduced the trees in the middle distance in *Derwentwater Morning* using the same pen and a soft layer of Dark Sepia. To distinguish between branches that were above

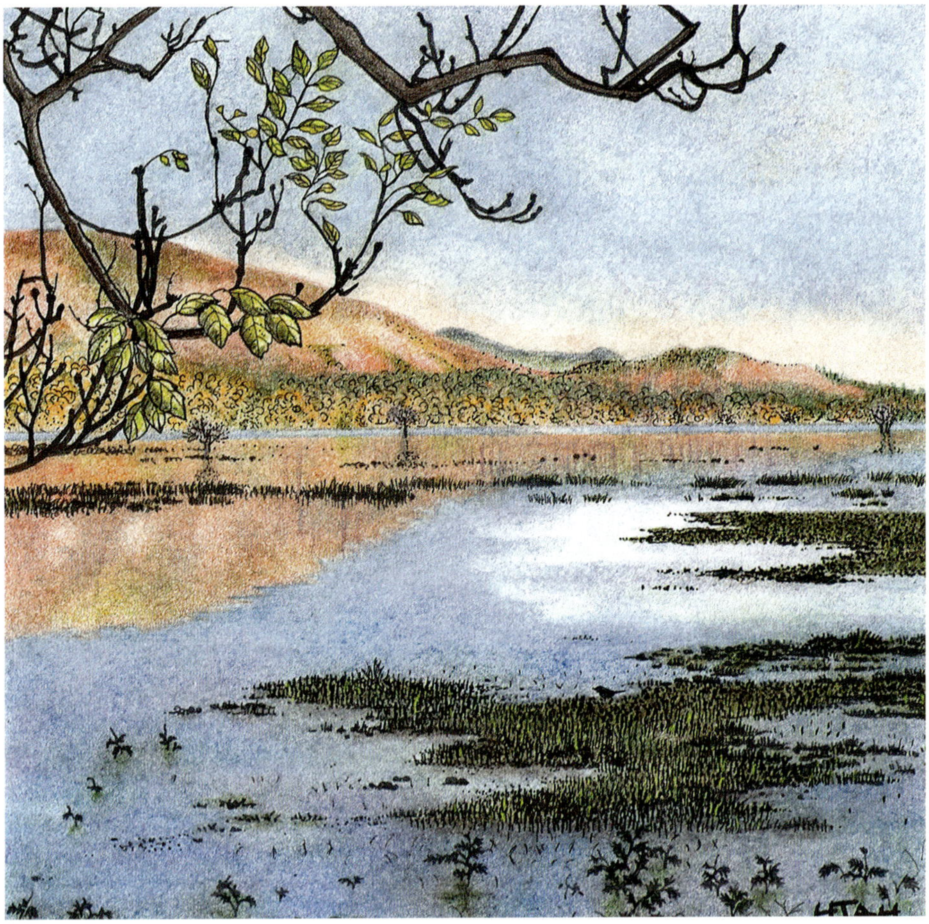

Bird in the Flood. The eye level is much higher in this image, so we see less mountainside and more foreground, with reflections in the flood and just a strip of lake. The little bird is pecking around amongst the plants that have emerged from the water, as the entire area should be rough pasture.

the water and those reflected below in *Quiet by Derwentwater* and *Derwentwater Morning*, I made the latter softer, using very little pen and only a gentle application of coloured pencil. These would eventually be covered by a layer of water to make them even less sharply defined.

Once the tree forms and leaves were established, I was able to add the shoreline, using coloured pencil only as a guide. Neither the lakeside nor the tops of the fells were defined in ink. However, at this stage the distant trees and bushes could be sketched in using an SX pen and an even finer Staedtler 0.05mm. I used an autumnal palette for the fells in *Derwentwater Morning* and *Bird in the Flood*: Light Flesh and Medium Flesh, Cinnamon, Sanguine and Indian Red, with touches of Permanent Green Olive and Pine Green. Dark Sepia, Mauve and Dark Indigo were also useful for shadowy areas. The same palette of colours was used for the reflections. As the lake water was an unusually pure blue, I chose a blend of Sky Blue and Light Ultramarine, adding Ultramarine for darker areas.

Using a putty rubber, I lifted out paths and gullies on the fells and added highlights in the water. I then used a very fine 0.03mm pen to create drifts of texture on the fells, keeping the markings very small to emphasize the distance. Patches of field and a few thistles were visible above the water in *Bird in the Flood*; I added these over the blue base in a mixture of pen and Chrome Oxide Green, and included the little bird feeding at the water's edge.

The fells seen from the opposite side of the lake in *Quiet by Derwentwater* and *Curving towards Derwentwater* shared the same palette, but with Permanent Green Olive and Chrome Oxide Green more dominant, and Dark Sepia, Mauve and Dark

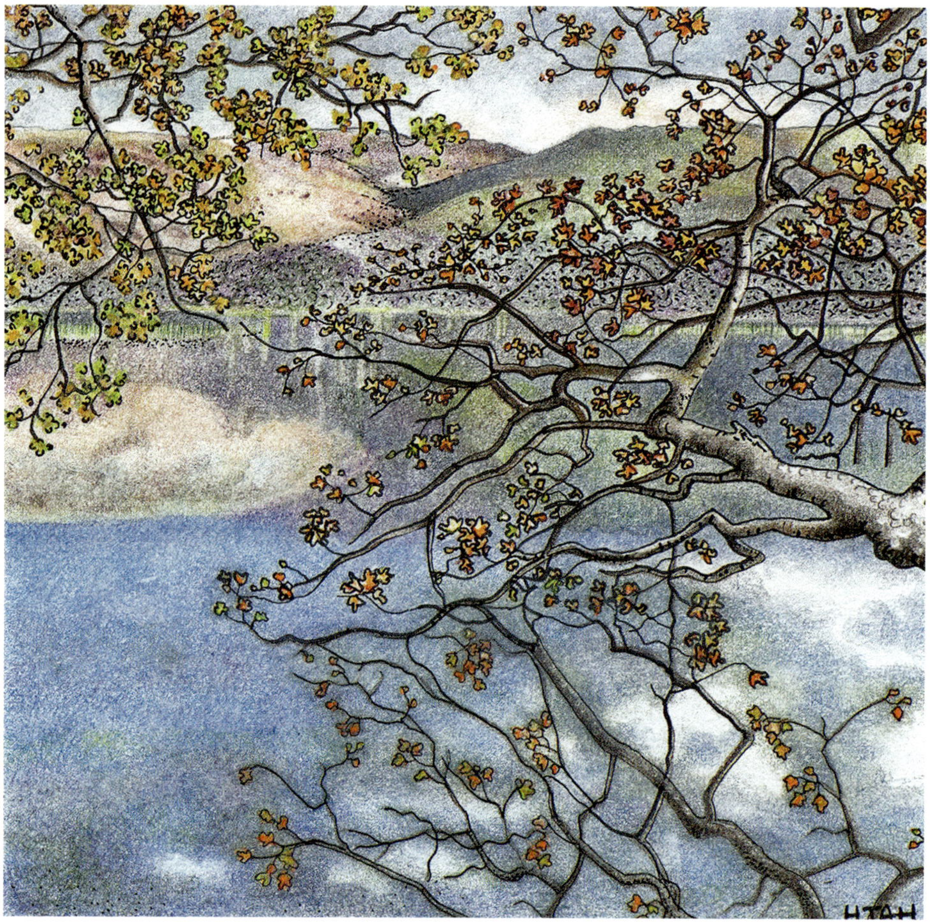

Quiet by Derwentwater. The high eye level allows us to see some of the folds of the fells, but the emphasis is on the nearside trees as they curve over the lake and create blurred reflections. They meet at a focal point on the opposite bank, where the lights are reflected in the water.

Indigo for the shadows and reflections. Both these images and *Bird in the Flood* featured overhanging branches with turning leaves, for which I used a selection of autumnal colours from the Prismacolor 'Premier' range, chosen for their softness and ability to add a strong pop of colour. These included Limepeel, Yellow Ochre, Spanish Orange, Orange and Pumpkin Orange. I also lifted out some small highlights on the leaves using a battery eraser.

The skies varied from picture to picture according to the time of day and the appearance of clouds. Although the day was sunny and the sky remained blue, the morning sky was calmer and the light rosier. I added some Light Flesh above the fells in *Bird in the Flood*, and kept a light strip of cloud in *Derwentwater Morning* to suit the still water. By afternoon more clouds had built up, and were reflected in the water on the opposite side of the lake. I used a combination of Sky Blue and Light Ultramarine, taking out clouds and reflections with Frisket and softening the edges with a putty rubber. I added some touches of Faber-Castell Warm Grey 11 to both, and smoothed the sky using Prismacolor Sky Blue as a burnisher.

A few finishing touches were needed as usual; some foreground branches required a fresh application of ink, as they inevitably merge into the background when colour is added around them. I lifted out a narrow line of light along the shoreline in *Curving towards Derwentwater* and *Quiet by Derwentwater*. Using a very pointed putty rubber, I erased a few vertical shafts of light and their reflections, creating a subtle focal point on the opposite bank.

Curving towards Derwentwater. This composition is similar, with a medium-high eye level and a focal point on the opposite bank. The foreground trees curve over the lake, meeting on either side of the reflections of light. The clouds that we see reflected in the water are those above the fells, plus more that are just above us.

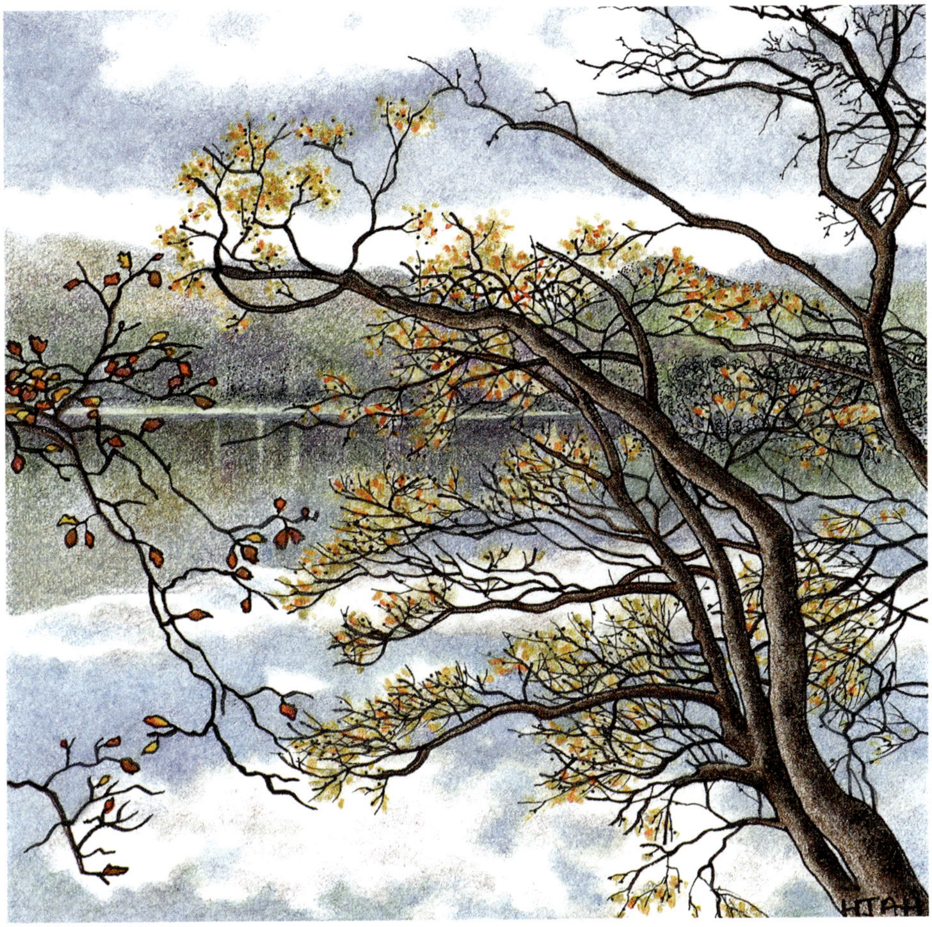

WINTER WOODLANDS

This series originated in a small nature reserve, utterly transformed on a winter afternoon by a heavy fall of snow. It was a strictly photographic outing in sub-zero temperatures, but the visual memory of the shadows on the snow, the dusty orange of the winter sun and the black rooks settling in the trees has stayed with me. I chose four images to create a winter series, envisaging stark ink marks against white, with just a hint of colour. I decided to use Lana Bristol board, which is very white, with an ultra-smooth surface. This would be ideal for the harder Derwent 'Artists' colours I chose to use. This Derwent collection had understated colours perfect for snow, which would only require one layer of application for the desired result. The Lana paper is one of the best surfaces I have used for ink, so this seemed a promising combination. I kept to a limited palette, some images taking up the warm orange palette of the sun and others the cool greys and blues of the snow. The image sizes are smaller than the previous series, measuring just 9×9cm. Recalling the rooks, I decided to have a bird theme running throughout.

As usual, I worked from very minimal drawings. All the branches had a covering of snow, so I limited ink lines to the underside only, leaving the upper parts completely white. I followed this with applications of coloured pencil in Sepia and Chocolate, keeping close to the ink line below and leaving an irregular upper edge to suggest a snow line. I chose a range of pen sizes for the branches and twigs, interweaving the lines, but always leaving space for the layers of snow where necessary. I added fine lines for the foreground grasses emerging through the snow, some in Derwent 'Linemaker' Graphite to introduce a touch of grey. I sketched in more random markings to indicate dead leaves, stones and so on, and to give variety.

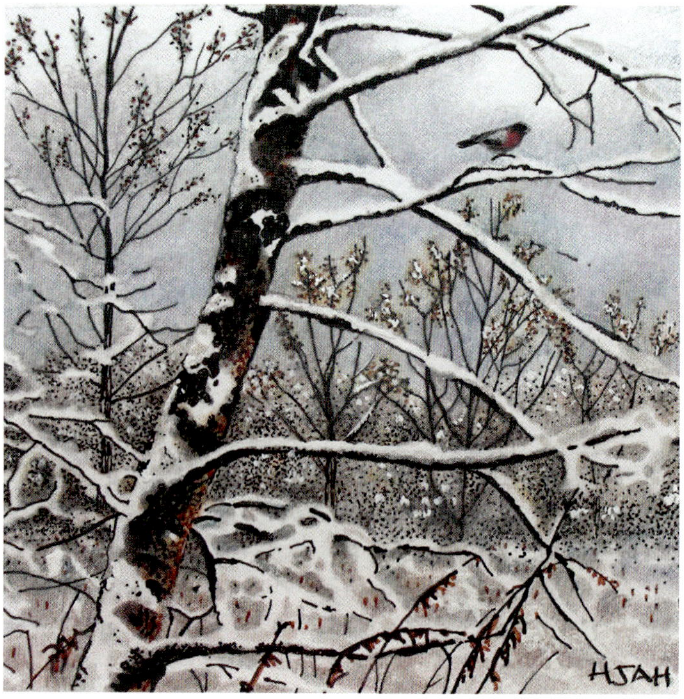

A Frozen Moment. The tree in the foreground, with its spreading branches, cuts through one side of the entire image. The combination of ink, dark colour and white paper shows where, and how deeply, the snow has settled. The palette is essentially cold, with touches of warmth on the leaves, bark and the bullfinch.

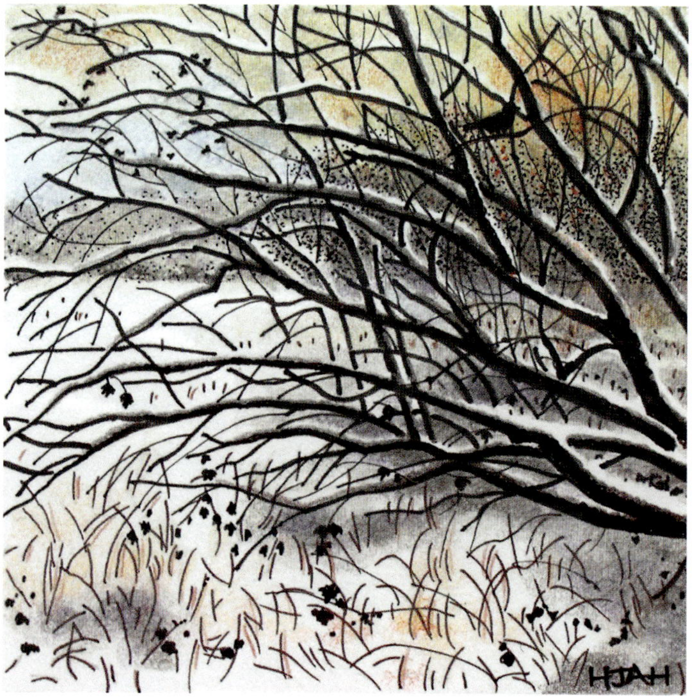

Evening Shadows Fall. Looking into the evening sun, this image has a warmer palette, with cooler shadows reserved for the areas under the tree and across the foreground. The use of different-sized ink marks, from the strong foreground branches to the dotted foliage, help to create a sense of distance within the small format.

Once the foreground branches were in place, it was possible to fit in the background, working carefully round the deposits of snow. I used a 0.03mm pen and soft colour for distant trees and bushes, keeping the mark-making appropriately small. For *A Frozen Moment* and *The Winter Visitors* I chose a bluish-grey palette; in both cases I used Sky Blue, Teal Blue, Silver Grey and Slate Violet in single-layer applications for sky, snow and shadows. *Evening Shadows Fall* and *Rooks at Solstice* had a late afternoon palette with Yellow Ochre, Sunset Gold, touches of Burnt Sienna and Slate Violet in the shadows.

This series was one that I enjoyed enormously. It was minimal in size and concept, but demonstrates that an effective combination of ink and coloured pencil does not have to be complicated or challenging. You can make a work of complexity or you can keep it simple; with the right materials and a bit of preparation, you can make either work.

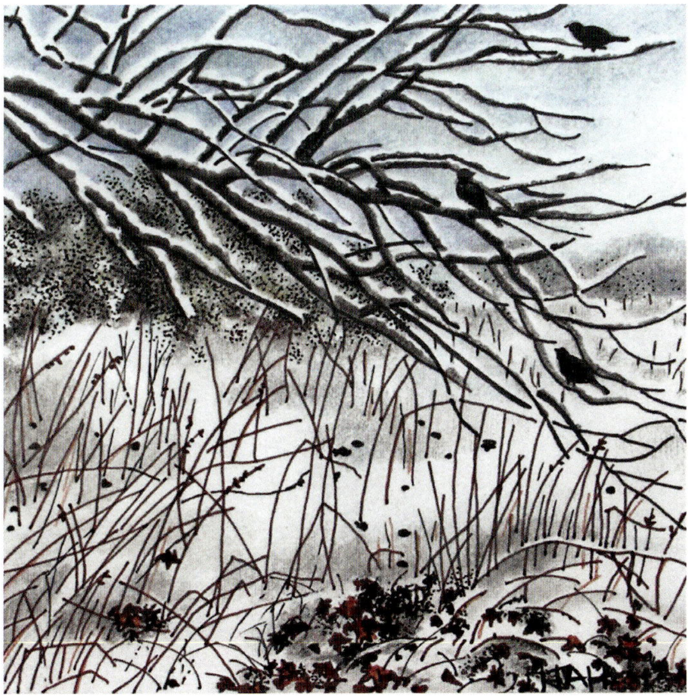

The Winter Visitors. This image has a completely cool palette with no touches of warmer colour. The emphasis is on the relationship between the three birds, seen in silhouette against the background. Once again, the relative distances are determined by the size and strength of the ink marks.

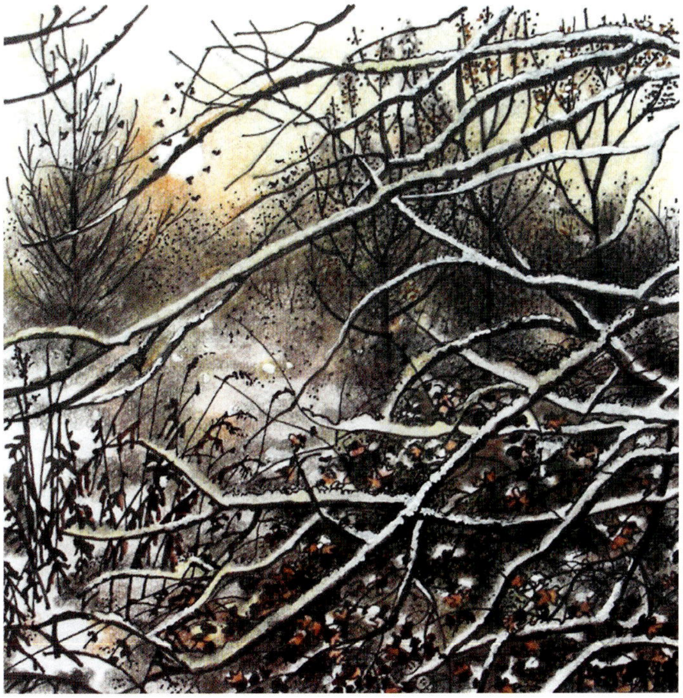

Rooks at Solstice. The rooks are circling round the trees before roosting, and the late winter sun casts a warm glow over the whole scene. The foreground is a tangle of brambles, created with ink, dark coloured pencil, patches of white paper and touches of Burnt Sienna.

LOCH ETIVE DUO

I first drove the long single track road through Glen Etive decades ago, and was overwhelmed by the sight of its magnificent lake. It was summer, but looking stormy, and the water back towards the glen was navy blue. At the end of the line in terms of remoteness, it must surely be one of the most spectacular cul-de-sacs in the country. It planted itself firmly in my visual memory, and since then Loch Etive has been part of my life as an artist, appearing in a series of etchings and more recently in this little duo in ink and coloured pencil. At 12×6cm the images are a diminutive version of the place itself and of my subsequent etchings, but every contour and colour still feels utterly familiar. I chose to use the original Fabriano 5 hot-pressed watercolour paper, with slightly more texture than Bristol board.

Both Glen Etive and Loch Etive had a rich range of greens in their local colour that I felt would suit Faber-Castell's 'Polychromos' selection. I began with drawings that merely indicated the lines of the mountains, river valley and the lake itself. I used no ink at all at this stage, but gradually introduced the shapes of a few bushes, rocks and larger stones along the riverbed, making sure to diminish their size as the eye travelled rapidly down the valley. I sketched in the sparse clumps of broom that were still blooming at intervals, and which would provide a little eye-catching yellow colour.

In both images I used a base of Cadmium Yellow Lemon, May Green, Earth Green Yellowish and Burnt Sienna for the nearer hillside, and a bluer blend of Chrome Oxide Green and Juniper Green for the more distant one. Small clumps of bushes and the main tree in *Loch Etive* were a mixture of ink, Chrome Oxide Green and Pine Green. I speckled the riverbed in *Glen Etive* with ink dots of different sizes, adding colour with Burnt Sienna, Burnt Umber and Sepia, as well as Dark Cadmium Yellow for the broom flowers. I trailed pathways and gullies down the hillsides to give texture and form, adding some tiny markings to the river and the loch to speed the eye along.

Glen Etive was unaffected by the incoming storm and the water was light blue, so I used a mixture of Sky Blue and Light Ultramarine, varying their distribution and intensity to include the sky and the distant mountains. Clouds were gathering over Loch Etive, casting a deep shadow over the more distant hills. I added Ultramarine and Deep Indigo to the mix and built up a cloudbank using Frisket, shadowing the base of the clouds quite heavily. The heather was just starting to come out, but there was still an abundance of earlier bell heather growing on the moorland alongside the loch; I used a mix of Magenta and Light Magenta, lifting out a few final highlights with a battery eraser.

I have always found that working on a series makes me more aware of my surroundings and the changes in weather, light and time of day. Artists such as Monet have embarked on a whole series just to explore differences in light and colour. Sometimes, one image is just not enough to convey what we want to say; at other times, the change is the point of the exercise. A few places, such as Loch Etive, just lodge in our memory and return to haunt us artistically, in the nicest possible way.

Glen Etive. The road down the glen to Loch Etive was memorable, and I wanted to convey something of its wide, open aspect. The four separate glimpses of the river, the receding perspective of the pebble banks and the folding hills do give the impression of a dramatic landscape, even on a small scale.

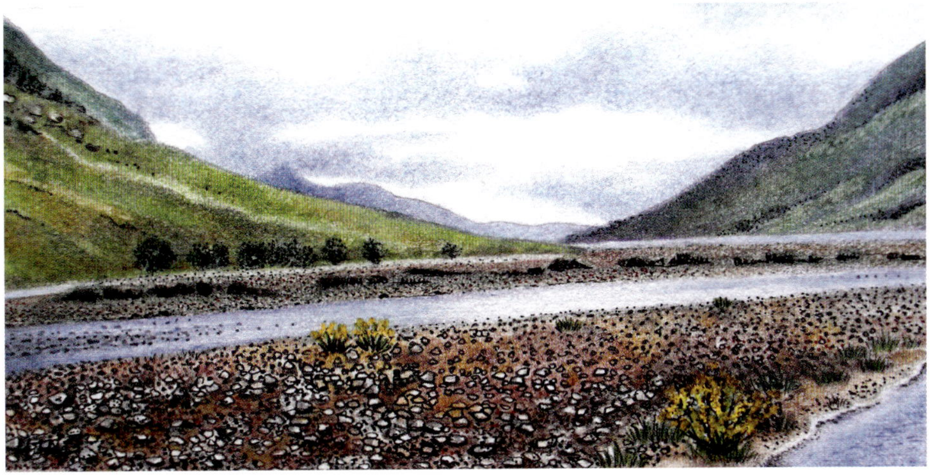

Loch Etive. The view down the lake was again panoramic and my approach was similar. The rapidly receding perspective covers a lot of ground, and a low eye level allows us to see several mountain ridges rising in the distance. This gives a sense of vastness and scale, even in a small image.

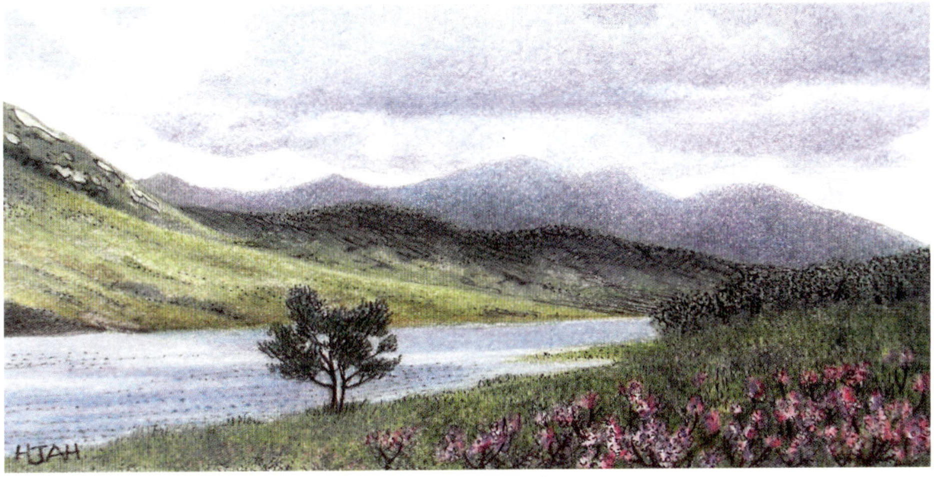

CHAPTER 11

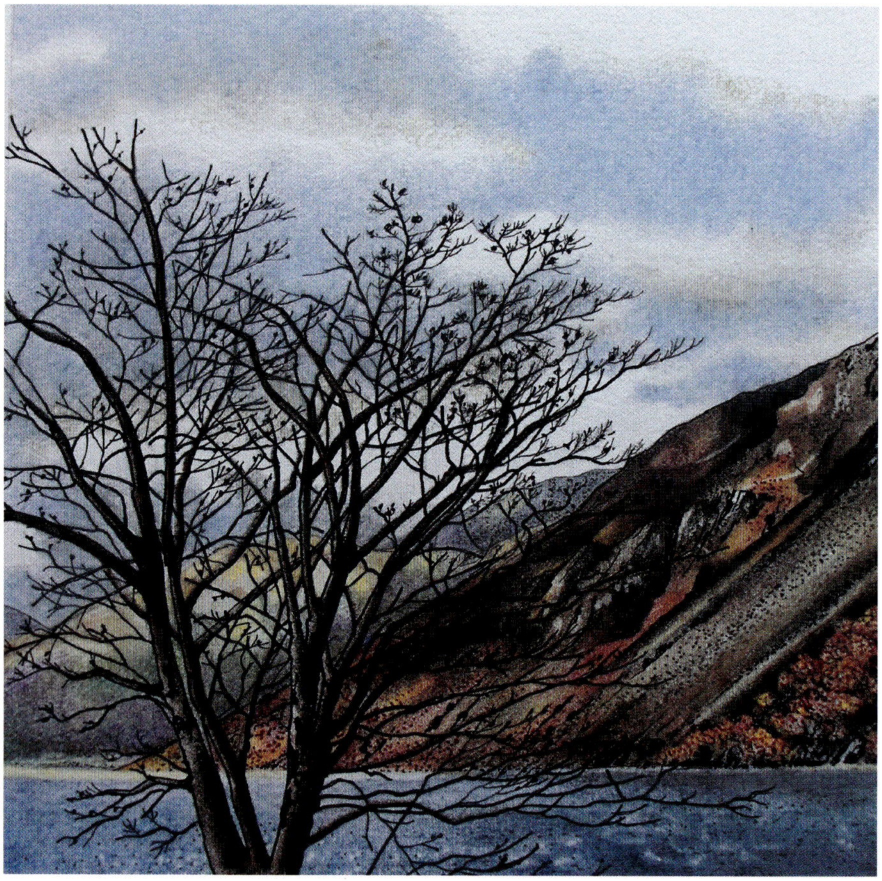

Tree by Wastwater.

Four Seasonal Projects

This chapter consists of four seasonal projects featuring different types of landscape, each with its own local colour and plant life. They are not recipes to be followed: in each case I have chosen to show how I work as an artist, making decisions, changing my mind and altering colours up to the very end. It is quite usual to apply a colour and later, on reflection, to get out the Frisket. Knowing when to stop is an art in itself; when nothing jumps out, looks incongruous or annoys, you have probably got there.

I have used different makes of coloured pencil, sometimes favouring one brand for a particular image. Although I have mentioned the specific colours I chose, it is quite possible to achieve a very similar look using another brand. Different makes have their own unique colours, but some are very close on the spectrum. Don't feel that you need to have a collection as extensive as mine! It is more important to follow the processes and order of working required for a particular image, so that you learn how to manage your own work.

SPRING

Fishcombe Woods

I visited these Devon woods in May when the bluebells and red campions were out, providing one of my favourite plant combinations. I decided on a low eye level, giving an interesting angle on the trees above; we mainly see their ivy-covered trunks as they stretch upwards, and most of the spring foliage is provided by the trees in the background. I simplified my original photograph considerably, cutting out several of the trees and avoiding an excess of greenery. I kept the sloping bank, but introduced drifts rather than a mass of bluebells. For this project I chose Faber-Castell 'Polychromos' pencils; their excellent range of greens, browns and greys provide all the right woodland colours, with some bright contrasts for the flowers.

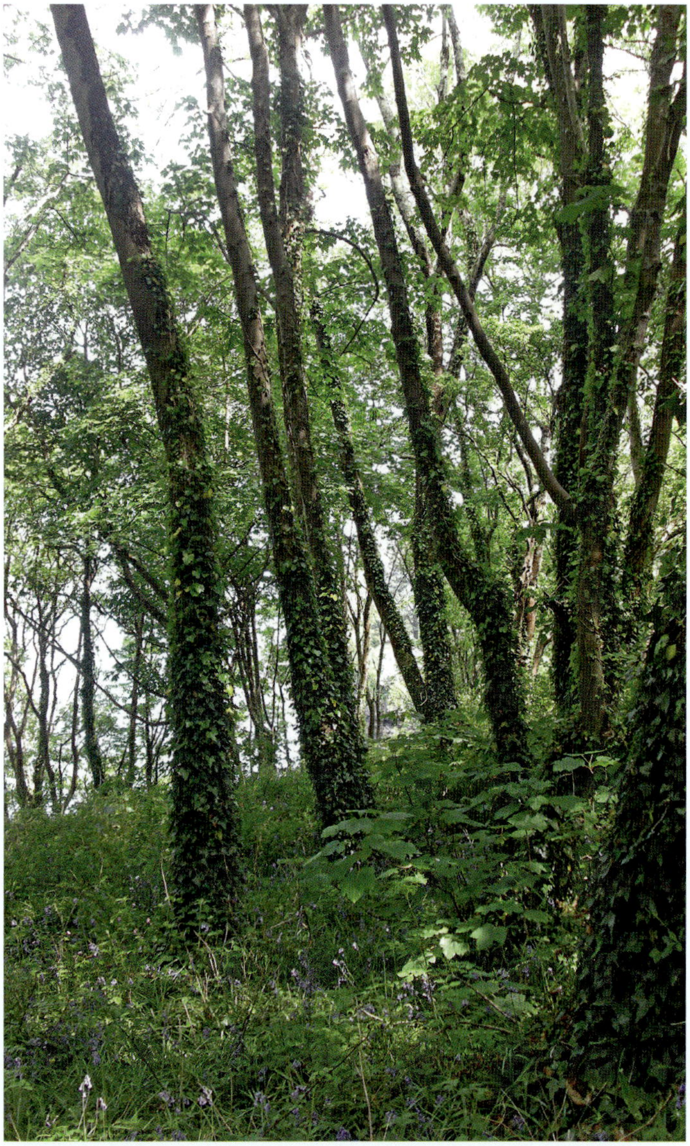

Fishcombe Woods: source photograph. My original photograph in Fishcombe Woods was just a starting point, with a collection of some of the flowers I wanted to use. I kept the slope, the tall trees and the sapling, but cleared away a lot of foliage, developing the picture in a way that owed more to the earlier *Bluebell Slope*.

STAGE ONE

I began with the foreground, pencilling in stems for the ivy leaves that twisted up the tree bark. I added the leaves with a 0.05 pen, following these lines. Once the leaves were in place, I removed the pencil lines, replacing sections that were still visible with Faber-Castell Bistre as a base for embossing. Using a medium embossing tool, I pressed into the lines to create the paler, fibrous stems. I added coloured pencil to the bark using (from the shadow side) Dark Sepia, Burnt Umber and Warm Grey III. I planned to add ink markings after colouring the ivy, as I wasn't sure how much detail would be required. Not everything you see in nature needs to be recorded in a picture; as the artist, you can make the decisions.

I outlined one of the saplings to provide a link between the foreground and the middle distance and a splash of spring green. I sketched roughly where the bluebell drifts might be, working out the appropriate size for plants in the distance. I wanted the bluebells and campions to show clearly in the foreground, so chose to ink their outlines in a fine 0.03 pen, bearing in mind which plants were in front as I worked. I added a few grasses behind, shaping their feathery heads with a fine embossing tool. Finally, I prepared the foreground for embossing over colour with a base of Earth Green Yellowish; I alternated this with Cadmium Yellow Lemon where the light would fall and Olive Green Yellowish for the patches of shadow.

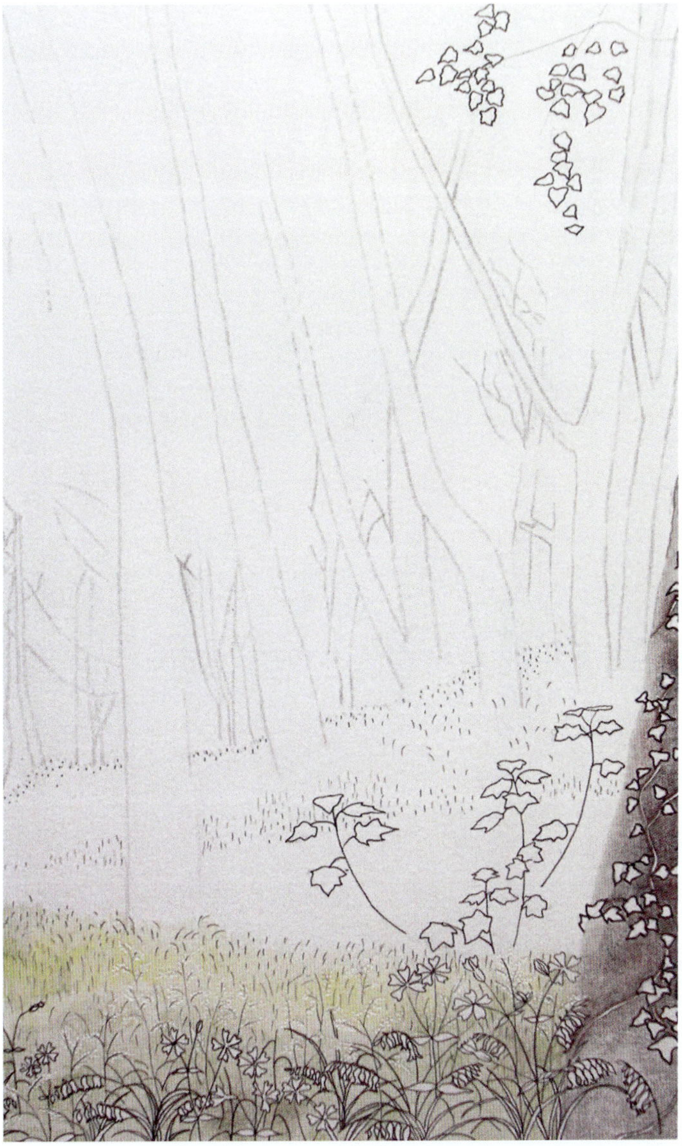

Fishcombe Woods: stage one. I began with ink drawings for the foreground: ivy, campions, bluebells, saplings and grasses. I used fine, linear embossing on the grass heads, and heavier embossing on the ivy stems twisting round the trunk. Base colours were added to the foreground in preparation for more embossing, and a first layer of browns on the tree trunk.

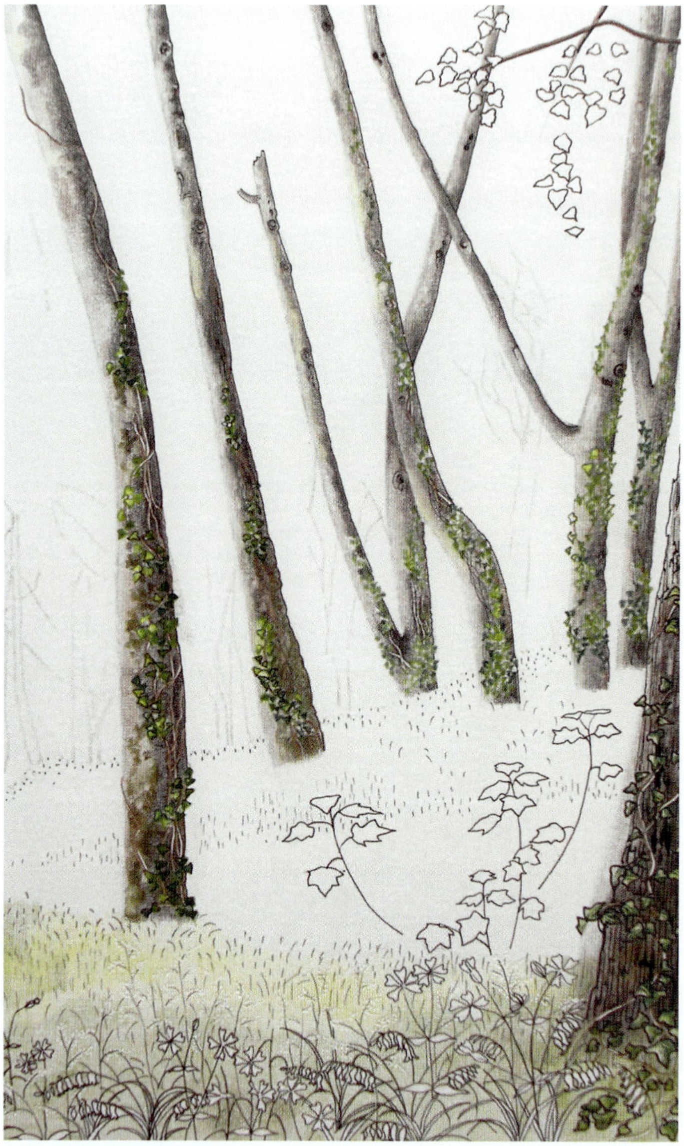

Fishcombe Woods: stage two. For this section I concentrated on the trees, creating ivy-leaf shapes in colour, then adding a few ink outlines for greater definition. I traced their twisting stems in Bistre and embossed them, before filling in the bark with colour and ink markings, progressing from dark to light.

STAGE TWO

I then worked on the bark and the ivy on the rest of the trees, starting with leaf shapes in Permanent Green Olive and Pine Green and adding a few ink outlines for greater definition. As for the foreground tree trunk, I threaded the ivy stems between the clumps of leaves using Bistre as a base for embossing lines. Observing the direction of the light (from the left), I used ink on one side of the tree trunks, progressing from Dark Sepia and Burnt Umber to Warm Grey III as before. Ink lines and knots were added round the ivy, with less detail visible on the more distant trees.

STAGE THREE

This stage involved the introduction of wider expanses of colour. In the foreground, I embossed fine lines over the coloured base to create pale blades of grass, adding more Earth Green Yellowish, May Green and Permanent Green Olive to make them visible. I then worked carefully round the grass heads I had embossed earlier, so that they emerged amongst the flowers.

Using Ultramarine, Light Ultramarine and Mauve, I started to create drifts of bluebells, combining curved markings in coloured pencil with softer applications of colour to create a misty look. For the remaining grassy spaces, I used May Green and Permanent Green Olive over darker, linear strokes in both ink and coloured pencil. Before working on the distant trees, I added May Green, Cadmium Yellow Lemon and Permanent Green Olive to any overhanging branches and leaves; behind them, I used small ink dots to create the foliage on the younger trees, blending Juniper Green and May Green with Cadmium Yellow Lemon where the light fell.

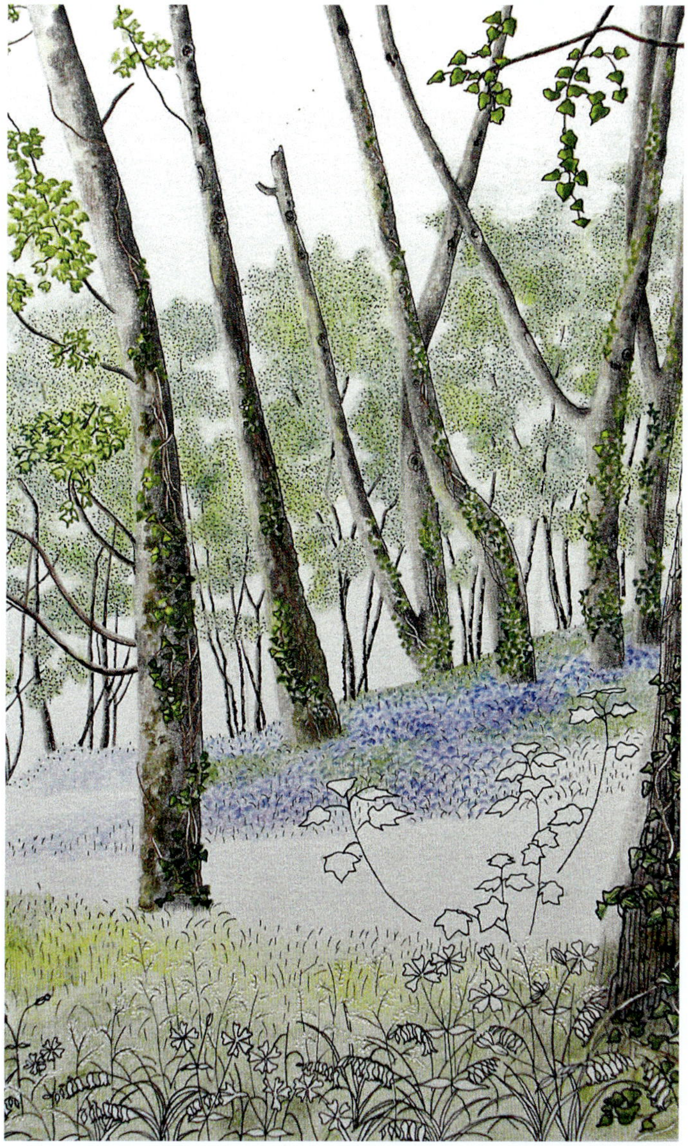

Fishcombe Woods: stage three. I started to build up larger areas of colour, creating drifts of bluebells interspersed with patches of grass. I embossed more foreground grasses over the base colour, and added foliage to the young trees using ink dots and blended colour. The few overhanging branches and leaves were outlined and given strong colour.

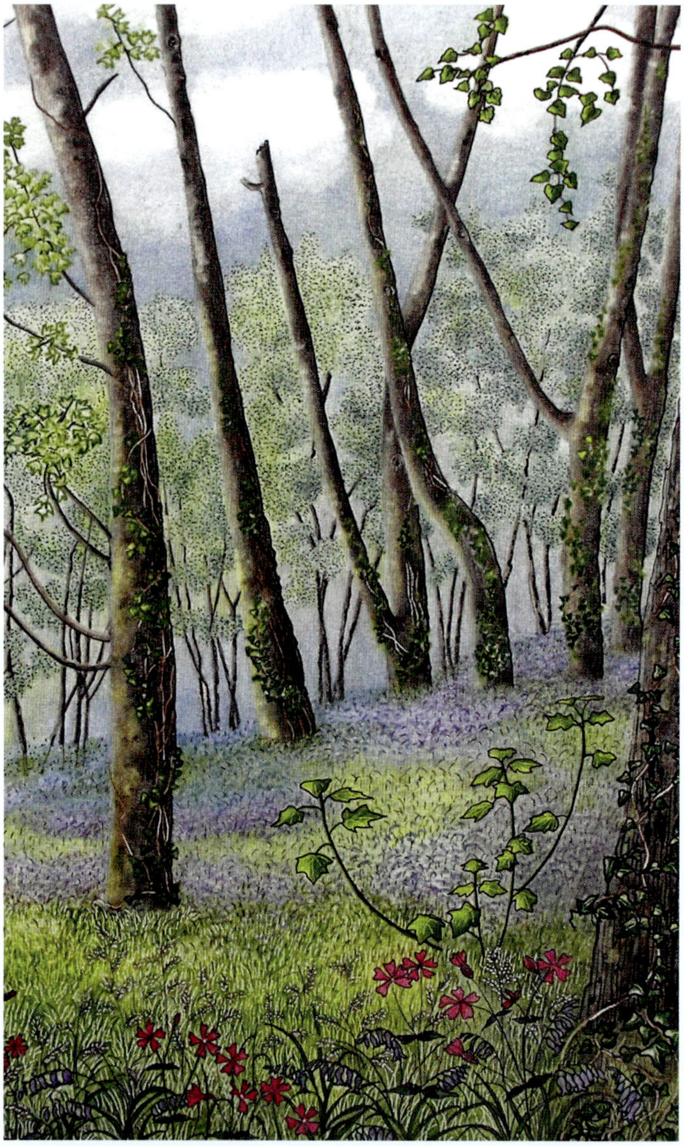

Fishcombe Woods: stage four. The foreground flowers were added, and finely inked grasses scattered up the slope to meet the bluebell drifts. The sapling, completed in bright greens, links the foreground and middle distance. I created a misty haze above the bluebells, merging it into the sky. As the picture was quite detailed, I kept the sky soft but unfussy.

STAGE FOUR

In this final stage, I brought together foreground and middle distance, adding more bluebell clusters and patches of grass. The foreground flowers were coloured in using Magenta and Light Magenta for the red campion, with the previous combination of Ultramarine, Light Ultramarine and Mauve for the bluebells. For the tree sapling I used bright May Green and Cadmium Yellow Lemon over lightly embossed veins. I shadowed the undersides of the tree foliage with Ultramarine, and used it with Light Ultramarine to create a soft, light sky with just a few drifts of cloud. Sometimes, as in this case, a picture develops a life of its own, and the source image is just a starting point.

SUMMER

Samphire Hoe

Samphire Hoe is one of my local nature reserves, which stretches below the white cliffs to the sea. On a hot July morning, the air was scented with restharrow and other grassland plants. I set off early, hoping to work on a larger, portrait version of *Flowers at Samphire Hoe*, done a few summers ago. Apart from the distinctive green and white of the chalk cliffs, the colour palette was quite muted. Bleached grasses dotted the area and fringed the water. Beyond them, at ground level, were large expanses of more colourful grassland flowers that I wanted to use as foreground. For this image, I worked predominantly with Caran D'Ache 'Pablo' pencils, using many of their 'in between' shades, which were perfect for the late summer grassland. I also added Faber-Castell and Prismacolor shades if they were ideal for a particular feature.

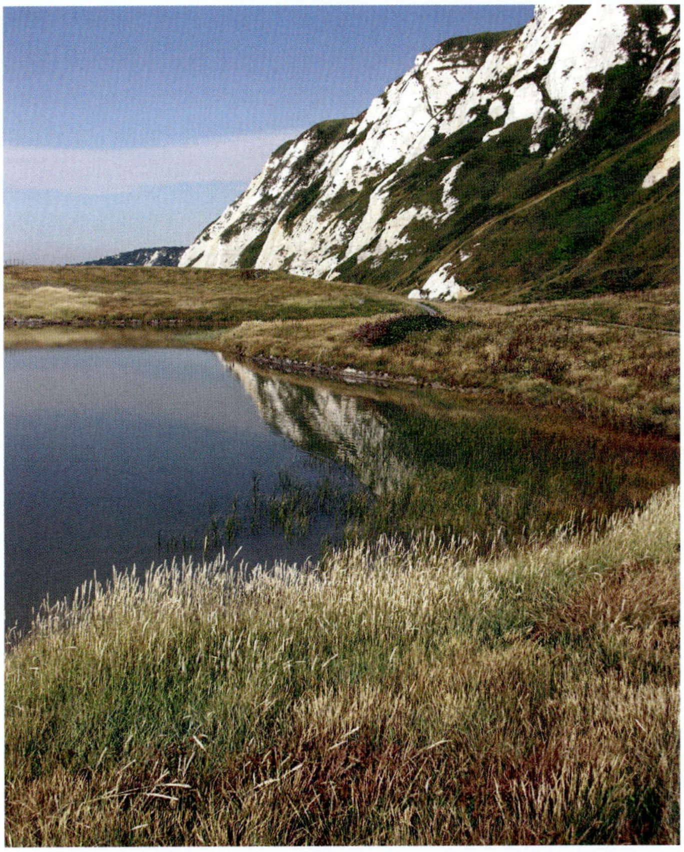

Samphire Hoe: source photograph. When the source image captures exactly what I want to include, I follow it quite closely, as in this example. The proportions are good, and the image divides comfortably into thirds. I did alter the foreground to include several locally abundant plants instead of more grassland, but otherwise kept the layout as in the photograph.

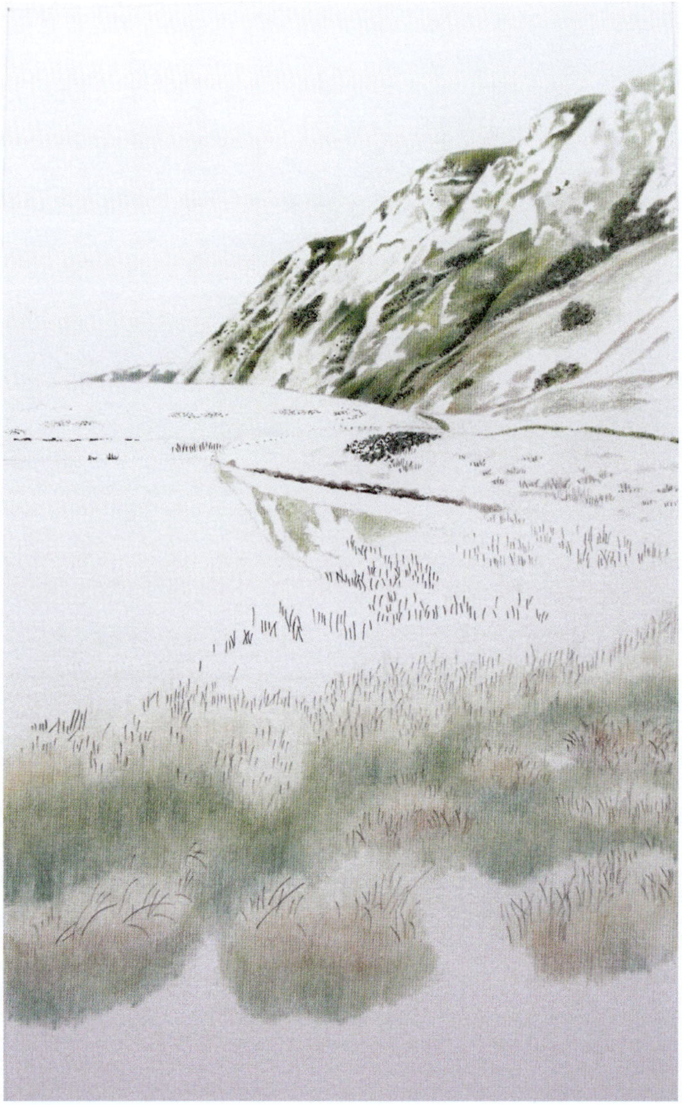

Samphire Hoe: stage one. I began with the cliffs, placing the areas of shadow first and some of the foliage, then adding a few directional marks to show the lie of the land. I sketched in some grasses in ink in the middle distance and foreground, establishing their approximate size, then put down some colour in preparation for embossing.

STAGE ONE

My preliminary drawing was minimal, with just enough markings to indicate the different sections of the image. I did pay close attention to the structure of the cliffs, lightly sketching in the chalk formations and the green areas so that I could apply coloured pencil later with confidence. This was not an image with tall foreground features, so I started at the top, choosing to set down a first layer for the white cliffs to establish their form, tonal values and distance.

I used a blend of Faber-Castell Chrome Oxide Green and Pine Green for the darkest areas and patches of foliage on the cliffs, applying these first to give some form. I then put down a first layer of colour using Caran D'Ache Moss Green, Olive Grey and Brown Ochre, carefully following the contours as they changed and steering round the chalk sections. Once I had worked out the lie of the land, I added ink, dotting in bits of texture, little paths and foliage shapes. I treated the very distant piece of coastline in the same way, but used a combination of Faber-Castell Juniper Green and Light Ultramarine to give some aerial perspective. I added touches of Caran D'Ache Cream and Beige to the chalk areas, leaving some of the off-white paper colour.

I then turned my attention to the middle distance and made a few marks in ink, picking out the edge of the path at the base of the cliffs, mud and pebbles along the borders of the scrape, and a tangle of plants on the bank. I also placed a few lines of reeds and added the reflections just visible alongside. Finally, I sketched in faint ink lines to indicate the size and direction of the foreground grasses. These would serve as guidelines, and would eventually blend in with the embossing and coloured pencil.

Working from the tops downwards, in preparation for embossing, I used a base of colours designed to suit bleached grasses: Caran D'Ache Cream, Luminance Olive Brown 10%, Brownish Beige, Brown Ochre and Moss Green, plus Faber-Castell Juniper Green. I applied these colours using a light touch and single linear strokes to suit the subject, rather than ellipses. I scattered these areas of grass along the waterside and across the foreground, leaving spaces at the front for the inclusion of grassland plants.

STAGE TWO

I introduced the cycle track connecting the two areas of grassland, making it a focal point. Although the terrain was similar throughout the landscape, I used more Olive Brown 10%, Brownish Beige and Hazel on the left-hand area, adding Moss Green, Olive Grey and Cocoa towards the water's edge. This suggested a more exposed, sun-bleached expanse and distinguished the two areas of grassland. I built up a blend of colours, shaped them into clumps, then lightened and roughened their appearance with a battery eraser without adding too much detail.

For the stretch of grassland on the right, I used some light ink lines, sketched in a few thistles, and added Luminance Naples Ochre to the palette for the highlights. To complete the section on the far side of the track, I needed to finish the hillside behind; I applied Chrome Oxide Green using downward linear strokes to feather the pale grasses, reverting immediately to ellipses and ink markings to create the foliage behind. This final section of cliff presented a smooth expanse of rich green, for which I used Caran D'Ache Moss Green and Olive Grey, with Faber-Castell Permanent Green Olive for freshness and Chrome Oxide Green for shade.

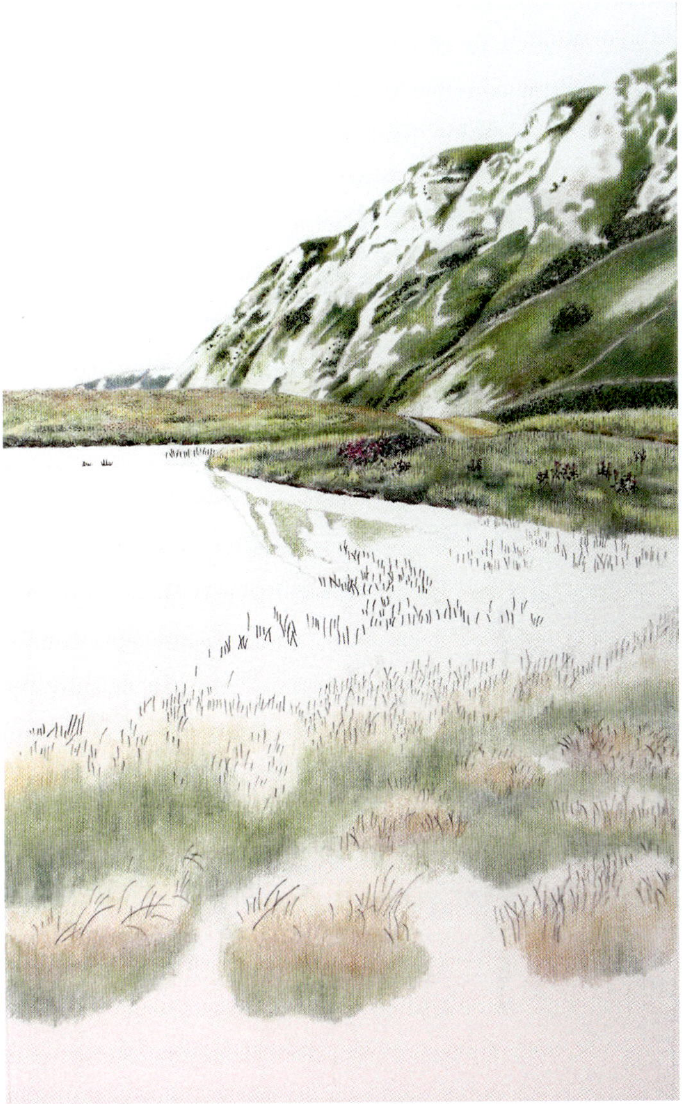

Samphire Hoe: stage two. I introduced the cycle path as a focal point, and developed the two stretches of grassland, differentiating between them in vegetation, colour and texture. More green areas were added to the cliffs, and neutral colours to the chalk. I used both ink and coloured pencil for the path and the dark edges of the lake.

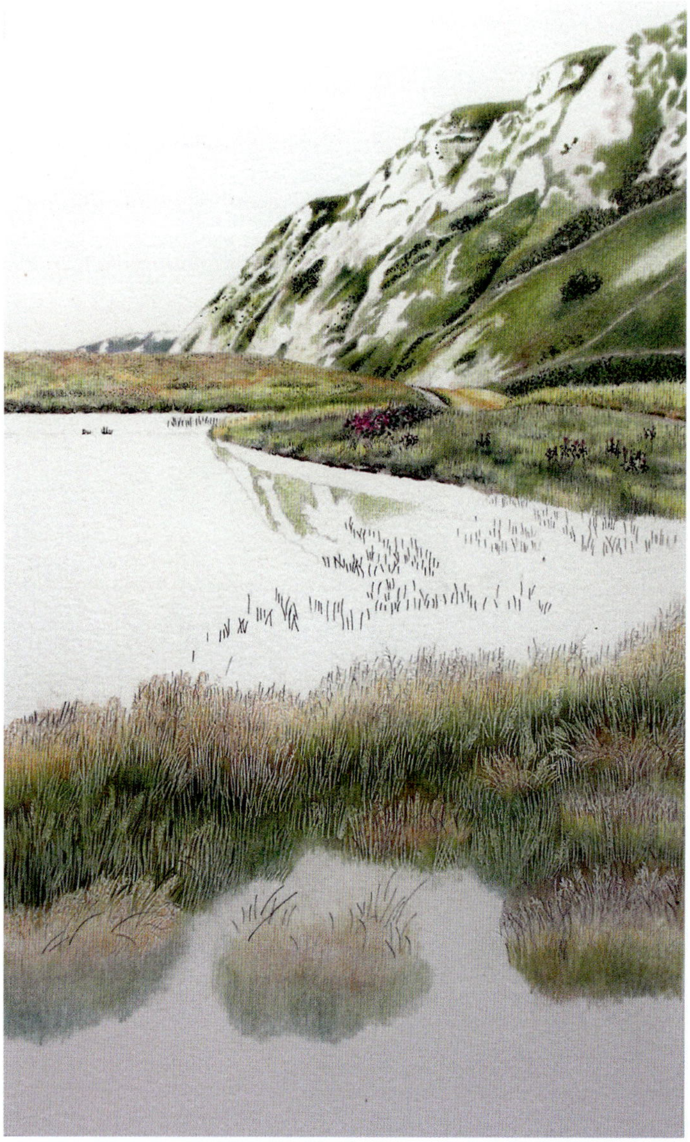

Samphire Hoe: stage three. The foreground grasses were finely embossed over the base colours I had put down earlier, so that subsequent layers of colour would reveal their form. Shadowing and lifting out then created direction, light and shade.

STAGE THREE

In the foreground I followed the areas of base colour established in stage one, embossing all the pale grasses using a fine line tool for the stalks and the smallest circular one for the heads. I then worked round them with more colour, using Caran D'Ache Moss Green, Olive Grey and Hazel and introducing Orangeish Yellow and Vandyke Brown. This warm brown created shadow, and when scumbled over the lighter colours, picked out the embossing in pinkish-brown. Grass shapes emerged where I had embossed earlier once I applied darker pencil. I left some clear areas at the front for foreground plants, which would be introduced at the next stage; these would gradually give way to grasses closer to the water.

STAGE FOUR

I based the foreground on close-ups I had taken of the grassland, identifying the species that were growing together at the time. These were mainly bird's foot trefoil, wild carrot and restharrow, interspersed with blades of new green grass and pale bleached grass. I began by sketching in the green grasses, using Faber-Castell Permanent Green Olive. I then added more strokes in Caran D'Ache Luminance Naples Ochre, immediately embossing over these lines to give a pale line. The heads of wild carrot were also white embossed at this stage, using a small circular tool to recreate their distinctive umbels. I scattered Caran D'Ache Yellow in clusters for the bird's foot trefoil, tinting the edges with Reddish Orange; I then trailed leaves and flowers of restharrow across the area, using Faber-Castell Juniper Green and Permanent Green Olive, with Light Magenta and Caran D'Ache Purple for the flowers.

Once the different species were in place, I added a light background in Moss Green and embossed more grasses on top; these would eventually show up under more coloured pencil layers. I also introduced leaves and stems for the wild carrot and bird's foot trefoil where visible, including touches of ink for definition and tufts of shorter grass.

For the final stage of the foreground, I built up patches of light and shade, bringing forwards the wild carrot heads and strengthening any flowers that needed more impact. I added Faber-Castell Mauve to the shadows behind the grasses and amongst the flowers. I integrated the area by the water with the grassland by using the same ground colours (Moss Green, Olive Grey, Brownish Beige and Hazel), so that the eye moves from one to the other without interruption. In contrast to the foreground, the water needed to be an area of calm. Apart from the reeds on the right, nothing interferes with the smooth surface. I built up the water using small ellipses and several colours: a base of Caran D'Ache Pastel Blue and Blue Jeans, with Faber-Castell Light Ultramarine and Light Magenta on the reflected band of cloud. For the darker water behind the grasses I introduced Caran D'Ache Olive Grey and Prismacolor Imperial Violet, working the colour in carefully between the fronds to help them stand out.

I used linear strokes for the reeds, blending Faber-Castell Permanent Green Olive, Pine Green and Chrome Oxide Green with patches of Caran D'Ache Chestnut and Umber. The tone is noticeably darker in this area, and I used more ink markings – lines, dots and a suggestion of leaves using 0.03 and 0.05 pens. I deepened the tone on the cliffs immediately above to suggest more shadow 'offstage' and to throw more light on the rest of the cliff face. The darker area of reeds also made the contrasting curve of foreground grasses appear lighter. At this stage, when all the elements of the picture are assembled, I usually need to make adjustments in tone. As we know, it is these variations that bring life to an image, and they can be achieved easily in coloured pencil by lifting or layering.

I kept the sky much as it appeared on the day; a drift of cloud lifted towards the cliff and was reflected in the water. There was a faint, early morning hint of pink, but otherwise everything was a calm blue. Sky and water belong together, and given the foreground detail, I wanted to avoid too much fussiness elsewhere. I used Faber-Castell Light Ultramarine and Ultramarine, with a little Light Magenta and a burnishing layer of Prismacolor Cloud Blue.

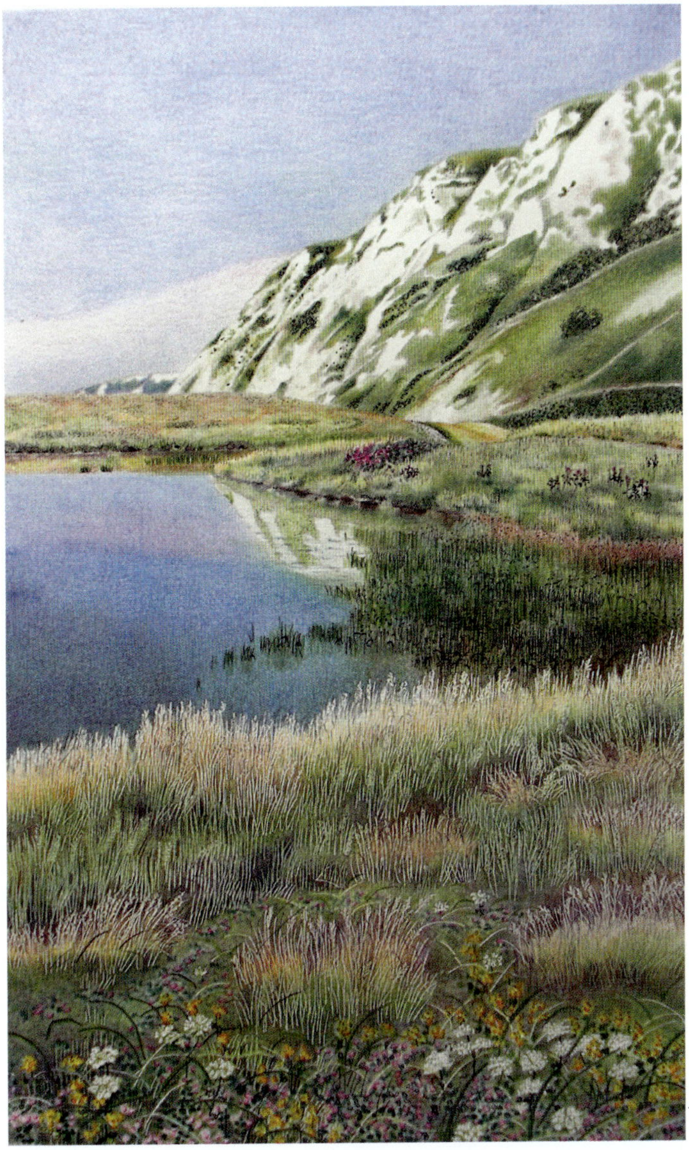

Samphire Hoe: stage four. The more detailed plants such as wild carrot, bird's foot trefoil and restharrow were woven into the foreground and individually coloured. I gradually built up the colours of the water, starting with Pastel Blue and Blue Jeans and introducing shadow where needed. I used linear, downward strokes for the reeds, mixing ink and coloured pencil. I deliberately created a more shadowy side on the right of the picture, continuing this up on to the cliffs.

AUTUMN

Rydal Water

Some of my favourite images of the Lake District have been based on a particular type of autumn morning: a pearly mist hangs low over the fells, and the landscape appears completely still. Light gleams on the water, background colours are muted, and bright autumn leaves draw the eye. I walked round Rydal Water on just such a morning, and have tried to capture the different types and colours of foliage as well as the utter stillness. I used three Derwent ranges: 'Artists', 'Procolour' and 'Coloursoft' pencils for this image, as their colours are perfectly attuned to the Cumbrian landscape.

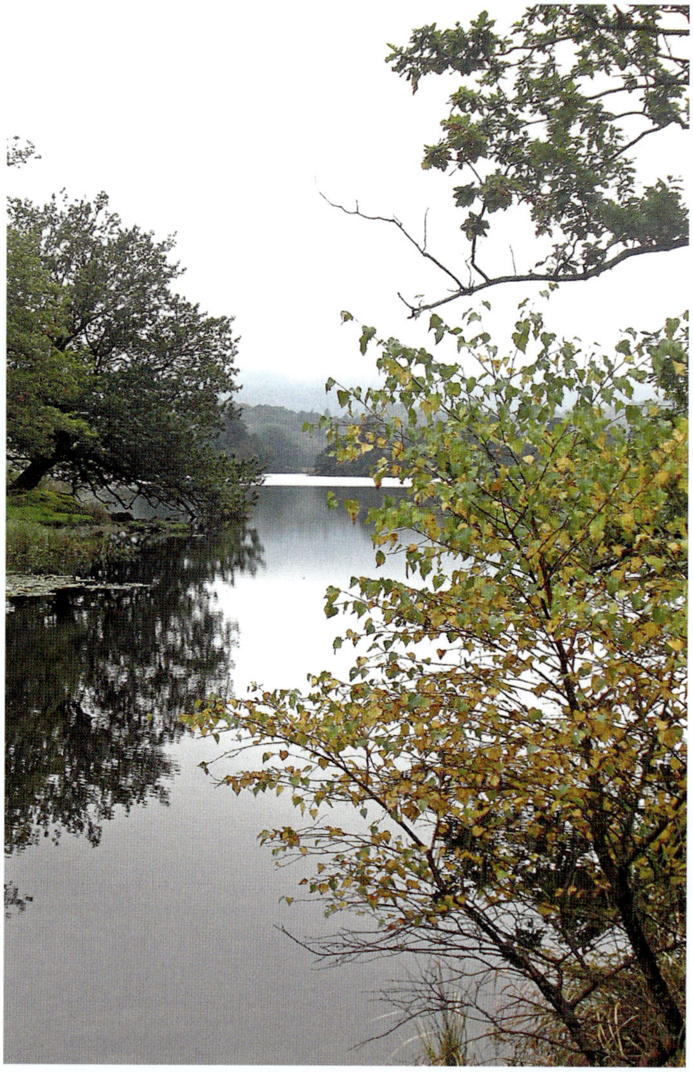

Rydal Water: source photograph. This was a cropped version of a larger photograph, focusing on the bright autumn tree and the misty landscape beyond. The image was far less complex than the previous two and depended largely on atmosphere for its impact. Getting the right colours and the right mood would be essential.

STAGE ONE

Different landscapes may need different starting points; this one was unusual in that I began with a lot of ink work alone. This was because I wanted to make a feature of the detail in the foreground trees, and fill in the brightly coloured autumn leaves. My plan was to outline some leaves for impact, then add less defined leaf shapes behind to create clusters of foliage. In addition, the two very different trees on the left-hand side required some definition. I used 1.0, 0.05 and 0.03 pen sizes to draw in the overhanging oak branches, the foreground tree and some of the foliage shapes on the left. I then applied coloured pencil to the branches using Derwent 'Procolour' Burnt Umber, Chocolate, Sepia and Copper Beech. I decided at this stage to put down a preliminary layer of Olive Green, marking the reflections in the water for future reference.

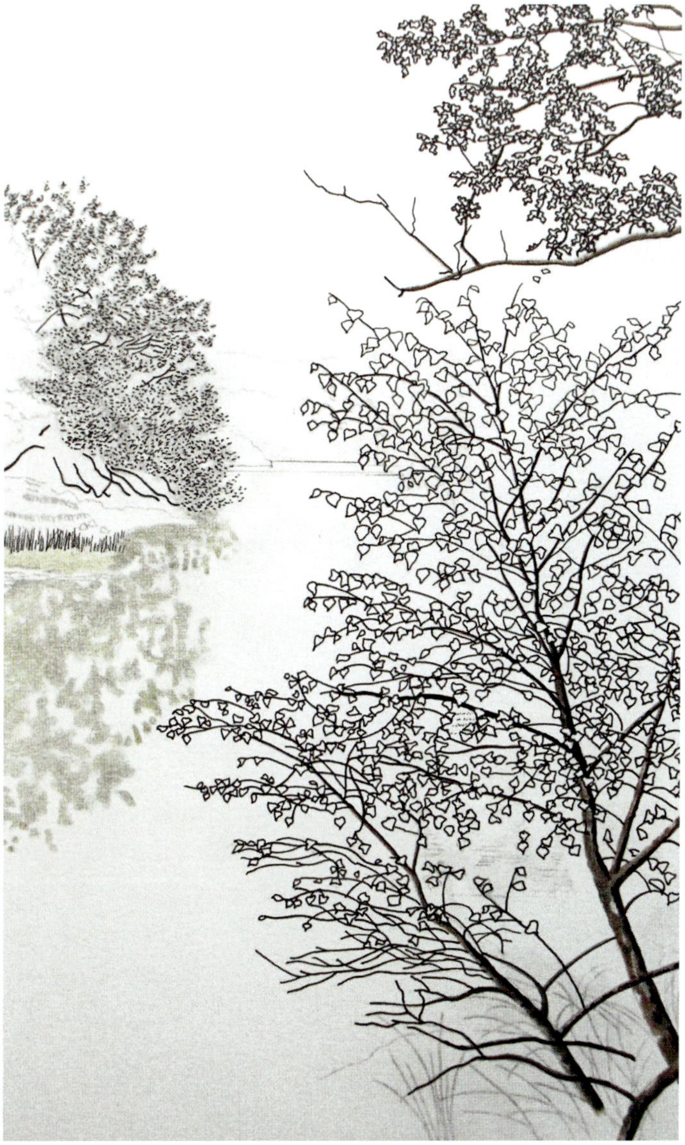

Rydal Water: stage one. It is unusual to start with an ink drawing of the subject, without any coloured pencil additions. However, in this case the foreground leaves were designed to be coloured in for extra impact, so I outlined them in ink. I added coloured pencil for the bark and branches and the reflections under the opposite tree.

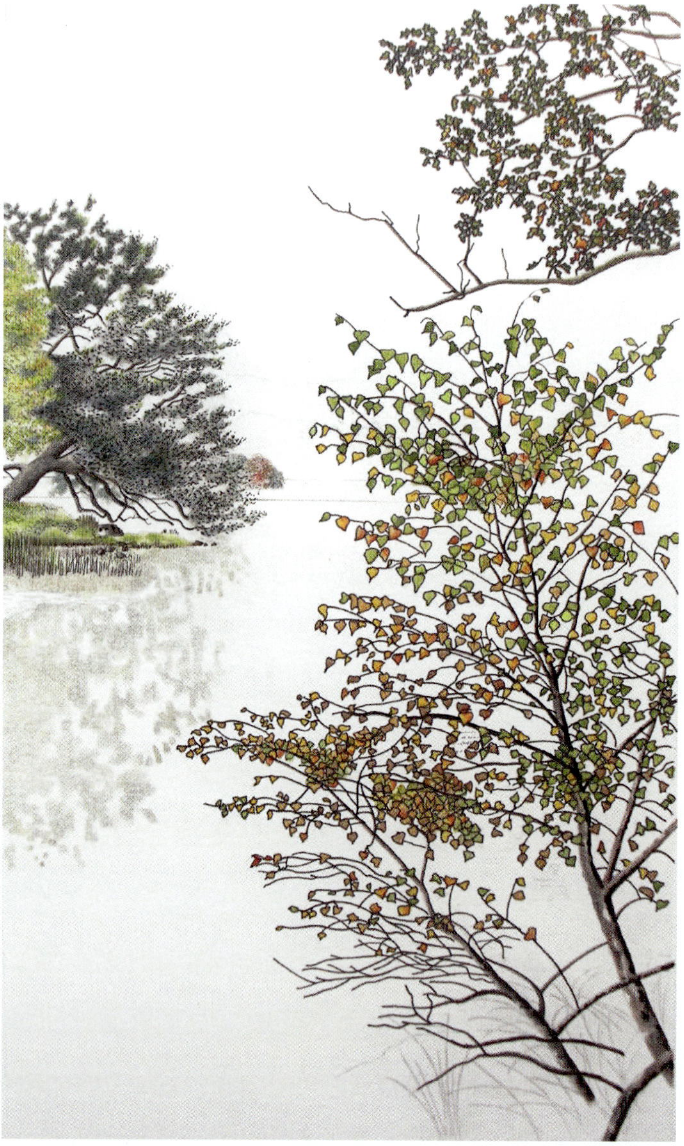

Rydal Water: stage two. I built up the different shapes of the trees on the left bank, following their form in ink and coloured pencil, adding grass, stones and reeds to the bank below and a little more colour to the reflections. Following a different palette for each tree, I coloured in the individual leaves and clusters in the foreground.

STAGE TWO

I chose to start on the left-hand side with the conifer overhanging the water, keeping to a bluish-green palette of Derwent 'Artists' colours: Spruce Green, Cedar Green and Sap Green, adding Indigo for the dark shadows. For the second tree, which was much lighter in colour, I used May Green, Golden Brown and a touch of Sepia, plus 'Procolour's excellent Foliage Green. I then built up the section of bank below the trees, inking in reeds, stones and the water's edge and using Moss Green, Olive Green and Foliage Green for the grass.

The overhanging oak branches needed strength and colour. I had drawn the leaf shapes in detail with a 1.0 pen and they were quite prominent. I chose the waxier Derwent 'Coloursoft' range and a single, strong application of colour rather than layering, selecting 'Procolour' Foliage Green with 'Coloursoft' Pimento and Pale Orange.

The delicate autumnal foliage of the tree in the foreground formed a pattern, with more green towards the top and down one side. Over the water and at the base the leaves were older and more yellowed. I followed this distribution, again blending Foliage Green with 'Coloursoft' Pimento and Pale Orange, plus Yellow Green, Ochre and Pale Brown. Once the individual leaves were finished, I added less defined leaf shapes behind to create more mass.

STAGE THREE

I began to work on the distant lakeside, keeping to a palette of blue-greens: Derwent 'Artists' Spruce Green and Cedar Green, with touches of Indigo and a focal point in 'Coloursoft' Pimento. I indicated some tree shapes in ink along the waterside, but used very little detail in the distance as I wanted to lose the landscape in a low-lying mist. I faded the treeline first into Blue Grey, then upwards into Iced Blue, repeating these last two colours above the clouds.

For the foreground grasses, I put down a pale base layer of Light Ochre, Yellow Ochre and Light Moss. I embossed lines, adding Burnt Umber and Golden Brown on top to make them visible. Introducing more fine ink lines gave variety and depth; I made sure that these were sketched in behind the pale embossed lines.

In preparation for working on the water I added another layer of Olive Green to the tree reflections and started to build up the reeds, bank and water's edge under the tree. I used colours from the general palette: Foliage Green, May Green, Olive Green, Indigo, Sepia and Persian Grey.

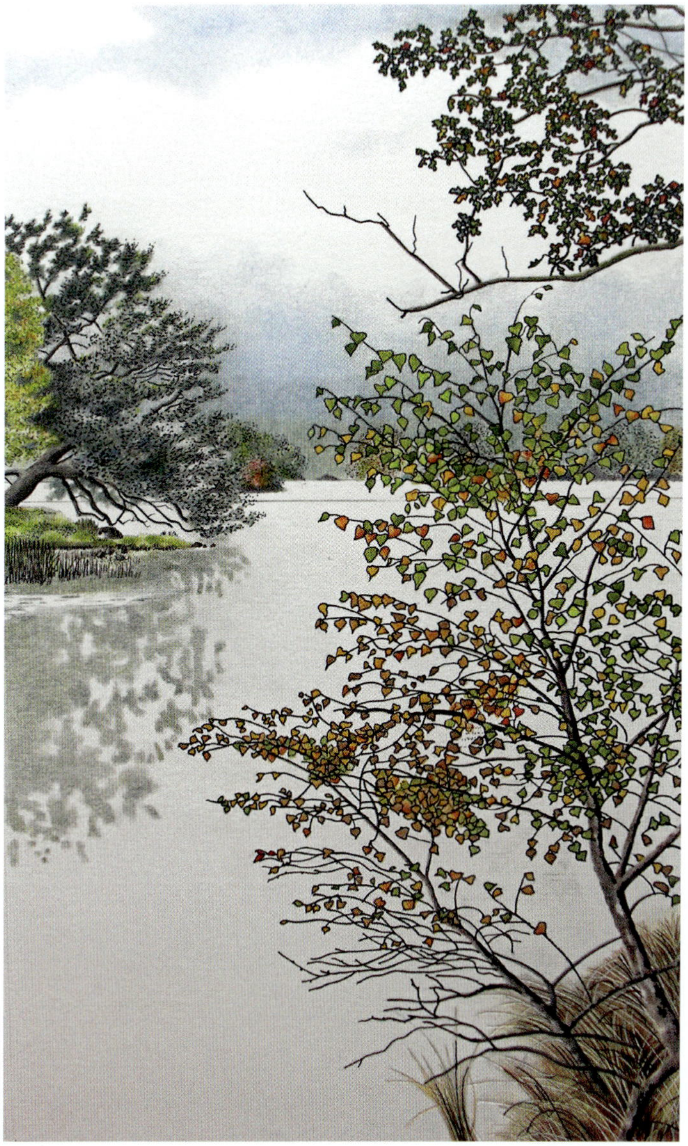

Rydal Water: stage three. I dotted tree shapes in ink on the far side of the lake, blending in some coloured pencil. Above this, I allowed the mist to merge with the colours of the sky, picking up some colour again above the clouds. In the foreground, I embossed the grasses over colour and added deep shadow.

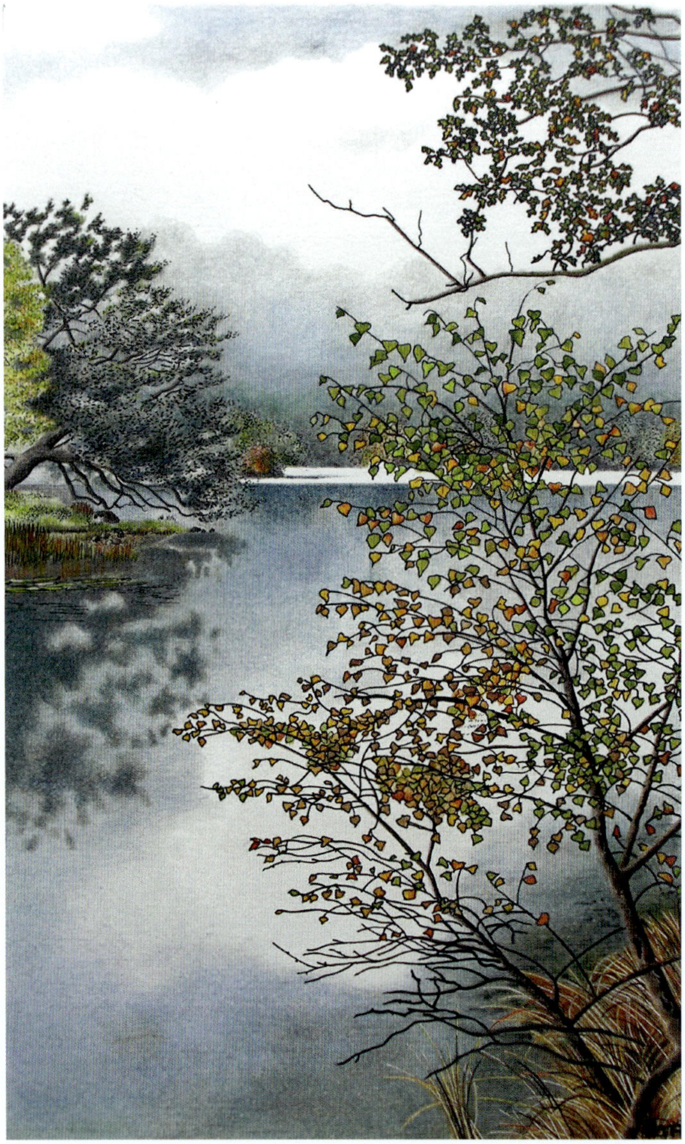

Rydal Water: stage four. Taking Smalt Blue as a base colour, I built up the layers of colour on the water, introducing shadows where necessary. I kept a bright band of light along the far shoreline and highlights in the centre. Finally, I strengthened the colours of the distant bank and the shadows under the tree.

STAGE FOUR

It is difficult to prescribe for water, as I add what it seems to need bit by bit; I also lift out frequently, and recolour until I have what I want. However, as a general principle, it is a good idea to start with a base colour that unites the expanse of water, and to create variations of colour, shadowy depths and lighter areas as required. For this image I chose Derwent 'Artists' Smalt Blue as it feels cool and understated. I started at the end of the lake, just below a gleaming band of light that I wanted to retain; this led to the focal point and set the mood for the entire scene. Below it, the water was at its darkest, so I used Indigo, Blue Grey and a touch of Spruce Green over Smalt Blue, fading them out gently to white towards the central area of light. This selection of colours also deepened and enhanced the shadows under the trees.

On the right-hand side, the water was muddier between the grasses, so I introduced patches of 'Coloursoft' Lincoln Green, Prussian Blue and Pale Brown. I frequently use a burnisher on areas of still water or clear sky; the satiny finish removes any unwanted texture. My favourite Prismacolor Cloud Blue has no equal as a coloured pencil burnisher, and I used it in addition to Derwent's own brand burnisher.

I also added some finishing touches, refreshing the tree trunks in the foreground and darkening them with more ink and 'Coloursoft' Brown Black and Brown Earth. Some grasses and foreground leaves needed another layer of colour, so I used autumnal colours from the previous palette.

WINTER

Brotherswater

I walked round this quiet little lake on a cold afternoon in February. The light was silvery, and the colours ranged from a cool, bluish grey to the warmer, cinnamon shades of the winter reedbeds. The trees were mostly bare, but a few early catkins dangled from the branches overhanging the lake. I chose a section of the lake with branches twisting over a patch of pale water, above some withered reeds. There were interesting features in the middle distance in the form of the reedbeds and the bare shapes of a winter wood. In the far distance the snow-capped fells disappeared into the sky. I liked the understated palette, with its limited number of cool and warm colours.
I used coloured pencils from several ranges: Caran D'Ache 'Pablo', Faber-Castell 'Polychromos', Derwent 'Procolour' and Prismacolor 'Premier'.

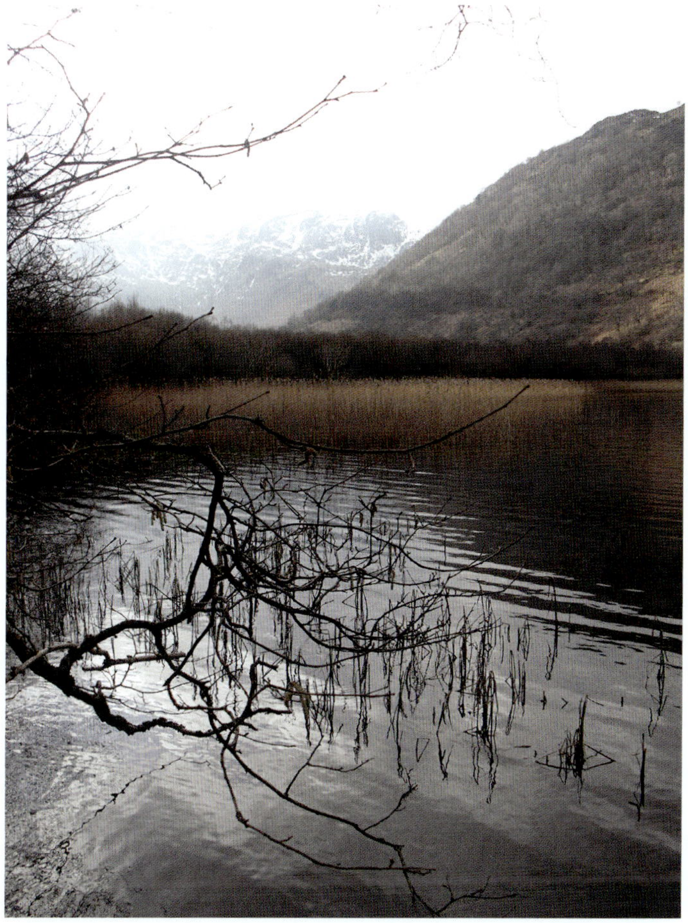

Brotherswater: source photograph. I liked the shape of the overhanging branches, the catkins and the movement of the water underneath. I felt that the image contained a variety of textures that would translate well into ink and coloured pencil. The muted palette contrasting warm and cool colours also appealed, and I kept very much to the mood of the original.

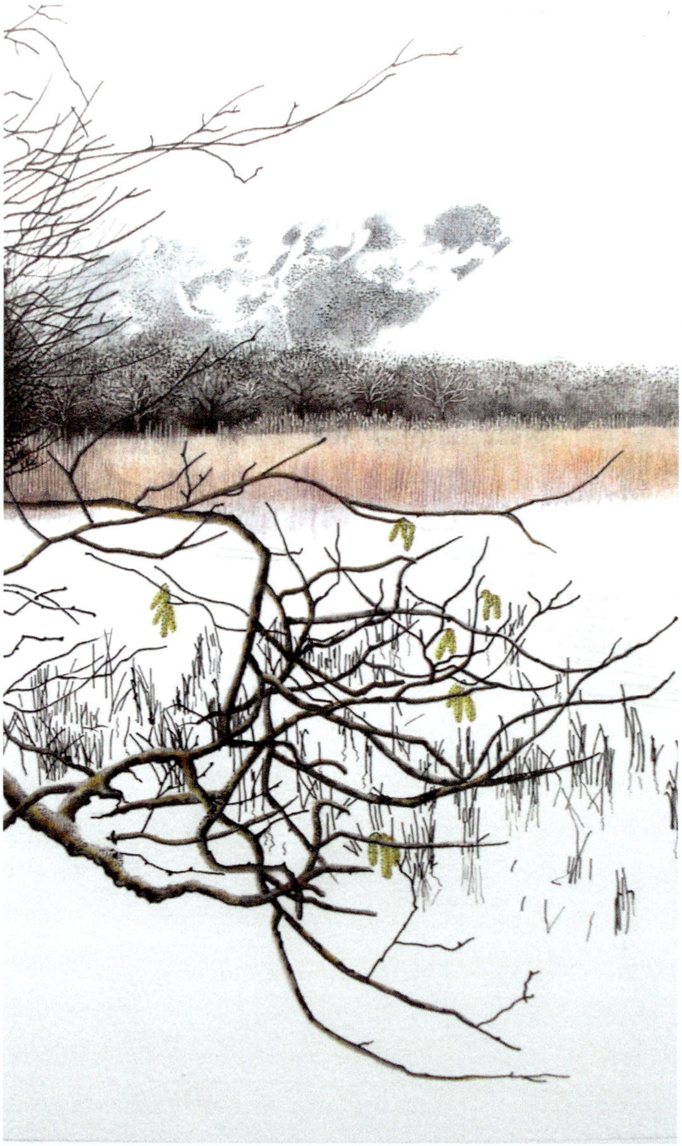

Brotherswater: stage one. I used both ink and coloured pencil to define the foreground branches, then placed the reeds behind them. I indicated the shapes of the distant fells, putting down coloured pencil first, then small ink dots. The reeds were embossed over a base colour, then the woodland behind was added using the same methods.

STAGE ONE

In my preliminary drawing I sketched in the shadow side of the main branches, the angle of the nearest hill and a few snow patches on the fells; I merely dotted in the upper edge of the reedbeds and the top of the wood. This was enough to give me the structure of the picture and keep me on track. I began with the largest branches in the foreground, using a 0.3 pen on the shadow side of each one, working out which branches crossed over the top and which passed below. I used a variety of pen sizes (0.3, 0.1, 0.05mm) to develop the tangle and add secondary branches. I applied Faber-Castell Dark Sepia in small ellipses immediately alongside the ink, blending it in to create dark shadow. I added a few ink knots to give a gnarled look, and followed up with two more colours, Prismacolor Artichoke and Faber-Castell Nougat, to suggest lichen.

For the lighter side of the main branches I used Caran D'Ache Brownish Beige and Faber-Castell Cool Grey III, dotting in some additional texture with a 0.03 pen. I could then ink in the lines of the foreground reeds, making sure that they all crossed under rather than over the branches. I included the catkins at this stage, creating their shapes without any lines, using a 0.03 pen for dots and Caran D'Ache Green Ochre and Prismacolor Jasmine.

I established the distance of the fells by using very small markings and soft colour. Resting my hand on a piece of clear acetate so that I could see the foreground but not smudge it, I put down a light layer of 'Procolour' Blue Grey, working around the patches of snow and following the contours. I added tiny dots with a 0.03 pen to give a sense of the rough terrain. I used Prismacolor Cloud Blue as a blender, leaving the lower part of the mountain pale and undefined for the moment, to hint at a misty valley beyond the wood.

The reed heads formed a pale, feathery line against the woodland and needed to be embossed before I could start on the trees. I used a light-coloured base over the whole area, mixing Caran D'Ache Venetian Red, Light Ochre and Prismacolor Deco Peach. I chose a fine line embosser for the reeds and dotted their tops before applying another layer of my three chosen colours. To darken the reeds at the waterline, I used Faber-Castell Violet and Caran D'Ache Cocoa.

Once the reeds were embossed I could add the woodland beyond. I started with coloured pencil, using Caran D'Ache Cocoa, Brownish Beige and Faber-Castell Nougat to build up the tree forms. This provided a neutral background into which I could emboss trunks and branches. I added darker marks, using a 0.03 pen and more layers of colour, gradually building up shapes and tones. I used Faber-Castell Dark Sepia at the base and for the interior of the wood, working in the colour round the pale reed heads. Wherever I felt the need to lighten an area, I used a pointed putty rubber to lift out patches or a battery eraser to take out tiny highlights.

STAGE TWO

Turning my attention to the hillside behind the wood, I used coloured pencil to place the bushes before committing myself to ink, choosing Caran D'Ache Olive Grey and 'Procolour' Spruce Green. I moved up from a 0.03 to a 0.05 pen to give a little more strength to the ink markings. The surrounding terrain was sparse and scrubby, and Prismacolor Clay Rose proved the perfect colour. I blended it with Caran D'Ache Cocoa to give some shadow, then lifted out random patches with a battery eraser to give a stony texture, filling them in with Faber-Castell Warm Grey II. I finished by applying Faber-Castell Dark Sepia to the bottom of the slope, working in the dark colour behind the paler branches, so that the hillside dropped behind the wood.

At this stage the hillside and woodland felt too similar tonally. The woodland needed more layers to give it a darker tone, so I worked round the trees, particularly at the base, using the previous colours and a lot more Dark Sepia. This made both the pale embossed trunks and branches and the reed heads in front stand out more effectively.

The addition of the water would change the overall balance of colour and tone. Browns and neutrals were dominant, and the image needed an injection of the icy blues and cool greys of a winter's day. As you add another strong element to a picture, relationships change, and earlier colours may seem less obtrusive. Frequently, the addition of any new section will mean a readjustment elsewhere. I started with a small amount of 'Procolour' Blue Grey and Caran D'Ache Marine Blue at the top of the lake on either side, just to see how this would affect the colour balance, and to test some base colours. Fortunately, coloured pencil allows you to proceed with caution: a colour that looks good as a sample may not always sit well with the general palette, but this can be easily remedied.

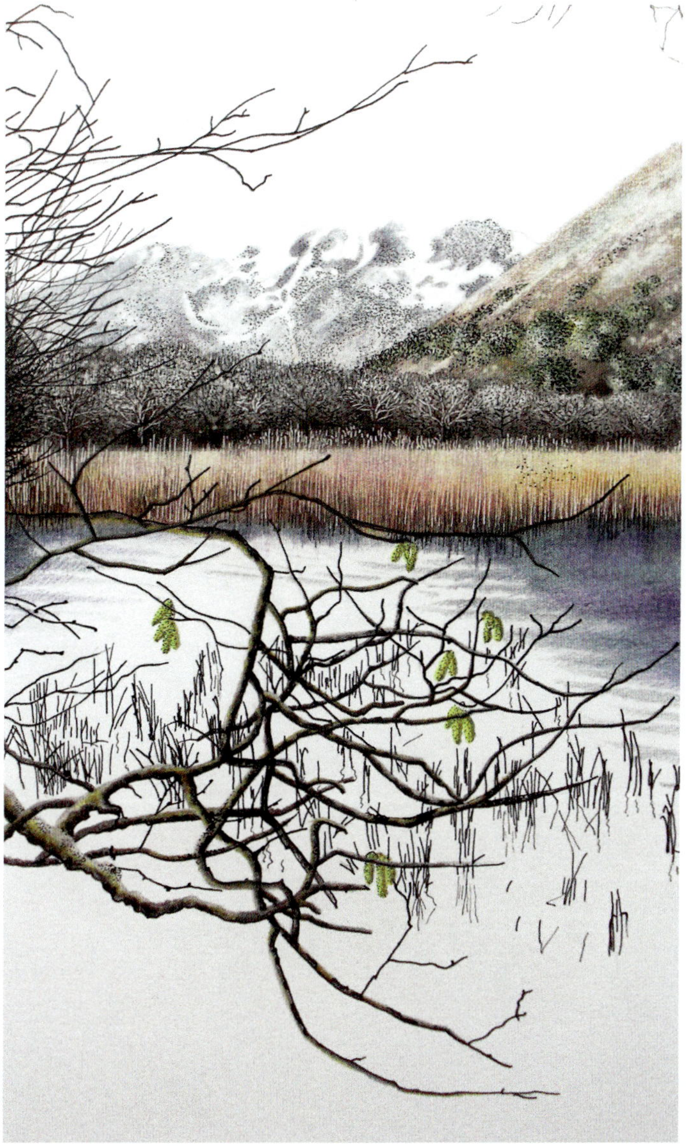

Brotherswater: stage two. I created bushes and rough terrain on the hillside, shadowing the base to drop it behind the trees. I then darkened the woodland and added layers of colour to the embossed reeds. Finally, I tried out a first layer of colour on the lake, blending it into the reeds and adding shadow and ink lines.

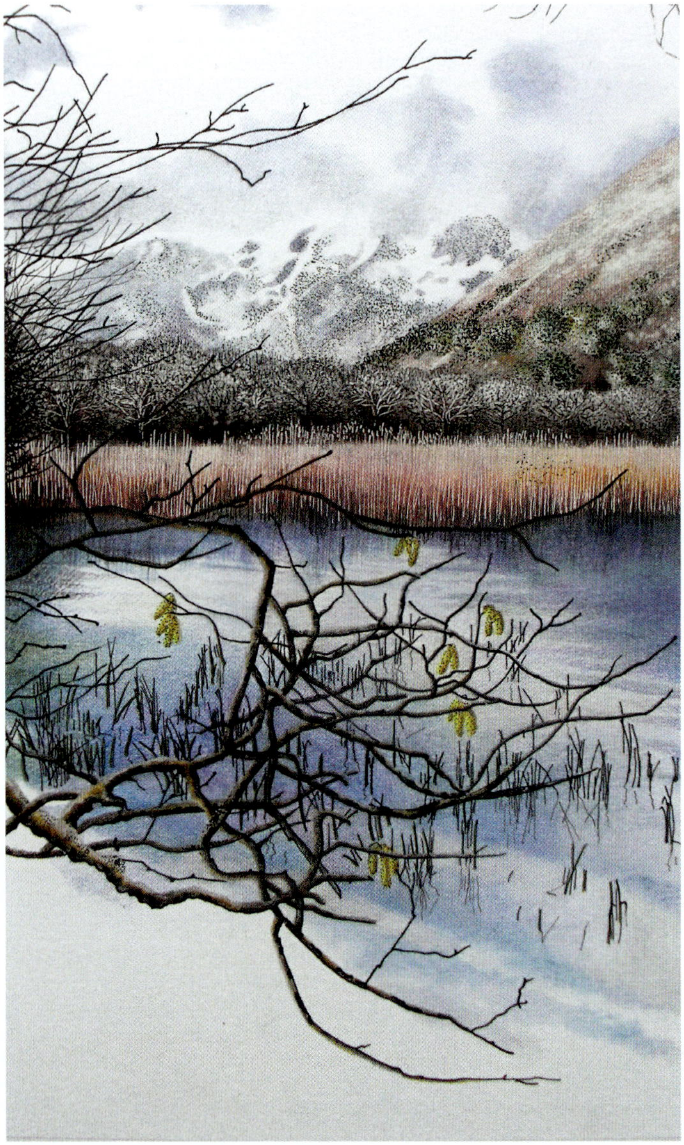

Brotherswater: stage three. I merged the sky with the fells, covering some of the peaks and skirting others. I kept to icy blues and greys and used a light touch. I started to introduce some diagonals into the water to draw the eye up the picture. The colours of the water and the reeds need modifying.

STAGE THREE

I decided to keep the sky simple, as the middle distance and the fells were already quite busy with textures. Adding fluffy or dramatic clouds would have created too much distraction. I chose pale colours – Caran D'Ache Light Grey and Prismacolor Cloud Blue – fading them out over the fells with downward strokes in putty rubber. I continued to apply ellipses of colour to the lake, following the gentle diagonal of the ripples and leaving some areas for highlights. I kept to 'Procolour' Blue Grey and Caran D'Ache Marine Blue as a first layer.

STAGE FOUR

There is always a certain amount of trial and error as you experiment with colours and techniques, but coloured pencil can always be altered. I decided to take out some of the lower clouds with Frisket and eliminate the downward strokes in the sky. I used circular movements with a putty rubber to make it mistier and indistinguishable from the mountain tops. I softened some of the light areas on the bushes to merge them into the hillside, and deepened the shadows in the wood. The reedbeds were too bright and dominant, so I added more subtle colouring with 'Procolour' Burnt Yellow Ochre, Sunset Gold, Olive Green and Sepia. I also used Prismacolor Parma Violet, a favourite shade for toning down grassland and introducing shadow. I added a few touches of Sunset Gold to the hillside as well, as echoing some colours in a landscape will help to create unity.

Building up a large stretch of water in coloured pencil takes time and patience. The combination of colours I had chosen for the base was veering too much towards turquoise, and I needed to introduce more to reach that elusive, watery colour that only comes from a good blend. I used a selection of pencils, mixing and matching them as I worked to introduce subtle changes of colour. Continuing with 'Procolour' Blue Grey and Caran D'Ache Marine Blue, I added Caran D'Ache Bluish Grey, followed by Cocoa and Sepia in the shadows, 'Procolour' Spruce Green and Prismacolor Blue Violet Lake, Periwinkle and Cloud Blue. The left-hand margins of the lake were more shadowy, so I continued this well into the foreground, using darker blends of colour. For the highlights on the water, I used a mixture of Caran D'Ache Silver Grey and Prismacolor Cloud Blue, leaving some patches of pure white. I kept the surface of the water smooth, but introduced diagonal ripples in the foreground to lead the eye into the picture.

Once I felt that the water suited the mood and colour palette, I reinforced some of the overhanging branches to restore them to prominence. I re-inked the branches, applied another layer of the earlier colours, and lifted out a few highlights with the battery eraser. Once the branches were revitalized, I introduced a hint of colour to the dead reeds below using Faber-Castell Permanent Green Olive and Caran D'Ache Olive Black. As a finishing touch I created a focal point in the form of a lone buzzard: the eye can travel up the diagonals, the overhanging branches and the hillside and then hover over the fells.

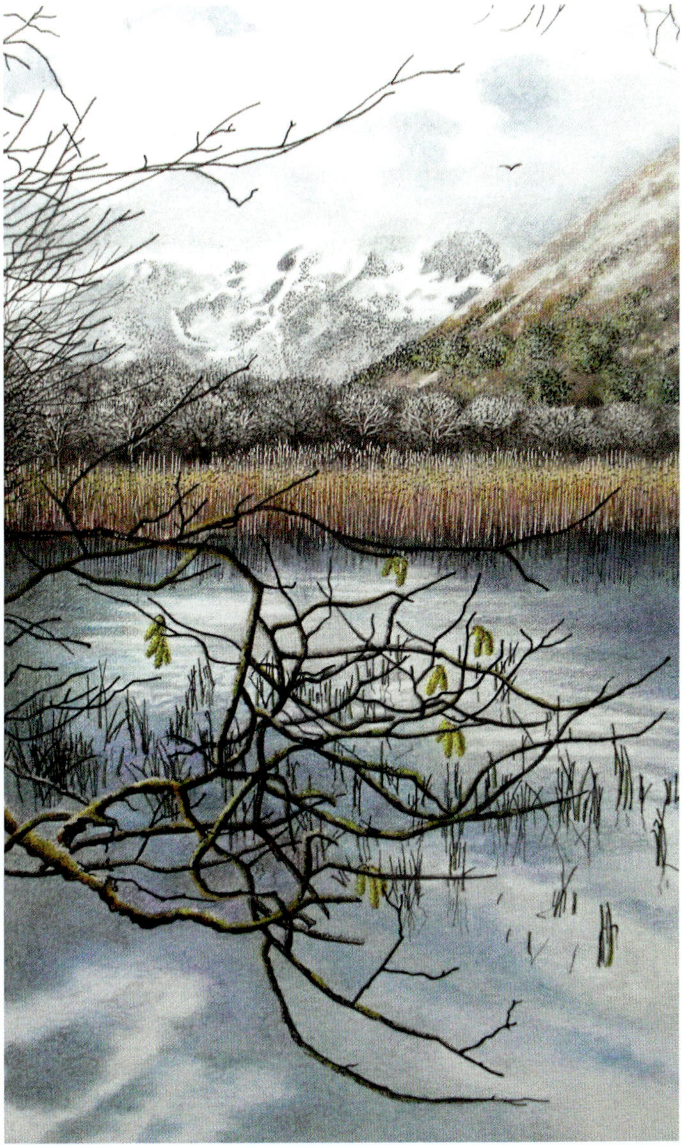

Brotherswater: stage four. The patterns on the surface of the lake have been completed, the colour modified, and patches lifted out with a putty rubber or battery eraser. I have darkened the reeds and introduced more ink detail. I have also strengthened and re-inked the overhanging branches and made the sky less busy. A buzzard has appeared.

CHAPTER 12

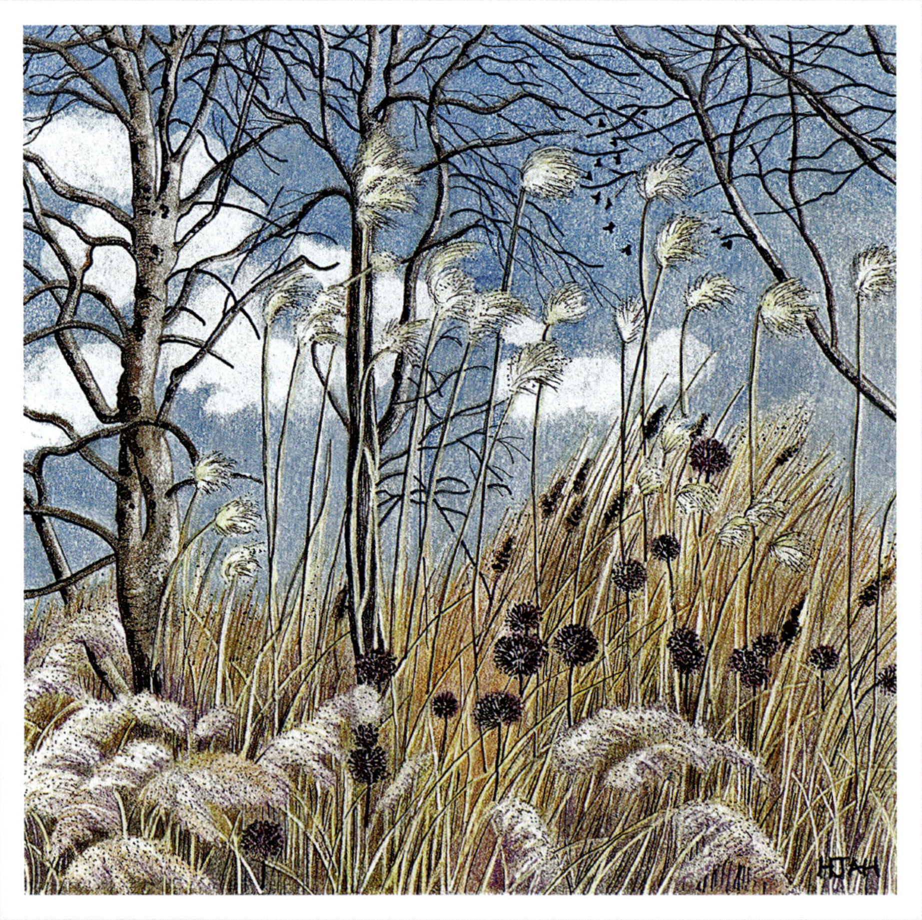

The Gravel Garden in Winter.

The Challenge of a Large Work

Tackling a large landscape is exciting, but inevitably more challenging. I like to do one annually, either taking a relaxed approach over a few months, or working in a concentrated way as a change from smaller pictures. Choosing and adapting a suitable image, finding a working order, applying appropriate techniques and keeping the whole image in mind all engage and tax the brain; however, we know that the process of applying pen and pencil is calming, meditative and encourages *flow*. A large work will progress steadily if you do just an hour a day; it does not need to be completed all at once, and can be tailored to fit into a busy schedule. It can be a very effective period of quiet time if you want to arrange it that way.

TACKLING A LARGE LANDSCAPE

Special Considerations

A more substantial work brings with it new considerations relating to composition and content. Even more than usual, it pays to do some forward thinking. If you are going to spend a lot of time on an image, choose something that will really work as a large piece: it should have balance, focus, variety and an area of calm. I always need to remind myself of this latter aspect because intricacies attract me; it is easy to allow things to become too 'busy'. The integration of ink and coloured pencil lends itself to creative detail rather than wide sweeps of colour, so I try to resist the temptation to over-embellish. Quieter areas such as sky or water can just be used to showcase skilful blending and beautiful colour.

Different Approaches

Covering the paper is more of a task in larger works, causing us to focus more on the method of assembly. I always work in sections, assessing what is in front, building up depth and adding immediate background; I then progress to the next area, linking them appropriately. I bear in mind the tonal values I want, and keep referring to the whole image as I work. This tendency to compartmentalize probably stems from my experience of etching, in which it is usual to 'stop out' (protect with varnish) some areas, whilst exposing others to acid. I am used to working on different sections, envisaging the whole and pulling everything together in the final stages.

However, there are no precedents or established ways of approaching a work in ink and coloured pencil. My method is what I have devised, but you can take a different starting point if that suits your way of working or your previous experience as an artist. You may prefer to work in a more tonal way from the start, establishing all the lightest areas, gradually building up deeper tones and introducing detail across the whole image. Watercolourists who are used to building up colour and tone and introducing detail at a later stage may find this more manageable. Experiment until you find a way of working that suits you, your style and your creative experience.

NOTE: The only disadvantage to working on a large area is that you are more likely to run your hand over, or smudge, existing colours. Artist-quality coloured pencils do not smudge easily, but it is always a good idea to keep the natural oil in your hands away from the paper. I resolve this by always resting my hand on a piece of clear acetate so that I can see both a particular section and the entire image, but am not touching the surface.

The Important Preliminaries

I keep the preliminary drawing very simple, merely indicating main features such as a shoreline, the extent of an area of foliage, and the lower, shadow side of overhanging branches. I need just enough information to begin to work directly on the different parts of the composition using ink and coloured pencil. As you put together all the components in pencil, it is a good idea to do a last-minute check for basic errors of composition: make sure that nothing slices the image in half horizontally or vertically, and decide whether anything needs moving. Make sure that all markings, especially those in ink, are of an appropriate size and strength for the distance. When deciding this, it is better to err on the side of caution, as ink marks can be reinforced later but not removed. Straighten horizon lines, shorelines and anything else that might look out of kilter, as basic faults look worse on a large scale. The more you work on them, the more they are accentuated. A drunken, upward-sloping waterline will remain an irritating distraction however hard you work.

Keeping an Eye on the Whole Picture

As your picture progresses, you will be able to see how the sections fit together; it is particularly noticeable in a larger work, as each change you make affects the whole image compositionally and tonally. A foreground section that seems very strong may appear less dominant once you have included foliage in the middle distance. The addition of water changes the balance dramatically. The final stages of the picture may involve some juggling so that the different areas of the image work together, make sense tonally and create believable distance. Dominant features such as foreground branches may need strengthening, and colours may require modification.

You can help to unify the picture by echoing some colours across the landscape, but stay subtle and do not overdo things. View shadow areas in relation to the whole, and deepen them where necessary; check the overall distribution of light, and use putty rubber or Frisket to lift out more if required. All alterations and embellishments at this stage should be undertaken in the context of the full picture. Eventually everything will fall into focus, and you will perceive the landscape as a harmonious whole.

SUMMER INTO AUTUMN

On my walks I often find myself catching the last vestiges of one season as it moves into the next. Over the years I have taken a particular interest in this seasonal no-man's land, when spring shoots appear amongst the dead wood, or dried-out summer flowers compete with the first berries.

Summer into Autumn, the large image I have chosen to illustrate this chapter, is just such a time. The image is of a fishing lake at one of my local nature reserves, captured on a late August afternoon. The week had been hot and dry and the weather was about to break: clouds were gathering and the light had a greenish tinge. The water's edge was a mix of semi-dried or seeding flowers and reeds: hemp agrimony, water mint, fool's watercress and curled russet leaves. Lichen-covered hawthorn branches hung over the water with the beginnings of a rather sparse crop.

Assessing the Image

The landscape divided neatly into areas, which suited a sectional approach: foreground plants, water, middle distance with reeds and bushes, the far distant bank, right-bank foliage and sky. When areas overlap, it is more difficult to establish what is in front and to show relative distances. The tonal values were also easy to distinguish; these had to be taken into consideration at every stage to make sure that the distant bank did not join the middle distance, and that the foreground plants and hawthorn remained dominant.

Materials

I chose to work on Strathmore Bristol board 300 series, with an image size of 50×40 cm. When choosing colours for a new work, I tend to use just a couple of makes of pencil rather than dip into my extensive collection. Brands have different qualities, and I like to consider the subject, its local colour and the paper surface. Caran D'Ache 'Pablo' pencils, with their excellent 'mixture' shades including olive greens and soft browns, seemed perfect for the transitional nature of *Summer into Autumn*. I added some of my favourite shadow, water and sky colours from Faber-Castell's 'Polychromos' range and a few indispensable Prismacolour 'Premier' colours to burnish, add a final layer or a rich pop of colour. If I know that a particular colour from my wider collection would be perfect, I add it; however, too much choice and too many different brands lead to confusion (for me). Different makes will mix, but well-chosen colours from the same one will always look good.

The basic palette for *Summer into Autumn* was made up of the following coloured pencils:

- **Caran D'Ache 'Pablo':** Light Lemon Yellow, Green Ochre, Light Ochre, Golden Yellow, Reddish Orange, English Red, Venetian Red, Granite Rose, Indigo Blue, Marine Blue, Bluish Grey, Blue Jeans, Spruce Green, Olive Yellow, Khaki Green, Light Olive, Moss Green, Olive Grey, Olive, Olive Brown, Olive Black, Brown, Russet, Hazel, Cinnamon, Brown Ochre, Sepia, Cocoa, Brownish Beige, Beige, Light Grey, Dark Grey.

- **Faber-Castell 'Polychromos':** Mauve, Dark Indigo, Ultramarine, Light Ultramarine, Permanent Green Olive, Pine Green, Chrome Oxide Green, Juniper Green, Olive Green Yellowish, Green Gold, May Green, Earth Green Yellowish, Chromium Green Opaque, Earth Green, Light Yellow Ochre, Dark Naples Ochre, Raw Umber, Nougat, Burnt Sienna, Dark Sepia, Warm Grey III.

- **Prismacolor 'Premier':** Artichoke, Sunburst Yellow, Crimson Red, Imperial Violet, Blue Violet Lake, Cloud Blue, Periwinkle, Yellow Chartreuse, Limepeel, Olive Green, Prussian Green, Kelp Green, Marine Green, Putty Beige.

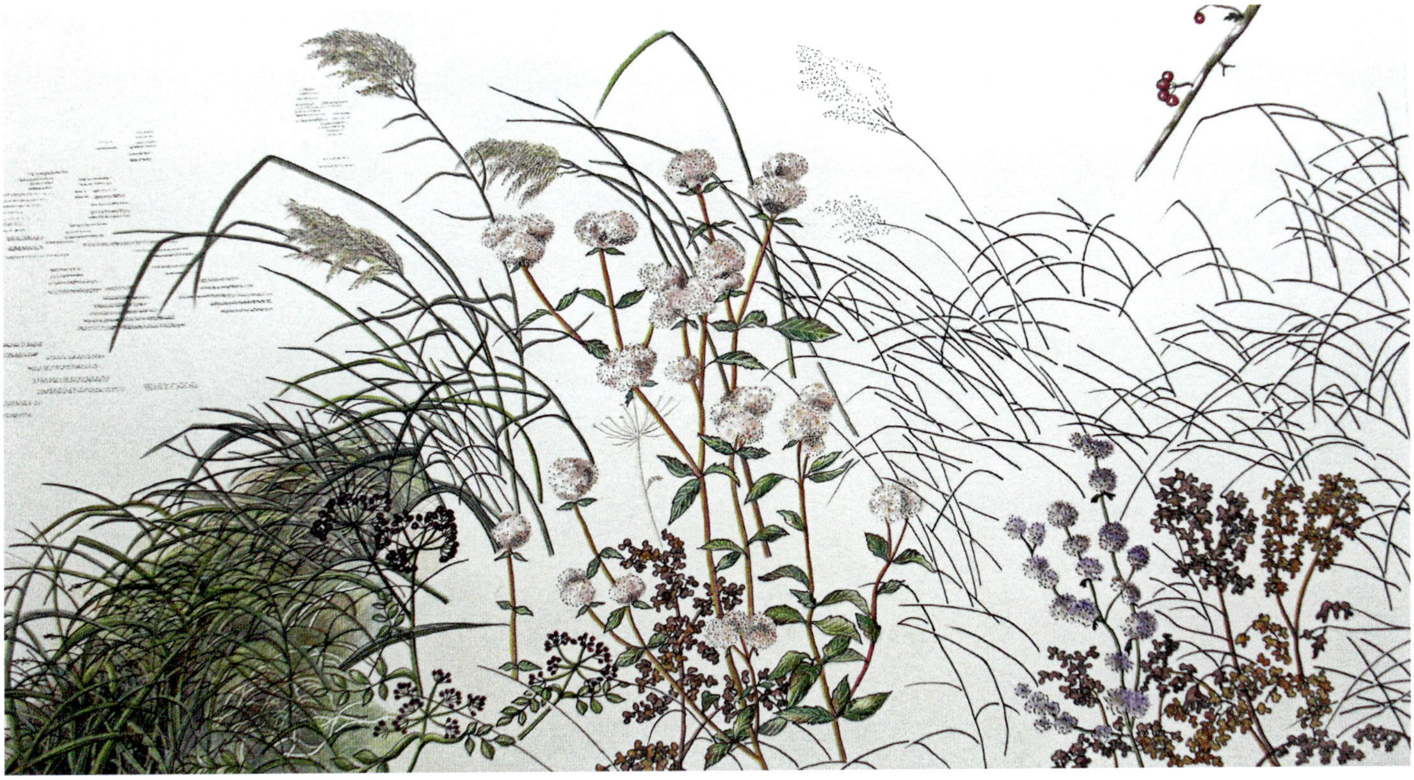

Summer into Autumn: preliminary foreground sketches. To build up the foreground, I chose the main waterside plants and created a composition based round their shapes, always bearing in mind which ones were in front. I introduced reeds in the background and dotted in their structure. As a guide for later, I sketched in single lines to plot the direction of the smaller grasses.

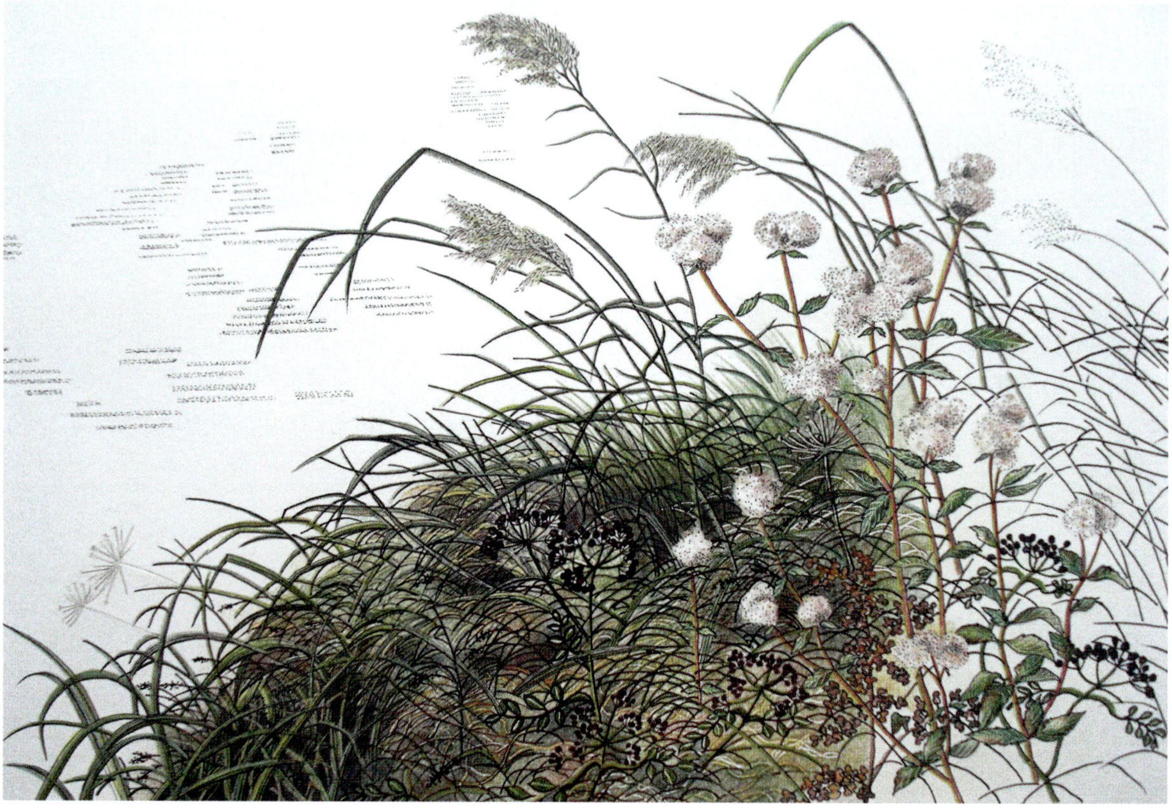

Summer into Autumn: stage one. The foreground plants were introduced gradually, starting at the front. Some, such as the fool's watercress, were outlined in ink for colouring in; others, such as the hemp agrimony, were created using ink and coloured pencil together. On the left-hand section I have used colour embossing, single ink strokes and blended coloured pencil to interpret the background grasses.

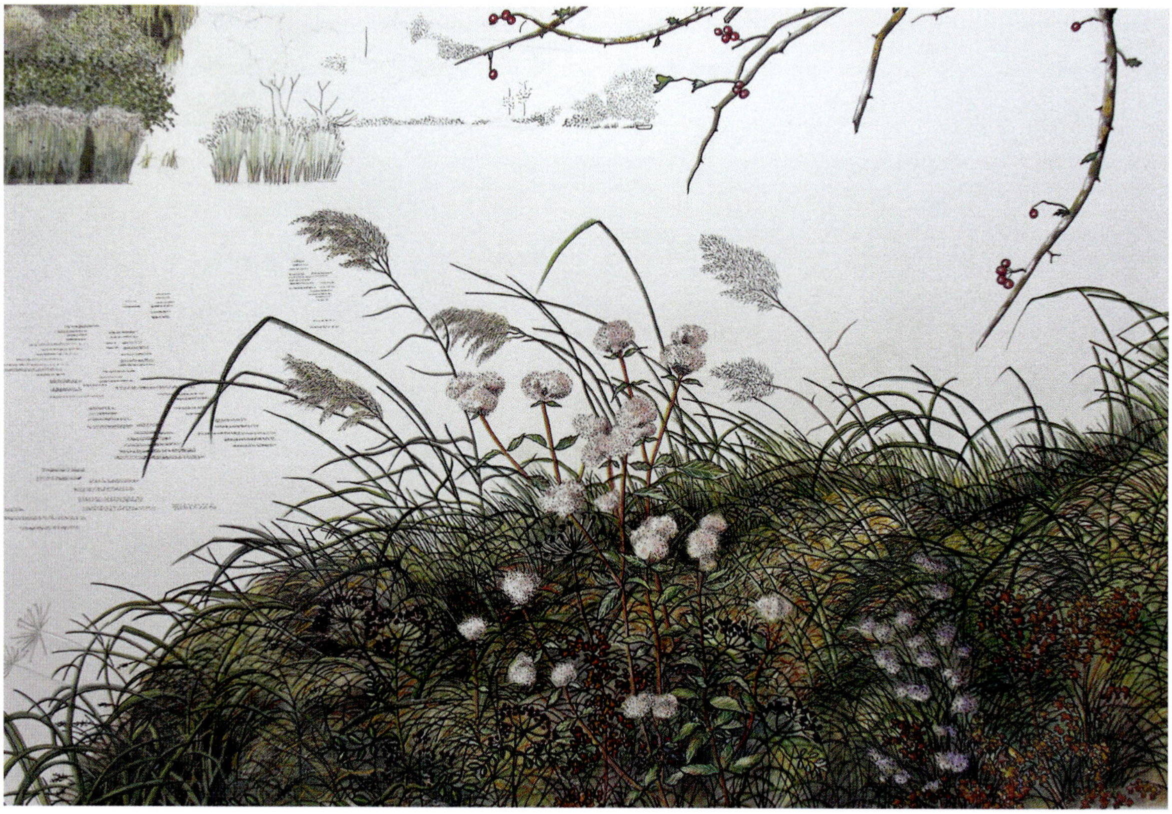

Summer into Autumn: stage two. The foreground is almost finished. Once the foliage and background had been established, light and shade were introduced to add form. I used shadow mixes behind the flower heads and leaves to bring them forwards, and to create dips and troughs on the bank. Highlights were lifted out with a putty rubber to provide light and contrast.

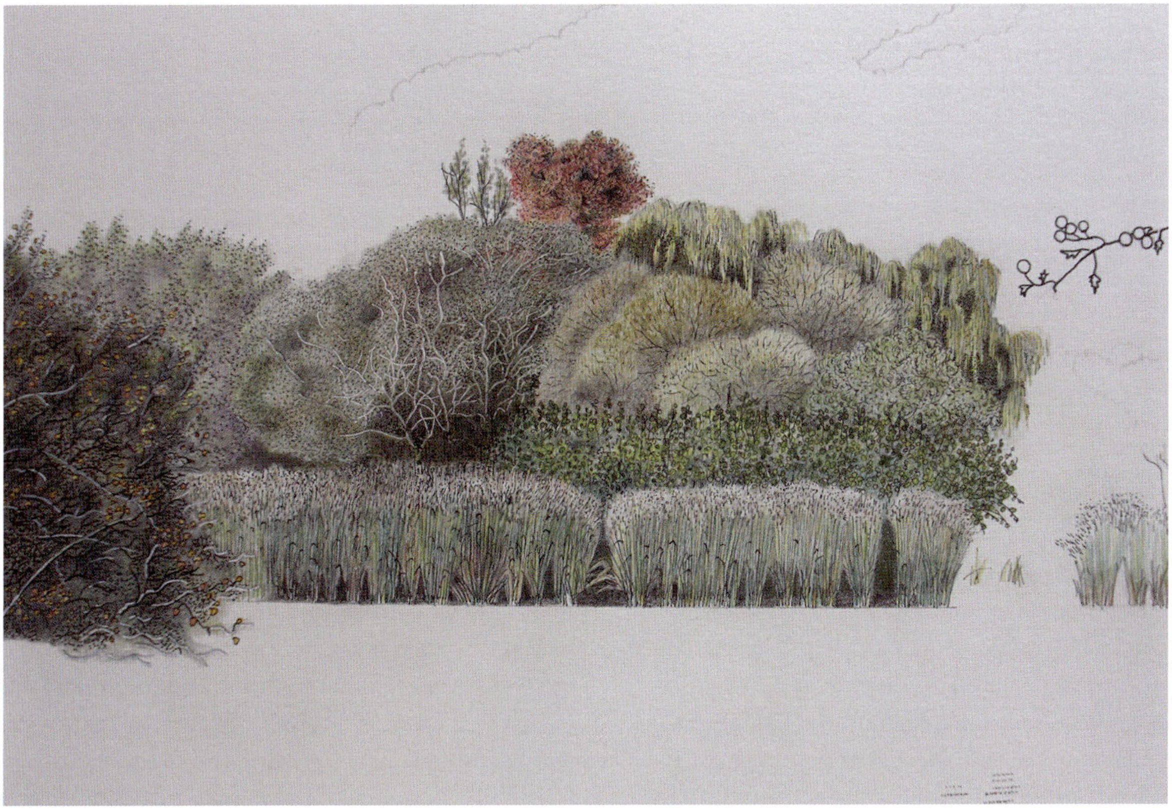

Summer into Autumn: stage three. I began the trees and reeds in the middle distance in coloured pencil, using small ellipses and a palette of soft, autumnal colours. I added embossing and ink, following their shapes and using a 0.03 or 0.05 pen. Shadows and highlights were introduced, keeping a medium tone and pressure to distance the area from the foreground.

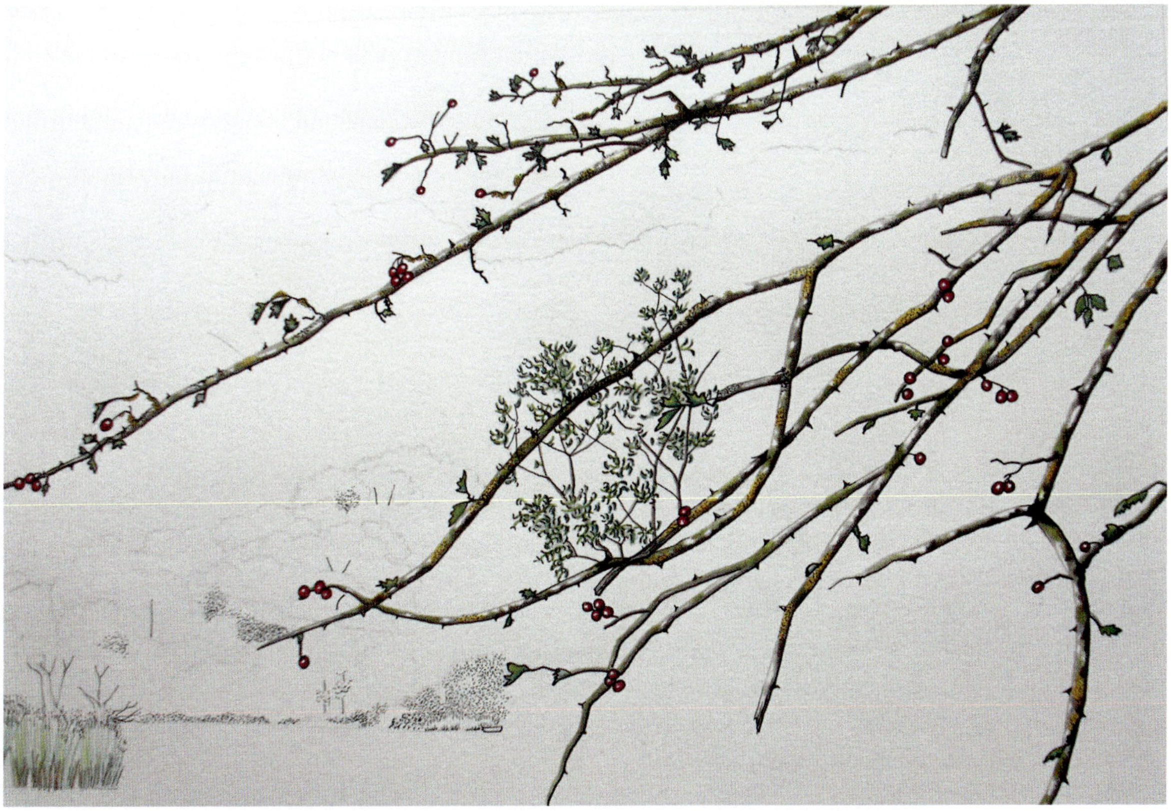

Summer into Autumn: stage four. On the right-hand side, the overhanging hawthorn branches needed to be clearly visible in front of the tree. I used a heavy 0.5 ink line on the underside, backed up by Faber-Castell Dark Sepia shading, with additional mid-browns and greys. I chose Prismacolor Limepeel and Sunburst Yellow for the lichen and Crimson Lake for the strongly highlighted berries.

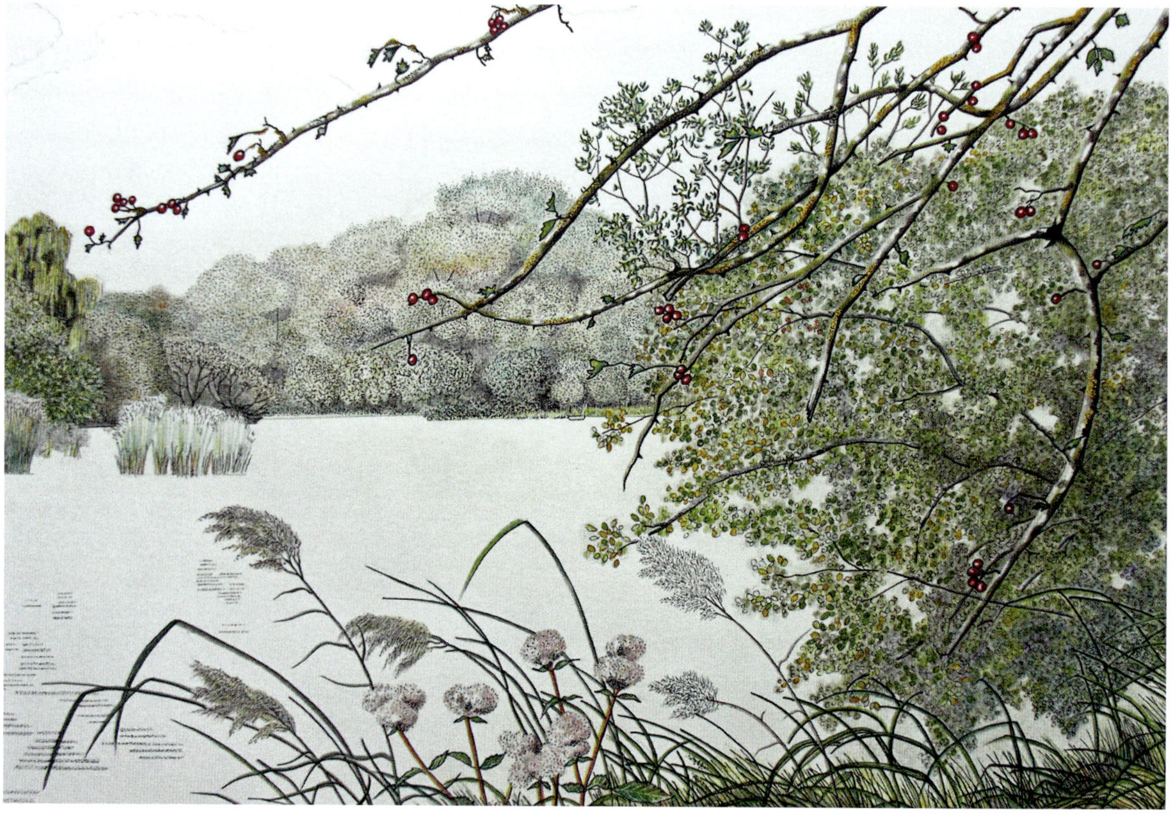

Summer into Autumn: stage five. For the waterside tree I used a mixture of ink outlines and coloured pencil alone, changing the colours and pressure to give depth and variety. The tree shapes on the far bank were created in pencil with markings in a 0.03 pen. The tone was kept light, even in the shadows, and the colour bluish to create distance.

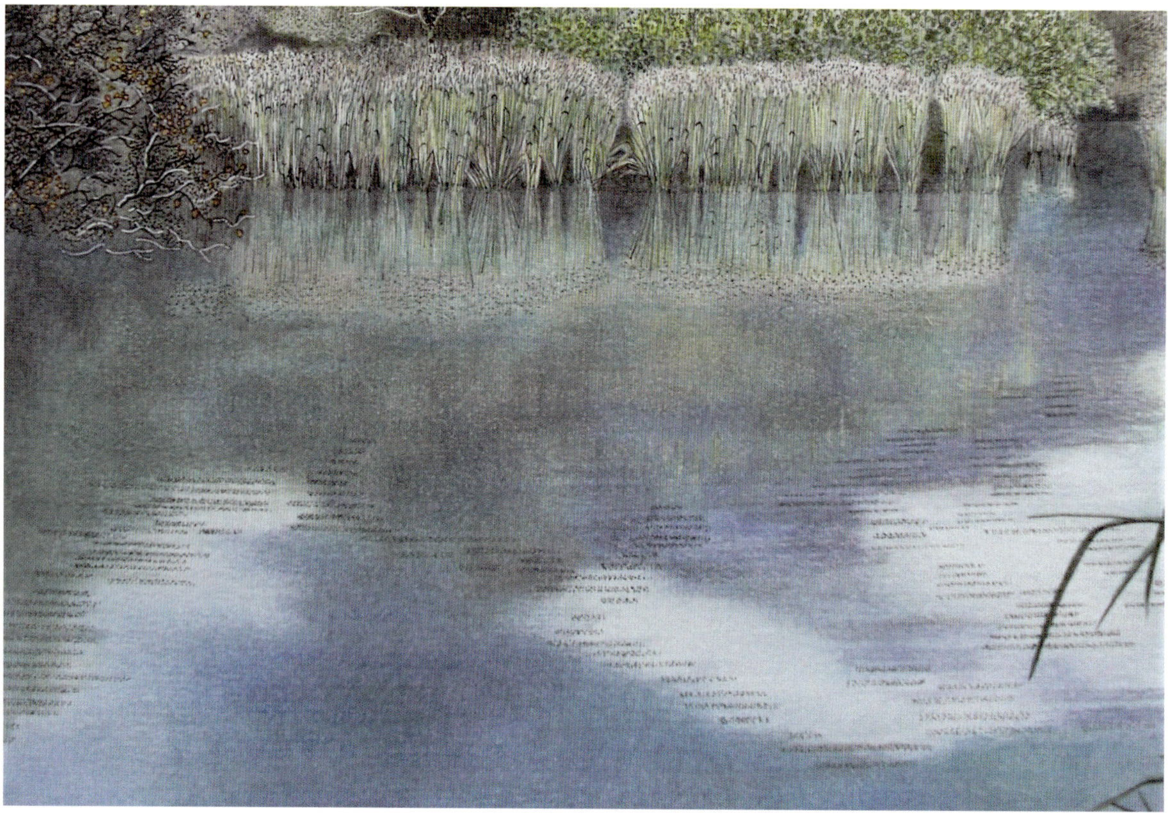

Summer into Autumn: stage six. I chose Caran D'Ache Blue Jeans as a base for the water, smoothing it with a paper stump. I added a range of Faber-Castell and Caran D'Ache colours for the reflections and deeper water, working horizontally and vertically rather than in ellipses until the required intensity was achieved. I then used Prismacolor Cloud Blue to blend and unify.

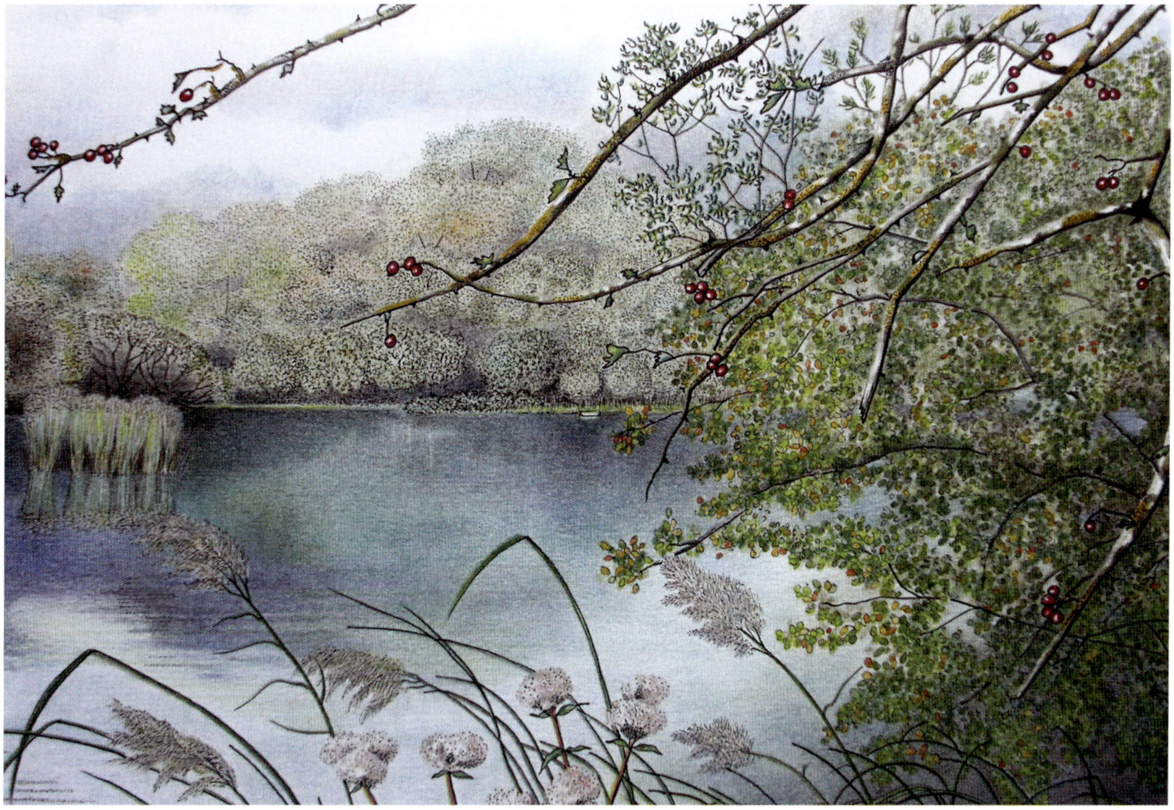

Summer into Autumn: stage seven. The base colour Blue Jeans was used for the entire stretch of water, with reflections added in colours appropriate to the foliage above. Edges were softened and highlights lifted with a rolled putty rubber. Water was added between the leaves, and shadows were reinforced along the bank. A small boat by the shore provided a focal point.

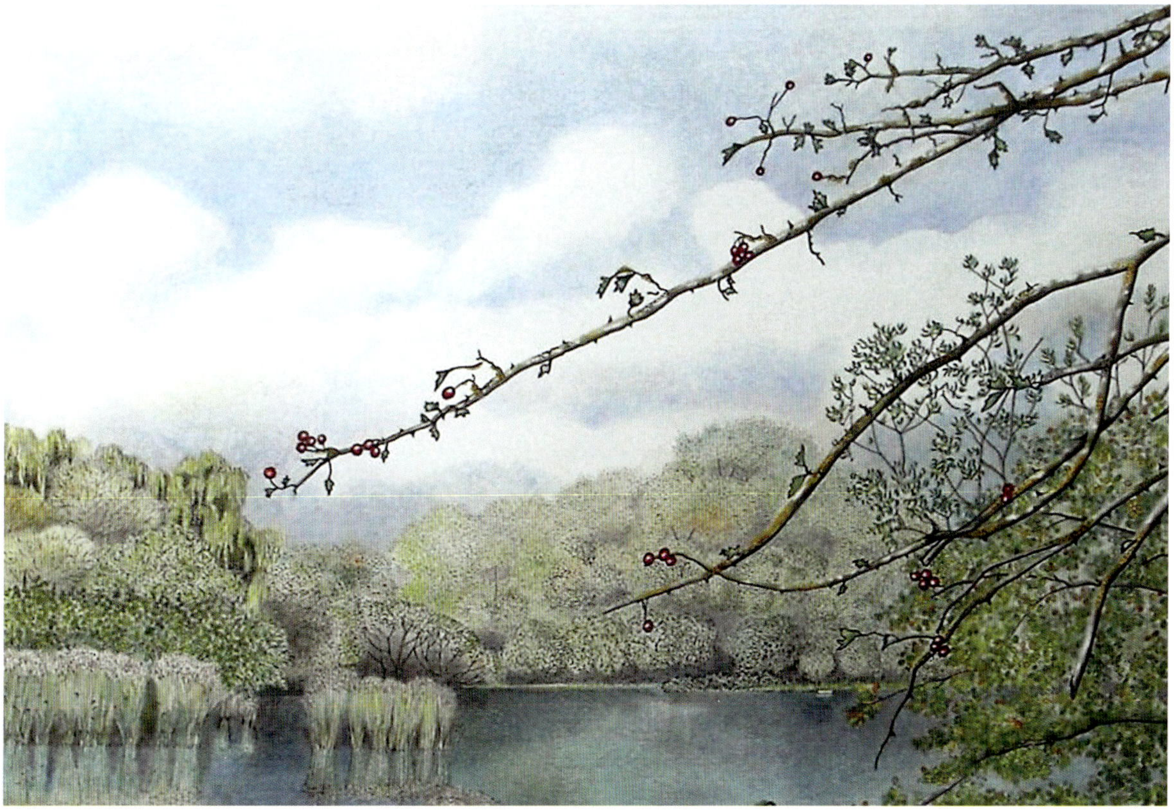

Summer into Autumn: stage eight. I kept the sky low key, choosing Faber-Castell Ultramarine and Light Ultramarine and fading them into each other. I followed up with Caran D'Ache Light Grey on the clouds to give a hint of bad weather to come. Cloud shapes were softened with a putty rubber, and uneven patches of colour smoothed with a clear blender.

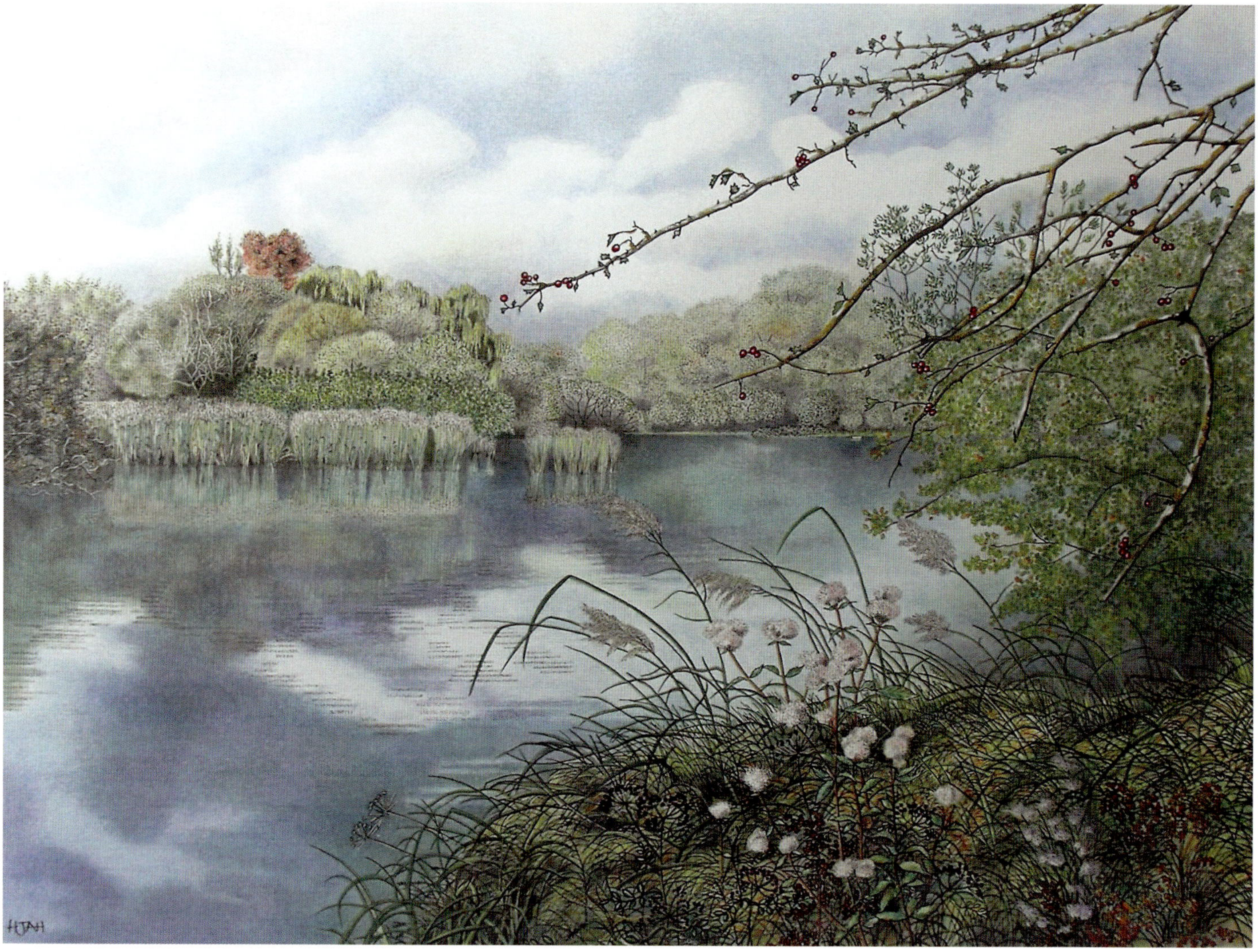

Summer into Autumn: the finished image. Once all the sections were finished, I checked that the image worked tonally, with a good balance between areas of light and shade. It is important in the final stages to concentrate on the whole picture; last minute adjustments to colour, and strengthening or lightening features, will bring the image to a harmonious conclusion.

MOVING ON

This large-size project marks the end of our adventures in ink and coloured pencil. If, like me, you enjoy using both, I hope this book has introduced you to a way of combining them to good effect. Even in well-established media, art always makes room for innovation; this field is wide open for you to explore new territory, working in your own way, or using the methods that I have suggested. I hope that you will find your own style, and in the process, continue to experiment with the richness of ink and the luscious pigments available to the modern coloured pencil artist. The gate is open: keep walking the territory, interpreting what you see and enjoying the process. Be bold, be creative, and to achieve that all-important sense of place, be authentic.

Index